Chinese Literary Forms in Heian Japan

Harvard East Asian Monographs 401

Chinese Literary Forms in Heian Japan

Poetics and Practice

Brian Steininger

Published by the Harvard University Asia Center
Distributed by Harvard University Press
Cambridge (Massachusetts) and London 2017

Printed in the United States of America

The Harvard University Asia Center publishes a monograph series and, in coordination with the Fairbank Center for Chinese Studies, the Korea Institute, the Reischauer Institute of Japanese Studies, and other faculties and institutes, administers research projects designed to further scholarly understanding of China, Japan, Vietnam, Korea, and other Asian countries. The Center also sponsors projects addressing multidisciplinary and regional issues in Asia.

Library of Congress Cataloging-in-Publication Data

Steininger, Brian, author.
Chinese literary forms in Heian Japan : poetics and practice / Brian Steininger.
Harvard East Asian monographs ; 401.
Cambridge, Massachusetts : Published by the Harvard University
Asia Center, 2017. | Series: Harvard East Asian monographs ; 401 |
Includes bibliographical references and index.
LCCN 2016028797 | ISBN 978-0-674-97515-6 (hardcover : alk. paper)
Kanbungaku (Japanese literature)—History and criticism. | Japanese literature—
Heian period, 794–1185—History and criticism. |
Japanese literature—Chinese influences. | Literacy—Japan—History. | *Kundoku.* |
Oral interpretation.
LCC PL719.81 2017 | DDC 895.609/0014—dc23
LC record available at https://lccn.loc.gov/2016028797

Index by Anne Holmes

♾ Printed on acid-free paper

Last figure below indicates year of this printing
21 20 19 18 17

Contents

Figures

Acknowledgments

This book grew out of a dissertation completed at Yale University under the direction of Edward Kamens. For over a decade Ed has continued to see more potential in me than I gave any reason to warrant and offered me opportunities to succeed regardless. I can only hope this book provides him some degree of satisfaction in return. While at Yale, I met Fujiwara Katsumi through the introduction of Robert Borgen. Every week during the summer of 2006, Professor Fujiwara invited me to his office at the University of Tokyo and patiently led me through texts in *Honchō monzui*, providing the core of my dissertation. When I returned to Tōdai the following year, I received an invitation from Satō Michio, first to join his seminar at Keiō University and then his *Chōya gunsai* reading group with Gōtō Akio and Kōno Kimiko. The guidance these scholars have provided is attested to throughout the following pages, but here I want to express my profound gratitude for their unstinting kindness and patience.

The development over the last several years in my approach toward this topic is almost entirely the result of conversations with and comments from my friends and colleagues in the field. My colleagues at Bates College, and later Princeton University, have been magnanimously supportive and have reshaped this project's goals and methodology. I have received feedback at numerous conferences and workshops over the years, and I am grateful to Torquil Duthie, Jennifer Guest, Martin Kern, Keiko Ono, and Robert Tuck for providing some of those opportunities. I must particularly thank those who gave of their time to read manuscript drafts as this work developed, most of all the three anonymous reviewers at

Harvard University Asia Center, whose perspicacious suggestions gave shape to the book's argument. Comments by Wiebke Denecke at the beginning of my dissertation research, and by Kang-i Sun Chang and David Lurie at the end, were a map through the wilderness of my own tangled ideas. Robert Borgen, Tom Conlan, Paize Keulemans, Peter Kornicki, David Leheny, Bryan Lowe, and Anna Shields all generously read drafts and provided invaluable feedback. David Wilson-Okamura, who shares with Sarah Pradt the blame for making an embryonic scholar of me during my time at Macalester College, kindly agreed to read through the introduction at the last minute. Deborah Del Gais and Bob Graham nimbly guided me through the editorial process, while Melissa McCormick suggested the perfect cover image.

I have been extremely fortunate to receive consistent institutional support as I pursued my studies: my dissertation research was conducted with grants from the Fulbright-IIE Program and the Yale University Council on East Asian Studies, and I completed the final draft of the manuscript while on a sabbatical leave supported by the Princeton University East Asian Studies Program and my home department. I have also been helped along the way by librarians at institutions across the United States and Japan, particularly Haruko Nakamura at Yale and Setsuko Noguchi at Princeton. In Japan, the Shidō Bunko at Keiō University has provided me with opportunities and support so frequent and generous that I would blush to list them all, and I can only express my sincerest gratitude to Horikawa Takashi, Sasaki Takahiro, Sumiyoshi Tomohiko, and the rest of the faculty there.

There are too many teachers and friends who have contributed to this book or supported my work over the years to list everyone, but I must particularly thank Heather Blair, Xing Fan, Nikki Floyd, Matthew Fraleigh, Josh Frydman, Fujikawa Masae, Aaron Gerow, Robert Goree, Frederick Green, Kendall Heitzman, Christopher Hill, Ishigami Eiichi, Reginald Jackson, Ashton Lazarus, Pauline Lin, Nan Ma, Maggie Maurer-Fazio, Lisa Maurizio, Arthur Mitchell, Muroki Hideyuki, Nagase Yumi, Jeffrey Niedermaier, Ono Yasuo, Ōnuma Haruki, John Phan, Christian Ratcliff, Saitō Mareshi, Patrick Schwemmer, Saeko Shibayama, Haruo Shirane, Ivo Smits, Sarah and John Strong, Satoko Suzuki, Tateno Fumiaki, John Treat, Bryan Vivier, Stanley Weinstein, Timothy Wixted, Yamada Naoko, Naoki Yamamoto, Yanagawa Hibiki, Mimi Yiengpruksawan, and the students in my 2013 *Wakan rōeishū* seminar. Yamazaki Akira has been a constant source of encouragement and skepticism in equal measure, and I am lucky to get both.

No words can express what I owe to my family. My parents and sister helped me to find and follow my passion and never questioned the result. In Tokyo, Yumiko, Hōsaku, Sora, and Haruka brought me into their home with truly selfless kindness. My wife Jenny has for ten years compounded my joys, distracted me from gloom, and refused to rise to the bait when I was a pill. This book is dedicated to all of them and to Richard and Shirley Magraw, whose adventures left a path for me to follow.

Conventions

When quoting texts in Chinese characters, I have standardized the orthography to traditional character forms and added punctuation for clarity. Character glosses are provided for proper names, work titles, and, where relevant, for specialized terms at their first appearance in the text. Glosses are generally not provided for office, ministry, and palace building names.

Chinese terminology is transcribed in Pinyin, Japanese terms in the modified Hepburn system. Passages and terms from classical Japanese are transcribed according to modern pronunciation; where necessary to the argument, the original text is provided (so, for example, the classical Japanese word for "today" may appear as either *kyō* or けふ, but not *kefu*). I distinguish between modern Japanese and Chinese pronunciations with the abbreviations "J." and "Ch." and indicate Late Middle Chinese reconstructions (from Edwin Pulleyblank's *Lexicon of Reconstructed Pronunciation in Early Middle Chinese, Late Middle Chinese, and Early Mandarin*) with "LMC."

Months and days are given according to the lunar calendar, but years are converted to their approximate equivalent in the Western calendar (so an event described as taking place in "the twelfth month of 948" actually took place in January of 949 by the Gregorian calendar). Ages are given according the traditional *kazoedoshi* enumeration of the total number of calendar years in which one had lived.

All translations are my own unless otherwise noted.

Introduction

The tenth and eleventh centuries were a period of tremendous cultural fertility for the nobles, whose lives revolved around the capital city of Heian in western Japan. A syllabary of *kana*—abbreviated Sinographs (Chinese characters) used to phonetically transcribe the local language—had become increasingly standardized, and writers developed new formal innovations that led to an efflorescence in vernacular literary forms. However, *kana* writing was still a relatively circumscribed practice: "writing" was more commonly identified with the written idiom of Chinese employed across medieval East Asia, which remained the orthodox standard of inscription. Throughout the Heian period (784–1185), administrative and religious documents were almost entirely written in variants of this "literary Sinitic" (a term discussed further below), as were most diaries, letters, and a great deal of poetry. A careful reading of Heian vernacular classics such as the *Tale of Genji* (early eleventh century) finds them woven through with threads of continental literary culture, which in modern scholarship has inspired both acclamation of and anxiety over the Chinese "influence" on classical Japanese literature.

This study treats the composition and reception of literary Sinitic genres of poetry and parallel prose in mid-Heian Japan. Rather than focusing primarily on such works' relationship to Chinese precursors, however, it takes a somewhat different tack by following not "vertical" lineages of textual adaptation and influence, but the "horizontal" networks of the mid-Heian literary quotidian: the day-to-day exchanges, performances, missives, commissions, banquets, and games that made up the lived practice of classical literary culture. Though it has received only limited scholarly attention, a world of literary Sinitic composition existed alongside the growing body of vernacular literature. In the Heian court, recitation of vernacular poetry (*waka* 和歌) occurred side-by-side with composition in the Chinese regulated verse format (*shi* 詩), the authors of Japan's earliest long narratives were intimately familiar with the Han dynastic histories, and calligraphers playfully juxtaposed *kana* with the "grass script" Sinographs from which they were derived. As writers moved between different venues of textual production, they created works that veered back and forth between vernacular, imported, and hybrid genres. In traditional accounts, this multiplicity has generally been treated as a step toward the synthesis or sublimation of Chinese influence into the native cultural tradition. I instead focus on the active invention and preservation of difference: the social practices that generated and surrounded literary genres served to align the multivalent possibilities of inscription into provisional and negatively defined categories of "literary," "plain," "spoken," "local," or "vernacular" discourse. Nor did these categories necessarily line up with a division between Japanese and Chinese languages; the retrospective history of vernacular literature's rise in the mid-Heian is premised on modern assumptions about the relationship between (national) language and writing, a relationship that was neither obvious nor immune to contestation in antiquity.

In some respects, the mid-Heian is a dark age. The tenth century is "the most poorly documented in Japanese history."[1] A tremendous cache of documents preserved in the Shōsōin archive at Tōdaiji (Nara), as well as a growing body of excavated materials, provide vivid insight into the late seventh and eighth centuries, and a series of official court chronicles contain detailed information on the ninth century (albeit from a state-centered perspective). From the end of the eleventh century onward, temple archives across the archipelago have preserved an extraordinary corpus of records, contracts, and deeds. For the decades in between, however, historians are mostly forced to rely on a few extant diaries of prominent noblemen. Perhaps for this reason, the field of Japanese history has developed institutional biases against the period. To grossly generalize, scholars

1. Farris, "Famine, Climate, and Farming," 278.

of "ancient" (*kodai*) Japan draw on Shōsōin documents to track the rise of the early state, while historians of "medieval" (*chūsei*) Japan employ temple archives to understand the development of local power in agricultural estates.[2] The intervening period becomes a kind of historical penumbra into which all manner of "transitions" must be projected.

Ironically, for the academic field of Japanese literature, the position of the mid-Heian could not be more different. Scholars of "classical" (*chūko*) literature hatch innumerable articles every year on the *Tale of Genji*, the *Pillow Book*, and other esteemed classics, a reflection of the crucial position of the period in the history of writing in Japan. The transmission of Chinese writing to Japan took the form not simply of a disinterested technology of inscription (Sinographs), but was deeply imbricated with a highly developed written language (the "Sinoscript," as it has been labeled) and a canon of literary classics. In this context, learning to write meant and could only mean learning to write literary Chinese (though its use was often heavily influenced by the local language). Nevertheless, Chinese literary convention also made provision for transcribing foreign words phonetically, using Sinographs exclusively for their sound value (a technique frequently seen in Chinese Buddhist sutras, for example). Eighth-century Japanese texts show this technique applied to individual words and relatively short texts such as songs, but the mid-Heian saw the mobilization of a set of conventions (including specialized shorthand abbreviations and rules governing spelling and the use of ligatures) that allowed for the intelligibility of lengthy documents in a vernacular register.[3] The tenth and eleventh centuries witness a string of poetic and prose experiments in this new *kana* syllabary, even as literary Sinitic retained its superior cultural prestige.

Because of these developments in orthography and aesthetics, the canonical position of Heian literature is integral to the definition of "national literature" (*kokubungaku*) as an object of scholarly discourse, which in late nineteenth-century Japan was identified with "the written expression of a people's unique ideas, feelings, and imagination *in their*

2. Hotate, *Heian ōchō*, i.

3. For a lucid discussion of the preconditions for *kana* prose, see Komatsu, *Nihongo shokishi genron*, 57–80.

national language."[4] The first formulations of this newly conceived body of national literature therefore presented a tradition of vernacular literature written in *kana*, excluding writings in literary Sinitic.[5] The opposition to and overcoming of Sinographs could be said to be the central dynamic of this new literary history, "a plot in the form of a romance" with Chinese as the antagonist that blocked the Japanese *kokutai* (national essence) on its journey toward full expression.[6] The Heian period played a pivotal part in this narrative: Tomiko Yoda has shown how early *kokubungaku* posited the figure of the Heian aristocratic woman, ostensibly cut off from true Sinographic literacy and confined to the *kana* syllabary, as a "passive medium linking the prehistoric masculinity of the native and the transcendent masculinity of the nation."[7] Heian *kana* literature filled a structural need in the narrative of the *kokutai*'s struggle and actualization, synecdochic evidence of a pure Japanese voice, uncorrupted by the transformation and hybridization so evident in the extant Heian textual corpus. In this romance, the enormous body of literary Sinitic by premodern Japanese was a distraction, if not a tragedy.

While domestic literary Sinitic was thus largely excised from the new national literature curriculum, many *kokubungaku* scholars were eager to investigate what they perceived as the influence of Chinese culture on the native tradition. Particularly following World War II, a generation of scholars who had come of age during the peak of Japanese aggression in China brought a new emphasis to the crucial role played by the Chinese literary heritage in reshaping Japanese literature. By seeking source texts or rhetorical techniques translated into *kana* works, this "tradition and influence" model presented a native tradition that was regularly overwhelmed

4. From the 1890 *Nihon bungakushi* 日本文學史 (History of Japanese Literature), quoted in Brownstein, "From *Kokugaku* to *Kokubungaku*," 451 (emphasis added). Such definitions were heavily influenced by the Romantic nationalism of the eighteenth and nineteenth centuries, which held that "a country's literature which is original and national must form itself in accordance with such a nation's original native language." Herder, "Fragments on Recent German Literature" (1767–68), translated by Michael N. Forster in *Philosophical Writings*, 50.

5. See for example Haga Yaichi's 1890 *Kokubungaku tokuhon* 國文學讀本 (Reader in National Literature), described in Shirane, "Curriculum and Competing Canons," 237–39.

6. Brownstein, "From *Kokugaku* to *Kokubungaku*," 454.

7. Yoda, *Gender and National Literature*, 70.

by waves of a prestigious continental civilization, each time eventually succeeding at incorporating and transforming the latter. This model was inherited in early Western scholarship, but attempts to combat misapprehensions of Japanese cultural purity often conversely resulted in a quarantining off of "native" elements by identifying and labeling influences.[8] The influence model structurally necessitates a recoverable "Japanese culture" prior to Chinese intervention, and the resulting "tendentious search for anything that does not seem marked as 'foreign'" tends to produce an anachronistic illusion of prelapsarian purity.[9]

Even as *kokubungaku* discourse was incorporating a renewed recognition of adaptations and borrowings from Chinese sources in vernacular literature, beginning in the 1960s a group of scholars led by Kawaguchi Hisao, Kojima Noriyuki, and Ōsone Shōsuke, building on pioneering prewar work by Okada Masayuki, Kakimura Shigematsu, and Kaneko Hikojirō, began a reappraisal of literary Sinitic works that had been excised from the "national language" model of *kokubungaku*.[10] Instead of measuring (and dismissing) local literary Sinitic by its capacity or failure to conform to Chinese norms, these scholars and their followers argued that the script and knowledge imported from China eventually became a "self-contained tradition" in Japan, with authors who looked to earlier Japanese models and teachers, often deviating from continental practices.[11]

The local life of Chinese literary lore and forms is a repeated theme of Sei Shōnagon's 清少納言 *Pillow Book* (*Makura no sōshi* 枕草子, ca. 1005). The following passage describes an encounter in the seventh month, the time of the autumn Tanabata Festival:

8. See Richard Okada, "Translation and Difference," a critique of Helen C. McCullough's *Brocade by Night*.

9. LaMarre, *Uncovering Heian Japan*, 3.

10. Though these scholars' work was crucial to the reincorporation of the literary Sinitic corpus into the discursive field of "Japanese literature" (*kokubungaku*) in the 1960s and 1970s, their research was in dialogue with, and in many cases dependent on, the efforts of scholars working in other fields, including bibliography (Nagasawa Kikuya and Ōta Tsugio), Sinology (Kanda Kiichirō), history (Ōta Shōjirō), and historical linguistics (Tsukishima Hiroshi and Kobayashi Yoshinori).

11. Ury, "Chinese Learning," 389; Smits, "Way of the Literati," 108–10.

> The Advisor Middle Captain Tadanobu, Captain Nobukata, and Junior Counselor Michikata came by and were chatting with us. Apropos of nothing, I said, "So what will it be tomorrow?" To my delight, Tadanobu responded without the slightest hesitation, "I'll do 'In the fourth month in the human realm.'" It's always wonderful when someone remembers something long past like that, but especially so when it's a man—women generally aren't so forgetful, but men often barely remember the poems they themselves have sent you. Neither the other ladies nor Tadanobu's companions understood what he meant at all, and no wonder: Back at the beginning of the fourth month, many of the privy courtiers had gathered at the corridor's fourth entryway. One by one they departed, until only the Chamberlain Captain [Tadanobu], the Minamoto Captain, and a sixth-rank chamberlain were left, and together we talked, chanted sutras, and sang songs. At dawn they were making to depart, when Tadanobu declared, "This dew must be their tears of parting." He and the Minamoto Captain then chanted it together very beautifully, but when I said, "This is quite an early Tanabata!" they were terribly chagrined. "What a disgrace—I just said the first line about a dawn parting that occurred to me. It's such a mistake to ever speak without thinking around here!" he said, laughing uproariously. "Don't tell anyone, I'll be a laughingstock."[12]

This anecdote revolves around the quotation of poems (underlined in the quoted passage), occasional appropriateness, and wit. It begins with Tadanobu making the apparently nonsensical remark that for tomorrow's celebration of the autumn Tanabata Festival, he will recite a poem about the early-summer fourth month. A flashback then reveals that Tadanobu is referencing a gaffe he had made a few months earlier: as he left a gathering, he recited a line about dawn parting, but what was intended as a clever and romantic quotation was undercut when Sei Shōnagon pointed out that the line came from a poem on Tanabata (a festival associated with legends of the Weaver Maiden, who can meet her lover the Cowherd only once a year), while they were still at the beginning of summer. Three months later, now on the eve of the Tanabata Festival, he makes a joke of his earlier mistake by promising to recite a poem celebrating the fourth month.

12. *Makura no sōshi*, "Kotono no onpuku no koro," 285–86.

The episode provides a useful inventory of phenomena frequently brought up in arguments about the "domestication" of Chinese literary culture. First, we find appropriation of imported literary texts. Tadanobu's "fourth month" line is by the Tang poet Bai Juyi 白居易 (772–846), from a poem describing delight at finding peach blossoms (a spring sight) still blooming at a temple high in the mountains: "In the fourth month in the human realm [the secular world below the temple], the fragrant flowers are spent" 人間四月芳菲盡.[13] In Tadanobu's recitation, the poem's meaning has little relevance beyond its easily recognizable reference to early summer, and scholars have often noted a pattern of Chinese literature quoted out of context or simply for imagistic value in Heian works (a topic examined in more detail in chapter 3). In a few cases, however, Heian writers actively magnify the significance of Chinese sources, as can be seen in Murasaki Shikibu's 紫式部 (fl. 998–1014) creative and illuminating applications of Bai Juyi.[14]

Second, there is local production in forms within the Chinese literary tradition. The second quotation in the excerpt comes from a "Chinese" poem—a poem in the *shi* 詩 genre—by Sugawara no Michizane 菅原道眞 (845–903). Beginning in the late seventh century, large numbers of poems in literary Sinitic were produced and circulated in Japan, and by the mid-Heian, aspiring poets were often directed to study the works of these forebears, rather than only learn directly from Tang models.[15] In addition to individual poems and essays, Heian writers produced anthologies compiling selections from Chinese works (such as the mid-tenth-century *Senzai kaku*, which contains the Bai Juyi poem quoted above), locally produced works (*Honchō monzui*, discussed in chapter 2), or examples of both (*Wakan rōeishū*, which contains the Michizane line quoted, and which is discussed in chapter 3). The compilation of such anthologies, along with dictionaries and manuals to aid in composition, produced a distinctive local canon of literary Sinitic.

Finally, the linguistic status of script is also a key concern. In the passage above, the lines are not quoted in the Chang'an dialect of Chinese

13. "Dalinsi taohua" 大林寺桃花, in *Bai Juyi ji jianjiao* 16.1023.
14. See for example Fujiwara, "Genji monogatari to Hakushi bunshū."
15. See for example *Gōdanshō* 5.49.

or some other variety of Sinitic, but rather in vernacular Japanese phrases incorporating some Sino-Japanese vocabulary (that is, Chinese words whose pronunciation has been adapted to Japanese phonology, so-called *on'yomi*).[16] The widespread use of the Chinese script in Japan occurred in a context without sustained communities of native speakers of any Sinitic language; literary Sinitic functioned as a prestigious written idiom for speakers of an utterly different Japonic family of vernaculars, a condition similar to what Sheldon Pollock has defined as "hyperglossia," the highly compartmentalized yet parallel usage of a prestige language (Sanskrit, in the case of Pollock's research) with an entirely different local language (though as we shall see, the status of literary Sinitic as a "language" in Heian Japan is highly ambiguous).[17] As a consequence of this gap, the most common form of reading in mid-Heian Japan was the practice of *kundoku* 訓讀 ("reading by gloss"), through which literary Sinitic script was vocalized in a modified, hybrid vernacular speech. From the vantage point of script then, both Bai Juyi's and Michizane's poems can be characterized as "Chinese," but read aloud by Tadanobu, they are just as equally "Japanese."[18] The questions of how Heian writers acquired literacy, and how they conceived of the relationship between script and language, will be taken up in chapters 4 and 5.

The divergent path pursued by literary Sinitic in the mid-Heian is related to specific historical circumstances: eighth- and ninth-century Japanese officials might exchange poems with visiting continental emissaries or even travel overseas themselves, but with the disintegration of the Tang empire, followed by the fall of the northeastern state of Parhae in 926, the literary rituals of diplomacy temporarily disappeared from Japan. This was by no means the end of commerce with the continent—in fact, control of the trade with Song and Koryŏ merchants was a crucial component of the Fujiwara regency's power—but their presence was

16. Respectively, "Jinkan no shigetsu" 人間の四月 and "Tsuyu wa wakare no namida narubeshi" 露は別れの涙なるべし.

17. Pollock, *Language of the Gods*, 50. Pollock uses the term "hyperglossia" in contradistinction to the more typical "diglossia" split between literary and colloquial forms of the same language.

18. On the indeterminacy of linguistic affiliation in logographic writing, see Lurie, *Realms of Literacy*, 180–84.

largely limited to seaports.[19] Foreign interaction with the capital literary sphere was thus mostly limited to encounters between merchants and provincially stationed officials, and the books the latter sent back to wealthy patrons.[20] Capital officials had almost no interaction with representatives of continental culture, nor any realistic opportunity for their writings to be read outside their peer group.

Postwar research has therefore frequently emphasized the selectiveness of continental influence, with elements of Chinese civilization taken up or discarded in patterns that seem to bear little relation to their original context, so that "'China' became a construct that was only tangentially related to the state across the East China Sea."[21] This "construct" has been termed the "China within Japan," stressing the independent life and evolution pursued by Chinese cultural forms within Japan and the quasi-imaginary nature of their relationship to China itself. Yet in recent years, many scholars have begun to problematize the ready distinction between Chinese and Japanese cultural elements or between a "real" and "imaginary" China. Instead, they posit a "dialectical process" in which "Japan" and "China" (or Yamato and Kara—*wakan* 和漢 is the most common term in Japanese) figured as "antithetical but complementary terms," a "binary structure" intrinsic to the self-recognition of the subject.[22] Such approaches promise an escape from the paradigmatic cul-de-sac of "influence" versus "innovation." In actual analysis, however, the structure of this binary frequently reduces to figures of agonistic opposition: a "traumatic fracture in Japan between oral and literate representation," "the bipolar psychology of admiration versus reflexive self-defense," or "exotic infatuations."[23] Thus, like narratives of Japanese "selection" or "appropriation" of continental forms, dialectical analyses have struggled to avoid

19. On regency power and continental trade, see Hurst, "*Kugyō* and *Zuryō*," 93–94. For an overview of Japanese trade with the continent during the mid-Heian, see Verschuer, *Across the Perilous Sea*, 33–47.

20. For poems sent to a Song merchant by an official serving as governor of Echizen, see *Honchō reisō kanchū*, 131–32. For a chronological overview of the transmission of Chinese texts to Japan, see Kornicki, *Book in Japan*, 277–96.

21. Smits, "Way of the Literati," 109. See also Pollack, *Fracture of Meaning*, 57.

22. Pollack, *Fracture of Meaning*, 227; Chino, "Gender in Japanese Art," 22–25.

23. Pollack, *Fracture of Meaning*, 11; Denecke, "Chinese Antiquity," 121; Sakaki, *Obsessions with the Sino-Japanese Polarity*, 19.

ascribing to culture a kind of collective agency, too easily identified with a trans-historical Japanese nation defined through its difference from the continental other.[24]

This study attempts to shift the terms of debate by abandoning the attempt to analyze composition in literary Sinitic genres as a nexus of interaction between the a priori abstractions of "Chinese culture" and "Japanese culture," and instead examining the processes by which categories of "literary," "vernacular," or "erroneous" inscription are defined within a synchronic field of cultural production that includes both texts themselves and the practices of commission, composition, recitation, and interpretation through which they were realized. I begin from the premise that the employment of script and literary form by Heian officials was multivalent and transitory, not susceptible to analysis in terms of an overarching relationship with the Chinese other running through Japanese literary production. There are (multiple) *wakan* binaries at work in Heian texts, but such oppositions have to be contextualized in relation to other definitional categories that are marshaled as provisional tactics in a continuous process of differentiation. The extant corpus of Heian writing provides vivid documentation of the repeated attempts and failures to fix such binaries, which play out on a field of complex semiotic possibility through the interaction of two basic principles:

1. Technically and practically speaking, writing and literacy in the Heian court were not characterized by a hard boundary between the Japanese and Chinese languages. Literacy based on *kundoku*, which deciphered Sinographs in terms of vernacular language, ensured that all writing—whether it adopted the grammar and lexicon of literary Sinitic, the syllabic transcription of *kana*, or some combination thereof—took place upon a spectrum of potentially infinite gradation and variation. However,

24. As Naoki Sakai points out, the fallacy here is not the premise of a relationally defined subject, but rather the presentation of such processes of identification through the foreign other as explicable in terms of a historical experience unique to Japan. "Modernity and Its Critique," 100–102. Recently, Wiebke Denecke has conversely posited a trans-national structure of engagement with an older "reference culture" in both early Japan and ancient Rome (*Classical World Literatures*).

2. The educated elite nevertheless worked to *establish* distinctions and oppositions—between native and foreign poetic forms, masculine and feminine calligraphic styles, orthodox and barbarous prose, and so on—which were treated *as if* they were natural. These are not necessary or essential differences, but ideological products generated through the reproduction of social hierarchy.

To put it in the broadest terms, the production of meaning proceeds through a dynamic of differentiation, in which formal potentials (lexical, grammatical, orthographic, vocal, etc.) are regulated and closed off. The use of literary Sinitic genres of verse and parallel prose by Heian officials offers a particularly visible confrontation between writing's underlying hybridity and the anxious desire to limit its potential for deviation and polysemy, thereby securing the social goals of inscription.

My attention to the dynamics of differentiation is indebted to the work of Thomas LaMarre, who sought to counter the anachronistic treatment of Heian literary works as phonetic transcriptions of an ethnolinguistic community, instead reading Heian poetics as generating a productive zone of indeterminacy—a "perpetual contest of doubles." This critique of a nation-based, phonocentric imaginary proceeds through analysis of literary texts as fundamentally figural, "a-grammatical" rebuses, and thus ultimately deprivileges linguistic signification in favor of a pre-discursive realm of sensation.[25] A useful corrective is offered by David Lurie's recent work on the history of writing in Japan. Where the traditional accounts LaMarre attacks focused on the importance of *kana* as a system of "phonographs" (each graph signifying a sound), Lurie's analysis centers on the notion of the "logograph," the use of a graph to signify a word or morpheme. Lurie shows that the use of writing in early Japan expanded concurrently with literacy techniques in which Sinographs were read as signifiers of semantic equivalents in the local language(s). Thus the grammatical order of inscription could be shaped by Chinese models studied in literacy education, but also by the writer's own native language, or elements of both, and in its use as a tool of communication and record among a community of Japonic speakers, writing frequently

25. LaMarre, *Uncovering Heian Japan*, 15–25, 41–49, and passim; Richard Okada, review of *Uncovering Heian Japan*.

deviated from Chinese norms of grammar and orthography.[26] Like LaMarre, Lurie conceives of writing without an *essential* linguistic affiliation (since a logographic text can be vocalized in multiple languages), but while such inscription is certainly not a transparent transcription of spoken language, as *logo*graphy it can likewise never be innocent of or prior to linguistic structures of communication. The question is how to engage with inscriptions as both historically pre-determined (grammatically, figurally, vocally), yet also as themselves the determining instrument by which arbitrary realities are misrecognized as aesthetic, cosmological, or political order. The chapters that follow thus seek to analyze how the "literary" (no less than the "Tang" or the "Yamato") functioned not simply as a normative value (as expressed, for example, in theoretical writings on poetics), but as the secondary effect of a web of practices operating across all levels of the representational act (social recognition as a poet, vocal performance in ritualized settings, form and symbolism within the text, etc.).[27]

The multivalent strategies of literacy in early Japan make analytical terminology a particularly vexing problem, and scholars have often argued over how to label the work of Japanese authors writing in Sinitic modes. In contemporary Japanese scholarship such writing is normally labeled as "*kanbun*" 漢文 (Han writing), a general term sometimes given the qualifier "*Nihon kanbun*" to distinguish local compositions from the broader corpus of literary Chinese. In Anglophone scholarship, J. Timothy Wixted has proposed the term "Sino-Japanese" to distinguish writing by Japanese authors, which frequently shows traces of their native language, from texts written by Chinese authors.[28] More recently, Peter Kornicki has lucidly critiqued the easy identification of text with nation or even language, providing a series of examples of works written by Korean and Japanese authors that circulated "as Chinese" in China and across East Asia.[29] Conversely, Lurie's work shows how even texts originating in China

26. Lurie, *Realms of Literacy*, 169–212 and passim.

27. The turn to embodied practice as a corrective to rationalistic theories of ideology is closely associated in cultural studies with the work of Pierre Bourdieu (*Outline of a Theory of Practice*), whose work in turn was influenced by Louis Althusser's analysis of ideology's "material existence" (see for example *Lenin and Philosophy*, 112–15).

28. Wixted, "*Kanbun*, Histories."

29. Kornicki, "A Note on Sino-Japanese."

could be read logographically in a register of Japanese. This emphasis on the trans-regional, trans-linguistic potential of Sinographic inscription accords with Victor Mair's postulation of "Literary Sinitic" (*wenyan* 文言) as a more-or-less self-contained system that early on diverges from vernacular speech in China and travels freely in other linguistic communities.[30] The historically contingent and multivalent set of signifying practices by which Sinographs in fact functioned as a trans-regional means of communication, however, should be distinguished from the ideal of a perfectly universal Sinoscript, which existed not in practice but as the aim of prescriptive discourse and canon-based education, fighting a rearguard battle against language change and diversity. The analyses below generally make reference to writing "in literary Sinitic" as a term of convenience to distinguish from the better known corpus of literature in *kana*-based Japanese idioms, but as chapter 5 shows, the definitions of what in fact constituted graphical and literary orthodoxy were under active construction and contestation in the mid-Heian. When it is necessary to refer to the native languages spoken by the authors of the documents examined below, I will use the anachronistic and over-generalized terms "Chinese" and "Japanese" for simplicity's sake. Finally, when discussing Heian recitation practices that mimicked Chinese phonology, I will refer to "Sinitic(-derived) pronunciation"; as will be detailed in chapter 4, the pronunciation employed in such recitation attempted to reproduce a prestige dialect imagined as Chang'an Chinese, but by the mid-Heian was heavily influenced by Japanese phonology.

The five chapters that follow treat the production and circulation of literary Sinitic poetry and parallel prose among mid-Heian officialdom, moving from panoramic identification of literature in its social context to close-up analysis of the mechanics of Sinographic literacy. The first two chapters look at the social life of writing, situating literary composition within its attendant interpersonal relationships, goals, and venues. Chapter 3 moves to the works themselves, outlining the formal features of what Heian writers referred to as "patterned writing" (*bunshō* 文章) and the aesthetic standards that shaped its reception. Finally, the two concluding chapters assess the underlying preconditions of these writings, examining

30. Mair, "Written Vernacular in East Asia," 707–9.

the mechanics of literacy education and the formulation of the category of the literary through practices of recitation.

In order to examine the literary as quotidian practice rather than preconceived ideological construct, the chapters regularly return to the writings and career of one figure, Minamoto no Shitagō 源順 (911–83), embedding broader questions of cultural performance in individual historical experience. Shitagō is a particularly useful heuristic device because of the length and breadth of his career. Born into a declining family (his great-grandfather was the son of Emperor Saga [r. 809–23], but his father failed to attain noble rank), Shitagō became a student at the State Academy as an entryway into officialdom. However, his career seems to have been crippled by a lack of consistent support at court: he was not able to advance into the bureaucracy until his forties, and after one governorship, spent almost a decade without office in the 970s. Shitagō's struggling career is in some ways typical of the declining status of regular officialdom in the mid-Heian, in response to which educated officials often sought to use scribal service as a means to establish lucrative patronage relationships with the upper nobility. In the case of Shitagō, however, this search for patrons generated a fascinating assembly of the diversity of mid-Heian literature, as he produced, in addition to a range of literary Sinitic documents, *waka* poetry, an encyclopedia, and allegedly a work of vernacular fiction.

Chapter 1 draws on this last work to introduce mid-Heian capital society and the circulation of literature within it. The surprisingly understudied *Utsuho monogatari* 宇津保物語 (Tale of a Tree Hollow, late tenth century) is the earliest extant long narrative in *kana* prose, and paints a satirical portrait of declining nobility, nouveau-riche provincial administrators, and impoverished students. One of the tale's central plots, the courtship and marriage of a powerful noble's daughter, maps out a social topography strictly divided between insiders and outsiders, but reconciled through rituals of reciprocity. At the banquets that served as the most prominent sites of exchange, poetry and other literary forms circulated alongside the gifts, favors, and marriages that structured capital society. An anonymously circulating work of fiction, *Utsuho monogatari* itself stands outside the field of publicly recognized literature examined in the rest of the study, but this liminal position allows for a uniquely penetrating representation of the struggles over service and commensurability at the core of mid-Heian cultural production.

The mid-Heian period examined in this study, roughly the early tenth through mid-eleventh centuries, corresponds to a flourishing of household record-keeping by the nobility, and chapter 2 draws upon these diaries to reconstruct the specific processes by which literary works circulated in networks of exchange.[31] The most prestigious venue for literary composition was court ceremony, which often made use of ritual documents in parallel prose, or celebrated with group composition in regulated verse. The mid-Heian, however, witnessed a reconfiguration of ritual space, which broke down official distinctions between public and private and centered ceremony on the person of the emperor, limiting direct participation to the inner circle of the oligarchy. Literary writing by lower-ranked officials, increasingly excluded from court ceremony, came to be understood as a technical skill of limited value. As seen in the mid-eleventh-century *Honchō monzui* 本朝文粋 (Literary Essence of This Court), the most canonical anthology of mid-Heian literary Sinitic prose, the literary sphere was defined through transactions of commission, in which skilled authors provided documents for use in rituals from which they were often excluded. The production of literary works thus simultaneously produced hierarchical relationships of obligation and relative prestige, which officials sought to exploit for practical advantages.

Chapter 3 turns to consider the formal dimension of Heian literary Sinitic, drawing on the evaluative and prescriptive discourse on "patterned writing" preserved in the mid-Heian composition manual *Sakumon daitai* 作文大體 (Essentials of Composition) and commentaries on the couplet anthology *Wakan rōeishū* 和漢朗詠集 (Collection of Japanese and Chinese Verses for Chanting, ca. 1012). The discussion of literary aesthetics (in both poetic and parallel prose genres) repeatedly emphasizes two rhetorical strategies: *hadai* ("topic decomposition"), the exposition

31. Diaries cited in this study include *Teishin-kō ki* (907–48), by Fujiwara no Tadahira; *Rihō ō ki* (920–53), by Prince Shigeakira; *Kyūreki* (930–60), by Fujiwara no Morosuke; *Shōyūki* (982–1032), by Fujiwara no Sanesuke; *Gonki* (991–1011), by Fujiwara no Yukinari; *Midō kanpaku ki* (998–1021), by Fujiwara no Michinaga; *Sakeiki* (1009–39), by Minamoto no Tsuneyori; and *Shunki* (1026–54), by Fujiwara no Sukefusa. The practice of diary-keeping by the nobility is taken up in detail in chapter 4.

on an assigned topic through restatement and circumlocution; and *jukkai* ("divulging feeling"), a formalized conclusion that describes the poet's humble gratitude at receiving the sponsor's favor, which gradually became associated with a discourse of aging and unrewarded virtue. Instructions on *hadai* rhetoric describe a compositional mode focused on technical flash and erudite one-upmanship, with group composition treated as an extension of the competitive format of the civil service examination. The supplication discourse of *jukkai* represents an alternative strategy that posited a direct relationship between poet and patron, but contemporary records suggest it was less effective as a device of differentiation than as the basis for a shared affective experience. Attention to these rhetorical modes shows how the essentially opportunistic strategies of individual actors could coalesce as a seemingly rigid devotion to formal aesthetic principles.

The literary activities discussed in these chapters are premised on a base of shared literacy, extending from basic character recognition to more abstract cultural knowledge. Chapter 4 examines the institutional structures that fostered classical education among officialdom. The question of Heian women's literacy or lack thereof has received considerable scholarly attention, but such arguments have often proceeded from a very abstract image of male literacy in the period, which this chapter aims to correct through examination of education both within and without the court's official organ of higher learning, the State Academy. Contemporary records and manuscript marginalia reveal a path of learning that proceeded from early-childhood rote memorization of Chinese primers, through *kundoku* recitation methods based on vocalizing literary Sinitic texts in vernacular language, culminating in interpretation of canonical works through imported commentaries. Classical education was exported to the homes of the nobility, who employed academy graduates as private household tutors. This admittance was not a wholesale adoption, however; noble families relied heavily on orally transmitted ritual knowledge for their cultural capital, challenging the academy's model of knowledge based on textual authority.

The reliance on *kundoku*-based literacy revealed in chapter 4 severely complicates the historical significance of Heian literary Sinitic, and chapter 5 takes up these implications by returning to the scene of literature's ritual use to consider literary works as vehicles for performance. Evidence shows that even literary genres that appear to conform exactly to Chinese models were primarily recited through *kundoku* in the Heian period, meaning that in performance many of the formal characteristics of "patterned writing" (particularly rhyme and tonal prosody) would be effaced. This chapter analyzes the fragile distinctions between literary and nonliterary as well as Sinitic and vernacular genres by examining surviving examples of one genre that seems to sit on the border between these categories, the property commendation. Such documents initially made extensive use of literary rhetoric, but increasingly abandoned it as they were required to incorporate more vernacular legal terminology. This tendency suggests a conscious rejection of colloquial language within literary inscription, a move that is repeated in the encyclopedia *Wamyō ruijushō* 和名類聚抄 (Categorical Miscellany of Yamato Names, ca. 934), which delineates a lexicon of orthodox inscription that is vocalized through a highly rarified and archaic vernacular. Heian literary Sinitic is thus paradoxically both embedded in a Japanese vernacular idiom and defined through its rejection of a register of lower, "colloquial" language.

The chapters that follow provide a detailed introduction to an important body of writing hitherto mostly ignored in English-language scholarship, but more importantly, seek to reconceptualize its place in the larger history of literature and inscription in Japan and East Asia. Modern histories tend to treat the development of phonographic writing in early Japan as inevitable and organic, but quirks of early *kana* documents suggest instead a laborious process of technological experimentation, and multiple modes of inscription remained the norm in Japan until the turn of the twentieth century.[32] This book reconsiders the continuum between works "written in Chinese" and the vernacular literary tradition by demonstrating that the division between the two was a calculated and fragile conceit with specific social origins. The literature of Heian Japan is a project that aims at naturalizing the relationships between language, script, social identity, and aesthetics, but it can never completely remove the possibility of contestation and redefinition.

32. On early *kana* inscription, see especially Okumura, "Kana monjo no seiritsu izen" and "Kana monjo no seiritsu izen, zoku." On the multivalent discourse of late nineteenth-century Japan, see Lee, *Ideology of Kokugo*, 7–53.

ONE

Gifts and Governors

Heian Capital Society in *Utsuho monogatari*

Like employees in any bureaucracy, Heian officials knew their place on a ladder of potential advancement and demotion. In literary works like the *Tale of Genji*, the acute awareness of status variation is manifested in the complex combinations and fine gradations of honorific and humilific language that characterize the dialogue. Onto a relatively one-dimensional hierarchy of status, however, was mapped an intricate web of vertical and horizontal alliances, as well as rivalries. Military and fiscal administration, personnel decisions and marriage politics, religious observances and artistic productions were all dependent upon and at times motivated by these partnerships and factions.

One of the central goals of this study is to model the cultural field surrounding literary Sinitic genres in mid-Heian Japan in its historical specificity. This chapter examines the late tenth-century *Utsuho monogatari* (Tale of a Tree Hollow), a fictional narrative attributed to Minamoto no Shitagō, to develop a framework for treating literary production as part of a network of material and performative exchange structuring Heian capital society. I begin with an overview of the changes overtaking rank, office, and extralegal power structures in the mid-Heian, which combined to disenfranchise lower officialdom, before examining how this social stratification serves as a theme in *Utsuho monogatari*. If reorganization of the bureaucracy threatened to alienate non-noble officials and even the lower nobility from the ruling oligarchy, in *Utsuho* this threat is countered through repeated acts of gift giving and exchange that serve to reaffirm vertical alliances.[1] Historians have shown that with the rise of the *zuryō* tax farmer as the primary intermediary between capital and province in the mid-Heian, central finances came to be organized through mechanisms of commission and reciprocal service, but *Utsuho* extends this web of exchange to social interactions and cultural production throughout capital officialdom. It thus suggests a model through which the commission, production, and circulation of literary Sinitic documents in particular can be examined in chapter 2. The chapter concludes by exploring how this sociality of exchange, glorified through much of the narrative, is ultimately challenged at the tale's climax, a rare voice of repudiation that will be pursued further in chapter 3's treatment of the literature of complaint.

The Stratification of Heian Officialdom

The Heian state inherited a model of sovereignty in which the will of the emperor was effected through a complex bureaucracy. At the head of this bureaucracy were the senior nobles (*kugyō*), representatives of several powerful *uji* kinship groups in Nara times but increasingly dominated by a few households in the Heian, who convened at the Council of State (Daijōkan). The relationship between the sovereign and the council was strategically ambiguous; theoretically, the emperor exercised dictatorial power, but he required the cooperation of the council for the drafting and promulgation of edicts. In mid-Heian practice, most day-to-day administrative decisions were made by whichever ranking senior noble (the *shōkei*) was in attendance, with difficult questions where precedent was unclear referred to the emperor (or his regent) for final judgment. The council as a body (as few as eleven men in the early ninth century, and as many as twenty-four by the late eleventh century) met relatively rarely, when the emperor sought their consultative opinion on important

1. On vertical alliances, see Kiley, "Estate and Property in the Late Heian Period," 109–14.

matters.[2] These "Guard-Post Judgments" debated governorship evaluations, foreign relations, and tax law in the mid-Heian.[3] However, such judgments legally only served a consultative function. The council thus held practical authority over the bureaucracy, but this authority was sharply bounded by precedent and the will of the emperor.

The bureaucracy underneath the council and the method of its administration were both changing dramatically in the mid-Heian. In the first place, the rank system established in the administrative code became increasingly hollowed out. This system defined nine ranks (with numerous subdivisions), with officials of third rank and above (effectively, the Council of State) as "nobles" (*ki*) and those of fourth and fifth rank (the heads and deputies of various bureaus and ministries, as well as governors of some important provinces) as "provisional nobles" (*tsūki*). These men were granted an array of benefits marking them out from the rest of officialdom, most notably additional salary and automatic ranks for their sons (*on'i*). The result of this overemphasis on the division between fifth and sixth rank was a simplification of the rank system. By the turn of the eleventh century, the bottom ranks of the bureaucracy had disappeared: men with named offices in the bureaucracy were almost all of senior sixth rank upper (the highest rank below fifth), assisted by various unranked functionaries (*zōnin*).[4] Early in the Heian period, the Council of State abandoned its evaluation system for approving advancement to fifth-rank-noble status, which came to be determined largely by seniority within particular offices, effectively removing the independent meaning of rank for the vast bulk of officialdom.[5]

Concurrently, the code-defined structure of bureaucratic office was undergoing massive revision. Three trends stand out in particular: First, the tendency for sons to succeed their fathers in administrative positions—already evident in the eighth century—continued to grow. Despite the

2. On the petition (*mōshibumi*) and judgment (*sadame*) administrative procedures that characterized the early and mid-Heian council, see Hashimoto Yoshihiko, *Heian kizoku*, 91–97; Soga, *Ōchō kokka seimu*, 14–57.

3. On the Council of State and Guard-Post Judgments (*jin no sadame*), see William H. McCullough, "Heian Court," 42; Hurst, "*Kugyō* and *zuryō*," 77–83; Mikawa, *Insei no kenkyū*, 15–39.

4. Kuroita, *Heian ōchō no kyūtei shakai*, 63–64.

5. Yoshikawa, *Ritsuryō kanryōsei no kenkyū*, 362–68.

establishment of the State Academy (Daigakuryō) as an institutional mechanism for reproducing the bureaucracy, household transfer of professional knowledge seems to have functioned more effectively.[6] Second, the bureaucracy became drastically simplified, with the original chain of command under the bureaus and ministries replaced by direct administration of offices by the controllers (*ben*) or secretaries (*geki*) of the Council of State, who reported to a particular senior noble with oversight over that office.[7] The four grades of administrative office (*kami*/*suke*/*jō*/*sakan*) became functionally obsolete, with most offices organized around a titular head from among the nobility, one or two low-ranked officials (called "annual charges," *nen'yo*) in charge of the actual administration, and a staff of unranked functionaries.[8] The third and most important change, however, was undoubtedly the bureaucracy's budgetary problems. The court had increasing difficulty allocating sufficient funds to pay officials' salaries, and by the mid-tenth century, centrally distributed salary for lower-ranked officials (always inadequate) had dried up completely. One attempt to address this problem was the allocation of land grants for particular offices, beginning in the late ninth century, which eventually created a system whereby offices were individually funded through privately managed estates.[9] The "tree" organization of the bureaucracy was thus flattened out, with many semi-independent offices each with a direct relationship to the council.

In the late Heian period, this method of finance would develop into the well-studied medieval *ie* system, whereby offices became sinecures belonging to particular households. Already in the mid-Heian, however, the bulk of officialdom effectively became retainers to either powerful

6. This tendency can already be seen in the Nara bureaucracy's heavy reliance on continental immigrant lineages (Inoue Kōji, "Daijōkan benkankyoku," 115–17). Note, however, that at least by the eleventh century, the maintenance of official lineages proceeded through adoption as much as through actual bloodline inheritance (Soga, *Ōchō kokka seimu*, 188–204).

7. Tamai, *Heian jidai no kizoku*, 12–20, 30–34; Nakahara, *Chūsei ōken*, 12–22. This structure was mirrored in the temporary "event offices" (*gyōjisho*) that managed annual ceremonies. Ōtsu, *Ritsuryō kokka shihai kōzō*, 249–63.

8. Kon, "Kanshi un'ei no tokushitsu," 9–23.

9. William H. McCullough, "Heian Court," 46; Satō Shin'ichi, *Nihon no chūsei kokka*, 43; Yoshikawa, *Ritsuryō kanryōsei no kenkyū*, 370–74; Ōtsu, *Michinaga to kyūtei shakai*, 217–20.

noble households or estate-funded offices. Officials clustered around these manors and offices, forming crowded neighborhoods that accelerated the urbanization of the northeast quadrant of Heian-kyō.[10] Through favored sponsorship from a senior noble or seniority in their office, they might ultimately be granted fifth rank and thus noble status, but otherwise they were largely invisible to the central administration. Increasingly, the Heian elite were split in two, with an accompanying division of labor: the nobility, who took center stage in imperial and religious ceremonies, and the lower-ranked officials, in charge of government administration.

Just as the Council of State adopted simplified forms of administration, the imperial household too developed a more direct interface with the bureaucracy outside codified procedure. The most visible feature of this transition was the establishment in the ninth century of several new offices under the direct control and appointment of the emperor, in particular the regent (*sesshō* or *kanpaku*), the chamberlains (*kurōdo*), the imperial police (*kebiishi*), and the residential attendance (*shōden*) policy. The Chamberlains' Office was created around 810 as Emperor Saga sought to retrench control during a power struggle with his brother Heizei (r. 806–9). It quickly took over the day-to-day management of the imperial residence, largely superseding the female-staffed Rear Court Offices.[11] The chamberlains were selected from nobles posted in the most important of the capital offices, giving the emperor a representative at each, and by the end of the eleventh century, ranked capital offices were almost all assigned based on petitions submitted through the Chamberlain's Office.[12] The imperial police force was begun around the same time, absorbing the soldiers and equipment of the palace gate guards (Emonfu) and supplanting the security role of the Capital Office (Kyōshiki).[13] Residential attendance was not an office as such, but rather admission to the emperor's living quarters (generally the Seiryōden from the late ninth century onward) within the residential palace. The number of these attendant "courtiers" (*tenjōbito*) included the chamberlains (nine to ten men), almost all senior

10. Toda, *Shoki chūsei shakaishi*, 178–80.

11. Yoshikawa, *Ritsuryō kanryōsei no kenkyū*, 104.

12. Tamai, *Heian jidai no kizoku*, 286–88.

13. Satō Shin'ichi, *Nihon no chūsei kokka*, 11–24. For a detailed description of the *kebiishi*, see Farris, *Heavenly Warriors*, 166–69.

nobles, plus any other fourth- or fifth-ranked nobles the sovereign chose to favor (perhaps a dozen men in the tenth century, and swelling to thirty-seven on one occasion in the early twelfth century).[14] As both ceremonial and administrative procedures increasingly moved within the residential palace after the ninth century (a development discussed further in chapter 2), it became necessary to assign "office directors" (*bettō*) to many offices from among the courtiers, who could freely move in and out of the palace.[15]

All of these posts created relationships of personal obligation with the emperor that were progressively systematized. While residential attendance began as permission extended by the sovereign to individuals, it quickly became a semi-official position with quotas and associated expectations: Emperor Uda (r. 887–97) established a system of "daily attendance tablets" in which all courtiers were registered, and their regular appearance (reported monthly) determined rank promotions.[16] Similar forms of obligatory "service" (*yaku*)—in the form of material and labor for ceremonies—were demanded of senior nobles and provincial governors as well.[17] Even as the administrative structure of bureaucracy became increasingly segmented, a small circle of elite office-holders were harnessed to relationships of personal obligation to the sovereign based on favor received and service rendered.

It was precisely the mismatch between these new posts and the codified rank/office system that gave them their alliance-strengthening potency (fig. 1). Originally, the most important division within officialdom lay between nobles holding fifth rank and officials below that, but generally half of the emperor's chamberlains were men of sixth rank. Sixth-rank chamberlains were granted fifth rank after six years of service, but this meant giving up their position as chamberlain, and the acquisition of noble status could seem a poor replacement for the loss of residential attendance rights, especially as the number of nobles swelled in the second half of the Heian period: Sei Shōnagon comically describes the pathetic sight of a "former-chamberlain fifth rank" who fills his empty

14. Fukui, "Heianchō ni okeru jige," 41–43; *Chōya gunsai* 5.112–16.
15. Kon, "Ōchō kokka chūō kikō," 158–60.
16. Furuse, *Nihon kodai ōken*, 344–46.
17. Endō, *Chūsei ōken*, 98–99.

days going to Buddhist sermons.[18] Similarly, the senior nobles on the Council of State ostensibly stood at the peak of the aristocracy, but a man excluded from the emperor's inner circle (those referred to in the *Tale of Genji* as "mere senior nobles," *namanama no kandachime*) had little influence. In rare cases, such a figure might even suffer the indignity of not being granted courtier status, becoming a "base senior noble" (*jige no kandachime*).[19] While regular offices were held for a fixed term or until a promotion, chamberlains and courtiers served at the pleasure of the emperor. A new roll was announced with the accession of a new emperor, and courtiers were even automatically stripped of residential-attendance permission with any change in rank or office, thereby being forced to repeatedly seek "re-admittance."[20] Office directors seem to have usually kept their position across reigns, but they too had their appointment renewed at least ceremonially with a change in reign.[21]

This was true as well of the most important of the new offices, the regent, who advised the emperor on all judgments and even acted in his place when the latter was a minor. The office of the regent grew out of the older post of prime minister (*daijō daijin*), to which were added new powers deriving from the figure's blood relationship to the emperor (usually a maternal grandfather).[22] Under the legal framework of the Council of State, ministers (*daijin*) held office until death or retirement, but because a regent was defined by his family connection to the emperor, he had to be reappointed with a new accession.[23] The so-called "regency politics" of the mid-Heian is thus defined by a core alliance (both administrative and genetic)

18. *Makura no sōshi*, "Sekkyō no kōji wa," 73. By the medieval period, it became common for a sixth-rank chamberlain to forego promotion in order to retain his place in the Chamberlain's Office.

19. As power was concentrated in the emperor-regent clique, the subordination of senior nobles became increasingly obvious: at the 999 entrance to the palace of Michinaga's daughter Shōshi, eleven of the senior nobles escorted her as a kind of honor guard, leading Fujiwara no Sanesuke to remark in disgust that "the senior nobles of these latter days are no different from the common rabble." *Shōyūki*, Chōhō 1/11/2 (2:68).

20. Fukui, "Heianchō ni okeru jige," 42–44.

21. Furuse, *Nihon kodai ōken*, 407.

22. On regents in the mid-Heian, see Piggott, "What Did a Regent Do?" For an overview of the institutional development of the office, see Tamai, *Heian jidai no kizoku*, 6–12.

23. Hashimoto Yoshihiko, *Heian kizoku*, 88.

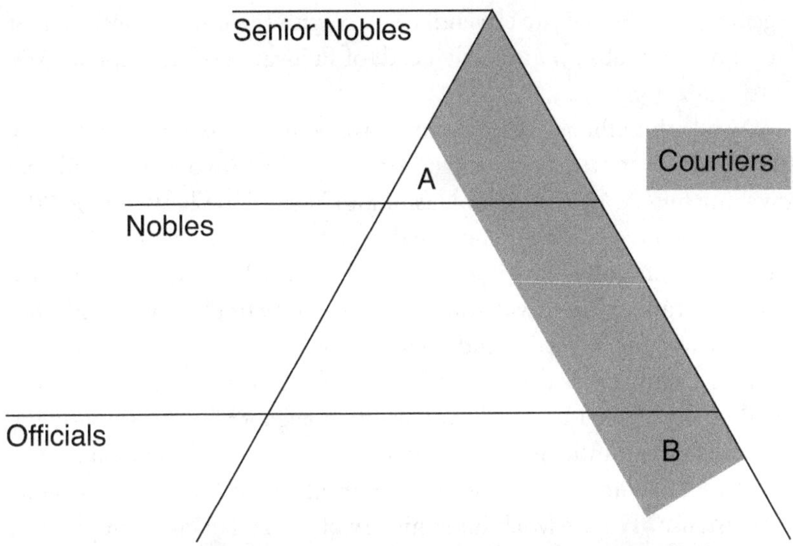

FIG. 1 Code-based rank divisions and the advent of "courtier" (*tenjōbito*) status. Residential attendance permission divided the nobility between courtiers and administrative nobles (including *zuryō*). It also created ambiguous positions, such as non-courtier senior nobles (A) or non-noble courtiers (B).

between two of the most powerful households in the archipelago—the imperial family and the Fujiwara Northern Branch—neutralizing procedural checks and the potential for conflict between crown and council.[24] The grand bargain at the seat of this alliance can be seen in Emperor Daigo's (r. 897–930) appointment of Fujiwara no Tadahira 藤原忠平 (880–949) as regent for the sickly child-emperor Suzaku (Tadahira's nephew, r. 930–46) in 930, just before Daigo's demise, with the imperial household still reeling from the deaths of two successive crown princes.[25] The partnership and intermarriage between the descendants of Daigo and Tadahira would become the fulcrum of court politics until the decline of

24. On the "regency politics" framework, see Hashimoto Yoshihiko, *Heian kizoku*, 60–70; Morita, "Toward Regency Leadership."

25. On this series of events, which was seen as revenge by the ghost of Sugawara no Michizane, see Borgen, *Sugawara no Michizane*, 308–14. On Daigo ordering Suzaku to abide by Tadahira's judgment, see *Rihō ō ki*, Enchō 8/9/26 (42).

regency power in the late eleventh century with the unlikely accession of Go-Sanjō (r. 1068–73) and early death of Fujiwara no Moromichi 藤原師通 (1062–99).

While this alliance based on marriage politics thus appears relatively stable from a macro perspective, for the players involved it could be anything but. As the historian Hashimoto Yoshihiko bluntly put it, "the history of Fujiwara development and expansion is simultaneously a history of schism and competition."[26] The Heian nobility did not practice primogeniture, so there was always the possibility of the younger brother outmaneuvering his elder and seizing control of the line of descent.[27] Although retrospective accounts have emphasized the tremendous personal power of men like Fujiwara no Michinaga 藤原道長 (966–1027), who radiated his influence over the world below like "a full moon uncovered by any cloud," these tend to treat accidents of fortune as foregone conclusions.[28] Hotate Michihisa's history of the Heian court emphasizes instead the anxious fragility of sovereignty at this time. When the line of succession split between the brothers Reizei (r. 967–69) and En'yū (r. 969–84) in the late tenth century, prospective regents such as Fujiwara no Kaneie 藤原兼家 (929–90) and his sons Michitaka 道隆 (953–95) and Michinaga found that they now needed to marry off their daughters into not one but two different royal lineages in order to ensure a stable relationship with the throne. Even despite such measures, human physiology could be uncooperative: when the ill-fated Prince Sanehito 實仁親王 was born in 1071, he was the first (recognized) son born to a sitting emperor in over sixty years.[29] The arbitrariness of fortune that raised one house above another must have been especially clear to Michinaga, the youngest son brought to power by a smallpox epidemic. He once remarked that

26. Hashimoto Yoshihiko, *Heian kizoku*, 105.

27. Minamoto no Shitagō seems to have been a victim of such a feud: his early career is marked by service to the family of Fujiwara no Morosuke, but after Morosuke's death, maneuvering among his sons erupted in the so-called "Anna Incident" of 969, in which Minister of the Left Minamoto no Takaakira, Morosuke's son-in-law and Shitagō's patron, was exiled from the capital. Shitagō subsequently spent the 970s without office. See my "Poetic Ministers," 205–12.

28. For Michinaga's famous poem comparing his glory to the full moon, see *Shōyūki*, Kannin 2 (1018)/10/16 (5:55).

29. Hotate, *Heian ōchō*, 126, 162.

if Emperor Reizei had not been born, "right now we'd be household retainers, clearing paths and running errands."[30]

If the above description paints a portrait of an oligarchy prone to infighting, teetering atop an increasingly disenfranchised officialdom, history shows that this power structure was remarkably stable, even surviving largely intact through the rise of eastern warrior power after the twelfth century.[31] The mid-Heian tale *Utsuho monogatari* presents these tendencies toward social entropy as counteracted through centripetal forces realized in patterns of exchange and reciprocity, in forms of both economic transfer and cultural production.

Atemiya's Suitors: Insiders and Outsiders in *Utsuho monogatari*

As status among the mid-Heian nobility became increasingly defined through proximity to an oligarchy centered on the emperor's household, the geographical imagination of access became a central motif in literature of the period, in which poets lament their exclusion from the court "above the clouds" and narratives romanticize the plight of highborn women raised in unforgivably provincial circumstances. The late tenth-century tale *Utsuho monogatari* thematizes a similar set of anxieties in its narrative of the courtship and marriage of Atemiya, daughter of a powerful senior noble, but represents the status-based disenfranchisement arising from these marriage politics as alleviated through rituals of gift exchange and communal literary performance. These ceremonies of exchange are overseen by senior nobles at the summit of capital society, but are materially dependent on the custodial governors (*zuryō*) of the provinces. In *Utsuho*, the recuperation of social equilibrium is ultimately accomplished through the ostracism of these custodian figures, scapegoats who both guarantee and critique the cycle of exchange that structures officialdom.

30. *Ōkagami*, 170.

31. On the continuation of Heian patterns of governance into the Kamakura period, see Mass, "Kamakura Bakufu."

Extending to twenty chapters (*kan* 巻), *Utsuho monogatari* is the earliest known tale of its scale in Japan. Like the *Tale of Genji*, which it preceded by at least two decades, it describes the lives and rivalries of the most powerful families in the capital elite, though because of the text's corruption and narrative discontinuities it rarely receives the same sort of attention for the title of "world's first novel." In the *Shimeishō* 紫明抄 (ca. 1294), a commentary on the *Genji*, the tale is attributed to Minamoto no Shitagō, though this attribution is naturally suspect, appearing as it does more than three centuries after Shitagō's death.[32] Based on the tale's subject matter and perspective, scholars generally agree that it must have been written by an educated man in the capital bureaucracy. Whereas the *Tale of Genji* presents a narrative voice situated among the personal attendants of the upper nobility, with a consequent emphasis on private space, the narrator of *Utsuho monogatari* speaks from the perspective of one of the courtiers, part of the daily action of court ceremony and yet a step removed from the royalty and senior nobles at the center of it.[33] Shitagō himself, though a direct descendant of the imperial household, was born into lower officialdom, and only entered the lower nobility late in life.[34] More important than the specific identity of the author (or more likely authors) of *Utsuho* is its unique voice, which presents a careful reckoning of debit and credit among the capital nobility.

Utsuho monogatari contains many subplots, and often gives the impression of a somewhat undigested assemblage of earlier narrative traditions, but the macro-level structure of the work is organized along two parallel narrative arcs. The first is a fantastical tale of music: Kiyohara no Toshikage, an envoy to the Tang court, is lost in a storm along the way and shipwrecked in "Persia" (Hashikoku). He encounters mysterious immortals and learns to play the *qin* (J. *kin*, a zither) from them, returning to Japan twenty-three years later after obtaining several magical instruments. After his death, his daughter is isolated, but through a

32. However, *Shimeishō* contains a great deal of Heian material, so the idea cannot be dismissed out of hand either. Inoue Yutaka, "Utsuho monogatari no sakusha," 287–88.

33. On the social positioning of the narrative voice in *Utsuho*, see Nakano, *"Utsuho monogatari" no kenkyū*, 240–45.

34. For records of Shitagō's grandfather Itaru and father Kozoru, see *Nihon sandai jitsuroku* Ninna 2 (886)/1/7 (603); *Sonpi bunmyaku*, 3:6. Timelines of Shitagō's life can be found in Okada Yoshio, "Minamoto no Shitagō"; and Kannotō, "Anna no hen."

chance encounter with a Fujiwara nobleman bears the latter's son, Nakatada, who is subsequently raised in the eponymous tree hollow and becomes one of the main protagonists of the tale. The central figure of the other extended narrative is Atemiya, the daughter of a powerful noble, whose hand in marriage is sought by an array of heroic, tragic, and ridiculous figures in a prototypical courtship tale. After she successfully weds the crown prince, the interest of the story turns to the political maneuvering to determine which of the prince's children will be named the next heir apparent. These stories meet but do not finally merge, since Nakatada's own courtship of Atemiya is unsuccessful. They can be seen as the tales of two different households: Nakatada trades on his musical ability to advance at court and ensure the secret teaching's transmission from his mother to his daughter, founding a new lineage, while Atemiya and her father Minamoto no Masayori strive to ensure the political supremacy of an already-established household by renewing their connection to the imperial line.[35]

Like historical figures contemporary to the work's composition, such as Fujiwara no Kaneie, Masayori is a powerful noble under pressure to sustain his lineage's success through marriage politics. A brother to the minister of the left, and senior councilor himself, he has a flourishing household, with two wives, twelve sons, and fourteen daughters, whose careers and connections are related in systematic detail.[36] His sons are advancing into posts in the Council of State and Chamberlain's Office, and his daughters are married to key political figures, including the current emperor and the minister of the right. His immediate political prosperity is assured—but the future is not so clear. Though one of Masayori's daughters is consort to the reigning emperor, her son by him was his third, and was not chosen as crown prince. The eldest son and crown prince was born to a Fujiwara mother, and this prince already has several consorts, none of whom are related to Masayori. The narrative makes clear that Masayori's success or failure at marrying his daughter Atemiya to a powerful figure, preferably the crown prince himself, will have enormous implications for the future of his household. Much of this plot's development takes place in a series of lavish banquets and excursions, mostly hosted by

35. Satō Atsuko, "Masayori-ke no seiritsu," 9.

36. *Utsuho monogatari*, "Fujiwara no kimi," 68–69.

Masayori, at which the guests partake of his hospitality and strive to win his approval or his daughter's attention. Eventually sixteen different men are identified as suitors of Atemiya in *Utsuho monogatari*, each contriving to send her poems through a lady-in-waiting, or petitioning her father directly. From the start, however, it is clear that it will not be a level playing field, as suitors are encouraged or ignored in direct proportion to their status. Princes and senior nobles receive replies from Atemiya and consideration from her father, while lower-ranked officials find their letters thrown away unread.[37]

While status dynamics thus lie at the heart of *Utsuho*'s narrative, in fact the most important division in Heian officialdom—between those party to the emperor/regent clique and those not—barely figures in the tale. Instead, the narrative of Atemiya's courtship takes place almost entirely within a narrowly circumscribed circle of insiders. As with the *Tale of Genji* and other classics of Heian literature, the action of the story is generally limited to the senior nobles and courtiers—who in the mid-Heian would have numbered perhaps three or four dozen men—and their families. The remainder of the nobility (approximately two to three hundred men of fifth rank and above), along with the thousands of officials and unranked functionaries who staffed the palace and bureaucracy—not to speak of the general populace—appear only around the edges of the narrative. The actors of the tale are almost all the children of senior nobles or princes. Even the suitors who are not taken seriously by Masayori—such as Yoshimine no Yukimasa, a renowned musician with a sixth-rank post in the Ministry of Ceremonial—are chamberlains to the emperor or otherwise permitted residential attendance. While *Utsuho*'s clear gradation of suitors thus on one level echoes the stratification of the official class into increasingly hardened caste divisions, its portrayal of a world composed exclusively of insiders at the same time effaces the reality of those divisions through fantasies of inclusion and social advancement. Atemiya's suitors are carefully differentiated based on their relative status, but access to this social circle of courtship and banquets is open to almost all the characters depicted in the tale.

A glaring example of this phantasmal inclusivity is the character Fujiwara no Suefusa, usually referred to by his literary sobriquet of Tōei.

37. Muroki, *Hyōgen to ronri*, 30–39.

Tōei is an orphaned and long-suffering student in the State Academy, the training ground for administrative officials. As will be discussed further in chapter 4, these students generally hoped to pass one of the civil service examinations, and thereby become eligible for an administrative post in a provincial governor's office. In *Utsuho*, however, Tōei's talents come to light when he has the opportunity to chant a poem at one of Masayori's banquets. Catching the host's ear, he goes on to describe his long toil in obscurity while less talented colleagues purchased promotions through money or influence. Within the space of a few months, he has sat for and passed the letters student examination, been promoted to noble status, and become tutor to the crown prince.[38] Though his courtship of Atemiya is never seriously entertained, Tōei is eventually allowed to marry one of Masayori's other daughters (as is Yukimasa), confirming his new place among the elite. Nevertheless, the rewards Tōei's talent receives are also implicitly dependent on the facts of his birth: though Tōei has been left orphaned and impoverished, his father was an advisor (*sangi*) on the Council of State, not a common official. In the world of *Utsuho*, even the administrative officials are always already insiders.

The Heian period was characterized by the formalization of an insider caste of senior nobles and courtiers, and the disenfranchisement of wider officialdom. Within *Utsuho monogatari*, this official class is not available for representation—the "officials" within the story are revealed to actually be nobles. In a kind of return of the repressed, however, the alienation of wider officialdom from the nobility is displaced onto a different object in *Utsuho*: the provincial custodian (*zuryō* 受領). Along with the princes and able social climbers introduced as Atemiya's suitors are three comic figures (traditionally referred to as the "three eccentrics"), whose ludicrous efforts to pursue Atemiya introduce an atmosphere of subversive absurdity: the Kanzuke prince, a recluse far removed from the line of succession; Miharu no Takamoto, another imperial son by a low-ranked woman who spends his life as a *zuryō*; and Shigeno no Masuge, an elderly advisor who rose up from serving as *zuryō* of Dazaifu. With Atemiya's final betrothal to the crown prince, her other suitors are mostly married off as well, their seemingly irrational desire ultimately resulting in interpellation into the new social order. Yet the efforts of these three men to win her are

38. *Utsuho monogatari*, "Matsuri no tsukai," 231, "Kiku no en," 313.

conversely repelled with further ostracization: the Kanzuke prince is tricked into taking one of Atemiya's servants as his wife, Masuge objects too strongly to Atemiya's marriage to the crown prince and is exiled to a distant eastern post, and Takamoto is driven mad by the news, burning down his estate and fleeing to the mountains. These figures are clowns in the narrative, symbolically excluded from its reconsolidation of the political status quo, but their alienation provides the sharpest note of contradiction and critique within the tale, connecting the narrative specifically to the role played by *zuryō* in Heian society.

The mid-Heian *zuryō* was a peculiar artifact of the transition between the census-based taxation of the early state and the medieval propriety-province (*chigyō-koku*) system. The *zuryō*, often but not always a province's governor, was the figure assigned responsibility for delivering tax income from the province to the court (as distinct from officials commissioned in name only). After 902, household land redistribution was completely abandoned, and over the course of the tenth century these custodians increasingly relied on agreements with local elites named as tax managers (*fumyō*) to requisition necessary products from the provincial populace. The 915 establishment of the evaluation system for *zuryō* who completed their term of appointment formalized the status of *zuryō* as tax farmers for the central government, who were desperate to recover a higher yield from the land's production.[39]

Defined by his role as state-authorized wealth amasser, the *zuryō* often appears in Heian fiction as a greedy crook or dissembling parvenu.[40] In *Utsuho monogatari*, this theme is taken up in the figure of Miharu no Takamoto. A quintessential miser, he has assembled vast riches through six consecutive governorships and become a senior noble, but resigns his position on the Council of State because of the expenses the job entails, returning to his career as a *zuryō*. Though he had hitherto avoided the costs of a wife and family, like the other men he conceives an irresistible desire for Atemiya and attempts to use his wealth to win her. Takamoto's parsimony is repeatedly made an object of mockery in the narrative: "He

39. Kiley, "Provincial Administration," 283–326.

40. For an overview of *zuryō* as villain figures in literature, see Murai, "Zuryō: Ōchō no akuyaku." Compare, however, *Konjaku monogatari shū* 28.38.

made his way to the palace in a clapboard cart with one wheel missing, pulled by a sickly cow and led by a young girl. . . . He dyed some thick floss-silk for a robe, and wore a hand-made train and trousers. Since he was assigned to the Palace Guard as well, he brought along some kids dressed up with wooden swords and branch bows as his retainers. The whole city laughed at him, but he paid no mind and went about his business."[41]

Yet while Takamoto's portrayal in *Utsuho* is exaggerated and humorous, he is not contemptible, and the narrative suggests a conflicted ambivalence toward him. His greed is less base appetite than a kind of sincere devotion to wealth and thrift, and this devotion paradoxically grants him a perverse integrity. When his newly hired servants demand lunch, Takamoto is appalled, declaring, "This is why I went so many years without servants. What tremendous cost! However I scrimp, if I give fifteen servants each a pod of soybeans, that's fifteen pods. If I planted them instead think how many more I'd have! If I gave them yam buds instead, it would still take more than ten, but if I harvested those after they grew, I'd have many yams. Even if I made jerky out of a skylark—if I let it live and used it as bait, I could catch a flock of birds!"[42] Takamoto's miserliness is farcical, but it is also what has made him a supremely skilled custodian, who rises to a position on the Council of State after governing six different provinces. The court tolerates his eccentric behavior because his skill at governance (*matsurigoto*) is enough "to calm wild warriors and beasts."

In the context of Atemiya's courtship, Takamoto is an eccentric clown with no relevance to the central question of Masayori's political victory. At the same time, his position as an "outsider" in the social geography of the narrative provides a lone vantage point from which the implicit values of the main narrative are subject to critique, never more so than when Takamoto expresses his own contempt for Masayori's glory: "As for that commander, just what is so glamorous about building nice houses on a big piece of land and inviting every gallant in the land over just to use everything up? He'd be smarter saving his things and opening up a shop. I may live like this, but I don't cause any grief to the peasants. It's men who go in for glamour that cause trouble to the throne and grief to the

41. *Utsuho monogatari*, "Fujiwara no kimi," 85–86.
42. Ibid., 86.

people."[43] There is no attribution of double-dealing or bad faith in this accusation; rather, Takamoto simply apprehends the same "glamour" that is celebrated as glory throughout the tale as scandalous waste. (Takamoto himself lives in the less desirable southern part of the capital, on a plot of land half the size of Masayori's, upon which "all of his men take up spade and hoe to work the field.") The symmetry of this inversion suggests a kind of structural necessity to the men's antagonism: the greedy *zuryō*'s need to acquire is matched by, and completes, the generous noble's "need to destroy and to lose," their antithetical relationship corresponding to roles in a mutually defining cycle of exchange.[44] Thus the tale's encomium to Masayori's glory cannot proceed without also depicting the *zuryō,* enabler of and uncanny counterpart to the noble economy of reciprocal service. The ambivalent attitudes toward *zuryō* displayed across Heian literature reflect their role as an official response to dramatic and sometimes frightening changes overtaking the Heian state. The insight of *Utsuho* is to narrate the interweaving of interests and roles between *zuryō*, the ruling oligarchy, and the lower nobility, which become clearest in the tale's many grand banquet scenes of ritualized exchange.

Zuryō and the Heian Network of Reciprocity

Mid-Heian writers often depicted their world as living through an age of decline—in religious terms as the "Latter Days of the Buddhist Law" (*mappō*) in which salvation was increasingly difficult, or in political terms by comparison with earlier "sacred reigns" (*seidai*) such as that of Emperor Daigo.[45] It is true that the mid-Heian was a time of menacing threats to order. William Wayne Farris has constructed a detailed argument showing that population growth in Japan stalled or even reversed in the early-to-mid Heian, only beginning to rebound after 1050. He argues that

43. "Kiyora suru hito koso, ōyake no ōntame ni samatage o itashi, hito no tame ni kurushimi o itase." Ibid., 87.

44. Bataille, "Notion of Expenditure," 121.

45. For famous examples of this discourse see *Genji monogatari*, "Wakamurasaki," 1:224; *Shōyūki*, Chōgen 2 (1029)/7/17 (8:144); *Honchō monzui* 196.

disease and drought repeatedly ravaged the archipelago during this time, exacerbating the weaknesses of code-defined administration. Particularly savage were the smallpox epidemics: one outbreak in 993–95 killed off a fifth of the nobility. The effects of the resulting disorder and lack of manpower can be seen in declines in roads, trade, and industries such as silk production.[46] In Heian literature, anxiety about such threats to their way of life was manifested in narratives of princesses and children of senior nobles declining into poverty through personal tragedies of orphanage, political ostracism, or legal punishment.[47] Modern historians have drawn upon such maudlin episodes to craft a narrative of mid-Heian decadence, which until recently scholars have generally characterized as the rise of feudalism concurrent with the collapse of the code-based state.[48]

Yet while the mid-Heian decline in the population base, together with the eastern and western rebellions of Taira no Masakado 平將門 and Fujiwara no Sumitomo 藤原純友 (from 935 to 941), represented enormous challenges to the central government, its reorganization into an oligarchic alliance between the imperial household and the Northern Branch Fujiwara, administered through the Council of State and the Chamberlain's Office, served as a practical response to this danger. The code-based census and taxation systems were largely abandoned, but *zuryō* custodians oversaw a flexible and effective program of wealth extraction that continued to support the ceremonial functions of the state. For this reason, institutional historians such as Satō Yasuhiro describe the mid-Heian, particularly the late tenth century, as the "end of antiquity," the final retrenchment of a centralized Yamato state before the full-scale transition to medieval decentralization beginning in the late eleventh century.[49]

Since the *zuryō* system was the pipeline between capital and provinces and the most important source of state resources, Heian capital society increasingly adapted itself to the key characteristics of the system, which

46. Farris, *Daily Life and Demographics.*

47. See Haruo Shirane's discussion of "fallen princesses" in the *Tale of Genji*. *Bridge of Dreams*, 133–50. In *Utsuho*, see the tale of Minamoto no Nakayori's impoverished in-laws. "Fukiage jō," 248.

48. See for example Ishimoda, "Utsuho monogatari ni tsuite."

49. Satō Yasuhiro, *Nihon chūsei no reimei*, 629–31. See also Tamai, *Heian jidai no kizoku*, 56–58.

have been lucidly explored by Nakagomi Ritsuko.[50] The first of these is the flexibility of taxation: almost all tax was delivered in commodity money (rice or silk), and rates of exchange were negotiable between the *zuryō* and various central offices. Furthermore, much taxation was carried out on an ad hoc basis, with senior nobles sending requests to *zuryō* to fund ceremonies and construction. Second, there was no distinction between government apparatus and the *zuryō*'s household: he employed his family and household retainers in administration and tax collection, and the taxes collected were not distinguished from his personal wealth. Finally, central and provincial administration were almost completely disconnected. The provincial rate of taxation was not tied in any direct way to internal budgetary financing, and the central government had no consistent means of measuring provincial production, population, or taxation. Thus while the ruling oligarchy was able to exercise rigid control over the appointment of *zuryō*, the *zuryō* had near total independence in their course of action once appointed—though their nominal power was checked by the influence of local elites.[51] This "age of the *zuryō*" continued until the mid-eleventh century, when the establishment of new tax laws, the growing tendency of *zuryō* (now increasingly courtiers) to remain in the capital and rely on representatives, and the explosion of imperial estates dissolved the custodians as a meaningfully distinct social entity.[52]

The fluctuating demands of taxation and administrative disconnect between capital and provinces naturally created many opportunities for *zuryō*, who often took advantage of the lack of central oversight to amass great personal wealth. The grasping *zuryō* figures that appear in literature of the period correspond to a growing resentment, not just from the peasantry they governed, but increasingly from the nobility, who both

50. Nakagomi, *Heian jidai no zei-zaisei*, 170–255.

51. Nakagomi's emphasis on the ignorance of capital administrators is in contradistinction to scholars who argue that central control was maintained through *zuryō* "evaluations" (*kōka sadame*); Nakagomi sees these as largely ceremonial and unable to track actual revenues by the end of the tenth century. Cf. Sasaki Muneo, "Court-Centered Polity," 234; Ōtsu, *Ritsuryō kokka shihai kōzō*, 349–70. For an overview of how *zuryō* carried out provincial administration, see Batten, "Provincial Administration," 124–32.

52. Satō Yasuhiro, *Nihon chūsei no reimei*, 619–21; William H. McCullough, "Heian Court," 72–73; Satō Shin'ichi, *Nihon no chūsei kokka*, 11–13.

appointed them and depended upon their remittances.[53] One mid-tenth-century diarist describes them as lowly figures who "groveled day and night" before the senior nobles who determined future postings, but the state's dependence on tax income from *zuryō* threatened to upend such status distinctions.[54] By the eleventh century, Fujiwara no Sanesuke 藤原實資 (957–1046) would record his exasperation at learning that a fellow senior noble had stooped to performing the capping at the coming-of-age ceremony for a *zuryō*'s son, and a sumptuary edict promulgated soon after suggests the nobility's growing anxiety over the potential for *zuryō* wealth to destabilize the social order.[55]

But if the rising wealth and power of *zuryō* could provoke intense antipathy among the nobility, to lower officialdom it made a *zuryō* appointment the best hope for meaningful financial reward through bureaucratic service. While *Utsuho* constructs a narrative universe eliding the difference between officials and nobles, in reality it was the *zuryō* who represented the ultimate career goal of officials. One such example is Minamoto no Shitagō, the ostensible author of *Utsuho*, who like many of his contemporaries devoted his career to gaining a *zuryō* governorship. He obtained his first such post at the age of fifty-six, but a loss of political support would then leave him without office for a decade, until he finally achieved a second governorship a few years before his death in 983. A petition to the court he submitted with a group of officials in 974 reveals how *zuryō* appointments had become the nexus coordinating relationships among the emperor, courtiers, and officials. The petition explains that in recent years (specifically since the death of Emperor Murakami in 967), *zuryō* appointments had tended to go to newly minted fifth-rank nobles, while men who had already served one governorship struggled to obtain a second one, even with a good record.[56] As a result,

53. The most famous complaint registered against a governor by his subjects is the Owari Province Petition of 988. Kiley, "Provincial Administration," 326–37. For a noble complaint, see *Shōyūki*, Chōgen 2 (1029)/9/5 (8:158).

54. *Kagerō nikki*, 205.

55. *Shōyūki*, Manju 4 (1027)/7/26 (8:11); *Nihon kiryaku*, Chōgen 3 (1030)/4/23 (2:277). A classic overview of the place of *zuryō* in capital society is Hayashiya, *Kodai kokka no kaitai*, 131–55.

56. On the *zuryō* selection process, see Hérail, "De la place et du role."

> All believe that *zuryō* is an official honor that comes only once in a lifetime. If [the court] does not employ those credited with reviving the state and soothing the people, what use is there in being known for "dumping the mallow" or "thrashing with bulrush"?[57] How could that be better than ignoring the sufferings in the commoners' huts to lay a lasting plan for a wealthy household? If this is the case, we fear the court will have few humble ministers, the state will have many rapacious officials; the state will be benighted and the people dispersed, and recovery will be beyond hope. It is not that we dare to block the path of the worthy and vie for the way to office, [but rather] we would only make the eyes and ears of all know the impartiality of the sovereign's favor.[58]
>
> 朝野皆以爲、受領者、一生一度之官榮也。興國安民之治迹不用、盡葵鞭蒲之政聲何益。豈如不慮編戸之苦、長迴潤屋之謀矣。如此則恐朝少廉恥之臣、國多貪婪之吏、國弊民散、興復難期。非敢塞賢路爭吏途、只令天下之耳目、知聖德之平均也。

Here the figure of the greedy *zuryō* is inverted, with provincial malfeasance depicted as a direct consequence of partiality by the ruling nobility. The petition is specifically concerned with establishing quotas for the apportionment of *zuryō* offices among competing parties, but the explanation at the document's opening that the "loyal devotion" 無貳之節 of those below responds to "undifferentiated beneficence" 均一之德 from above hints at an ongoing negotiation over the terms of official service and reward.

Modern scholarship has often followed the lead of Heian literary accounts by depicting the growth of *zuryō* wealth as symptomatic of the breakdown of central authority. But while the central government granted *zuryō* tremendous leeway to amass riches, they also made use of a variety of procedures to recover wealth from them. Even as the code-defined system of taxation became a legal fiction, ad hoc demands and customary donation practices were used to mobilize *zuryō* wealth as a kind of state

57. The figures reference two stories of gentle governors from Chinese history: Gong Yixiu 公儀休 plucked out the mallow in his garden to avoid competing with local farmers, and Liu Kuan 劉寬 carried out flogging punishments using a bulrush stalk in place of a whip. *Shiji* 119.3101–2; *Hou Hanshu* 25.887.

58. *Honchō monzui* 157.

revenue, funding construction and ceremonies.[59] Historians such as Ōtsu Tōru have even argued that despite the apparent "decline" of legally defined provincial administration, the custodian/tax-manager system actually extended central control over and demands on provincial resources.[60] In any case, there can be no doubt that the ruling oligarchy encouraged *zuryō* wealth as a means of ensuring access to funds.

The central government's most obvious method of leveraging *zuryō* wealth was the "(meritorious) achievement" (*jōgō*) system through which lucrative *zuryō* appointments were granted on the condition of constructing government offices or temples, effectively contracting out the maintenance of central infrastructure. Less immediately visible, but far more important in the mid-Heian, was the broad network of gift-giving and service relationships that obliged *zuryō* to provide material support to the imperial household and senior nobility. *Unshū shōsoku* 雲州消息 (Izumo Letters), a mid-eleventh-century epistolary handbook, provides a glimpse of the breadth of these exchanges:

- A soldier in the Palace Guard has been assigned the duty of serving as one of the dancers at the Iwashimizu Special Festival; he writes to a *zuryō* hoping to borrow a horse.
- An administrative noble writes to a *zuryō* to request fruit and fish to cater a banquet two days later.
- One *zuryō* writes to another, relaying an order from the minister of the right to produce robes for the Gosechi dancers at the Harvest Festival.[61]

Within the collection, such letters appear side by side with orders demanding the delivery of rice taxes, and indeed one letter conveying a *zuryō*'s remittance of silks ends with a party invitation for the supervising

59. For a treatment of *zuryō* wealth as state revenue see Terauchi, *Zuryōsei no kenkyū*, 83–110.

60. Ōtsu, *Ritsuryō kokka shihai kōzō*, 375–76; Ōtsu, *Michinaga to kyūtei shakai*, 217–20. Nakagomi notes that *zuryō* wealth was overwhelmingly concentrated in storehouses within the capital, emphasizing the continuity in wealth extraction from periphery to center, even as agents and methods changed (*Heian jidai no zei-zaisei*, 184–201).

61. *Unshū shōsoku*, 393, 416, 401.

administrator.[62] These examples suggest that while *zuryō* were the most crucial source of capital wealth, they were not commissioned through a unique structure of employment by the bureaucracy or oligarchs. Instead, they were integrated into an expansive network of reciprocal relationships that connected all of capital officialdom. These relationships were not limited to *zuryō*, and the obligations did not follow a simple hierarchy: a noble might be obliged to pay a visit to a man ranked below him, or a *zuryō* might be retainer to one senior noble, but provide goods to another.[63] In these transactions, we can glimpse how the social topography of the Heian capital as central site of exchange was realized through a fluid network of goods, services, and rituals.[64]

Several of the *Unshū shōsoku* letters suggest the ways that literary service and production could appear as one more element in these reciprocal relationships:

- A courtier writes to a professor of letters inviting him to a chrysanthemum banquet where *shi* poetry will be composed; he asks him to bring one or two other poets with him, and to supply the wine.
- A chamberlain has been invited to a banquet and, apprised beforehand of the topic that will be assigned for *waka* composition, he writes to another courtier hoping he might secretly supply a poem to use.
- A low-ranked scholar writes to the crown prince's tutor, sending him several collections of *waka* he had requested, and seeking in return to borrow some works of literary Sinitic poetry in order to make copies of them.[65]

If the historical record clearly documents the ways in which government finances and capital society were dependent on the regular circulation of *zuryō*-funneled resources, examples such as these hint that cultural

62. Ibid., 419, 434.

63. Endō, *Chūsei ōken*, 49–56. Such service obligations were enforced as much through mutual peer oversight as through clientage agreements. Satō Yasuhiro, *Nihon chūsei no reimei*, 535–39.

64. This characterization of Heian-kyō draws on Kyōraku, "Toshi no tensei," 12–18. See also Toda, "Kyoto and the Estate System."

65. *Unshū shōsoku*, 400, 424, 413–14.

production too was based in the same network of reciprocity. This is not to reduce cultural artifacts to mere trade goods; on the contrary, it is rather economic exchange that seems to emerge as a secondary "residue" of the larger field of symbolically organized exchange.[66] As gifts, the literary texts and material goods of the Heian capital move back and forth through the same paths of reciprocation. The dynamic through which exchange relationships produce literary performance comes out clearly in *Utsuho monogatari*'s many depictions of ceremonies and banquets accompanied by poetic exchanges.

Utsuho has sometimes been referred to as "literature of festivities" (*shukusai no bungaku*) for its exhaustive attention to a parade of ceremonies and banquets, often described in almost documentary detail. In these events, Masayori in particular is represented as using ritual to situate himself as the locus of material redistribution: banquet provisions are ordered from *zuryō*, raw materials are procured from estates and processed for consumption by women in his household, and gifts are distributed to attendees.[67] These banquets are usually accompanied by poetic exchanges between the host and guest. Such poems are in both literary Sinitic (*shi*) and "Yamato song" (*waka*) formats, but consistent with other *kana*-inscribed literature from the period, the former are only referenced, not quoted; by contrast, the text repeatedly transcribes long sequences of *waka* exchange (the longest is thirty-eight consecutive poems) between the host and his guests.[68] These sequences are organized through a call-and-response dynamic in which elements are introduced and reaffirmed by the event's attendees, who might take turns celebrating the host's longevity, or bestowing praise on a musical performance. Heian poetic discourse treats such group composition dynamics as the manifestation of cosmological patterns of stimulus and response, and modern scholars have suggested an underlying sociological utility to

66. Baudrillard, *Mirror of Production*, 78–79.

67. For *zuryō* providing provisions, see *Utsuho monogatari*, "Saga no in," 187, "Matsuri no tsukai," 206. For procurement and preparation of materials, see ibid., "Saga no in," 189, "Kiku no en," 309. For gifts to guests and performers, see ibid., "Fukiage ge," 285, "Kasuga mōde," 149.

68. While *Utsuho* is only sixty percent as long as the *Tale of Genji*, it includes almost two hundred more *waka* poems.

sequences that produce a "sense of solidarity" among the participants.[69] Nevertheless, the banquet descriptions in *Utsuho* also make clear that such symbolic exchanges are inextricable from concrete material exchange. Each banquet attendee's poem is a token of symbolic recompense for Masayori's welcoming reception, largesse, or political assistance, anticipating the relationship of mutual support he has entered into by accepting the host's hospitality.

The tale devotes long passages to describing the paths gifts take as they are presented, augmented, and re-gifted in cyclical displays of wealth and fealty, so that the gifts themselves can take on the role of important characters.[70] This is especially true when the gifts exchanged are women: several times, the hand of Atemiya is bestowed as a banquet reward (*roku* 祿) for a musical performance by Nakatada or his rival Minamoto no Suzushi. Each time, in the cold light of day, this reward is recognized as a jest or trick. It is the celebration that provides a carnivalesque atmosphere in which lower-ranked men such as Nakatada or Tōei can present themselves as suitors for Atemiya's hand.[71] When Atemiya's inevitable marriage to the crown prince occurs, many of her other suitors are consoled with marriage to her younger sisters, affirming the constancy of their relationship with Masayori. It thus becomes clear that the courtship of Atemiya is an extension of the exchange-based alliance structure underlying Masayori's banquets.

This underlying continuity is represented through the formal presentation of the suitors' courtship poems within the narrative as well: poems sent to Atemiya generally appear immediately following banquets in the narrative, in long sequences (each suitor taking a turn) whose structure mirrors the group composition of banquet poetry. While *Utsuho monogatari* describes at length the "tears of blood" wept by men suffering for love, the form of the text at the same time conflates erotic desire and the

69. Wixted, "*Kokinshū* Prefaces: Another Perspective;" Ōida, *"Utsuho monogatari" no sekai*, 225. On theories of *waka*'s role in the "communal body" (*kyōdōtai*) of early Japan, see Richard Okada, *Figures of Resistance*, 91–99. Similarly, Gustav Heldt's *The Pursuit of Harmony* argues that the Heian state employed *waka* as a generator of ritual "harmony."

70. Nishiyama, "Utsuho monogatari 'mono.'"

71. Mitamura, "Utsuho monogatari no ronri," 177–91.

alliance building of banquet composition. In a political sphere organized by households, marriage—and love poetry—had wide-reaching implications.[72] The long sequences of group composition that thread through *Utsuho monogatari* figure literary composition's inextricable entwinement with material exchange and political alliance.

If the courtship of Atemiya produces discomfiting echoes of the very real obstacles social stratification was placing before much of Heian officialdom, these anxieties receive at least temporary comfort in Masayori's banquets, where all attendees, low and high, participate in celebration and reciprocation. An idealization of the noble magnate who draws his power not from traditional rank and office (his older brother Sueakira stands at the peak of government as minister of the left), but rather through giving and receiving, Masayori is the agent of status differentiation as he picks and chooses from among the suitors, but also reconciliation, as he welcomes both political winners and losers into his manor. But where contemporary ritual discourse presents an inevitable correlation between human and cosmological orders, *Utsuho* denaturalizes the harmony of Masayori's banquets. Through its detailed accounting of material accumulation and rewards, the narrative reveals a machinery of symbolic investment, strategic delays, and productive malfunctions liable to rationalized exploitation (including Masayori's false promises of Atemiya's hand).[73] Even as the tale portrays the provisional success of Masayori's consolidation of power, skeptical voices such as the *zuryō* Takamoto repeatedly intrude at the margins. In a utopia guaranteed by ceaseless exchange, however, no critique is as threatening as the renunciation of a gift, as is made clear in the tale of *Utsuho*'s other central protagonist, the musical noble Nakatada.

72. Lower nobility often depended on romantic relationships with palace ladies-in-waiting to establish a line of communication with influential imperial consorts or empress dowagers. Yoshikawa, *Ritsuryō kanryōsei no kenkyū*, 446–48. Secondary representations of such love affairs could also have political motives. Mostow, *House of Gathered Leaves*, 1–38; Heldt, "Writing Like a Man," 11–18.

73. On "cunning" and the rationalization of ritual exchange, see Horkheimer and Adorno, *Dialectic of Enlightenment*, 39–49.

Conclusion: Service and Reward

The discussion thus far has focused on one of the twin strands of *Utsuho monogatari*'s narrative, the courtship of Masayori's daughter Atemiya, suggesting ways that its representation of her suitors encodes the social anxieties and contradictions of the mid-Heian. The narrative of Kiyohara no Toshikage and his musical descendants, which runs parallel to the story of Atemiya's politically fraught marriage, is one type of imaginary solution to these contradictions. Toshikage's wanderings through foreign lands earn him a set of magical *qin* and the secret techniques to play them. When the emperor attempts to make him music tutor to the crown prince on his return, however, he refuses, declaring,

> When I was just a child I left my parents to cross the sea to China. Pulled by a cruel wind and powerful waves, I was taken to a strange country. There can be no grief greater than this. When I finally returned, I found an empty house, my parents already dead. Long ago, I followed the court's orders, passed all my tests, and was sent to China. I'm full of sadness at losing my parents without seeing them again, but as for the spirit to teach this to the prince I have none. Though it be a crime against the throne, I will not teach another this *qin*.[74]

Going into hiding, Toshikage instead passes his musical knowledge on to his only child, but when she reaches the age of fifteen her mother dies, and Toshikage follows soon after, declaring, "I leave my daughter to the gods (*tendō* 天道). If heaven decrees it, she may yet be a consort or mother to an emperor."[75] The young girl is left with one elderly servant in a decaying house on the outskirts of the city.

It is here that she is discovered by the young Fujiwara no Kanemasa, who fathers her son Nakatada, one of the tale's central protagonists. Though Nakatada never progresses very far as one of Atemiya's suitors, his parentage and musical skill (passed down from his mother) earn him a place among the courtiers, and he marries the emperor's eldest daughter

74. *Utsuho monogatari*, "Toshikage," 21.
75. Ibid., 22.

soon after Atemiya becomes consort to the crown prince. When his daughter Inumiya is born, he has Toshikage's old manor rebuilt and devoted to the secret musical training of the girl by her grandmother. The final chapters of the novel dedicate increasing attention to Nakatada's efforts to leverage his grandfather's cultural legacy into a lasting place within the upper nobility by acquiring prestige for his household. As plans are made for Inumiya's climactic recital, we find the newly acceded emperor reassuring his consort Atemiya, jealous that she cannot hear Inumiya's music, that she will "hear it all she likes when the crown prince [their son] comes of age."[76] If Inumiya's musical ability is enough to make her a desirable consort for the next emperor, Nakatada might eventually become maternal grandfather to a crown prince, the regency-associated position Atemiya's marriage guaranteed for Masayori.

In the final chapter, Nakatada's old rival Suzushi secretly listens in while Inumiya plays with her father and grandmother, "the moon, stars, and clouds moving" in resonance with the sound, then is brought to tears as Nakatada recites several of Toshikage's old poems on "gazing on an empty house after his return" from overseas, invoking the memory of his grandfather's sacrifice.[77] The tale concludes with a recital attended by all the nobility, in which Inumiya's music provokes a series of supernatural wonders. Afterwards, the two retired emperors discuss what ranks and offices to bestow on Nakatada, his mother, and even the departed Toshikage, in hopes "that old spirit will feel better."[78] However, Nakatada refuses the proffered post, just as his grandfather had long ago rejected the position of music tutor to the crown prince in a gamble with fate to establish a more durable legacy for his lineage. These repeated refusals suggest a reckoning or bargaining with the system of services and rewards that defined capital society. As is hinted at through the repeated references to Toshikage's unfilial sin of leaving his parents to die without him, the price of his knowledge was too high, and the rewards for official service too low.[79] Nakatada, who was promised Atemiya's hand for his own *qin* performance,

76. *Utsuho monogatari*, "Rō no ue jō," 856. By the final chapter, Masayori reports that Suzushi is withholding his own daughter from palace service because he is sure Inumiya will become the crown prince's principal consort. Ibid., 888.

77. Ibid., 906.

78. Ibid., 937–38.

79. Takahashi Tōru, "Utsuho monogatari: Hajimari," 168–74.

only to see her married to the crown prince after all, knows better than to accept the first reward offered.

Nakatada's ascent at the tale's end in no way supersedes the political triumph of Masayori's clan: Atemiya is successfully married to the crown prince, and when he succeeds to the throne her son is named heir apparent, reinforcing the stability of Masayori's power. Despite the fact that they are the two primary protagonists of the tale, the narratives of Atemiya and Nakatada at a certain level are incompatible and disconnected. The eventual merger of their households through a marriage between Atemiya's son and Inumiya is hinted at, but never resolved in the tale. If the narrative of Masayori and Atemiya depicts the successful manipulation of the Heian capital's network of exchange culminating in power and glory, the narrative of Toshikage and his descendants suggests skepticism toward this give-and-take, a fundamental incommensurability at the heart of the capital bureaucracy, in which some are not rewarded for their labors. The myth of the magical *qin* resolves the practical impossibility of recompense for official service by projecting an ever-greater reward into an always-delayed future.

The tale of Toshikage and his descendants presents a mystical alchemy whereby, through lineal transmission and secrecy, talent and learning can be transmuted into a durable position within society. But this was a fantasy prompted by the realities of mid-Heian officialdom, in which men like Minamoto no Shitagō desperately maneuvered for the patronage of senior nobles and other courtiers, whose support was the only path to prestige and income. The following chapter takes up the largest corpus of writings by these officials, parallel-prose documents produced for use in noble rituals, to demonstrate how the social dynamics of the capital exchange network fueled and shaped mid-Heian literary production.

TWO

Honchō monzui and the Social Dynamics of Literary Culture

Gift exchange was an organizing principle of both government finance and elite society in the mid-Heian, and homologous structures ordered the production and reception of artistic forms such as literature as well. Numerous events at the palace, temples, and noble households necessitated the performance of literary Sinitic documents—poems presented at banquets, sermons recited at Buddhist assemblies, memorials offered up at an imperial audience—and all such scribal production was generally reciprocated with a material token of some sort recognizing the service rendered. *Utsuho monogatari,* however, repeatedly depicts the breakdown of this principle of reciprocity, particularly in regards to forms of cultural service, as when a *qin* master flees his palace post, declaring, "Though I served, I was never respected at court. Palace service through learning is a waste of time (*zae no miyazukae kai nashi*)."[1] In the mid-Heian, the unreliability of official remuneration forced officials to seek new outlets for technical expertise.

At the same time, the upper nobility, led by the imperial and regent households, increasingly pursued ritual practices that emphasized exclusivity, restricting the direct participation of the lower-ranked officials most active in compositional service. This change in ritual practice both provoked an ideological shift in the valuation of scholarly ability and

1. *Utsuho monogatari*, "Fukiage ge," 294.

increased the importance of freelance commissions outside the purview of direct ceremonial participation. Comparing records from contemporary diaries and the works preserved in the eleventh-century anthology *Honchō monzui*, it is possible to reconstruct an economy of patronage, in which scholar-officials provided commissioned works to senior-noble magnates in exchange for material and social rewards. By treating literary composition within its broader praxis of client sponsorship, material remuneration, and ceremonial performance, this chapter argues that while literature was heavily conditioned by the rigid status hierarchy of Heian officialdom, this social structure was itself generated through those same documents, with the active participation of lower-ranked scribes.

Within a notoriously sparse historical record, ritual assemblies are perhaps the most consistently well-documented cultural form in the Heian period. The seventh-century installation of a centralized, code-based state was accompanied by the institution of a yearly calendar of ritual with the sovereign as ritual coordinator at the center. This calendar included courtly ceremonies of obeisance, promotion, and gift giving that defined the relationship between ruler and subject, as well as invocations of divine protection or placations of divine wrath (which concurrently served to demonstrate the ruler's own sacred power). Ritual affirmed the proper order of an earthly state reflecting cosmological principles, and assured the continued prosperity of the realm through the protection of deities.[2]

Many of these rituals entailed the recitation of texts. In some cases these were sacred texts invoked anew at each iteration of an event, while in other cases a ritual could necessitate the composition of a document specific to that instance. Very commonly both were needed: Buddhist assemblies, for example, generally included both the recitation and explication of a sutra, as well as recitation of a prayer text specifying the particular goal of the assembly's sponsor. Thus texts played an essential role in coordinating ritual performance's signification and ensuring ritual efficacy. For this reason, the question of literature's ritual function is central to early Japanese cultural history. In recent studies on early Heian literary culture by Gustav Heldt and Jason Webb, for example, the

2. Piggott, *Emergence of Japanese Kingship*, 139–49; Ooms, *Imperial Politics and Symbolics*, 105–31; Duthie, *"Man'yōshū" and the Imperial Imagination*, 94–107.

presentation of literary Sinitic *shi* poetry in royal banquets (*sechie*) is analyzed as a state ritual; both argue that the presentation of poems by the assembled officials legitimated the sovereign's authority through a staged expression of imperial virtue, loyal subjecthood, and harmonious cooperation.[3]

In focusing on the ritual qualities of banquets and poetry composition, these analyses raise definitional questions about the nature and extent of "ritual" in Heian society. The numerous events and ceremonies in the Heian court calendar were diverse, and demonstrate varying degrees of formalization, conventionalized behavior, symbolic or sacral meaning, and visibility, to name some of the characteristics scholars have used to define ritual.[4] Nor do they all belong to a calendar as such (as for example a state funeral), and many have limited or ambiguous relationships with the cosmology of imperial rule (as for example the various coming-of-age ceremonies). The banquets of Masayori discussed in chapter 1 clearly mimic the sovereign-subject relationship in royal banquets discussed by Heldt and Webb, and thus encourage a similarly ritualistic interpretation, but what then about smaller gatherings among the lower nobility, which might produce poetry making use of largely identical tropes of praising the host and celebrating conviviality?

In this manner, attempting to define ritual categorically tends to generate a sorites paradox where we are left asking what degree of routinization turns a party into a ceremony. By contrast, Catherine Bell rejects the notion of ritual as a sphere of action to argue instead for the study of "ritualization" as a cultural strategy of differentiation. The question for Bell is how, cross-culturally, certain activities are made to evoke "strategic, value-laden distinctions" from other types of practice.[5] This approach is useful for understanding the production and circulation of literary Sinitic texts in the Heian capital, because it draws attention to the way a textual artifact can be both the *object* of ritualization, imbued with status through special modes or venues of performance, and also an *agent* of ritualization, serving to guarantee the differentiation of composer, reciter, or sponsor. Poems and other documents composed for ceremonial occasions often

3. Heldt, *Pursuit of Harmony*, 51–59; Webb, "In Good Order," 77–92.
4. See Tambiah, *Culture, Thought, and Social Action*, 123–66.
5. Bell, *Ritual Theory, Ritual Practice*, 88–93 and passim.

express particular ideologies, but Bell's work suggests that rather than seek to decode the texts as representations or mystifications of preexisting belief systems, we should consider the ideological work generated through the broader praxis of composition and performance.

The Transformation of Ritual Space

In the codified procedures of the various annual court banquets, the value of poetic performance is confirmed through the presentation of material reward. Ceremony participation in general was understood as a type of official service, compensated with rewards (*roku* or *kazukemono*), usually cloth, presented to all noble attendees as supplemental salary. Nevertheless, at banquets where group poetic composition was featured, such as the late-autumn Chrysanthemum Banquet (Chōyōen), separate rewards were designated specifically for those who had contributed a poem. A 967 set of procedures specifies that additional gifts beyond the standard amount are bestowed on those men who served as "poets" (*monnin* 文人) by presenting a poem on the banquet's set topic of composition.[6] Already in the ninth century *monnin* seems to have become an assigned role within poetic banquets, with quotas based on status: manuals of court precedent most frequently mention *jusha* 儒者 (professors and other elite academics who had passed the highest level of the civil service exam), palace secretaries (*naiki*), students in the State Academy, and graduates now serving as chamberlains or as clerks in the Palace Library (*uchi no goshodokoro*).[7]

Most commonly, composition at such large, formal banquets was in literary Sinitic verse (*shi*), with an assigned topic and rhyme scheme. Poets were expected to expatiate on the occasion (the season, event, host, and

6. A fourth-rank attendee would receive 30 *ton* of silk floss (*wata*) normally, but an additional 20 *ton* if he submitted a poem. Sixth-rank and lower attendees normally received no emoluments at all, but could obtain 10 *ton* of silk floss if they were a *monnin* (*Engi shiki* 30.736). The same criteria applied at the annual Residential Palace Banquet (*Saikyūki*, 1:75). Verschuer has a *ton* at approximately 168 grams (*Across the Perilous Sea*, 7).

7. Kudō, *Heianchō ritsuryō shakai*, 75–110.

location) in a clever and felicitous manner. An early poem by Sugawara no Michizane from an 868 Residential Palace Banquet (Naien) on the topic "No Thing Does Not Encounter Spring" 無物不逢春 gives a sense of the idiom:

寒光早退更無餘	The cold light of winter long since retreated, no more remains;
萬物逢春渙汗初	The myriad things encounter spring as it seeps out.
問著林前鶯語報	We ask what news the warbler's chatter has brought to the forest's edge,
看過水上波文書	And gaze upon the letters waves write on the water.
詩臣膽露言行樂	As the rhyming officials show their mettle, discoursing on these revels,
女妓粧成舞步虛	The dancing girls, their makeup set, perform the "Buxu."[8]
侍宴雖知多許事	Though in serving at a banquet, we know there are many such events,
一年一日忝仙居	Only one day in a year are we privileged [to attend at] the immortals' dwelling.[9]

In Michizane's poem, the world responds to encountering the spreading influence of spring by dispatching messages (報, 書) to the court, who celebrate with poetry, song, and dance. The poet's role in court celebration is thus also his place in the natural order of seasonal progression, and by extension the annual Residential Palace Banquet, like the coming of spring, is an event paradoxically both regular and rare. At this point in his life a graduate student in the State Academy, Michizane uses the final couplet to emphasize that, for "poeticizing officials" like himself, the banquet was a precious opportunity to enter the residential palace.

Such service was in fact one of the only chances for officials and lower nobles to receive some of the court's largesse at these affairs. At a flower-viewing banquet attended by three generations of emperors in *Utsuho*

8. "Pacing the Void," the title of a song used in Daoist ritual.
9. *Kanke bunsō, Kanke kōshū* 27.

monogatari, the *monnin* are assembled from "professors, twenty former letters students, and some provisional letters students," the latter of which are identified as men "of the fifth or sixth rank"—that is, not courtiers.[10] These students are given assigned topics and gather outside to work on their compositions. Meanwhile, the festivities continue inside the enclosure where the reigning and retired emperors are waited on by courtiers, and gifts are bestowed on the more senior *monnin* together with the musicians, reward for the entertainment they provide. The low-ranked provisional students, on the other hand, provide a different form of amusement: at the appointed hour, "when the host requested the provisional students submit their compositions, some had completed them, but others were only half done. As they rushed over in confusion, their arms raised in offering, some even tripped over. Their turmoil was the day's greatest diversion (*kyō no monomi*)."[11] The exaggerated pratfalls here are ridiculous, but it is a satire that is essentially sympathetic to the students' desperate eagerness for recognition.

For *monnin*, the hope was that one's poem might be recited at the assembly (many banquets seem to have ended before the poems could be read), and attract praise from the host. In these events, ritual constructs power relations through what Bell characterizes as a simultaneous objectification of and consent by the participants. Participation in ritual schemes produces relations of domination and subordination embodied by the participants, but though this participation may be "instinctive" (i.e., socially cultivated within a subject that misrecognizes the arbitrary schemes it has internalized as a transcendental order), it is never an "indiscriminate" abnegation of free will: ritual agents experience their participation as a negotiated relationship that provides the actor with some manner of empowerment.[12] While Michizane's poem emphasizes the latter aspect in its celebration of the banquet as opportunity, the portrayal in *Utsuho monogatari* caricatures the former; *monnin* attendees could

10. The State Academy's curriculum in letters is explained in chapter 4.

11. *Utsuho monogatari*, "Kuni-yuzuri ge," 819. The provisional students had already been the object of fun earlier in the banquet: as they go to receive their assigned composition topic from the emperor, he praises those that are presentable and mocks the flustered, ugly ones. This scene is echoed in the opening passage of *Genji monogatari*, "Hana no en," 1:353–54.

12. Bell, *Ritual Theory, Ritual Practice*, 206–9.

hardly be unaware of the implicit subjection in their ceremonial role, yet willingly participated in these events with the prospect of concrete rewards.

Over the course of the ninth century, the capital's calendar of ritual grew longer, drawing on a syncretic blend of Buddhist, Daoist, and local traditions, whose relative merits were weighed in terms of their efficacy in promoting prosperity.[13] New rituals such as the *shihōhai* (prayer to the four directions by the sovereign) and *kochōhai* (offering of new year's jubilation by the courtiers) seem to reflect a shifting model of sovereignty, emphasizing the emperor's personal and familial relations with a small subset of the nobility, particularly the regent's household. Increasingly, the "ritual topography" shifted from mass ceremonies (in outer palace buildings such as the Chōdōin) to more circumscribed events centered on the sovereign's person.[14] If the eighth century had witnessed the transformation of the imperial residence from a sacred and forbidden space into an "open palace" populated by nobles, in the mid-Heian the sovereign's living quarters themselves, the Seiryōden, became increasingly visible.[15] Furuse Natsuko analyzes this as a transformation in ritual space characterized by a merger between formerly public and private realms: the emperor's place of residence was opened up to a growing circle of courtiers, while the expansive public space of large-scale rituals was increasingly closed off and replaced by more exclusive alternative ceremonies. Particularly from the reign of Emperor Uda, the ritual privileges of courtiers were formalized, exacerbating the insider/outsider bifurcation of capital society.[16] The ritual calendar that consolidated in the early tenth century around these new developments would serve as the model for the remainder of the Heian period, with certain noble lineages established as masters of ritual knowledge.[17]

A rejection of codified distinctions between public and private was widespread in the Heian period, even within the bureaucracy: by the

13. Conlan, *From Sovereign to Symbol*, 18–19; Ruppert, *Jewel in the Ashes*, 43–101.

14. Heldt, *Pursuit of Harmony*, 90–95.

15. I take the term "open palace" (*hirakareta dairi*) from Yoshikawa, *Ritsuryō kanryōsei no kenkyū*, 102.

16. Furuse, *Nihon kodai ōken*, 202–5, 344.

17. Precedents cited in later courtier diaries generally go back no further than the Engi Era (901–23). Kojima Kogorō, *Kuge bunka no kenkyū*, 184.

mid-tenth century, *zuryō* governors brought a staff of dozens of personal retainers to assist in tax collection and administrative duties, and in the capital clerks tended to keep official documents in their own homes and pass them down to their children.[18] The restructuring of ritual space, however, was most specifically connected to the development of a dispersed sovereignty based on collusion between the imperial and regency households. Esoteric rites that had been reserved for the emperor were extended to the crown prince, and then the latter's maternal family. The ladies-in-waiting that served an empress were palace-appointed officials, but also the same women who had served her since she was a child, and they would accompany her on frequent visits back to her natal home. In many cases, the imperial household, the regent's household, and the bureaucracy were indistinguishable: the supplies for celebrating the assumption of a new empress or birth of a crown prince were provided to the palace by provincial governors at the command of the regent's household office.[19] The changed structures of the exercise of political power were accompanied by a correspondingly reimagined logic of ritual legitimation, based on shared secrets and privileged intimacy rather than mass assembly and visibility.

By the second half of the tenth century, the large-scale ceremonies centered on poetry composition (particularly the Chrysanthemum Banquet in the fall and flower-viewing banquets in the spring) had mostly disappeared. Following Fujiwara no Sumitomo's burning of Dazaifu in 941, the court had difficulty acquiring sufficient silk to provide the decreed banquet emoluments.[20] Such economic restrictions, together with the exclusivity that increasingly defined court ceremony, led to the replacement of many palace events with "hidden banquets" (*mitsuen*), attended only by the emperor and his high-ranked allies within the nobility.[21] If poetic entertainments were desired, a handful of lower-ranked poets might be summoned as well, and by the eleventh century *monnin*

18. Mori, *Zaichō kanjin*, 130–69; Soga, *Ōchō kokka seimu*, 131. Such phenomena can be seen already in the eighth century; see for example Lowe, "Rewriting Nara Buddhism," 100–110.

19. Grapard, "Religious Practices," 541–43; Yoshikawa, *Ritsuryō kanryōsei no kenkyū*, 443; Endō, *Chūsei ōken*, 49–56.

20. Yoshikawa, *Ritsuryō kanryōsei no kenkyū*, 371–72.

21. Takigawa, *Tennō to bundan*, 94–144.

often refers specifically to these low-ranking officials invited as entertainers, not to those among the courtiers who did compose poems.[22] In other cases, the sovereign might simply have the day's set topic sent over to the clerks in the Palace Library, enjoying some of their compositions after the banquet's conclusion.[23]

Literary composition and performance, particularly of *shi*, also occurred in venues outside the palace. The banquets of Masayori discussed in the previous chapter are an idealization of the type of hosting and excursion frequently sponsored by wealthy nobility and members of the imperial household. Other gatherings suggest more egalitarian participation: the employees of a capital office might gather together to celebrate a holiday; the homes of wealthy *zuryō* seem to have been a frequent site for feasts; and officials and lower nobles often made outings to suburban temples together to enjoy the scenery.[24] Produced in liminal spaces, such poems sometimes deviated from the stringent formal requirements observed on official occasions.[25] These gatherings imitated the format of shared food and drink, gift bestowal, and harmonization on shared topics found in the larger events of the court and great houses, but although they were open to a broader class of officials, the attendant social and material rewards were correspondingly reduced. Thus, although *shi* composition remained an important component of banquets and ceremonies in the mid-Heian, gatherings open to non-courtier officials presented few opportunities for recognition and reward. The large-scale events that

22. See, e.g., Michinaga's description of the ceremonial "first reading lesson" (*onfumihajime*) for Prince Atsunaga in 1015, which describes the different seating areas of senior nobles, courtiers, and *monnin*. *Midō kanpaku ki*, Chōwa 4/12/4 (3:35).

23. Kudō, *Heianchō ritsuryō shakai*, 102.

24. For poetic gatherings held among the clerks of the Palace Library, see *Honchō monzui* 271; *Sakeiki*, Chōwa 5 (1016)/4/7 (17); *Chūyūki burui shihai kanshishū* 30. Bryan Lowe identifies a similar gathering among scribes in the Nara Office of Sutra Transcription ("Rewriting Nara Buddhism," 145–51). For a poetic banquet hosted by a *zuryō*, see *Chūyūki burui shihai kanshishū* 4. The mostly twelfth-century poetic prefaces recorded in a manuscript in the Imperial Household Agency Archive almost all derive from private gatherings at the homes of lower nobles (*Kunaichō Shoryōbu zō shijoshū*). For excursions to suburban temples, see *Chūyūki burui shihai kanshishū* 34 and passim; *Honchō mudaishi zenchūshaku* 516–23 and passim.

25. On the social spheres of different forms of *shi* composition, see Horikawa, *Shi no katachi*, 33–61.

defined the ritual calendar of the imperial-regency alliance provided a shrinking outlet for the literary performance of lower-ranked officials, which was increasingly confined to ad hoc, informal events. Conversely, the multiplication of exclusionary ritual spaces generated a corresponding need for nobles who could fill the void left behind by the specialists whose low rank now precluded them from participation in court ceremony: In recreational palace musical ensembles (*gyoyū*), the instruments were generally played by courtiers, with lower-ranked musicians only used when there were not enough performers. At birth celebrations (*ubuyashinai*) for imperial princes, academy scholars were invited to recite auspicious texts from the classics, but only men of noble status were eligible.[26]

The monopolization of ritual performance by the upper nobility was rationalized through a systematic undermining of talent and learning as objective qualities distinguishable from the privileges of birth. Traces of this ideological process are ubiquitous in the literature of the period, most notably the *Tale of Genji*. Delighting over the beautiful dance performed by Genji and his rival Tō no Chūjō, the Kiritsubo Emperor remarks that, "In dancing and gesture, the wellborn [*ie no ko*] are different. One admires the renowned professional dancers, but they lack that easy grace."[27] The culminating justification of aristocratic amateurism in the tale is the "picture contest" between these same rivals several chapters later, where Genji's "leisurely" (*shizuka ni*) painted scenes from his exile in Suma overwhelm the works Tō no Chūjō has secretly commissioned from craftsmen for the contest. "Among the wellborn," Genji's brother Hotaru exclaims in admiration, "there are some exceptionally gifted people who seem to love every art and do wonderfully well at them all."[28] While Western accounts have often emphasized a "cult of beauty" in Heian aristocratic society, such characterizations can obscure the ways in which the strength of status-based forms of social stratification served to circumscribe the value of skills like musical performance, dance, calligraphy, or *shi* or *waka* composition.[29] If a high-born noble could be praised for easy mastery of

26. Iso, *Setsuwa to ongaku denshō*, 361–87; *Sakeiki*, Chōgen 7 (1034)/7/20–24 (357–58).

27. *Genji monogatari*, "Momiji no ga," 1:312–13; trans. Tyler, *Tale of Genji*, 135.

28. *Genji monogatari*, "Eawase," 2:390; trans. Tyler, *Tale of Genji*, 329.

29. Influential statements on Heian aestheticism are found in Sansom, *History of Japan*, 178–96, and Morris, *Shining Prince*, 170–98. A new valorization of specialization

all the arts, so a "specialist" was often derided for his ignorance in other areas.[30] Even in their fields of expertise, the aesthetic potential of the lowborn was inherently limited: "Do give your attention to the dancer's preparations," Genji asks the courtier Kashiwagi, as they make ready for the retired emperor's fiftieth birthday celebration. "Though tutors [*mono no shi*] have their areas of strength, they are so disappointing."[31]

There is something belated about this discourse of aristocratic superiority—both in its appearance decades after the major shifts in ritual participation during the late ninth century, and in its embarrassment over the ostensibly redundant presence of the experts—that suggests a kind of reaction formation. Even as the *Tale of Genji* celebrates the glory of the aristocratic paragon, it also incisively suggests that noble birth lacks the ontological weight to support such beliefs, provoking a recurring note of anxiety in the narrative. "I wonder about these levels of yours, though—the high, the middle, and the low," the protagonist innocently asks, in one of his first lines of spoken dialogue, "How can you tell who belongs to which?"[32] The constant revalidation of noble superiority appears as a symptomatic compulsion betraying an underlying absence.

The contradictions in this discourse of expertise become most acute in the arena of classical scholarship. When Genji's youthful affairs and the success of a rival faction undermine his standing at court, he withdraws and surrounds himself with "idle" professors, their alliance signaling both a shared alienation from practical power and the lingering threat of a possible alternative source of authority.[33] Several years later, when his son Yūgiri comes of age, Genji makes the idealistic decision to enroll the boy in the State Academy, depositing him in the sixth rank even as his peers have all begun to progress up the ladder of noble ranks. Reflecting on the vicissitudes of his own fortunes, Genji insists that developing "knowledge of the classics" will help his son become a "pillar of the state" (*yo no omoshi*) even after his father's support is gone. However, it is a bizarre

is one of the most significant cultural shifts in the medieval period. See Konishi, *High Middle Ages*, 146–57.

30. The regent Fujiwara no Tadazane marveled over the discrepancy between Ōe no Masafusa's mastery of classical learning and ignorance of music. *Chūgaishō*, 277.

31. *Genji monogatari*, "Wakana ge," 4:277; trans. Tyler, *Tale of Genji*, 668.

32. *Genji monogatari*, "Hahakigi," 1:58; trans. Tyler, *Tale of Genji*, 23.

33. *Genji monogatari*, "Sakaki," 2:139–43.

move by the standards of his circle, and the ceremony accompanying Yūgiri's acceptance into the letters curriculum hardly inspires confidence in Genji's decision:

> With desperately affected composure [the professors] shamelessly wore odd, ill-fitting clothes that they had had to borrow elsewhere, and everything about them presented a novel spectacle, including their manner of taking their seats with grave voices and pompous looks. The younger nobles could not stifle their grins. . . . Any buzz of talk [the professors] put a stop to, and rebuked any cheeky remark. But as the night wore on and their stridently disapproving expressions stood forth a little in the lamplight, they took on instead a comical and pathetic shabbiness [*sarugōgamashiku wabishige ni hitowaroge*], and this among other things made the occasion a strange and curious one indeed.[34]

The tone of this episode may seem "strange and curious" to the reader as well. Genji presents a compelling argument for the importance of classical learning, drawing on a vision of the transformative power of education that already had a long tradition in Japan.[35] At the same time, however, the narrative seems to undermine or relativize his point; the relationship between the idealized mastery of classical learning Genji himself embodies and the parodic anachronism of the old Confucians seems strained and ambiguous.[36]

Justifying his decision, Genji insists that a man may more dependably earn respect in the world when his "Yamato spirit [*yamato-damashii*] has a foundation of [classical] learning [*zae*]." Yamato spirit (or sometimes just "spirit," *tamashii*) refers to a combination of wit, shrewdness, and practicality, and was often contrasted with academic learning (*zae* 才 or

34. *Genji monogatari*, "Otome," 3:24–25. Translation (with minor alterations) from Tyler, *Tale of Genji*, 381–82.

35. See for example Kibi no Makibi's 吉備眞備 (d. 775) collection of maxims, *Shikyō ruijū* 私教類聚, which quotes Yan Zhitui's contention that "a man with learning will always have a place to stand in the world," while the illiterate nobleman may conversely be reduced to "plowing fields or tending horses" (46).

36. Fujiwara, "Osana-koi to gakumon"; Borgen, "Heian Love."

gakumon 學問), two sides of competence for the Heian nobleman.[37] Genji's speech echoes a similar formulation in *Utsuho monogatari*; protesting to the empress that he is not showing partiality to the relatives of a favorite consort, the emperor remarks, "Though you say [I am favoring] the relations of the one I love, it is best that the minister of the left run this country with Lord Nakatada. The prime minister [the empress's brother] is a good man, but he lacks learning. Men without learning are not suited to being protector of the realm [*yo no katame to suru ni namu ashiki*]."[38] Repeatedly, we find classical learning associated with notions of stability—of political acumen, of the country's stewardship—but the logic of base and superstructure here only reinforces the subordinate position of learning. Among the upper nobility, a grounding in classical scholarship has value, but by itself its worth is insignificant, as is made clear by the portrait of the bumbling professors.

The contradictions of Genji's idealism reflect an unbridgeable disconnect between the legacy of classical models, which was implicit in the codified Heian bureaucracy, and the realities of decision making by the noble oligarchy. Murasaki Shikibu's depiction hints that the interdependence between *zae* and *tamashii* espoused by Genji was increasingly untenable in her own day. Genji himself repeatedly demonstrates his mastery of classical scholarship, amazing learned elders with his poetry, but a century later the real-life scholar Ōe no Masafusa 大江匡房 (1041–1111) would straightforwardly insist, "Whether a regent has learning in Chinese [classics] or not, with a splendid Yamato spirit he can rule the land."[39] If there was a denigration of the authority of classical learning that is reflected in the humorous portrayal of academics in the *Tale of Genji*, however, it has to be read as part of a larger pattern extending across nearly all spheres of official activity.[40] The exclusionary ritual space that

37. For an overview of *tamashii* discourse, see Helen C. McCullough, *Ōkagami, The Great Mirror*, 43–53.

38. *Utsuho monogatari*, "Kuni-yuzuri ge," 752.

39. *Chūgaishō*, 338. Similarly, the contemporary *Ōkagami* insists that Fujiwara no Yoshichika 藤原義懐 (957–1008), despite being "illiterate" (*monmō* 文盲), was clever and possessed of "splendid spirit" (*onkokorodamashii ito kashikoku*), crediting him with excellent governance. *Ōkagami*, 192–93.

40. Cf. Mostow, "Mother Tongue," 135–37.

characterized mid-Heian court functions limited the outlets for performance by lower-ranked officials across literary, artistic, and intellectual fields, reconfiguring core patterns of Heian culture.

In this context, it is not surprising to find similar expressions of ambivalence in many contemporary writings by scholars themselves, including Minamoto no Shitagō's striking "Song of the Tailless Ox" 無尾牛歌, which allegorizes his classical learning through the eponymous animal as a diligent beast of burden that society scorns because of its disfigurement. The speaker alternates between defending the ox and lamenting its inutility:

無尾々々汝聽取	Tailless, tailless, hark to what I say!
我未以汝耕田疇	Never have I used you to plow paddy or field,
又不東西爲僦載	Nor driven you east and west, fetching and hauling,
一僦載之賃無收	And the rare times you hauled a load, I charged no fee.
我心不是偏愛汝	It's not that I can't bear to see you put to work;
家貧自忘農商謀	Poor, I've forgotten how to make a living at farming or trade.[41]

As with Murasaki Shikibu's professors, Shitagō's song mixes pathos, apologia, and satire in equal measure. Crucially different, however, is that here the question of value is figured in terms of labor and compensation, as the poet, no longer able to rely on the "skimpy" salary of official service 官俸薄, struggles to find a way to convert scribal or pedagogical employment into reliable material support.

Such anxieties among officialdom are directly connected to the mid-Heian shift in the ritual practices of the imperial-household/regency oligarchy, which increasingly employed strategies of exclusion to validate both the special efficacy of certain ceremonies and the close bonds between a chosen inner circle of upper nobles. This transformation of ritual

41. *Honchō monzui* 41. Translation by Burton Watson from Shirane, *Traditional Japanese Literature*, 487–88.

space and accompanying social stratification effectively barred most officials from direct access to the economic and social rewards distributed through ritual, encouraging the center of literary production to move up the social ladder. Yet as the persistent presence of tutors and experts in the *Genji* suggests, the employment of lower-ranked officials remained an important means by which ceremonies affirmed power relations. Neither was it practically feasible for the insider clique of the courtiers to fulfill all of its own needs for literary ritual implements. Instead, contemporary records reveal that officials' writings came to circulate through private, provisional relationships of patronage and commission. In the mid-Heian, specialists in document composition such as Shitagō could not depend on regular official employment, but would need to "drive east and west" to seek sponsorship where they could find it.

The "Splendor" of Commissioned Composition

Among the many lists in Sei Shōnagon's *Pillow Book* is one of "splendid things" (*medetaki mono*), which includes the following among its items: "Of course it goes without saying that a professor with learning is splendid. His face might be ugly and his rank low, but one can't but envy his splendor when he appears before the great, answering their questions and explaining the text. It's also so splendid when he is praised for composing a prayer, memorial, or preface."[42] Sei Shōnagon's list focuses mostly on instances of personal glory (the green robes of a chamberlain, the installation of a new imperial consort), and the praise a professor receives for his compositions is one example. With characteristically pithy insight, the author here sketches the basic dynamic of service through literary Sinitic composition in the mid-Heian: the expertise of trained scholars was valorized, but only in the context of subordinate relationships of service.

One of the best sources for investigating literary Sinitic in the mid-Heian is the anthology *Honchō monzui* (Literary Essence of This Court), which contains numerous examples of the genres mentioned in the *Pillow Book*. These are works in a stately idiom based on early Tang parallel prose.

42. *Makura no sōshi*, "Medetaki mono," 167.

The anthology shows a preference for pieces containing particularly admired couplets, mostly by academics of the late ninth through early eleventh centuries, such as Sugawara no Michizane or Ōe no Masahira 大江匡衡 (952–1012). It seems to have been intended as a companion to the *Fusōshū* 扶桑集 (Fusang Collection, ca. 997), a sixteen-volume anthology of locally composed *shi*; *Honchō monzui* includes one volume of miscellaneous poetic forms, and thirteen volumes of various genres of prose. The names of both works emphasize the local origin of their contents (Fusang being a poetic epithet for Japan), and together they would be thirty volumes, the same length as the most revered Chinese anthology, *Wenxuan* 文選 (Literary Selections, ca. 526), forming a fitting monument to the literary achievements of "this court."[43] However, while the editor of the anthology, Fujiwara no Akihira 藤原明衡 (d. 1066), is identified in an early catalog, little can be determined about its compilation. On the one hand, the scope of the materials Akihira was able to assemble suggest he had the backing of some powerful sponsor, but there is no extant preface identifying any patron. This absence, together with other internal anomalies, suggests that for whatever reason the work was never formally publicized.[44]

Instead, the first audience of *Honchō monzui* was likely Akihira's own household. Akihira was born into a lineage that had not previously been associated with scholarly posts, but became a very successful graduate of the State Academy (serving as tutor to the crown prince at one point). He had two sons very late in life, and the anthology likely served as a textbook for the types of writing they would find necessary in their careers as scholar-officials. While the anthology contains examples of more than thirty different genres of writing (again mimicking the thirty-seven genre headings in *Wenxuan*), many are represented by only one or two examples, and the vast majority of the work is taken up by only a few genres. Prayers (*ganmon* 願文), memorials (*hyō* 表), and prefaces (*jo* 序), the works Sei Shōnagon identifies with the potential for glory, together make up just

43. Ōsone, *Ōchō kanbungaku ronkō*, 84–106. In Chinese mythology, Fusang is a tree from which the sun rises, which came to refer metonymically to a land in the far east. See Schafer, "Fusang and Beyond."

44. For a summary of the contradictory evidence on *Honchō monzui*'s origin, see Gotō, *Honchō kanshibun shiryōron*, 42–47.

over half of the of 432 items in the collection.[45] Ōsone Shōsuke argued that practical use value was central to the compilation goals of *Honchō monzui*: after commissioned genres, the next largest categories in the collection are petitions for promotion (*sōjō* 奏狀) and sample essays from the civil service exam (*taisaku* 對策), both of which are directly concerned with the career advancement of academy-graduate officials.[46] *Honchō monzui*'s assembly of genres thus maps a literary sphere tightly integrated with the careers of lower-ranked officials.

Prefaces, the genre with the most entries in *Honchō monzui*, were parallel-prose documents most commonly produced in conjunction with major banquets of the court calendar and other gatherings where *shi* poetry was composed. A preface served as a commemorative record of the gathering, standing at the beginning of collected poems from the occasion when they were recorded for posterity.[47] Such works were widely composed in medieval China (the most famous being Wang Xizhi's 王羲之 "Orchid Pavilion" preface), and are found already in eighth-century Japanese anthologies like *Kaifūsō* and *Man'yōshū*. A 953 example by Minamoto no Shitagō served to introduce a set of poems produced by a group accompanying Prince Shigeakira 重明親王 (906–54), Emperor Murakami's half-brother, on an outing to Seikaji, a temple west of the capital. This temple had been established by Shigeakira on the grounds of the Seikakan, an estate owned by Minamoto no Tōru 源融 (822–895), Shigeakira's maternal ancestor.[48] The name Seikakan 栖霞觀 (Ch. Qixiaguan, Vista of Dwelling in Auroras) apparently derives from an abbey built for the famous Chinese "immortal" Zhang Guo 張果 by Emperor Xuanzong (r. 712–56). The first portion of Shitagō's preface thus contrasts the compound's Daoist origins and Buddhist reinvention. The topic chosen for group composition was "Frosted Leaves Fill the Forest with Scarlet" 霜葉滿林紅:

45. Gotō Akio points out the parallels between Sei Shonagon's discussions of writing by "professors" and the genres prevalent in *Honchō monzui*. Ibid., 108–24.

46. Ōsone, *Ōchō kanbungaku ronkō*, 56–83. Satō Michio explicitly characterizes the anthology as a practical manual. *Heian kōki Nihon kanbungaku*, 6–10.

47. For an example of this format, see *Dairi sanseki gyokai shikaishi utsushi* (Imperial Household Agency Archive Fushiminomiya Collection no. 480), a copy of the preface and poems from a 1410 palace banquet. Horikawa, *Shi no katachi*, 136.

48. The temple, now known as Seiryōji, is in the Saga district of modern Kyoto.

Seikaji is the former Seikakan. When long ago the minister took pleasure here, he left behind the burbling of the stream. Now that the prince has inherited it, he makes offerings of incense and flowers. What [the Prince of] Jiangdu enjoyed was athletics, but his seven-foot screen was needlessly tall. What [the Prince of] Huainan sought was immortals, but what use is there in one day riding the clouds?[49] How glorious! Our prince does not enjoy athletics, does not seek immortals, but delights in the mountains and rivers at his leisure, takes pleasure in the scenery at autumn's end.

Gazing around: the frost meets winter with whiteness; the leaves fill the forest with red. The trees are crossed by wind from Brocade Village; the branches are loaded with fire from the Flaming Lands. When they block the cave's mouth, piling up at dawn, and plug the rocky stream, floating in the cold, Deer Park is buried, not an inch of green moss to be seen; Heron Pond is transformed, not a foot of frothing flow remains.[50]

Now, winds and strings ring clear, as the Turtle Mountain tune is played; poetry and wine's delight is exhausted, and the Rabbit Estate's carriage makes to depart.[51] Shitagō broke the cassia bough late in life, sleeps among reeds on cold nights.[52] To have the fortune to serve midst the shining dust of the noble prince—how could it not be a great blessing for a small man? Allow me to record these splendid scenes, and thereby leave them to later days.[53]

栖霞寺者、本栖霞觀也。昔丞相遊息、所遺者泉石之聲、今大王紹隆、所供者香花之色。彼江都之好勁捷也、七尺屏風其徒高、淮南之求神仙也、一旦乘雲而何益。猗乎、我王不好勁捷、不求神仙、樂山水於閑中、翫景物於秋後矣。

49. *Xijing zaji* 西京雜記, a medieval collection of tales about the Early Han, records that the Prince of Jiangdu (Liu Jian 劉建, d. 121 BCE) was so strong and quick he could leap over a seven-foot folding screen (4.29), while the Prince of Huainan (Liu An 劉安, ca. 179–122 BCE, famous for the philosophical text *Huainanzi* 淮南子) was enamored of magicians and alchemists (3.16).

50. Deer Park and Heron Pond refer to sites where the Buddha preached, and thus to the grounds of the temple.

51. "Turtle Mountain" was a *qin* piece attributed to Confucius (*Chuxueji* 16.386). Another Han prince, Liu Wu 劉武 of Liang, built Rabbit Estate for his banquets (*Xijing zaji* 2.15).

52. Shitagō is thought to have passed the letters student examination ("broke the cassia bough") in 953, and Shigeakira died the next year in autumn of 954, so this excursion must have taken place the winter in between. Kannotō, "Anna no hen," 56.

53. *Honchō monzui* 311.

觀夫霜迎冬白、葉滿林紅。樹々傳錦里之風、枝々帶炎州之火。至夫鎖洞門兮曉積、掩巖泉兮寒浮、鹿苑跡埋、寸步無青苔之地、鷺池影變、尺波非曝布之流者也。

於是管絃韻清、龜山之曲間奏、詩酒興盡、兔園之駕將歸。順暮年折桂、寒夜臥蓬。幸陪大王之光塵、豈非小人之景福。請記勝事、貽于方來云爾。

The tripartite structure of the preface mimics an expository format of *shi* that came to dominate composition at such formal occasions in the mid-Heian (examined in the following chapter). First, the author introduces the locale, the event's host, and the occasion of the event, using a series of hyperbolic comparisons. Second, he expounds on the day's set topic for composition, using many of the same rhetorical tropes of circumlocution (the arrival of colorful foliage becomes "spreading wind from Brocade Village") and allusion ("Deer Park" as an eponym for a Buddhist temple) that the banquet's attendees would likely employ in their *shi* compositions. Finally, the third section returns to narrate the imminent poetic performance that will cap the night, concluding with a humble message from the preface author leading into the poems themselves.[54]

The style is typical of works found in *Honchō monzui*, characterized by syntactic parallelism, allusions to Chinese lore, and tonal prosody. The composition of such pieces naturally required a great deal of specialist knowledge. It is no coincidence that Sei Shōnagon attributes these works to "professors of letters" (*monjō hakase*). While poetry composition at banquets often centered on the host and other high-ranked nobles, the preface was always composed by someone (generally an official or lower noble) who had graduated from the State Academy. For more formal occasions, such as banquets in the palace, the bar was even higher: the preface must be provided by a professor of letters or other academic who had passed the highest-level civil examination. In either case, prefaces thus provided one of the few regular outlets for service and self-promotion by lower-ranked scholars.

Prayers and memorials differed in content, but not substantially in form from prefaces. The memorials in *Honchō monzui* are almost all letters

54. Satō Michio discusses the structure of Heian prefaces in *Heian kōki Nihon kanbungaku*, 173–204.

of resignation, which were technically required to be submitted to the throne by any official of fifth rank or higher seeking retirement, but seem mostly to have functioned as a ritualized show of humility at being granted a high office such as minister or regent.[55] Prayer texts show somewhat more variety, but by far the most commonly recorded are funerary (*tsuizen* 追善) prayers, presented in conjunction with offerings to pray for karmic benefits for a deceased family member. While the author of a preface spoke in his own voice, or at least for the assembled guests, almost all extant memorials and prayers are written from the standpoint of the sponsor, rather than the composer. At the service (*hōe*) for the deceased, such works were recited by a lecturer appointed from among the attendant monks, bringing an emotional climax to the proceedings. The historical narrative *Eiga monogatari* 栄花物語 (Tale of Flowering Fortune, late eleventh century) contains several descriptions of funerary services that include prayer-text recitation:

> The prayer [for the forty-ninth day service for Fujiwara no Seishi] was provided by Senior Secretary Sugawara no Tadasada. His description of her resting place was particularly moving. I can only record a bit of it:
>
> > Since her golden chariots were lined up,
> > And the jeweled doors closed,
> > Who is there to serve her?
> > Only the dawn visage of the setting moon.
> > Who is there to guard her?
> > Only the evening cries of the forest birds.
>
> These lines were particularly moving. After this [the service] concluded with readings from several sutras.[56]

As will be discussed further in chapter 5, passages such as these suggest the important performative dimension to the reception of literary Sinitic poetry and prose. Commissioned documents such as prayer texts played

55. A newly appointed minister conventionally submitted three letters of resignation before acquiescing to his sovereign's demand and assuming office. *Saikyūki*, 2:237; *Hokuzanshō* 4.393.

56. *Eiga monogatari*, "Mine no tsuki," 2:473. For a similar passage see also *Utsuho monogatari*, "Kiku no en," 329. On the performance of prayers, see Watanabe Hideo, "Ganmon," 144–50.

a central role in the legitimation of court ritual, but the text was in turn itself "ritualized" (to borrow Bell's terminology) through the elaborate ceremonies of recitation practiced in such assemblies, accentuating the authority and aesthetic appeal of its language.

The rewards for service through literary composition seem to have come in three forms. First, if the composer was able to participate in the banquet or ceremony in question, he might be privy to the general emoluments distributed to all participants, or singled out for an extra gift by the host.[57] Second, a composition that received acclaim at a very public venue might be rewarded through official advancement: at the conclusion of a flower-viewing banquet in 1006, Ōe no Masahira was rewarded for his preface by having his son Takachika 擧周 named a chamberlain.[58] Similarly, Fujiwara no Arikuni 藤原有國 (943–1011) received a rank promotion for producing a prayer text for Emperor En'yū, and later was restored to a revoked post after writing a prayer on behalf of then regent Fujiwara no Michitaka.[59]

Finally, and most commonly, composers could be remunerated outright for their work. Fujiwara no Michinaga twice mentions bestowing "gifts" (*roku*) on the supplier of a prayer for use in his Buddhist services.[60] Fujiwara no Sanesuke provides one of the most explicit discussions of such rewards for a resignation memorial: "This morning Professor of Letters [Yoshishige no] Tamemasa brought over the (third) memorial, and I gave him one oversized gown. . . . When his late lordship [Fujiwara no Saneyori] first was appointed minister of the right, [Ōe no] Asatsuna provided him with all three [memorials]. For the third, he bestowed one oversized gown. There is this precedent; it is not just my invention."[61] Fujiwara no

57. The most famous such incident is the robe a young Emperor Daigo bestowed on Sugawara no Michizane for a poem at the 900 Chrysanthemum Banquet; this became a key episode in later accounts of Michizane's life. Borgen, *Sugawara no Michizane*, 258–60. For a later example, see *Chūyūki*, Kanji 5 (1091)/3/16 (1:77).

58. *Midō kanpaku ki*, Kankō 3/3/4 (1:177).

59. Imai, "Fujiwara no Arikuni den," 276, 287.

60. *Midō kanpaku ki*, Kankō 1 (1004)/5/19 and Kankō 2/10/19 (1:89, 163). The men who bring Michinaga prayer texts are Ōe no Mochitoki and Ōe no Masahira, both former letters students.

61. *Shōyūki*, Jian 1 (1021)/10/26 (6:62). In *Utsuho monogatari*, the scholar Tōei twice composes resignation memorials for the powerful noble Masayori, for which he is plied

Tadahira similarly records rewarding the monk Ningaku with a white gown for delivery of a prayer text in 939.[62] The rewards were the same for court-sponsored functions: Ōe no Koretoki 大江維時 (888–963) was rewarded with a white gown for providing the prayer text to accompany a palace *Lotus Sutra* lecture series (*gohakkō*) in 954.[63]

The value of such gifts was considerable: court precedent manuals prescribe the same sort of white, oversized gown as the appropriate gift to a prince or other guest of honor at a formal banquet, and silk was often employed as a type of commodity money because of its exchange value and minimal weight.[64] Nevertheless, these gifting practices are not reducible to a form of payment, as in an economy of general equivalence.[65] Wealthy senior nobles such as Sanesuke regularly bestowed such gowns on *zuryō* as they left for the provinces; whatever the value of the gown, it would be repaid many times over through goods or raw materials sent back to the capital.[66] Rather than a purely economic transaction, "the passing on of wealth is only one feature of a much more general and enduring contract."[67] As the mimicry of rewards presented within official banquets and Sanesuke's concern with precedent both suggest, such exchanges served to reconsolidate literary service into the patterns of ritual—and its reinscription of power relations—at a step removed from the exclusive space of court ceremony. Like the poems presented to Masayori by his guests discussed in chapter 1, the non-equivalent form of the gift (Masayori's hospitality rewarded with a poem, Tamemasa's memorial rewarded

with "beautiful" (*kiyora*) things. *Utsuho monogatari*, "Kiku no en," 325; "Kurabiraki jō," 524.

62. *Teishin-kō ki*, Tengyō 2/3/20 (185).

63. *Daidai shinpitsu gohakkō ganmonra ki*, quoted as "Ganmon shū" in *Sandai gyoki itsubun shūsei*, 107.

64. Yamashita, *Kokka to kyūyosei*, 231; Umemura Takashi, *Nihon kodai shakai keizaishi*, 380–82. Officials received coarse silk (*ashiginu*) as part of their regular emoluments, but higher-quality taffeta silk (*kinu*) was not distributed as part of normal emoluments, being ostensibly reserved for the imperial household. Verschuer, "Life of Commoners," 316.

65. Cf. Ditter, "Writing in Tang Dynasty China," 252–59.

66. Murai, *Heian kizoku no sekai*, 273–78. For an exhaustive catalog of goods exchanged between one senior noble and his followers, see Watanabe Naohiko, *Nihon kodai kan'i seido*, 201–58, with gowns as "*makarimōshi*" gifts discussed at 249–50, 254. See also Hurst, "*Kugyō* and *zuryō*," 88–89.

67. Mauss, *The Gift*, 5.

with a robe) turns a simple repayment into a circulating token establishing persistent bonds of patronage and obligation.[68]

Gift exchange positioned literary production as a service relationship between individuals, and it is not a coincidence that this same period sees a dramatic decline in editorial and compositional projects associated with office rather than personal patronage. In the early Heian, five chronicles were commissioned by the court (beginning with *Shoku Nihongi* 續日本紀, 797), all attributed to named compilers charged by imperial command, and such an appointment was the pinnacle of prestige for learned officials. The last of these was completed in 901, however, after which the Council of State relied on the personal diaries of senior nobles and records kept by the council secretary (*geki nikki*).[69] Similarly, no new anthologies of literary Sinitic poetry and prose were commissioned by the court after 827. The *Kokin wakashū* 古今和歌集 (Collection of Yamato Songs Ancient and Modern, 905–20), a collection of *waka* poetry, attempted to revive this practice of court-sponsored anthologies, imitating the format of the earlier works by using a named group of editors, a preface, and presentation of the work to the throne (though it was not officially commissioned through an imperial proclamation to a senior noble as the earlier anthologies had been). Nevertheless, the model it proffered was not successfully continued in the following decades, and it was not until the *Goshūi wakashū* 後拾遺和歌集 (ordered in 1075) that the practice of imperially commissioned *waka* anthologies (*chokusen wakashū*) was fully established.[70] Scholar-officials continued to be employed in the bureaucracy as clerks, and might be asked to provide reports on inauspicious marvels or candidates for a new reign name, but their labor as authors and editors

68. See also Bourdieu, *Theory of Practice*, 5–6, 179–80.

69. A seventh court history was commissioned in the mid-tenth century, but seems to have never been completed. Similarly, the Engi era *kyaku* and *shiki* were the final compilations of court legislation and protocols (promulgated in 907 and 967, respectively), after which their role was largely subsumed by household transmissions of precedent.

70. The first sequel to *Kokin wakashū*, *Gosen wakashū* 後撰和歌集, seems to have been officially commissioned, but the death of the reigning emperor left the work as an unfinished draft. The next anthology, *Shūi wakashū* 拾遺和歌集, was compiled by a retired emperor who had been cut off from the central bureaucracy. On the lack of continuity between the first three so-called imperial anthologies, see Masuda, "Chokusen wakashū."

was no longer a part of their official duties, instead finding commission and reward through individual relationships with powerful senior nobles.

Composition of vernacular *waka* poetry exhibited similar patterns of commissioned patronage, though there are crucial differences in its historical background. Very little is recorded of *waka* composition during the century and a half between the latest poem in the *Man'yōshū* 萬葉集 (Collection of Myriad Ages), dated 759, and the presentation of the *Kokin wakashū* (905), but sporadic records in the official chronicles suggest that it was an important feature of public life, despite the flourishing of *shi* poetry under Emperor Saga. In the ninth century, poems in the vernacular served as decorations on screens and other accessories, or might be chanted by a banquet guest, most frequently as a kind of toast to the event's host.[71] However, such practices treated *waka* as a form of occasional entertainment, equivalent to a musical performance, rather than a composition whose specific contents were worthy of record.[72] *Waka* in this sense was "song" rather than "poetry"—it was not generally seen as categorically equivalent to *shi*, and was typically not preserved for posterity in the way that *shi* compositions often were.

This attitude began to change in the late ninth century, a shift marked most clearly by the compilation of *Shinsen man'yōshū* 新撰萬葉集 (Newly Compiled Collection of Myriad Ages, 893–913) and *Kudai waka* 句題和歌 (Yamato Songs on Topical Lines, 894), two anthologies that explicitly juxtaposed *waka* with *shi*.[73] Beginning in this period we have several records of "poetry contests" (*utaawase*)—light-hearted affairs centered on the matching and judging of poems between two sides. Poetry contests would become a serious pursuit in the late Heian, with the poems as a rule provided by the team members (*kataudo*) themselves, and judged by a renowned poet. Before the late eleventh century, however, the teams of such a contest were made up of the friends, family, and associates of the host, and the focus of the event was on matching and comparing poems, not extemporaneous composition. The poems might be provided

71. For a detailed inventory of *waka*'s use in public functions in the Heian period, see Hashimoto Fumio, *Ōchō wakashi no kenkyū*, 211–63.

72. Murase, *Kokinshū no kiban*, 17.

73. On these anthologies see Helen C. McCullough, *Brocade by Night*, 254–75.

by a lady-in-waiting or low-ranked official, but the author's presence was not required. At the 959 palace *shi* contest, the poets sat among the spectators in the courtyard to the east of the Seiryōden, where the main event took place among the emperor and senior nobles; records of the palace *waka* contest the next year, however, make no mention of any poets in attendance.[74] When lower-ranking officials were invited to such an event, they served as entertainers rather than guests. At a 977 "garden contest" (*senzai-awase*) given by a senior noble, a group of poet officials were posed in an elaborate garden display amid oil lamps and bell crickets in wicker cages, performers for the assembled guests watching from the veranda above.[75] Such experiments were exceptions, however, as contest *waka* increasingly came to be provided from among the highborn themselves—men like Taira no Kanemori 平兼盛 (d. 991), a prince-made-commoner, or Fujiwara no Norinaga 藤原範永 (fl. 1016–70), a chamberlain under Go-Ichijō (r. 1016–36).[76]

While lower-ranked officials thus had fewer opportunities to provide *waka* for banquet performance, their poems often hung silently in the background of these and other court events, inscribed on painted screens (*byōbu*), the significance of which has recently been analyzed by Gustav Heldt and Joseph Sorensen.[77] During the tenth century, senior nobles frequently had such works produced to celebrate rites of passage, such as a child's coming of age or a sixtieth birthday. The poems used in these productions tended to be commissioned from a small group of specialists, overwhelmingly officials associated with the compilation of an imperial anthology (e.g., Ki no Tsurayuki or Ōshikōchi no Mitsune), children of renowned *waka* poets (Nakatsukasa, daughter of the poet Ise), or both (Kiyohara no Motosuke). All of these people came from the middle ranks of court society: the men are fifth- or sixth-rank officials, and the women

74. *Tentoku 3-nen dairi shiawase* and *Tentoku 4-nen dairi utaawase.*

75. *Jōgen 2-nen sanjō sadaijin Yoritada zensai utaawase*, 120–21. For further discussion of the status-based layout of *utaawase*, see Heldt, *Pursuit of Harmony*, 81–86. On the cosmological basis for this ritual emphasis on hierarchy, see Hérail, *Cour du Japon*, 50–57.

76. Kudō Shigenori discusses what he calls "courtier poets" (*tenjō no utayomi*) as a prominent feature of the transitions of the tenth century. *Heianchō ritsuryō shakai*, 166–68.

77. Heldt, *Pursuit of Harmony*, 241–84; Sorensen, *Optical Allusions.*

are ladies-in-waiting (never the primary wives of the highly ranked). The implications of status hierarchy inherent in screen-poem composition were so strong that when Fujiwara no Michinaga broke with precedent to seek poems from peers on the Council of State for screens to be used in his daughter's 999 entrance to the palace, the councilor Fujiwara no Sanesuke considered it a shocking affront: "Is a senior noble's job now to haul firewood and draw water?" The outrage is compounded when Michinaga has the poets' names inscribed on the screens with their contributions, "a humiliation for later generations."[78] The strength of Sanesuke's negative reaction conversely indicates the potency of the forces coordinated in Michinaga's screens. The poems he elicited from senior nobles and courtiers were gifts fueling a cycle of symbolic exchange. Like the composition of prefaces and prayers for senior nobles documented in *Honchō monzui*, we can be certain that, in one fashion or another, this service did not go unrewarded, the principle of reciprocity continuing the cycle and validating hierarchies of power.

Conclusion: Inscribing Difference

As the discussion above has indicated, literary composition was conditioned on the assumption of particular social positions, oftentimes explicitly labeled: contemporary bylaws make provision for the invitation and reward of "poets" (*monnin*) at banquets, and Sei Shōnagon notes the glory "professors" (*hakase*) earned through their writing. Occupying such a role entailed taking a place in a social hierarchy, with attendant costs and rewards. The senior noble Sanesuke is in a position to flatly refuse a request he considers unworthy of his station, but more telling is the reluctant compliance of the author of *Kagerō nikki* 蜻蛉日記 (Mayfly Diary, ca. 975) when her husband asks her to contribute poems to a screen: the commission both affirms her poetic talent and demeans her status (particularly in relation to the man's other wives).[79] Lower-ranked officials

78. *Shōyūki*, Chōhō 1/10/23–30 (2:66–68). On this event see Sorensen, *Optical Allusions*, 202–22.

79. Heldt, *Pursuit of Harmony*, 267–68; *Kagerō nikki*, 184–87.

were often dependent on composition's social and economic rewards. Social recognition as a "scholar" (*jusha*) skilled at composition provided a basis for practical alliances, as officials exchanged technical knowledge for career advancement.

The rituals of exchange that accompanied compositional service validated both the literary document itself and its composer's status as a learned scholar and author, as well as instating an alliance of reciprocity between patron and client. This cycle of exchange might continue with promotion to a *zuryō* post, the new provincial appointee then expected to provide material support back to his original sponsor. Access to such service opportunities was therefore competitive, and often determined by hierarchies of rank, post, and lineage. Fujiwara no Morosuke 藤原師輔 (908–60) records the following exchange at the 950 Chrysanthemum Banquet, on a dispute over the assignment of preface-composing duties between two men who both held the post of Professor of Letters, Tachibana no Naomoto 橘直幹 (fl. 937–59) and Mimune no Motonatsu (fl. 937–57) 三統元夏:

> The minister [Fujiwara no Saneyori] asked Naomoto, "Who should compose the preface?" Naomoto replied, "Either myself or Motonatsu could, as you command." The minister ordered that Naomoto compose. (The day before I had summoned Motonatsu and privately asked him, "Is the matter of the preface determined by the presiding noble's command? Or is it first decided on by the professors?" Motonatsu said, "Earlier Chrysanthemum Banquet prefaces were determined by the order in which [the professors] had passed the civil service examination. After [930], this banquet was no longer held.[80] If we follow order of examinations, I should compose. If we go according to seniority [in the post of professor] Naomoto should compose. Only if we abandon procedures could [Ōe no] Asatsuna compose.")[81]

80. The Chrysthanemum Banquet was held on the ninth day of the ninth month, but after Emperor Daigo's death in the ninth month in 930, the banquet went unobserved until it was revived as a tenth-month "Lingering Chrysanthemums Banquet" (*zangiku no en*) by Murakami in 950.

81. *Kyūreki*, Tenryaku 4/10/8 (78). Naomoto took the civil service examination several months later than Motonatsu (in 937), but was appointed professor of letters in 948, while Motonatsu did not achieve the post until 950 (*Dai Nihon shiryō* ser. 1, 10:535–36, 19:226–29). The text enclosed in parentheses is parenthetical in the original.

Motonatsu makes an argument for his own priority over Naomoto, the other professor of letters at this time, but more important is his premise that the opportunity to compose the event's preface could not be arbitrarily assigned, but was an entitlement based in a particular office: the far more senior scholar Ōe no Asatsuna 大江朝綱 (886–958), who no longer held the post of professor, could not be eligible.[82]

Motonatsu's discourse on precedent recasts his own subservience—obliged to provide compositional service in hope of reward—as privilege and hierarchical superiority over other unrecognized and unnamed scholars lacking his prerogative to participate in palace ceremony. Scholars actively sought to stabilize their service obligations/opportunities by championing precedents that forged a link between ritual, literary genres, and particular posts and households. This effort was particularly fraught as the role of "scholar" itself was altered by the mid-Heian changes in ritual space, disrupting established prerogatives such as the authority of the older scholarly lineages. For example, Fujiwara no Arikuni, a graduate of the State Academy, parlayed the favor of the regent Fujiwara no Kaneie into a series of official posts and eventually senior noble rank. His sons followed into the academy in his footsteps, but their father's status meant they became courtiers at an early age, giving them an advantage in positions directly serving the imperial household, such as tutor to the crown prince.[83] In the second half of the Heian period, Fujiwara lineages like Arikuni's came to dominate the scholarly posts previously controlled by lineages who were excluded from courtier status.[84] *Honchō monzui* occupies an ambivalent position in this environment: it focuses on works from a generation or two earlier, mostly ignoring the rising Fujiwara scholars (Arikuni receives only a single selection). Instead, the anthology instrumentalizes the past glories of the traditional scholarly houses, the editor

82. Following the 943 Residential Palace Banquet, Fujiwara no Tadahira criticized the conduct of the ceremony, in which Emperor Suzaku had commanded Naomoto to provide the preface, because the preface composer should have been decided ahead of time by the invited professors. *Rihō ō ki*, Tengyō 6/2/2 (119).

83. Hironari (977–1028) was made a courtier in 996, and Sukenari (988–1070) in 1005. Both were made chamberlain at the age of twenty-one. *Kugyō bunin* 1:269, 297.

84. During the eleventh and twelfth centuries, twenty-nine men of Fujiwara lineage (including Hironari and Sukenari) would be appointed as professor of letters, with only ten such appointments for Ōe and Sugawara scholars. Hisaki, *Nihon kodai gakkō*, 295.

Fujiwara no Akihira superseding them with his own upstart scholarly lineage by consolidating and mastering their corpus.

Like Sei Shōnagon's discussion of the glories attendant on professors, *Honchō monzui*'s juxtaposition of texts establishes a positive connection between patterned writing and social positions while marking off the boundaries within which such writing could be used. Because of its heavy emphasis on commissioned ceremonial documents, however, it also serves to map the differentials established between scholars of different lineages, providing a vivid picture of how differences in status and access determined whose compositions were presented for public audience (and preserved for later readers). Minamoto no Shitagō, who never passed the highest-level civil service examination and peaked at junior fifth rank upper, has seventeen poetic prefaces included in the collection, but almost all derive from excursions or banquets of princes and other high nobility, rather than official rites of the court calendar. A telling example is a 966 lecture on the *Analects* sponsored by Minamoto no Nobumitsu 源延光 (927–76), for which Shitagō provided the preface, even as the lecture itself was given by Professor of Letters Fujiwara no Nochiō 藤原後生 (907–70).[85] By contrast with these numerous banquet prefaces, not a single one of the resignation letters or prayers in the collection is attributed to Shitagō. The many prefaces by Shitagō in *Honchō monzui* thus illustrate both the recognition accorded his compositional skills and the limits of his status.

His contemporary Sugawara no Fumitoki 菅原文時 (899–981) makes a good object of comparison: like Shitagō, he studied in the letters curriculum, but had the advantages of descent from a renowned scholarly lineage, academic posts that came with passing the highest-level examination, and higher rank (at his death, junior third). Fumitoki's works in *Honchō monzui* include a prayer text for minister and regent Fujiwara no Koretada 藤原伊尹 (924–72) and resignation letters for several other ministers. He also contributed prefaces to palace events overseen by the sovereign, such as a Residential Palace Banquet in 966.[86] When the wife of Shitagō's most important patron, Minamoto no Takaakira 源高明 (914–82), died in 947, Shitagō was commissioned to write a prayer on behalf of

85. *Honchō monzui* 259.

86. Ibid. 422, 112–13, 124–26, 132–33, and 340.

the woman's nurse. By contrast, when Takaakira presented a prayer under his own name after the death of his half-sister Kōshi 康子 in 957, it was written by Fumitoki, then professor of letters.[87] The anecdote collection *Gōdanshō* 江談抄 (The Ōe Conversations, ca. 1108) contains a conversation that well illustrates the perceived differences between these men:

> [Ōe no Masafusa] said, "Do you understand Fumitoki's work, 'Song of an Old Man's Retirement'?" I replied no, but I had heard about the format. . . . It begins with a couplet of one-character lines, and increases to twelve characters per line. He said, "Yes. It's like a fan's edge [spreading outward]. Fumitoki made this song with careful thought over a period of three years. When he finished, he first showed it to Shitagō. Shitagō read it, and in the space of a night composed a response in the same format and sent it to Fumitoki. Fumitoki was very upset, calling [Shitagō] witless. Other people of the time also criticized him. It's not that the composition was mediocre, but he showed no thought or tact."[88]

In an echo of Genji's complaints about the inadequacy of "tutors," here it is Shitagō's technical mastery that conversely becomes symptomatic of a lack, differentiating him from Fumitoki, whose ancestry, office, and rank give the latter an unimpeachable cultural authority. Masafusa, himself a descendant of one of the most revered scholarly lineages, insists elsewhere, "Among Japanese collections, for poetry one should study Fumitoki's style."[89] The validation of Fumitoki's compositions as exemplars to be imitated is inseparable from the lineage and rank that provided him the most esteemed service opportunities.

This chapter has analyzed the hierarchical structures through which literary Sinitic documents were produced in the mid-Heian, as nobles eligible to participate in ceremony were cordoned off from document-composing officials, who in turn were ranked in terms of their relative prerogatives to provide scribal service. As the quotations from Motonatsu and Masafusa above suggest, this hierarchical differentiation was not simply a top-down imposition, but actively generated from within the

87. *Chōya gunsai* 2.30–31; *Dai Nihon shiryō* ser. 1, 10:346–47.
88. *Gōdanshō* 5.73.
89. Ibid. 5.49.

stratum of academy-educated officials whose lives it shaped. The validation of particular genres of ornamented prose and poetry provided a social outlet for the technical expertise produced in the State Academy, but the stratified patterns of the extant corpus cannot be explained simply through discrepancies in the degree of education or literacy among officialdom. Rather, there is always an imperfect overlap between more-or-less objective formal distinctions—parallel prose obeys certain rules, and the production of it requires extensive training—and socially defined correspondences with those distinctions.

While the preceding pages have shown repeatedly the strong identification between specific social roles and corresponding forms of writing, the incessant repetition of such concerns is itself testimony to the fragility of those associations. The codified definitions of banquet "poets," the anthologization of writing by a few recognized scholarly lineages, and the preoccupation with precedent governing composition service and its reward all point to the laborious maintenance of fundamentally arbitrary classifications. It is the praxis of literature broadly conceived—the stipulation of seniority in office as a qualification for service opportunities, the robe given each time in return for service, the recitation of the document by a talented monk before an audience of formally dressed nobles—that naturalizes the arbitrary, physically embodying a set of power relations that are textually represented in documents that praise hosts, mourn rulers, and beg for the recognition of one's talents.

Contemporary diaries and other sources reveal that the mid-Heian literary sphere operated through a complex economy of exchange. The rising exclusivity of ritual barred scholar-officials from direct participation in the most prominent ceremonies, so their work instead circulated through private commission. These commissions were a precious opportunity to establish relationships of reciprocity with the upper nobility and were thus jealously guarded as prerogatives of seniority, rank, or lineage. But while the rigid restrictions of precedent and hierarchy at times seem inescapable, it would be a mistake to treat these social regulations as pre-existing phenomena, with literary production simply reflecting underlying power relations. Rather, literature stood in a mutually constitutive relationship with the imagination of capital society: even as socially defined privileges and restrictions shaped literary production, literary writing in turn served to delineate and enforce social distinctions.

The perlocutionary force of these documents was self-justifying through their form, the complexity and decoration that differentiated literature as a distinct and superior class of writing. The next chapter considers the aesthetics of literary Sinitic by analyzing contemporary prescriptive discourse of ornament and pattern in writing. The above discussion has detailed the motivations of and demands upon officials seeking to advance their careers through writing; the mastery of technical poetics establishes the boundaries of action within which they maneuvered for advantage.

THREE

Couplet Collections and Aesthetic Strategy

Unable to depend upon a regular salary, low-ranked officials drew on their education to find employment as scribes for the upper nobility, producing documents for use in ceremonies and banquets. Such patronage was based on demonstrated mastery of recognized genres of literary Sinitic (including poetry, prefaces, and prayer texts) that demanded a classical education beyond the typical bureaucrat. The patterns of service and exchange discussed in the previous chapter are thus predicated on a shared recognition of a separate sphere of inscription, the "literary," that was particularly suited to ritualistic uses and could only be reliably produced by so-called "scholars," generally graduates of the State Academy. This chapter examines how this category of literature was defined through reference to internal formal features, drawing on Heian prescriptive discourse to reconstruct the devices by which writers enacted literariness and assessed the relative quality of competing literary works. Reconstructing these emic definitions of the literary provides the basis for analyzing the interplay between ostensibly universal formal principles and the exigencies of quotidian practice. Such discursive formulations of literary form are further problematized in chapter 5, which returns to the same problem of the distinction of the literary from the standpoint of recitation performance.

The genesis of a literary sphere in ancient Japan, meaning first and foremost the cultivation of a critical mass of people able to read and write, was intimately connected with new forms of political control. The modes of administration pursued by the Asuka and Nara governments necessitated the mobilization of large staffs of clerks and scribes, whose numbers only increased over the course of the eighth and ninth centuries.[1] In the mid-Heian, contemporary accounts such as Fujiwara no Sanesuke's diary *Shōyūki* 小右記 make reference to a seemingly endless river of petitions, reports, proclamations, records, and letters produced by and circulating around the Heian court. The apparatuses of state provided some of the most powerful and enduring motivations for writing, and collections like the *Ruijū fusenshō* 類聚符宣抄 (Classified Collection of Directives and Orders, early eleventh century) preserve hundreds of directives and communiqués that circulated between the Council of State and various bureaus, temples, and provincial administrators.

As the previous chapter demonstrated, this administrative use of writing was complemented by the performance of documents in rituals that served to legitimate the cosmological role and numinous authority of the court. Early Japanese discourse on writing, however, portrays an ambiguous relationship between these two uses of script: they can be conflated as two aspects of governance through writing *qua* civilization, but in other cases the peculiar virtue of literary writing is distinguished from the broader realm of quotidian inscription. According to the preface of the *Kaifūsō* 懐風藻 (Verses Commemorating the Past, 751), Japan's earliest surviving poetic anthology, composition in literary Sinitic first became widespread during the reign of Emperor Tenji (roughly 662 to 671), presented in the preface as an enlightened era cut tragically short by the violence of the Jinshin War. However, the preface draws a distinction between the basic technology of writing (whose advent is ascribed to the centuries-earlier reign of Emperor Ōjin [ca. 400]), and the "embossed poetry and beautiful prose" that arose through and that completed the regulation and ritual of the new, code-based state.[2]

The *Kaifūsō* preface draws upon a Chinese tradition of literary thought based upon the classical identification of "pattern"/"patterned writing" (Ch. *wen*[*zhang*], J. *bun*[*shō*] 文章) with civilization through ordering and refinement. "Language must be adequate to intent. . . . If one puts [intent] into language without *wen*, then when he puts it into practice it will not go far," as Confucius is quoted in the *Zuo Commentary*

1. Mesheryakov, "Quantity of Written Data."
2. *Kaifūsō*, Preface (58–59).

(*Zuozhuan* 左傳).[3] In Warring States philosophical discourse, the "patterning" of *wen* was a concept equally applicable to culture, ritual, and writing. By the end of the Han dynasty, however, scholars were increasingly conscious of the "literary" as a category of writing distinct from scholarship or history, defined specifically by its formal ornamentation. The sixth-century Chinese anthology *Wenxuan* ("selection of *wen*"), which would become one of the central texts in the State Academy curriculum in Japan, presents in its preface a narrative of crude antiquity brought to order through the medium of writing, whose patterning in turn becomes steadily more refined.[4] For this reason, the collection is dominated by belletristic and persuasive pieces, while for example philosophical writings that aim at "establishing doctrine" rather than "skillful writing" are excluded from the collection.[5] In this formulation, refinement—in the form of rhetoric, parallelism, prosody, and rhyme—is integral to the mission and efficacy of pieces, and writing that possesses these elements occupies a privileged place within the wider world of inscription.

This definition is echoed in the Japanese anthology *Keikokushū* 經國集 (Collection for Governing the Realm, 827), whose preface declares:

> Literary writing [*bunshō*] is that which exhibits the images of high and low, clarifies the order of human affairs, exhausts underlying principles and thereby seeks the fitness of the myriad things. Furthermore, "pattern and substance in balance is what makes the gentleman." This may be compared to decorated silks among clothing, or goose wings among the birds.[6]
>
> 文章者所以宣上下之象、明人倫之敘、窮理盡性、以究萬物之宜者也。且文質彬々、然後君子。譬猶衣裳之有綺穀、翔鳥之有羽儀。

3. Owen, *Chinese Literary Thought*, 29–30.
4. Bol, *This Culture of Ours*, 88–89.
5. *Wenxuan* [*xu*].2b; trans. Knechtges, *Wen Xuan*, 1:89. The only genre of administrative documents in the *Wenxuan* represented by more than a few examples is the memorial (*biao* 表), and widely used formats like the commission (*fu* 符) and explanation (*jie* 解) do not appear at all. On formats of administrative documents in Six Dynasties China, see Nakamura, *Gi Shin Nanbokuchō*. *Honchō monzui*, discussed in the previous chapter, follows this example.
6. *Keikokushū*, 490. "Pattern and substance . . . " is a reference to the *Analects* 6.18 (*Lunyu zhushu* 6.23).

The last line makes reference to a passage in the *Classic of Changes*, which explains that because the goose flies so high, its feathers can serve as "emblems" (*yi* 儀), plumed ritual implements.[7] Martin Kern has argued that the late Han invention of "literature" occurs through a strategic slippage, in which the emblematic power of ritual practice's ornamentation is transferred onto the textual canon and classically motivated writing.[8] The presentation of poems at banquets discussed in the previous chapters implies the same premise, with the symbolic exchange between guest and host dependent upon language ritualized through the adherence to a customary literary format.

Thus in formulations like that of the *Keikokushū*, the characteristic features of *bunshō* that set it apart from other inscription are ornament and ritual use, which go hand in hand. Early Japanese discourse exhibits a sustained distinction between writing in the broadest sense and the literary genres whose ornamentation set them apart from the herd, but ornamentation does not here imply that the literary is purely decorative or lacking in instrumental efficacy—rather, it is understood as a manifestation of the laborious cultivation of civilization. The title *Keikokushū* derives from an oft-quoted passage attributed to the Wei emperor Cao Pi 曹丕 (187–226), "Literature [*wenzhang*] is a great enterprise for governing the realm," emphasizing the political efficacy of the anthology's artful contents: fifteen volumes of rhymed verse (*fu* rhapsodies and *shi* poetry) and five of parallel prose genres (poetic prefaces and civil service examination essays). The formal ornamentation of literary genres is conceptualized not as superficial or supplementary decoration, but as pattern or ordering, contiguous with the wider organization of the state through laws, schools, ranks, offices, and other venues of writing.[9]

This chapter first takes up a corpus of technical discourse on literary writing to reconstruct the parameters by which formal correctness was judged. This poetics was conceptualized at two levels: assorted types of parallelism within couplets and expository development organizing these

7. *Zhouyi zhengyi* 5.51.

8. Kern, "Ritual, Text, and the Formation of the Canon," 61–81.

9. For a translation and analysis of Cao Pi's essay, see Owen, *Chinese Literary Thought*, 57–72. On *bun* as a distinct category of writing in the Japanese context, see also Borgen, "Politics of Classical Chinese," 215–17; Webb, "In Good Order," 165–67, 206–15.

couplets into complete works. As depicted in poetic manuals and couplet collections, literary composition is homologous to an academic examination, the success of which depended on the ability to fulfill these formal requirements while demonstrating erudition through adroit allusions and wordplay. Where erudition can be seen as a tactic of horizontal differentiation from other competing poets, authors might also seek to enact a vertical alliance through a rhetoric of supplication, which becomes increasingly prevalent in banquet poetry and other literary genres in the mid-Heian. I argue, however, that there was a fundamental disparity between these two positioning strategies: while erudition was expressly asserted as the core criteria of literary evaluation, supplication was largely effaced from technically oriented manuals, its formalization as the basis for group affective response conversely enervating its utility as a strategy for seeking support and recognition. By reading Heian poetry in the context of the manuals and anthologies that preserve it, this chapter ultimately seeks to understand formal aesthetics not as a priori principles, but as constructs whose meaning was retrospectively articulated through social practice.

Parallelism and Topical Exposition

> I'll bring along some oranges and some good wine. I have no talent for linked verse, but if you'll let me use the *Qieyun* [rhyming dictionary], I can join the gathering.
>
> —letter in response to a banquet invitation, *Unshū shōsoku*

By the Tang period in China, discourse on the proper ornamentation of literary genres, particularly *shi* poetry, was standardized and propagated through a growing library of rhyming dictionaries and poetry manuals (*shige* 詩格).[10] In the early Heian, Japanese works such as Kūkai's 空海 (774–835) *Bunkyō hifuron* 文鏡秘府論 (Treatise on the Treasury of the Literary Mirror, ca. 820) and Sugawara no Koreyoshi's 菅原是善 (812–80) dictionary *Tōkyū setsuin* 東宮切韻 digested much of this knowledge in domestically compiled works, in the same way that *Honchō monzui*

10. On *shige*, see Yugen Wang, "Popular Poetics."

provided a local supplement to prestigious imported literary anthologies. Among extant works, the one most directly connected to mid-Heian practice is the manual *Sakumon daitai* (Essentials of Composition). This work survives in an array of disparate manuscripts, but one fourteenth-century example provides a facsimile of a late Heian recension of the text. Even at this stage, however, the manual shows evidence of several layers of compilation: a tenth-century set of ten basic rules for poetic composition (attributed to Minamoto no Shitagō in some manuscripts), to which were added sometime in the eleventh century instructions for parallel prose composition titled "Essentials of Prose" and a list of poetic precedents for various types of unconventional rhetorical maneuvers (the opening "Ten Rules" and some of these precedents are translated in Appendix A).[11]

Sakumon daitai follows the Tang *shige* in apprehending poetry as rhetoric; the analysis of literature is couched in terms of technical requirements and formal possibilities, with almost no attention to ideology or theory. The paradigm of rhetorical technique was in turn the couplet, whose two lines were coordinated through tonal and syntactic parallelism. According to *Bunkyō hifuron*, parallelism is the defining feature of the literary, distinguishing it from other language:

> In literary writing [*bunshō*], one must observe parallelism throughout, with only one or two places not in couplets. If one consistently uses non-parallel [constructions], it is not ultimately literary writing (if it is never parallel, then it is no different from common language).[12]
>
> 在於文章、皆須對屬、其不對者止得一處二處有之。若以不對爲常、則非復文章(若常不對、則與俗之言無異)。

The formal features discussed in composition manuals can be conveniently classified according to James Robert Hightower's schema of "Metrical, Grammatical, and Phonic" forms of parallelism.[13] These rules will

11. This MS also has a preface that seems to have been grafted on from a different work. On the compilation stages of the work, see Yamazaki Makoto, "Sakumon daitai no gensho keitai."

12. *Bunkyō hifuron*, "Hoku," 740. The text enclosed in parentheses is parenthetical in the original.

13. Hightower, "Parallel Prose."

be well known to readers familiar with the Chinese poetic tradition, but it will be helpful at the outset to summarize the broader characteristics, as well as a few of the tendencies specific to Heian literary Sinitic.

METRICAL PARALLELISM

Rules 2 and 3 of *Sakumon daitai* allow for poetry in five-syllable or seven-syllable lines, conforming to the standard format of Chinese "regulated verse" (*lüshi*, J. *risshi* 律詩). A few unusual forms are listed elsewhere in the manual, but in general, discussion of poetry is limited to pentasyllabic or heptasyllabic regulated verse, in poems of four or eight lines. In actual practice, the majority of *shi* composed in the mid-Heian were heptasyllabic verses in eight lines (four couplets). The discussion of parallel prose is largely devoted to the various types of line lengths available in prose composition. With the exception of "unfettered" (nonparallel) lines used at the opening and closing of the essay, prose should alternate among "contracted" couplets (four syllables per line) and "long" couplets (between five and nine syllables per line). There is a particular emphasis on "alternating couplets" (*kakku* 隔句), made up of four lines of alternating syllable counts. This passage, from the preface on autumn leaves by Shitagō quoted in the last chapter, is made up of a contracted couplet, two long couplets, and an alternating couplet of 4/7/4/7:

觀夫	Gazing around:
霜迎冬白、	The frost meets winter with whiteness;
葉滿林紅。	The leaves fill the forest with red.
樹々傳錦里之風、	The trees are crossed by wind from Brocade Village;
枝々帶炎州之火。	The branches are loaded with fire from Flaming Lands.
至夫	When
鎖洞門兮曉積、	They block the cave's mouth, piling up at dawn,
掩巖泉兮寒浮、	And plug the rocky stream, floating in the cold,
鹿苑跡埋、	Deer Park is buried,
寸步無青苔之地、	Not an inch of green moss to be seen;

鷺池影變、	Heron Pond is transformed,
尺波非曝布之流者也。	Not a foot of frothing flow remains.

As here, these sequences of couplets are periodically broken up by two- or three-syllable interjections (e.g., 觀夫, "gazing upon it," or 於是, "thereupon"), which often mark "paragraph breaks" in the exposition's development.

GRAMMATICAL PARALLELISM

Most of the examples quoted throughout *Sakumon daitai* demonstrate fairly exact syntactic parallelism, with every word in the first line matched in the second by a word of equivalent function (nouns with nouns, verbs with verbs, etc.).[14] Such oppositions can be extended further with forms of semantic parallelism, opposing words with complementary meanings, such as colors, directions, numbers, or names. Nevertheless, compared to *Bunkyō hifuron*, which lists twenty-nine different types of this sort of lexical parallelism, *Sakumon daitai* is relatively vague on the topic, only listing a handful of varieties. In addition to basic semantic complements, the work also notes that homonyms can be used to create unorthodox parallels, such as opposing the word "hundred" 百 with the word "sandalwood" 栴, since the latter is homophonous with the word for "thousand," *sen* 千. Such devices allow for the creation of what Hightower labels "complex" parallels, in which two elements form complements in two different senses (Deer Park and Heron Pond are both sites where the Buddha preached, but also both incorporate the name of an animal), a technique used with increasing frequency in Japan from the mid-tenth century onward.[15] The art of parallelism lies not in the endless pairing of opposites, but in the subtle variations and deviation into partial and "pseudo-parallelism."[16] Furthermore, rule 6 of the poetry section notes that grammatical parallelism is limited

14. This is an oversimplification, since often in literature the grammatical ambiguity of Chinese morphemes is specified precisely *through* parallel construction. See Gentz, "Zum Parallelismus," 242.

15. On the use of such punning parallels in Japanese *shi*, see Kudō, "Engo kakekotoba-teki hyōgen."

16. See Plaks, "Where the Lines Meet," 48.

to the two middle couplets of an eight-line poem, excluding the first and last couplets, a point discussed further below.

PHONIC PARALLELISM

Like *Bunkyō hifuron*, *Sakumon daitai* invokes some of the discourse of "poetic maladies" associated with the so-called "Yongming style" of the fifth- and sixth-century Southern Courts, but much of its explanation of tonal patterns, as well as the examples cited, accords more closely with Tang regulated verse. Whereas the former distinguished syllables into level, rising, falling, and entering tones, and established rules prohibiting certain kinds of repetition of the same tone, the latter was based on a binary division between level and "deflected" (any of the other three) tones, which were arranged in mirrored patterns in successive lines.[17] *Sakumon daitai* provides schematic diagrams of such tonal patterns, such as the following:

○○●●○○●
●●○○●●○

where ○ represents a level-tone syllable and ● a deflected tone.[18]

Heian writers strove to observe these tonal patterns and were largely successful. Surviving *shi* from the seventh century show little awareness of tonal prosody, but eighth-century poems in the *Kaifūsō* already display partial tonal alternation.[19] By the late ninth century, writers such as Shimada no Tadaomi 島田忠臣 (828–92) and Sugawara no Michizane experimented with extremely complex tonal patterns, showing a ready grasp of Tang poetics. In the mid-Heian, however, the tonal patterns observed

17. On the shift in tonal prosody from the late Six Dynasties to the Tang, see Matsuura, "Rikuchō shintaishi."

18. An introduction to regulated verse prosody is provided by Downer and Graham, "Tone Patterns." For more detail, see Wang Li, *Hanyu shilüxue*, 72–142. *Sakumon daitai* uses the characters 平 ("level") and 他 ("other") to diagram these patterns.

19. Tsuda, "*Kaifūsō* no hyōsoku."

in *shi* became somewhat simpler.[20] The poems in the collection *Honchō reisō* 本朝麗藻 (Beautiful Verses of This Court, ca. 1010) show mirroring of syllables 2, 4, and 6 of alternating lines, as well as each line's final syllable. Syllables 1 and 3 seem to have been treated as prosodically irrelevant.[21] The status of the fifth syllable is ambiguous: many poems display mirroring here, but others do not. This suggests a degree of leeway in compositional standards: at a 1006 flower-viewing banquet at the estate of the powerful statesman Fujiwara no Michinaga, poems by the scholars Ōe no Masahira and Fujiwara no Hironari 藤原廣業 (977–1028) observe perfect tonal alternation in the fifth syllables, while courtier guests show occasional lapses, and the host ignores this rule altogether.[22]

In the case of parallel prose, *Sakumon daitai* suggests a very limited attention to tonal prosody. There is no explicit discussion of tones in the prose sections of the work, and the example pieces given have tones labeled only for the final syllable of each line, which alternate between level and deflected. This is somewhat simplified from the dominant style of Tang parallel prose, elucidated by David Branner, in which tonal mirroring is typically observed in two or three words per line.[23] Nevertheless, examination of actual mid-Heian examples suggests that at least some writers went beyond line-final syllables to create more complex parallel patterns. The tonal prosody of the final couplet by Shitagō quoted above can be represented (following Branner's scheme) as:

※●※○ ※●※○○※●
※○※● ※○※●●※○

with ※ representing a prosodically irrelevant syllable.

20. On the changing standards for tonal prosody in the early to mid-Heian, see Huang, "Nara Heianchō Nihon kanshi," 146–69, 222–57.

21. Thus Heian writers frequently violate the so-called *guping* 孤平 restriction (a fourth-syllable level tone should never be sandwiched by deflected tones on both sides), one of the most carefully observed rules in Tang regulated verse. Ibid., 249.

22. *Honchō reisō kanchū* 11–21. The study of Chinese pronunciation through chanting was one of the first steps in elementary education in the Heian period, as discussed in the following chapter.

23. Branner, "Tonal Prosody."

In addition to tonal prosody, the other main form of phonic parallelism is rhyme. *Sakumon daitai* notes the rules for determining a word's rhyme according to the *fanqie* (J. *hanzetsu*) glossing system, and explains that the even-numbered lines of a poem should rhyme (generally using a level-tone rhyme), cautioning against mistaking two similar rhymes (e.g., 青 and 清).[24] The discussion of parallel prose contains no mention of rhyme, and indeed this is the defining distinction between poetry (*bun* or *shi*) and prose (*hitsu* 筆) in *bunshō* discourse, categories that appear in Liu Xie's 劉勰 *Wenxin diaolong* 文心雕龍 (Literary Mind and Dragon Carving, ca. 500) and are carried on in various Heian period treatises.[25] "Prose" in this model lacks the rhyme of poetry, but is still heavily ornamented with metrical, grammatical, and tonal parallelism. Thus, this apprehension of the literary excludes unadorned discursive writing: in the anthology *Honchō monzui*, almost every piece is in rhymed poetry or parallel prose, with the only exceptions a handful of records and biographies that adopt the documentary idiom of the official court chronicles.[26]

Heian writers defined literary writing through its ornamental patterning, drawing on a well-established Chinese aesthetic of sentences structured through parallelism. The macro-level organization and content of a piece in turn was premised on a dynamic of exposition, seen most frequently in the context of group composition on an assigned topic (*dai* 題) at poetic banquets. As the first rule of *Sakumon daitai* puts it, "The way of poetry is to first consider the topic, and only then dip one's brush." Composition manuals were primarily pitched at the level of the individual couplet, but they did provide some guidance on the process of topical exposition, which was based on the "tripartite form" frequently observed in medieval Chinese poetry: an opening couplet setting the scene, two middle couplets that describe the moment and must make use of grammatical

24. The *fanqie* 反切 method indicates a character's pronunciation using two other characters, the first indicating the initial consonant, and the second the rhyme (the vowel and any final). On the history and accuracy of *fanqie* glosses, see Branner, "*Fǎnqiè* Phonology."

25. *Wenxin diaolong jiaozheng* 44.267; *Bunkyō hifuron*, "Sei," 716; *Kuchizusami chūkai*, 205.

26. Ōsone, "Kanbuntai," 423–24.

parallelism, and a final couplet that reacts to the occasion described.[27] A typical example of this form is Bai Juyi's poem "On Seeing Master Xiao Off on His Travels to Qiannan" 送蕭處士遊黔南, sometimes praised in the mid-Heian as his greatest poem:

能文好飲老蕭郎	A fine writer and great drinker is old Xiao,
身似浮雲鬢似霜	His body like a floating cloud, his temples white as frost.
生計拋來詩是業	Since he cast off his livelihood, poetry is his work;
家園忘却酒爲鄉	Once he forgot his household, wine became his hometown.
江從巴峽初成字	After the Ba Gorge, the Yangtze loops into a rune;
猿過巫陽始斷腸	South of Wu Gorge, the gibbons' [cries] pierce your gut.
不醉黔中爭去得	Unless you're drunk, how will you leave for Qianzhong?
磨圍山月正蒼蒼	For the moonlight on Mount Mawei glows so soft.[28]

The first couplet introduces the subject of the poem, who is celebrated here as a cultured gentleman of leisure. The middle two couplets make use of parallel constructions, first describing Xiao's abandonment of home and office to pursue his travels, then evoking the wild and haunting terrain he will be entering. The final couplet brings us back to the matter at hand, another round to stiffen the subject's resolve as he prepares to depart.[29]

In the mid-Heian, the topic for poetic exposition at banquets and other group composition settings was almost always a five-character

27. Owen, *Poetry of the Early T'ang*, 234–55.

28. *Bai Juyi ji jianjiao* 18.1179. For this poem described as Bai Juyi's finest, see *Gōdanshō* 4.54. On the figure of poetry as "work" in Bai's poetry, see Owen, *Late Tang*, 53–55.

29. My translation of the final couplet is based on the Japanese reading tradition of this poem, which glosses Qianzhong with the dative particle *ni*. See for example the thirteenth-century collection of Bai Juyi selections *Kankenshō* 管見抄 (2.52a). The object of the verb 去 is more commonly the location departed *from*, in which case the final couplet imagines Xiao after he has arrived at his destination, and the seductive beauty he will find below the Yangtze.

literary Sinitic phrase. Originally the phrases were quotations from well-known Chinese poems, but by the eleventh century they were often simply invented to suit the occasion, usually referencing the season ("At Year's End, We Think of Spring Flowers") or place ("Rain Makes the Mountain Colors Lush"). This genre of *shi* came to be labeled "topic line poetry" (*kudaishi* 句題詩). Composition manuals explain the sequence of exposition by assigning specific roles to each of the four couplets in a standard heptasyllabic poem. The couplets are labeled the Subject Matter (*daimoku* 題目), Topic Decomposition (*hadai* 破題), Metaphorical Comparison (*hiyu* 譬喩) or Classical Anecdote (*honmon* 本文), and Divulgence of Feeling (*jukkai* 述懐).[30] These labels provide a logic of exposition that governs how the individual couplets of the poem link together:[31]

1. In the first couplet (*daimoku*), each of the five characters of the phrase designated as the topic for group composition (henceforth, the "topic phrase") must be incorporated, preferably divided between the two lines of the couplet.

2. Each line of the second couplet (*hadai*) should restate the elements of the topic phrase using synonyms or metonymic associations. *Sakumon daitai* gives an example of the topic phrase "Palace Warblers Twitter in the Dawn Light" 宮鶯囀暁光 with a *hadai* couplet of

   西樓月落花間曲 Moonlight falls on the western tower, a song among the flowers;
   中殿燈殘竹裏音 Lamplight fades in the central pavilion, a tune in the bamboo.

   Here the topic-phrase element "palace" is replaced by "western pavilion" and "central hall" (locations within the Imperial Palace), "warblers twitter" by "song among flowers" and "notes within bamboo," and "dawn light" by "moonlight falls" and "lamplight fades."

3. The third couplet (*hiyu*) also demands a restatement of the topic phrase, but the practical difference between "decomposition" and

30. The earliest source for these labels is the 970 children's primer *Kuchizusami* (221).

31. The following summary draws on Horikawa, *Shi no katachi*, 33–61, and Denecke, "Topic Poetry." The authoritative treatment of *kudaishi* will be Satō Michio's forthcoming *Kudaishi ronkō*.

"metaphorical comparison" is not entirely clear. The thirteenth-century composition manual *Ōtaku fukatsushō* 王澤不渇鈔 (Compilation of Unexhausted Royal Blessings) replaces the term *hiyu* with "classical anecdote" (*honmon*). The expectation seems to have been that the couplet should refer to historical or literary figures that are associated with words in the topic phrase.

4. The fourth couplet (*jukkai*) presents the poet's individual mindset (generally gratitude toward the host or a humble declaration of the poet's lack of talent or age), preferably employing figurative language related to the topic phrase's theme.

The model presented in composition manuals is an idealized abstraction; prior to the eleventh century, poets regularly deviated from the strictest formulations of these guidelines. Even in later periods, the distinction between the second and third couplet remained fuzzy—the practical implementation seems to have been to treat both couplets as pursuing a kind of *hadai* restatement of the topic phrase, with a bias toward including some clear classical reference in one or the other couplet.[32]

An unambiguous example is provided by a composition by Ōe no Mochitoki 大江以言 (955–1010), from a late-spring banquet at the home of Michinaga in 1007, on the topic phrase "Tree Flowers Fall Sprinkling into the Boat" 林花落灑舟:

春暮林花枝漸空	At the end of spring, trees' flowers gradually clear the branches;
紛々散落灑舟中	They scatter and fall in profusion, sprinkling into the boat.

The first, *daimoku* couplet uses all five of the topic-phrase characters (trees, flowers, fall, sprinkle, boat) in what amounts to an expanded recapitulation of the phrase.

32. The Kamakura-period manual *Shinzoku tekkinki* 眞俗擲金記 (Record of Buddhist and Secular Composition) condemns poems without any classical anecdote, but also poems containing such references in both the second and third couplets. Horikawa, *Shi no katachi*, 40.

棹郎忽怪黃頭雪	The oarsman is suddenly nonplussed at the snow upon his yellow cap;
畫鷁應迷繡羽紅	The painted heron must be confused by the crimson of its embroidered wings.

The first parallel couplet restates the topic phrase using elegant associations, describing white and red flowers ("snow" and "crimson") falling upon the rower and the figurehead on the prow, synecdoches for the boat. The introduction of analogy through a pose of confusion (the flowers are mistaken for snow or for embroidery) is typical of Heian *shi*, and shows clear continuities with the *waka* mode of *mitate*.[33]

粧勝郭家歸路日	This decoration outdoes the day when Guo returned home;
榮嘲傅氏濟川風	This bloom mocks the wind [by which] Fu crossed the river.

The first word of each line ("decoration/face powder" and "bloom") are words associated with flowers, which are described as overwhelming two historical figures associated with boats. This is the use of historical anecdote referred to in *Ōtaku fukatsushō* as *honmon*. In this case, the top half refers to the scholar Guo Tai 郭泰 (128–69), who befriended the statesman Li Ying 李膺 (110–69) and became famous in Luoyang; when he cast off to return to his home village, accompanied by Li, their grandeur was said to resemble immortals. Fu Yue 傅說, referred to in the second line, was prime minister to King Wu Ding of the Shang dynasty, who famously said to Fu, "If I am iron, you will be my whetstone; if I will cross a great river, you will be my oarsman."[34] Both stories deal with men raised up from lower beginnings, prefiguring the final couplet's humble gratitude:

池亭頻侍華筵末	At this lakeside pavilion, I've often served at the margin of florid festivities;

33. Helen C. McCullough devotes extensive discussion to the *shi* precedents for *mitate* in *waka* in *Brocade by Night*.

34. *Mengqiu* 100; *Shangshu zhengyi* 10.62.

枯幹先歡道欲通	Now a withered trunk, I'm already glad for the way that will carry us on.[35]

The final couplet draws on the topic phrase's botanical imagery to describe the poet's humble gratitude at being invited to participate in such an exalted occasion, punning on the name of his host to allude to the "way" of enlightened rule that Michinaga ("path/way long") has brought to the realm.

Similar expository formats with set structures of development were followed in parallel prose genres as well. *Ōtaku fukatsushō* analyzes poetry banquet prefaces and funerary prayers into five-part and ten-part templates respectively, with subject matter prescribed for each part.[36] There were precedents for such structures among Tang technical manuals. The ninth-century *Fupu* 賦譜 (Manual on the Rhapsody), for example, explains that "the body of the rhapsody is divided into sections and each [element] has its place," describing an eight-part division of "new-style" rhapsodies that can be found imitated in some tenth-century Japanese works.[37]

By regulating the structure of expository development, the *kudaishi* format stabilizes the social function of group composition, ensuring a harmonious echoing of themes and imagery across each poet's contribution to the event. The format also provides a template upon which less poetically inclined participants could safely rely. While parallel prose documents such as prefaces and memorials were almost exclusively drafted by State Academy graduates, any wellborn courtier was expected to be able to provide a *shi* at a flower-viewing banquet or temple excursion. While the requirements for adherence to tonal prosody could be adjusted to the

35. *Honchō reisō kanchū* 6.

36. For the preface: praise of the host/setting/season; description of scenery in parallel couplets; statement of the poem topic; exposition of the topic; humble reference to the preface's composer. For the prayer: introductory statement on transience/filial piety/dharma; description of the deceased in life; the deceased's illness; the deceased's death; the sadness of the survivors; how many days have passed since; the sutra recited at the assembly; the season and scenery; comparison to famous historical personage; prayer for salvation. Ōsone, *Ōchō kanbungaku ronkō*, 288–312.

37. Bokenkamp, "*Ledger on the Rhapsody*," 83; Wu, "Hanyu shengdiao de zhangwo," 174. See also the discussion of paragraph divisions in *Bunkyō hifuron* ("Nan," 487–502), translated in Bodman, "Poetics and Prosody," 438–49. On similar structural schematics in Dunhuang liturgical texts, see Teiser, "Shilun zhaiwen de biaoyanxing."

background of the composer, the uniformity of the *kudaishi* format conversely provided a kind of level playing field upon which senior nobles and scholar-officials could demonstrate their shared cultural attainment.

The value and ritual efficacy of literary documents was explained in terms of the ornamentation that distinguished them from ordinary discourse, and this ornament was systematized through a technical vocabulary of couplet-level parallelism and expository development. These aesthetic principles were so fundamental that they could even be universalized to apply outside of the realm of literary Sinitic composition: the earliest surviving composition manual for *waka* vernacular poetry closely imitates the language of *bunshō* aesthetics, arguing that "[r]hyme is what distinguishes [*waka*] from customary language," and attempting to apply the "poetic maladies" of literary Sinitic tonal prosody to *waka*, despite the incompatibility of these formal categories (*waka* is defined exclusively through metrical prosody, and has no rhyme).[38] These apparently rigid principles could also, however, be flexibly aligned in a variety of ways with the dynamic social distinctions that ordered capital officialdom. If the technical aesthetics of parallelism and exposition provide a kind of compositional rulebook, the remainder of this chapter is devoted to examining two strategies that Heian writers adopted in playing the game of literary composition, positioning themselves advantageously in relation to other actors, both literary competitors and potential patrons.

The Rhetoric of Erudition

Literary Sinitic parallelism is based upon the unit of the couplet, whose individual elements partake in what Stephen Owen has called an "epistemology . . . based on correlatives and counterparts," such that the "two lines face in upon one another, not forward or backward to lines from other couplets."[39] The individual couplet generates a self-contained and self-sufficient aesthetic, and can thus often be read and appreciated

38. Rabinovitch, "Wasp Waists and Monkey Tails"; Denecke, *Classical World Literatures*, 92–93.

39. Owen, *Traditional Chinese Poetry*, 85–91.

without reference to its function in the poem or essay as a whole. It is this couplet-based aesthetic that gave rise to the arrangement of excerpts we find in the early-eleventh-century anthology *Wakan rōeishū* (Collection of Japanese and Chinese Verses for Chanting), undoubtedly the most influential and widely circulating collection of Heian literary Sinitic. Like the technical discourse of poetic manuals, the fad for couplet collections (what Wiebke Denecke labels "couplet culture") provides a vital avenue for analyzing mid-Heian poetics.[40] In the commentarial tradition that accompanies *Wakan rōeishū* manuscripts, we find a detailed exploration of the variety and repercussions of *hadai* rhetorical operations, which serve as the scholar-official's arena for competitive performance.

Wakan rōeishū collects couplets from *shi* and parallel-prose compositions by both Chinese and Japanese authors, together with *waka* poems, all organized into seasonal and other thematic categories (spring nights, fireflies, Tanabata, music, old men, etc.). The autumn category "Dew" is short and convenient for citation:

可憐九月初三夜	We can cherish this third night of the ninth month,
露似眞珠月似弓	With the dew like pearls and the moon like a bow.
	—Bai [Juyi]

露滴蘭叢寒玉白	The dew drips through thoroughwort, white as cold jade;
風銜松葉雅琴清	The wind's gathered up pine needles, crisp as the noble *qin*.
	—[Minamoto no] Fusaakira

saoshika no	Midst the autumn clover
asa tatsu ono no	where stands a stag
akihagi ni	this morn,
tama to miru made	the dew lies white
okeru shiratsuyu	as pearls.
	—[Ōtomo no] Yakamochi (nos. 338–40)

40. Denecke, "Topic Poetry," 14–21.

While the *waka* collected in *Wakan rōeishū* are complete, thirty-one-syllable poems, the literary Sinitic couplets are all excerpts from larger works. In the sequence above, the Bai Juyi lines come from a poem on "Evening by the Yangtze" and Minamoto no Fusaakira's 源英明 (911–39) from a poem on the topic phrase, "The Autumn Air is Brisk and New." Mid-Heian literary works often depict nobles singing or chanting lines of *waka* or *shi* (as in the *Pillow Book* passage quoted in the introduction), and the content of *Wakan rōeishū* seems to build off of this fashionable practice, organizing the excerpts into categories based on shared themes.

According to the most widely circulated tale of the anthology's compilation, it was edited by the influential courtier Fujiwara no Kintō 藤原公任 (966–1041) as a wedding gift for his son-in-law; but whatever Kintō's own intentions for the work might have been, it quickly became recognized as an ideal textbook for elementary literary education, and the vocabulary and imagery of its selections reappear incessantly in the war chronicles and Noh drama of the medieval period. The couplets of *Wakan rōeishū* provided a repertoire of imagery and rhetoric to draw on, but also a kind of veneer of educated sophistication that could be applied to new literary genres in need of cultural prestige.[41]

Judging from the large number of extant manuscripts, as well as printed editions in the early modern period, *Wakan rōeishū* was read regularly and widely for centuries after its initial compilation. However, the basis for this valuation was not consistent; instead, the variety of forms that *Wakan rōeishū* manuscripts take suggest the shifting applications and reevaluations that were applied to the work in different time periods and

41. A typical application is found in the concluding lines of the *Taiheiki* 太平記 (Chronicle of Great Peace, ca. 1371) description of Emperor Kōgon's visit to the grave of his grandfather Fushimi (chap. 23), interpolating language from the Bai Juyi couplet quoted above:

> With all the various small services, the autumn sun set in no time. How moving, the moon on the third evening of the ninth month, as it hides and reappears among the clouds; the cries of the geese, falling before this false bow, echo forlornly across the paddies of Fushimi, and even the sounds of the villagers' evening activities had ceased, so the Emperor had torches lit and made his return (3:147).

For a comprehensive review of scholarship on the compilation and reception history of *Wakan rōeishū*, see Smits, "Song as Cultural History."

contexts. This is particularly visible in relation to the generic features of *kudaishi*, which became the standard for aesthetic judgment in poetry from the eleventh century onward.

Wakan rōeishū was compiled in the same period that the *kudaishi* genre was being standardized, and its selections show considerable overlap with the features of *kudaishi*: many of the selections by Japanese poets are taken from *kudaishi* compositions, and the selections by Chinese authors are overwhelmingly drawn from heptasyllabic regulated verse poetry (particularly the middle, parallel couplets), rather than so-called "ancient style" poetry that disregarded the prosodic rules of regulated verse. Yet other aspects of the anthology ignore *kudaishi* aesthetics: while many of the selections are quotations from *shi* poems, others derive from rhapsodies (*fu*) or parallel prose essays, not to speak of the *waka* poems that make up approximately a quarter of the more than eight hundred selections. Moreover, the anthology's arrangement of different types of excerpts within broad thematic categories encourages their reception as examples of pleasing imagery or skillful parallelism, rather than providing any clue to their function in the multi-stage development of a completed poem. Compiled as a gift, *Wakan rōeishū* seems to have been primarily intended as an object of great physical beauty. The oldest manuscripts emphasize superlative calligraphy, often making use of highly decorative paper to offset the juxtaposition of "*mana*" and "*kana*" character forms (so-called running or grass-style calligraphy for the literary Sinitic couplets, and the more abbreviated *hiragana* calligraphy for *waka*).[42]

Extant manuscripts of *Wakan rōeishū* from the twelfth and thirteenth centuries, however, often take a very different form. To put it simply, the anthology begins to be consumed not as a model of calligraphic beauty, but as a textbook to be studied for its content. This is most immediately evident in the pronunciation guides and diacritics that litter the page in many later manuscripts, which sacrifice visual beauty in the service of proper recitation and accurate comprehension. Even more important, however, is the expanded system of attribution in these later manuscripts. The earliest manuscripts of *Wakan rōeishū* contain only an abbreviated name for each excerpt (e.g., *Haku* 白 for Bai Juyi or *Ya* 野 for Ono no Takamura), with no further information on the couplet's provenance. By

42. See LaMarre, *Uncovering Heian Japan*, 116–39.

contrast, twelfth-century and later manuscripts (such as the "Taga-gire" 多賀切 family of fragments) provide the topic (*dai*) of the original poem each excerpt derives from as well, which in the case of Japanese excerpts is usually a five-character topic phrase (fig. 2).[43]

In the context of the *kudaishi* generic model, this new information transforms the anthology into an encyclopedia of *hadai* techniques of replacement and circumlocution.[44] Consider, for example, this couplet by Shitagō:

隨嵐落葉含蕭瑟	The falling leaves blown by the gale carry lonely sighs,
濺石飛泉弄雅琴	While the pouring stream upon the rocks plays a noble *qin*. (no. 313)

Read through the thematic organization of Kintō's anthology, where it appears under the category "Falling Leaves," the interest of the couplet is essentially imagistic. However, through reference to the topic phrase of the original poem, given in later manuscripts as "The Light of Autumn Changes the Mountains and Rivers" 秋光變山水, the reader can see how Shitagō's description of the falling leaves and flooding waters of autumn implements the topic phrase by matching a mountain scene in the first line with an aquatic image in the second. More subtly, each line contains an allusion to "change" or "transformation": "lonely sighs" references a line in the *Chuci* 楚辭 (*Songs of Chu*, second century CE), where the phrase describes the sound with which "flowers and leaves flutter down and change to decay."[45] "Noble *qin*" occurs in Sima Xiangru's "Rhapsody on the Tall Gate Palace" 長門賦, in the phrase "I take up the noble *qin* and change the mode."[46] The reintroduction of the original topic phrase, excised in Kintō's anthology, implies that the rhetorical interest of Shitagō's

43. Miki Masahiro provides a valuable comparison of characteristic features of various *Wakan rōeishū* manuscripts in *"Wakan rōeishū" to sono kyōju*.

44. Satō Michio, *"Wakan rōeishū" eiin to kenkyū*, 166–68.

45. 蕭瑟兮草木搖落而變衰 ("Jiubian" 九辯, in *Chuci buzhu*, 182). This phrase is also quoted in Pan Yue's "Rhapsody on Autumn Inspirations" 秋興賦 (*Wenxuan* 13.5a).

46. 援雅琴以變調兮 (*Wenxuan* 16.10b). The couplet hinges on a punning parallel of "noble *qin*" 雅琴 with the onomatopoeia *shōshitsu* 蕭瑟, because the second syllable of the latter happens to be written with a character meaning "harp."

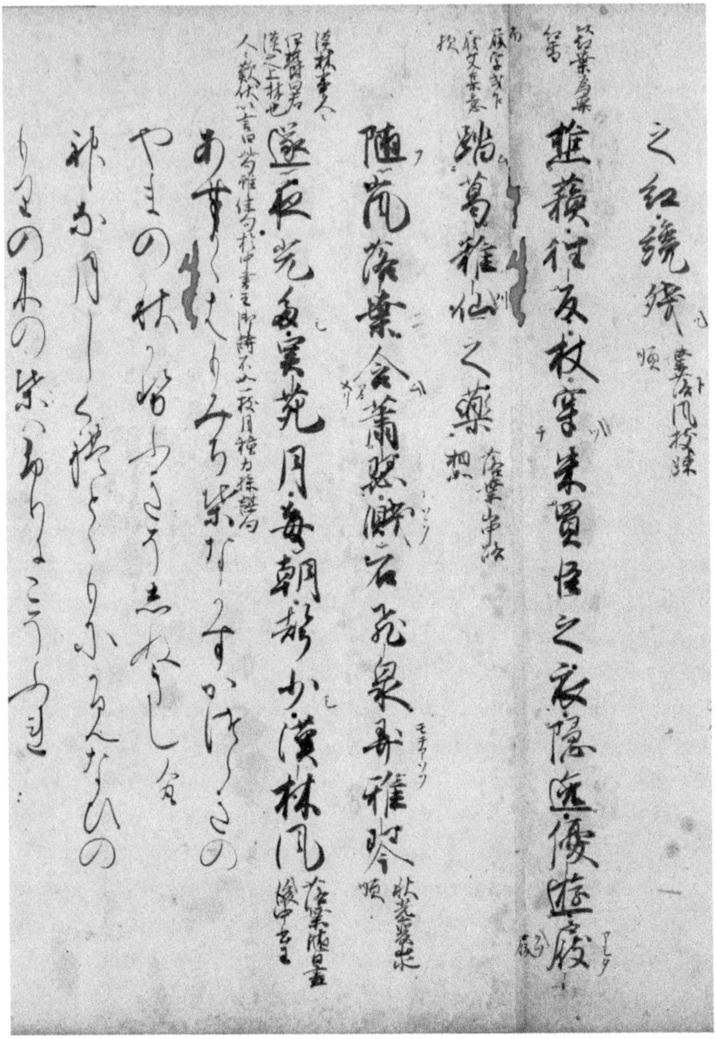

FIG. 2 Section from a 1339 manuscript copy of *Wakan rōeishū*. Photograph courtesy of Satō Michio.

couplet depends on recognizing the way it develops the topic phrase through *hadai* techniques.

One family of early manuscripts contains further marginalia for many of the literary Sinitic couplets, including quotations of allusive references and anecdotes surrounding the original composition of many of the sources. These have been identified as a commentary by the Heian scholar and statesman Ōe no Masafusa.[47] Recently, Satō Michio has published extensively on this commentary, showing that Masafusa's notes repeatedly emphasize the importance of *hadai* techniques in poetic composition.[48]

A clear example is Masafusa's commentary on the following couplet, from the "End of Autumn" section of the anthology:

文峯案轡白駒景	Reining it in on the peak of letters, the flash of a white colt;
詞海艤舟紅葉聲	Mooring a boat off the sea of words, the sound of red leaves.
	—[Ōe no] Mochitoki (no. 276)

The lines anthropomorphize autumn, which bids farewell to the poets who adore it. According to later manuscripts of the collection, the topic phrase of the original poem was "Autumn Has Not Yet Left the Realm of Poetry" 秋未出詩境. Masafusa's commentary provides a telling anecdote surrounding the poem's composition:

> Mochitoki originally composed [the poem] with [the line-ending phrases] as "flash of a passing colt" and "sound of falling leaves." It was a composition from a day when Mochitoki and [Ki no] Tadana were being tested. The Rokujō Prince saw this draft and wrote that it needed to include the word "white," so Mochitoki revised it. Tadana ever after resented this. . . . When Tadana was on his deathbed, the Prince visited him, and Tadana

47. Kuroda, *Chūsei setsuwa*, 1–27. For a recent refinement of Kuroda's argument, see Esaka, "Ikuta-bon *Wakan rōeishū*."

48. Satō Michio, *"Wakan rōeishū" eiin to kenkyū*, 166–84. Satō argues that Masafusa must have produced it in the early 1090s as part of the education of his young son Masatoki. Ibid., 193–99.

said, "The favor you have shown me is an overwhelming honor. But I cannot forget about that word 'white.'"[49]

According to the story, Mochitoki was able to best Ki no Tadana 紀齊名 (957–99) in an examination with the help of Prince Tomohira 具平親王 (964–1009), who improved Mochitoki's poem to accord with *kudaishi* aesthetics. The original version would also be a perfectly adequate parallel, and in some ways might seem superior (the "sound of falling leaves" makes more literal sense than the "sound of red leaves"). However, it would not represent a complete restatement of the topic phrase. In both lines, the first four characters ("tug reins on the peak of letters" and "dock boat on sea of words") correspond to "not yet leave the realm of poetry" 秋未出詩境, meaning that the final three characters must express the element "autumn" 秋未出詩境. Mochitoki's original draft apparently accomplished this in the bottom half (with "falling leaves"), but not the upper line of the couplet, which alludes to the *Zhuangzi* description of life passing by "like a white colt past a crack [in a wall]."[50] Tomohira suggested using a different word from the same passage, because white was associated with autumn in traditional Chinese cosmology. The revised couplet recapitulates each element of the topic phrase in both lines, a successful *hadai* exercise.[51]

A similar story about Tomohira's revisions accompanies a couplet in the "Wind" section of the anthology:

班姬裁扇應誇尚	Consort Ban, trimming her fan, ought to boast of her regard;
列子懸車不往還	Master Lie retires his chariot and no more wheels about.
	—[Yoshishige no] Yasutane (no. 400)

The poem makes reference to Consort Ban's (ca. 48–6 BCE) famous "Song of Resentment" 怨歌行, which compares loss of imperial favor to a fan being thrown aside with the arrival of the "chilling winds" of autumn, and

49. *Rōei Gōchū*, 110.
50. *Zhuangzi jishi* 7[*xia*].746.
51. Satō Michio, *"Wakan rōeishū" eiin to kenkyū*, 180–81.

the *Zhuangzi*'s description of the Daoist philosopher Liezi, said to be able to "ride the wind and fly, cool and skillful," two well-known literary references related to wind.[52] Masafusa's annotation gives the topic phrase of the original poem as "Where Does the Clear Wind Hide?" 清風何處隱, a line from a Bai Juyi poem on seeking to escape the heat, so it was likely produced for a late summer or early autumn gathering. The lines describe two historical counterfactuals: the cool autumn wind has not arrived as expected, so Consort Ban and her fan are not abandoned, and Liezi is not able to soar about. According to Masafusa's commentary, however, the author Yoshishige no Yasutane 慶滋保胤 (fl. mid- to late tenth century) originally wrote the first half of the couplet as "The common people spread their mat and must wait for it," until he was corrected by Tomohira.[53] This line makes reference to Song Yu's 宋玉 (fl. late-fourth century BCE) "Rhapsody on the Wind" 風賦, wherein the poet assures King Xiang that the cool wind he enjoys is utterly different from the hot, damp wind of the common people.[54] Yasutane's first draft is problematic because the "common people" have only a negative relationship to the clear, cool wind of the topic—in Song Yu's rhapsody, it is King Xiang who is associated with the cool wind—so the logic of the two lines does not match, confusing the topical restatement.

The changing appearance of the *Wakan rōeishū* suggests a feedback loop between interpretive framework and compositional idiom, in this case a mode of reading predicated on the formalization of *kudaishi* as a genre. By the end of the eleventh century, the more generalized categories of Kintō's original anthology were no longer sufficient to appreciate the meaning and quality of the couplets he had chosen. Clever restatement of the assigned topic phrase was the fundamental measure of poetic success, so the anthology's use as a tool of literary education demanded that its couplets be read in the context of their original topics.

We see this mode of reception extended further in an unusual anthology from the same period, the so-called *Ruijū kudaishō* 類聚句題抄 (Miscellany of Classified Topic Lines). Almost nothing is known about this collection, which survives in only a few incomplete and relatively

52. *Wenxuan* 27.17a; *Zhuangzi jishi* 1[*shang*].17.

53. *Rōei Gōchū*, 163.

54. *Wenxuan* 13.1b–4a.

recent manuscripts (even the name is a later interpolation). However, the latest datable poem it excerpts is from 1033, so it was likely originally compiled in the mid-eleventh century.[55] Most entries in the anthology consist of a five-character topic phrase, followed by two parallel couplets:

叢香近菊籬	Grasses Are Fragrant near the Chrysanthemum Hedge[56]
江相公	Ōe [no Asatsuna]
如入牛頭秋霧岫	Like entering the autumn-misted peaks of Ox Head;
似尋雀卵曉鑪傍	Like seeking out the dawn-lit censer of the Sparrow's Egg.
匂襟洛媛出波色	The Luo maiden with her scented collar, their beauty pierces the waves.
染夢呉娃專夜粧	The Wu belles who perfume my dreams, their makeup lasts through the night.[57]

It is clear that rather than complete poems, these must be excerpts: the middle, parallel couplets of what were originally eight-line poems on set topics. Stripped of any identifying information regarding the poem's occasion or audience, the couplets become pure rhetorical exercises, illustrations of the techniques espoused in composition manuals like *Sakumon daitai*. In this case, the first couplet alludes to fragrance by making reference to legends of powerful incense, and the second uses figures for chrysanthemums drawn from earlier poems on the topic.[58] Just like the

55. Honma, "*Ruijū kudaishō* kenkyū oboegaki," 54.

56. The topic line is taken from a Bai Juyi poem, "Ziti xiaocaoting" 自題小草亭, in *Bai Juyi ji jianjiao* 33.2240. The organization of the anthology is based on shared words in the topic lines (the example given is part of a string of poems whose topic contains the word "near").

57. *Ruijū kudaishō zenchūshaku* 425. "Suffusing dreams" 染夢 is a very peculiar construction, suggesting a possible corruption in the text here.

58. The fragrance produced by sandalwood grown in the Ox Head Mountains is mentioned in many sources, including the *Lotus Sutra* (*Taishō shinshū daizōkyō* 262 [9:18]). "Sparrow's Egg" refers to the shape of a legendary "spirit-startling incense" said to resurrect the dead (*Shizhou ji* 十洲記, quoted in *Taiping yulan* 983.4354). Cao Zhi's *fu* on the Luo River goddess compares her beauty to an autumn chrysanthemum (*Wenxuan* 19.12b). The beautiful dancers of Wu appear in a Chrysanthemum Banquet poem

expanded *Wakan rōeishū* manuscripts, this anthology would have served as a composition guide for poets learning the possibilities of *hadai* rhetorical transformations. Asatsuna's poem, apparently composed in 951 during the earliest stages of the development of the *kudaishi* genre, does not itself strictly follow the rules of *kudaishi* composition as they were later understood, since the first of the couplets makes no direct reference to the "chrysanthemum" element of the topic phrase, but it is nevertheless reappropriated in the anthology as raw material for new composition.[59] The mutilated preservation of Asatsuna's poem indicates the force *kudaishi* principles had achieved by the eleventh century: his complete poem could no longer serve as a viable model for composition, but the individual rhetorical techniques employed within it were a valuable source to be reapplied in *hadai* couplets. As with the transformation of *Wakan rōeishū* manuscripts, the *Ruijū kudaishō* collection demonstrates how developments in poetics could be retrospectively applied to earlier materials, canonizing the earlier Japanese poetic tradition through reinterpretation.[60]

The technical poetics of *kudaishi* provide a template format to be filled in through a series of operations (i.e., *hadai*) on a given object; this is essentially the structure of an examination, and it is no coincidence that the anecdote of Tomohira's advice to Tadana quoted earlier occurs in the context of a test. There are two somewhat contradictory implications of this poetics: on the one hand, the heavy formalization of *kudaishi* provides a scheme by which it was fairly easy to compose a serviceable poem, fulfilling the basic requirements by making regular reference to each of the two or three major elements of the topic phrase, and certainly for most courtiers that was sufficient. But even as they lowered the bar for

by Bai Juyi ("Jiuriyan jizui ti junlou, jian cheng Zhou, Yin erpanguan" 九日宴集醉題郡樓兼呈周殷二判官, in *Bai Juyi ji jianjiao* 21.1406).

59. This topic was used at a palace "Lingering Chrysanthemums Banquet" (*zangiku no en*) in the tenth month, the second such event contrived to replace the Chrysanthemum Banquet, which was traditionally scheduled in the ninth month but had been abandoned since the death of the Emperor Daigo in that month in 930. *Kyūreki*, Tenryaku 5 (951)/10/5 (81).

60. Similarly, Fujiwara no Mototoshi's 藤原基俊 (ca. 1056–1142) sequel to *Wakan rōeishū*, *Shinsen rōeishū* 新撰朗詠集 (Newly Selected Collection of Verses for Chanting, ca. 1116–26), incorporates the original topics of its excerpts, imitating the format not of the original *Wakan rōeishū*, but of the expanded later manuscripts.

participation, formal restrictions increased the potential for direct comparison, and thus competition, among the presented poems. For scholar-officials, poetic composition was an opportunity to seek advantage (and a test that could damage a reputation), and *hadai* rhetoric provided a venue for virtuosic performance. As depicted in Masafusa's commentary to *Wakan rōeishū*, this virtuosity was found in demonstrations of unusual adroitness through the choice of a particular metaphor, image, or reference that perfectly aligned with occasion and topic line. The commentary to a couplet on the topic "Facing the Rain but Yearning for the Moon" by Minamoto no Shitagō reads, "He composed this poem and held on to it for several years until it rained on the autumnal equinox, then went to the Rokujō Prince's manor and presented it."[61] The autumnal equinox was a night when moon-viewing parties were held, and Shitagō has carefully prepared and set aside a poem that matches the predictable topic of longing for the absent moon.

The foundation of this occasional aptness lies in a certain kind of erudition. The ideal poet will have an encyclopedic access to an endless web of synonyms and anecdotes and, furthermore, will be able to cite his sources:

逐夜光多呉苑月	With every night, its light increases— moon of the Wu gardens;
毎朝聲少漢林風	Each morning, its sound diminishes— wind of the Han forest.

—Prince in the Central Ministry [Tomohira] (no. 312)

> Some were dissatisfied with the term "Han forest," saying "Does this refer to the Han dynasty's Shanglin Park? He has just arbitrarily invented a phrase." The prince provided a source in the [*Wenguan*] *cilin* and silenced them.[62]

As the commentary suggests, the potential for inventive language in composition was very circumscribed. To show that one's exposition made an effective literary reference, it might be necessary to provide a locus classicus. We find very similar anecdotes focused on source citation in other

61. *Rōei Gōchū*, 100.

62. Ibid., 124. This passage is corrupt in the surviving *Wakan rōeishū* MSS, but can be reconstructed from *Gōdanshō* 4.64.

medieval sources, as well: "When [Sugawara no] Fumitoki's students were lined up into two companies, [Yoshishige no] Yasutane was at the head of the literature [*bunshō*] group and Shōmon was at the head of the scholarship [*saigaku*] group. However, Fujiwara no Motosada, a graduate student, stepped forward to argue with this. When Fumitoki asked his reason, Motosada said, 'Among the usage quotations [*honmon*] for characters in the *Qieyun*, there is not a single one I do not know.'"[63] *Wenguan cilin* 文館詞林 (Institute of Literature and Grove of Lyrics, 658) was an imperially commissioned anthology of poetry and prose and *Qieyun* 切韻 (Divided Rhymes, 601) was a rhyming dictionary that defined a standardized set of literary pronunciations. Chinese reference works like these are some of the most frequently quoted works in Japan's early literary corpus. Along with the composition manuals discussed at the beginning of this chapter, rhyming dictionaries, categorical encyclopedias, and other tools were imported and used widely in support of the technical poetics of regulated verse. The promulgation of these works in China and their distribution in Japan bespeaks the integration of poetry into the institutions of education, particularly the civil service examination.

A growing emphasis on literary talent in official recruitment is visible from the early sixth century in China, and by the mid-eighth century poetic composition became a standard component of the *jinshi* examination.[64] This model was imitated along with many other aspects of the Tang educational code by Japan's State Academy: when Tadana's poem is bested by Mochitoki's through Prince Tomohira's intervention, they are competing to qualify for the status of student of letters (*monjōshō*) in a test administered by the Ministry of Ceremonial. The emphasis on erudition in composition observed throughout the corpus of poetic manuals and commentaries reflects an understanding of poetic composition as a demonstration of skill and learning, systemized in Heian educational institutions. The highest-level examination for academics, modeled on the Tang *xiucai* (J. *shūsai*) examination, presented candidates with a pair of open-ended questions, to be answered in elaborate parallel-prose essays

63. *Kojidan* 6.36. For a gloss on this tale, see Satō Michio, "'Bunshō' to 'saigaku.'"

64. Dien, "Civil Service Examinations," 105–7; David McMullen, *State and Scholars*, 229–32. However, the use of poetic genres in the examination process was a point of contention throughout the Tang dynasty. Yu, "Poems for the Emperor," 75–76.

(*taisaku*) full of classical references. The test was designed to select out "gentlemen who had heard much and observed widely" (*tamon hakuran no shi* 多聞博覽之士), that is, who could demonstrate copious knowledge arranged in neat parallels.[65] The essay format extends the valuation of erudition already visible in the "evidentiary catalog" (*zhengshi* 徵事) contests of China's fifth- and sixth-century southern courts, in which scholars were presented with a common object and competed to offer the most extensive list of related classical references.[66] The same term, *zhengshi* (J. *chōji*), is used in Heian documents to refer to the individual subheadings of an examination question, hinting at the underlying continuity between these modes of learning.[67] Poetic composition was studied and practiced as one part of a field of scholarly activity defined through erudition and eloquence.

The Tang civil service examination fostered an imbrication of literary composition with scholarly modes of analysis and presentation, what Wen Yiduo once characterized as a cycle of "regularization and differentiation": from commentaries (such as Li Shan's line-by-line annotation of the *Wenxuan*, presented 658) that explicate by reference to allusive sources, then to categorical encyclopedias that index and categorize those same allusions, and finally to the vast corpus of occasional verse that poets used those encyclopedias to compose.[68] This same cycle of reception, exegesis, and reapplication was continued and extended in Heian Japan as the quintessential mechanism of scholarship. Successful presentation of oneself as a scholar demanded composition that participated in this cycle, not only during examinations, but across almost all genres of

65. *Ryō no shūge* 22.645. On the subject matter and style of these essays, see Ceugniet, *L'office des etudes supérieures*, 131–66.

66. For descriptions of evidentiary catalog contests, see Zhang, *Leishu liubie*, 25. Histories of this period give repeated examples of scholars being tested on the breadth of their knowledge in this way (see for instance the biography of Wang Chi 王摛 in *Nanshi* 49.1213), which contrast sharply with the emphasis on argument and paradox in the numerous third- and fourth-century "pure talk" (*qingtan*) anecdotes found in *Shishuo xinyu* or the *Weishu*.

67. For use of the term *chōji* to describe the various parts of the essay question, see *Kanke bunsō, Kanke kōshū* 594; *Gōdanshō* 5.64 and 5.66. For more on *chōji*, see Hamada, *Heianchō Nihon kanbungaku*, 279–313.

68. Wen, "Leishu yu shi." For similar phenomena in a slightly earlier period, see Tian, *Beacon Fire and Shooting Star*, 96–110.

literary Sinitic, from prayer texts to poetry.[69] As the preface to a tenth-century Japanese rhyming dictionary declares, "The path of learning begins with composition. One who only chants the classics without learning poetry is like a box of books without any use."[70] Such formulations both valorize literary writing and circumscribe its range of expression: poetry must be, and must make evident that it is, a manifestation of tremendous learning.

By concretizing aesthetic principles, rhyming dictionaries and other reference materials served not simply as tools to assist in composition, but responded also to a social need for criteria by which literature could be measured in terms of its "correctness." As in China, this standard was engendered through the examination system, but persisted as an available mode of reception in other contexts as well. The standardization of poetry both lowered potential barriers to participation in group composition and made direct comparison (and therefore competition) among participants unavoidable. Like the rules of a board game, the regular patterns of *kudai-shi* delineated a space of action in which both academy-graduate officials and less-educated senior nobles could participate together, ensuring the viability of group composition, but they also provided the opportunity for competition through virtuosic performance. The rhetoric of *hadai* turns occasional verse into an implicit test, in which the poet's knowledge and wit are judged by the banquet's host.

Jukkai and Decontextualized Poetry

Couplet anthologies, commentaries, and composition manuals provide one perspective on Heian *shi*, presenting poetry as technique, the epideictic amplification of an assigned topic through adroit couplets and obscure anecdotes. Yet this rhetorically oriented corpus also obscures some aspects

69. On virtuosic erudition in funerary prayers, see Yamazaki Akira, "Ōe no Masafusa no ganmon."

70. Preface to the 939 dictionary *Wachū setsuin* 倭注切韻, quoted in *Sakumon daitai*, 6. This insult was originally leveled at the academic Lu Cheng 陸澄 (425–94) for amassing great knowledge but not really understanding the classics or producing any work of his own. *Nan Qishu* 39.685–86.

of poetry's social life, as poems are dissected into couplets, removed from their context of composition, and lose any communicative function. On the one hand, the incompleteness of literary fragments only makes more visible an interpretive lacuna inherent to any piece of writing, "more rather than less typical than texts that have not been thus truncated."[71] Nevertheless, the process of excerption that has produced these couplets was no random accident of history, but a deliberate aesthetic criteria that cannot help but mold—even as it enables—our retrospective understanding of the Heian literary sphere.

This chapter's heavy reliance on fragmentary sources is not an arbitrary expedient, but rather an unavoidable result of the historical circumstances of Heian literary Sinitic: compilation practices have combined with accidents of manuscript transmission to make isolated couplets the center of the surviving corpus. To give representative numbers for some of the mid-tenth-century poets mentioned in this study, there are eleven extant complete poems by Minamoto no Fusaakira and eighteen fragments; for Ōe no Asatsuna we have thirty-two complete poems and twenty-seven fragments; and for Sugawara no Fumitoki twelve complete poems and forty-four fragments. From Fumitoki's student Yoshishige no Yasutane, one of the most respected poets of his day, we have sixty-six fragments, but only five complete poems.[72] After a few prominent poets of the late ninth century (notably Sugawara no Michizane), almost no personal collections of literary Sinitic poetry and prose by Heian authors survive, but rather couplet anthologies and poetic manuals.

The shape of the extant archive reflects the use value of different types of texts. Consider the diary of Fujiwara no Sanesuke, *Shōyūki*, cited as a source repeatedly in the last chapter. His original autograph diary was first copied by his adopted son Sukehira 資平 (986–1068), and the two manuscripts that supply modern editions of the text were both copies of Sukehira's version made by his descendants. These two manuscripts were held by the Sanjōnishi household through the Muromachi period, until the bulk of the transmitted text was acquired by the bibliophile daimyō Maeda Tsunanori 前田綱紀 (1643–1742) in the late seventeenth century.[73]

71. De Man, "Shelley Disfigured," 55.
72. Numbers based on *Nihon shiki* and *Nihon shiki shūi*.
73. Momo Hiroyuki, "Kaidai."

Such diaries were carefully preserved because of the vital advantage they could provide their owner, given the heavy reliance on precedent in court ritual and bureaucratic procedure.[74] For high noble houses of the medieval period such as the Sanjōnishi, knowledge of precedent provided a source of authority in their role as managers of court ritual, buttressing their lineal prerogative to court offices. The diary functioned as an essential educational apparatus for the preservation of a household (*ie*) as an institution. The survival of these works is thus intimately connected to their political value. By contrast, although many kinds of poetry and other belletristic writing had important social uses in Heian Japan, they only rarely enjoyed sustained connection with long-lived institutions whose survival and success depended on them.[75] For example, a recent study of the Sugawara lineage in the fifteenth and sixteenth centuries finds that while such scholarly lineages were still responsible for drafting ritual parallel-prose documents such as prayer texts, *shi* poetry was no longer a prominent part of their activities.[76] Even as literary tastes changed and *shi* composition increasingly became the purview of Zen monks, *Wakan rōeishū*'s use as an elementary educational text ensured its survival while many other poetry collections disappeared.

Though few survive today, bibliographic records show that many personal collections of the poems and prose of a single author were produced in the mid-Heian.[77] One of the only extant examples, Sugawara no Michizane's collection, was compiled and presented to Emperor Daigo by Michizane himself in 900, along with collections of writing by his father Koreyoshi and grandfather Kiyokimi 清公 (770–842), forming a monument to the endurance of his family's literary prestige.[78] The twelve-volume collection is divided between poetry and prose, with each

74. Yoshida, "Aristocratic Journals." The role of diaries is discussed in detail in chapter 4.

75. The Reizei household, with its Shiguretei Library, is perhaps the quintessential example of a lineage whose dependence on authority in the literary sphere (*waka* poetry, in this case) led to the preservation and reproduction of literary writings. See Carter, *Householders: The Reizei Family.*

76. Itō, *Kuge shakai to bunji*, 2.

77. See, for example, the fourteen such titles in one "chest" of the so-called *Tsūken nyūdō zōsho mokuroku*, a twelfth-century bibliography (198).

78. *Kanke bunsō, Kanke kōshū* 674. See Borgen, *Sugawara no Michizane*, 222–26.

volume of the first half collecting poems from a different period of Michizane's life as he grew up, advanced in the academy, took a post in Sanuki Province (Shikoku), and returned to elevated power in court. If *Wakan rōeishū* and other couplet collections suggest an aesthetic of ratiocinated rhetorical mechanics, Michizane's personal collection would seem to be premised on diametrically opposing principles. As in all such personal collections, each poem is accompanied by a "title" (*hashizukuri*), including not just the topic for composition but date, occasion, host, others present, and so forth; the apparatus thus encourages reading the poem as a moment of interpersonal "address," the rhetorical mechanics deriving meaning from their application within the poet's social relationships.[79] Michizane extends this contextualization further with footnotes that clarify his age, career status, and other shifting circumstances, making autobiography the principle validating textual meaning. While technical poetics analyze couplet-level ornamentation, personal collections present poems as individual responses to experience.

The technically oriented corpus that provides most extant documentation of mid-Heian *shi* attests to a standardized aesthetic of topical exposition that came to dominate poetic practice (and itself likely accelerated that standardization). But while this corpus provides a valuable index to contemporary poetics, the very different hermeneutic implied by personal collections suggests that it can also act as a filter on the literary field. By channeling the multiple reception possibilities open to poetry in a specific direction, such works tend to ignore or even actively obscure the poem's potential to refer to the world outside the set topic, particularly its relationship to the lived experience of the poet.

Many commentators have observed this filtering effect in the editorial practices of *Wakan rōeishū*, which selects and organizes its excerpts largely based on the themes and language of the individual couplets, rather than the topic of the original poem as a whole (so that, for example, the excerpts under the "Falling Leaves" category do not all come from poems whose ostensible topic was falling leaves, even if that image appears in the specific couplet quoted). The personal or political referents active in a poem's original context disappear, leaving an exercise in

79. Owen, *Traditional Chinese Poetry*, 236.

wordplay or pure description within the thematic organization of the anthology. For example, while almost all of Bai Juyi's poetry excerpted in *Wakan rōeishū* (as well as in one of the former's main sources, the anthology *Senzai kaku* 千載佳句, ca. 940) consists of parallel couplets taken from occasional poems in the regulated verse style, it also includes eight selections from his *Xin yuefu* 新樂府 (New Ballads, 809) series. These are highly political poems in "ancient style" (non-regulated-verse) prosody, yet the lines quoted are largely descriptive, appearing within topical sections like "Cicadas" or "Autumn Evening" where the political allegories of the original poems are invisible.

The same abstracting process can be seen in some of the Japanese selections as well: Prince Kaneakira's 兼明親王 (914–987) "Rhapsody on Retirement," an angry and frank castigation of his enemies at court, supplies these lines to the "Thoroughwort" section:

扶桑豈無影乎	How could Fusang have no light?
浮雲掩而忽昏	The clouds cover over and it suddenly darkens.
叢蘭豈不芳乎	How could the thoroughwort have no fragrance?
秋風吹而先敗	The autumn wind blows and wrecks them.
	(no. 287)

In Kaneakira's original poem, Fusang (the sun) and thoroughwort (eupatorium, an intensely fragrant flowering grass) are figures for the sovereign, whose innate virtue is obstructed by outside forces.[80] The metaphor here is hardly obscure, but flanked by lines on autumn scenery and dew glistening on petals in *Wakan rōeishū*, the excerpt is drained of specific reference. This blurring of signification is clearest in such allegorical works, but the same general tendency applies as well to the occasional verse that makes up the main source of the anthology's material. These propensities of *Wakan rōeishū* are further systematized in *Ruijū kudaishō*, which collects from each poem only the middle two couplets that employ technically elaborate parallelism, but omits the opening "subject matter" (*daimoku*) couplet and the concluding "divulgence of feeling" (*jukkai*).

80. The lines are adapted from *Huainanzi*. *Huainan honglie jijie* 17.572.

While the opening couplet is the most formulaic portion of a *kudaishi* poem, an expanded restatement of the topic line (as in the Mochitoki example quoted above), the *jukkai* couplet is more complex, generally representing the poet's personal response to the topic and occasion of composition. A typical early Heian example is the following by Shimada no Tadaomi, from a ninth-century Chrysanthemum Banquet:

黄衿侍宴恩多澤	In yellow lapels at the banquet, wet with so much grace,
應似菊花冒雨開	We must seem like chrysanthemums blossoming through the rain.[81]

Playing with two meanings of the character *taku* 澤, as moisture and as beneficence bestowed by a superior, Tadaomi ends his poem on the late-blossoming chrysanthemums with an expression of his gratitude at being allowed to participate in the event, comparing himself and his fellow favored officials to the bright flowers they had gathered to celebrate. Such statements of gratitude or festive felicitations drawing on imagery from the topic were the most appreciated conclusion to a formal poem.

As discussed in the previous chapter, however, in the mid-Heian officially sponsored outlets for poetic service by officials like this decreased dramatically. Those eleventh-century officials who managed to find opportunities for poetic composition in the banquets of powerful senior nobles adopted a different rhetorical strategy, using the final couplet to invoke lamentations of the poet's age or misfortune and entreaties for aid from the host, as in this conclusion to a poem presented at a late-spring gathering in the home of Fujiwara no Michinaga in 1006:

爲吾未有陽和德	But for me there is yet no taste of spring's warm blessings—
鬢雪甚寒任陸沈	My snowy brow freezing, I might as well "sink in dry land."[82]

81. *Denshi kashū chū* 203.

82. *Honchō reisō kanchū* 10.

Here "sunk in dry land" is a euphemism for abandoning one's official career; the poet compares the vernal festivities that surround him to the unseasonable cold of his own lack of favor and hair whitened with age. Such complaints could be tremendously affecting for the assembled party: at another gathering the prior year at Michinaga's home, Fujiwara no Korechika 藤原伊周 (974–1010), who just a few days earlier had been granted courtier status again for the first time since his 996 exile, produced a poem that "moved all assembled to tears."[83] There are also numerous anecdotal records of poets acquiring rank or office promotion through a poem's convincing complaint.[84] The *jukkai* couplet is thus the portion of the poem in which the poet's position as a social actor is directly thematized. The mid-Heian brings a peculiar double movement here: at the same time that complaint rhetoric is becoming more prevalent in *kudaishi* poetry, it disappears from the growing body of couplet collections.

An authorial stance of aggrieved misfortune became prominent across literary genres in the mid-Heian, as officials sought strategies to maneuver through the increasingly rigid stratification of capital officialdom. The most important outlet for an official seeking redress for his career difficulties was the petition (*sōjō*), presented to the crown via the Council of State.[85] Petitions seeking office or rank promotion (sometimes called *mōshibumi* in vernacular writing) became widespread in the tenth century (such as the example quoted in chapter 1). Sugawara no Michizane's personal collection contains only one *sōjō* seeking promotion (written on another's behalf), out of twenty-seven total petitions dated between 866 and 900.[86] The eleventh-century collection *Honchō monzui*, by contrast, contains thirty-seven petitions, twenty-one of which are directly concerned with rank or office promotion (in addition to several dealing with closely related issues such as scholarships or permission to take the civil service examination). The typical format relates the petitioner's past service to

83. *Shōyūki*, Kankō 2/3/29–4/2 (2:106–7). According to a report Sanesuke received, Michinaga was particularly moved by the poem, and bestowed a gift on Korechika. The poem is recorded in *Honchō reisō kanchū* 27.

84. E.g., *Gōdanshō* 4.25.

85. Petitions could also be submitted through unofficial channels. See *Kojidan* 1.26.

86. The rest are mostly resignation letters, as well as Michizane's famous petition to end official envoys to the Tang court. *Kanke bunsō, Kanke kōshū* 583–609.

court and his current lowly status, lists various prior examples of similar cases who were granted the office in question, and expresses hope that the sovereign will show the same wisdom as prior rulers by promoting such examples of loyalty and virtue as the petitioner. These works were written in the same elaborate parallel-prose style as prefaces or prayers, and were sometimes admired as examples of literary beauty: several couplets in *Wakan rōeishū* are taken from such petitions.[87]

The formalization of the *jukkai* couplet in *kudaishi* is part of a larger pattern of petition language being adapted into other literary genres. We see a similar development in prefaces (*jo*), the celebratory pieces in parallel prose that commemorated a banquet or festival celebration. In early Heian examples of the preface (and their early Tang models), the writer describes in turn the place or host, the season, the celebration or banquet activities, and then finally proclaims that the assembled guests, moved by the occasion, will compose verse about it. Sometimes this final section might dwell on the great honor his invitation extends to the composer, and his own inadequacy to the occasion—a "self-effacing couplet" (*jikenku* 自謙句).[88] While at the end of the ninth century such expressions are only used for the most formal occasions (when the emperor himself is present), by the beginning of the eleventh century a "self-effacing couplet" is found in nine out of ten prefaces, with little regard to the occasion.[89] The tone shifts as well: earlier prefaces mostly treat the author's own inadequacy (in terms of talent or learning), but later examples dwell on his misfortune (in terms of rank and office). The preface no longer speaks on behalf of the assembled participants, but rather adopts the individual voice of the preface composer. As nominations replaced testing as the primary means of advancement for scholar-officials (a development detailed in the following chapter), the preface became a valuable means of direct appeal to a higher-up, without passing through the Council of State or other official intermediaries.[90]

87. See, for example, *Wakan rōeishū* 437. This petition, written by Tachibana no Naomoto, became the subject of a set of legends concerning the wise rule of Emperor Murakami, including a Kamakura picture scroll, the *Naomoto mōshibumi ekotoba*.

88. *Gōdanshō* 6.25.

89. Kido, "Heian shijo no keishiki." The "self-effacing" conclusion was also a standard part of the *taisaku* examination essay. Hamada, *Heianchō Nihon kanbungaku*, 390–403.

90. Ono, *Heianchō Tenryakuki no bundan*, 130.

Concurrently, we can see echoes of the petition's inflated rhetoric of imperial service in vernacular genres as well. *Waka* poetry appropriates common *jukkai* tropes of hair whitened by frost, a lonely pine tree deep in a valley, or sinking in obscurity, such as this example, purportedly sent to an imperial lady-in-waiting the morning after the annual Appointments Ceremony (*jimoku*):

toshigoto ni	Perhaps it is because
taenu namida ya	my endless tears collect
tsumoritsutsu	year after year,
itodo fukaku wa	that I am sinking
mi o shizumuran	ever deeper.[91]

There are records in the tenth century of such *waka* poems being affixed to petitions for promotion, which makes clear the continuity of expression.[92] By the late Heian, the term *jukkai* becomes a frequently used topic for *waka* composition, even appearing as a shared object for exposition at poetry contests.[93] Just as in the *jukkai* couplet of a *kudaishi* poem, the poet is here expected to lament his age, failure to be recognized or advance in office, and desire to leave the secular world.

As the language of supplication became increasingly common across literary genres, officials progressively turned to hyperbole. Over the course of the mid-Heian, petitions show increasing length, increasing rhetorical elaboration, and even increasing exaggeration of the petitioner's resume.[94] This policy of escalation had inherent limitations as a strategy of differentiation, producing such inflated examples as Ōe no Masahira, a professor in the academy and deputy commissioner of ceremonial, comparing

91. *Shūi wakashū* 443. Attributed to Kiyohara no Motosuke 清原元輔 (908–990). The key word for the *waka* topos of *jukkai* is "*mi*": "myself/I," but also "my life" or "my fate."

92. Ono, *Heianchō Tenryakuki no bundan*, 277–93.

93. In an 1119 contest judgment, Fujiwara no Akisue 藤原顯季 (1055–1123) condemned all appearance of *jukkai* poems in poetry contests, but this protest reflects the growing popularity of the style. An 1126 contest is the first recorded instance of a *jukkai* topic being set, and by the late twelfth century this had become commonplace. Minegishi Yoshiaki, *Heian jidai waka bungaku*, 290–328.

94. Ono, *Heianchō Tenryakuki no bundan*, 169–88.

himself to Liang Hong 梁鴻 (first century CE), the hermit poet who eschewed an official career to herd pigs.[95] The bathos of this self-aggrandizement is suggested by the portrait of doddering scholars in the *Tale of Genji* or Shitagō's *Song of the Tailless Ox*, discussed in the previous chapter.[96] This deficiency of *jukkai* rhetoric as a venue for distinguished performance is in turn reflected in the neglect of the final couplet in couplet collections and poetics discourse, by contrast with the recognition one could obtain through the middle, *hadai* couplets.

The relative effectiveness of these two modes is in some ways predetermined through the primary venue of poetic performance, the banquet. As seen in chapter 1, group composition takes place in a structure of symbolic exchange, within which the assembled guests respond together to a topic set (or approved) by the host, echoing his felicitous sentiment and reciprocating his largesse. Whereas the *hadai* rhetoric of erudition provides a venue for virtuosity by which the poet seeks to differentiate himself horizontally, in relation to other poets, the *jukkai* couplet attempts to establish an individual vertical relationship between poet and host, beseeching change rather than celebrating harmony. The standardization and lassitude of *jukkai* discourse reveals the strength of the binary structure of group composition, in which all assembled guests stand in an equivalent relationship of hierarchically differentiated reciprocity with the host; the only possibility for stepping outside the repeated discourse of supplication and celebration is to seek a different venue for composition entirely.

Perhaps the most radical examples of such an experiment are two poems labeled as "anonymous letters" (*rakusho* 落書) in *Honchō monzui*. Amid all the lamentation of poverty and low rank, it is extremely rare to find any attempt in Heian literature to address the blanket debasement

95. *Honchō monzui* 324. Nagase Yumi discusses a letter Masahira addressed to Fujiwara no Yukinari in which he compared the poor status of scholars in his day to the Qin Emperor's infamous "burning of books and burying of scholars" ("Ichijō-chō bunjin," 245–48).

96. The *Genji* often mimics the rhetoric of petition, as when Genji admonishes his adopted daughter Tamakazura to "take [her suitors'] efforts into account" (*rō o mo kazoetamae*), lampooning the standard language in petitions for describing one's years of service in a particular post. *Genji monogatari*, "Kochō," 3:178.

of lower officialdom, but these works explicitly complain about corruption and bribery in the capital bureaucracy:

官爵專非功課賞	Rank and post never come as reward for accomplishments,
公私寄致贖勞求	Openly and secretly men spend, pursuing credit with cash.
除書久待貢書致	The assignment letter will wait at length until your tax return arrives,
直物遲期獻物收	The corrections notice is slow because they hope for a receipt of offerings.

The assignment letter and corrections notice are both official proclamations of new post assignments for the coming year, which the poet complains are issued in direct response to material payments to state offices. Similarly:

登高只是銅山動	If ascent to the top comes when a mountain of bronze is spent,
在下猶因金穴空	Then stagnation at the bottom is also because the gold chest is empty.
不信宣尼貧樂道	I cannot believe Confucius "enjoyed the way in poverty,"
祇看後輩富成功	For I witness my juniors' Achievements come through wealth.[97]

The Heian practice of "Achievements" (*jōgō*) allowed officials to purchase rank or office promotion through donations to fund infrastructure and ceremony. These works still make use of the petition rhetoric of undeserved misfortune, but are striking for their frank language of accusation—one goes so far as to condemn explicitly the minister of the left for "harming the sovereign's designs" 損皇猷.

97. *Honchō monzui* 388–89. "Enjoy the way in poverty" refers to *Analects* 1.15 (*Lunyu zhushu* 1.2). For an overview of *rakusho* in the Heian, see Gotō, *Heianchō kanbun bunken*, 216–23.

It is a touchstone of modern scholarship to characterize the Japanese literary tradition as apolitical or lyrical (implicitly compared with Chinese literature), and for this reason the *Honchō monzui* "letters" seem quite unusual and exciting.[98] Ono Yasuo sees them as an adaptation of the "explicit criticism of the court" found in Bai Juyi's socially critical poems (*fengyushi* 諷諭詩), almost unique among the extant Japanese corpus. He emphasizes, however, the important difference between Bai's public poetry, premised on direct address to the emperor, and the anonymous, privately circulated *rakusho*. Even if it is possible to equate the works based on a shared language of criticism, their paths of circulation and reception were radically different.[99] The *rakusho* reveal an underexamined side of Heian literary culture, but at the same time their exceptionality underlines the prohibitions attendant on poetry's socially recognized sites of circulation. There are other contemporary references to such works, but they are overwhelmingly negative, focused on the inherent illicitness of anonymity.[100] Indeed, the very label "anonymous letter" is primarily a legal category rather than a literary genre, referring to a crime punishable with three years of penal servitude.[101] The potential for critique in this case is won only through the abandonment of audience. Even in the *Honchō monzui*, compiled after both the authors and the objects of their criticism were long dead, the second poem is listed under

98. For a representative characterization of the apolitical Japanese aesthetic, see Brower and Miner, *Japanese Court Poetry*, 427–28. On the postwar establishment of an "aesthetic, lyrical" Japanese literary canon, see Shirane, "Curriculum and Competing Canons."

99. Ono, *Heianchō Tenryakuki no bundan*, 202–17. As Shizunaga Takeshi argues, the special support Bai enjoyed from Emperor Xianzong in the early 800s provided him a unique venue for this poetry. "Haku Kyoi no fūyushi," 149–56.

100. *Kanke bunsō, Kanke kōshū* 98 and 118. Sugawara no Michizane claims that in 882 he was unjustly suspected of writing an anonymous poem that criticized a Fujiwara senior noble (probably Fuyuo). At almost the same time, events in China underlined the force and danger of anonymous poems: following the sack of Chang'an by Huang Chao in 880, a poem mocking the rebels appeared on the gates of the Department of State Affairs. Huang's lieutenant Shang Rang responded by blinding and stringing up by their heels the bureaucrats and guards of the ministry, searching out and executing all poets remaining in the capital, and conscripting any other literate men into servitude. The dead totaled "more than three thousand." *Zizhi tongjian* 254.8247.

101. *Seiji yōryaku* 84.688; *Hōsō shiyōshō*, 93.

a pseudonym.[102] If the systematization of petition discourse in literature limited the author to repeated gestures of supplication, the *rakusho* are able to adopt a more expansive range of argument at the expense of the poem's phatic connection, sacrificing its tactical value as a gambit in an ongoing negotiation between two parties.

Conclusion

Couplet anthologies present figural language stripped of a social aim; the laments and prayers of the *jukkai* couplets drop away, leaving rhetorical mechanics floating out of time. The radical decontextualization of these anthologies suggests an understanding of composition and aesthetics at odds with the presentation of poems in other venues, most notably personal collections, in which poetry is presented as an outgrowth of individual occasions and the historical experience of the poet. However, this contradiction is only apparent, bespeaking rather a model of rhetoric and affective response central to the East Asian literary tradition. Each poem in the *Book of Odes* (*Shijing* 詩經) is the manifestation in language of an emotional reaction to some circumstance, according to its "Great Preface."[103] At the same time, this expressive origin of the poem does not fix the scope of its performative applications; in the *Zuo Commentary*, lines from the *Odes* are often quoted out of context as a conversational tool, their meaning reconstrued to further immediate social goals.[104] In this respect, the couplet collection is not the antithesis, but rather a complementary twin to the personal collection, in which both extend poetry's essential relationship with a sphere of interpersonal performance. The

102. The second *rakusho* is attributed to one Fujiwara no Moroumi, but Gotō argues that the poem was in fact composed by Tachibana no Aritsura, and dates both pieces to the mid-tenth century. *Heianchō kanbungaku ronkō*, 201–20.

103. "The poem is that to which what is intently on the mind goes. In the mind it is 'being intent'; coming out in language, it is a poem. The affections are stirred within and take on form in words" (Owen, *Chinese Literary Thought*, 40–41). This theory informs the *Kokin wakashū* prefaces; see Wixted, "Kokinshū Prefaces: Another Perspective."

104. Van Zoeren, *Poetry and Personality*, 35–44. See also Lewis, *Writing and Authority*, 155–76.

couplet is released from the poem only provisionally, a step toward its re-application (through quotation or imitation) in a new situation that is at base the same, another iteration of the guests' response to their host's proposition. The rhetoric of *hadai* transformations suggests a self-contained, purely formal beauty, but it is a beauty that gains value only through the contingencies of appropriate application, the adroit use of a clever reference on just the right occasion.

The formalization of the *jukkai* couplet is a quintessential example of the complex relationship between rhetorical and affective poetics. Originally, the language of supplication, presented as a sincere expression of the suffering poet's spirit, was a useful tactic for low-ranked officials to advance personal alliances via literary composition. As the strategy became widespread and formalized, however, it no longer sufficed to differentiate a performance, and technical manuals therefore devote little attention to it. The ubiquity of the *jukkai* couplet thus cannot be understood in terms of the individual instrumentalism of *hadai* rhetoric, but rather as a component in the standardization of literary form that served a less obvious, more dispersed purpose by enhancing group composition's potential for shared emotional experience. As H. Mack Horton has recently argued in the context of eighth-century poetic gatherings, successful poetic performance was predicated on a set of shared conventions that guaranteed the possibility of sympathetic affect.[105] From this perspective, the rules of the *kudaishi* format were not a sclerotic rigidity threatening poetry's capacity to represent the world, but rather productive guidelines that ensured the coordination of group composition by delineating a realm of expressive potential.

Generic conventions proved an effective means of productively orchestrating ritualized acts of exchange between officials and patrons. Nevertheless, exceptional examples such as the "anonymous letters" suggest that such conventions could be felt as confining laws when writers encountered the limits of composition's actual efficacy. Within the framework of technical poetics, formal standards were ideologically justified as universals, self-similar iterations of the literary's constituent "patterning." Historically, of course, they underwent constant adaptation to changes in social access to venues of composition, in literacy education, and in

105. Horton, *Traversing the Frontier*, 329–58.

awareness of contemporary practices in China, among many other factors. The growth of the *kudaishi* format itself demonstrates how conventions (including the requirements of *hadai* circumlocution and *jukkai* supplication) were established practically, through strategies demanded by socially defined venues of performance. The literary imagination could only be meaningfully actualized through the constant renegotiation of the practical applications of its standards and prohibitions.

Because the aesthetic principles of *bunshō* were largely based on Chinese sources, a discourse of local and foreign was one means of mediating the status of prescriptive standards of legitimacy. By and large, Tang poetics were figured not as simply one custom among many, but as eternal and fundamental principles, integral to a monolithic vision of civilization extending outward from a central paradigm. For example, in a 997 petition to the throne arguing over the results of a poetry composition examination, Ki no Tadana responded to his opponent's citation of earlier Japanese examination results with dismissal: "By what right could we heedlessly reject the unchanging *bun* of the Tang based on the ad-hoc decisions of this court?"[106] The prescriptive discourse of aesthetics presented in technical manuals depended on the premise of a universal authority, deviations from which were dismissed as errors and colloquialisms. Such a standard could only ever be illusory: the Tang dynasty had of course already fallen when Tadana was writing, but more importantly, the history of writing within the Chinese heartland is one of continuous reconceptualization of the relationship between script and the evolving language, both prior to the Tang and after.[107] This relationship was even more troubled in peripheral communities in which the primary spoken language was not Sinitic: Tadana's argument was unsuccessful, and his insistence on the superiority of universals over the expedients of "this court" (*honchō*) was preserved for posterity in the *Honchō monzui*, an anthology whose compilation and circulation testified to the need for local supplements to ostensibly comprehensive authorities.[108] The remaining chapters take up the imagination of this relationship between universal and particular

106. 何以本朝隨時之議、猥背唐家不易之文. *Honchō monzui* 177.

107. See for example Mair, "Rise of the Written Vernacular."

108. Similarly, *Sakumon daitai* refers to *kudaishi* as a phenomenon of "our court" not found in "poems by the Tang." See Appendix A.

more closely. Chapter 4 details the education system in classical Japan, which relied on the demonstration of mastery over a classical Chinese curriculum that was primarily performed through vernacular modes of recitation. Chapter 5 considers the ramifications of this literacy environment for the universalized aesthetic of literary Sinitic poetry and prose, demonstrating a complex process of negotiation underlying notions of the literary in Heian Japan.

FOUR

Glosses and Primers

Heian Education and Literacy

Early Japanese literacy education adapted a continental pedagogical model centered on the classical canon. During the Heian period, the official organ of education charged with preserving and interpreting this canon was the State Academy (Daigakuryō). Scholarship and argument in the academy took place within a framework of textual authority that was rarely open to challenge through material verification. The academic model of learning was promulgated through the nobility by tutors hired from among the academy's ranks of professors and students, but investigation of court procedures shows the limits of its influence, as decision-making primarily relied on precedent-based forms of authority associated with lineal oral transmission. More influential was the academy's program of literacy pedagogy, which provided the basis for Heian engagement with literary Sinitic. Previous chapters detailed the processes by which the social role of scholar-officials was delineated in the mid-Heian, and explored how these officials sought to position themselves advantageously through their writing, particularly through performances of scholarly erudition. The most fundamental justification for this positioning was classical scholarship institutionalized within the academy, but as this chapter demonstrates, the practical articulation of that scholarship—the demonstration of textual mastery through lectures, reports, and compositions—was itself profoundly reshaped by the same dynamics of exclusive ritual and service exchange that defined mid-Heian officialdom.

The educational background of the ladies-in-waiting who produced celebrated works such as the *Tale of Genji* or the *Pillow Book* has long been a subject of scholarly interest, and the chapter begins by briefly summarizing this scholarship and the question of Heian noblewomen's apparent prohibition from using Sinographs. Discussions of women's literacy have tended to take for granted men's Chinese literacy as a more or less self-evident point of reference, without interrogating the historical specificity of Heian officials' education. Extant traces of State Academy pedagogy reveal a core reliance on glossing in a hybrid Japanese idiom guided by imported Chinese commentaries. Academic pedagogy initially exercised great influence on the private education of the upper nobility, but competing standards of knowledge blunted the academy's ideology of textual authority. After establishing in the following pages how officialdom learned to read and write, the final chapter will turn to reconsider the place of "literature" (*bunshō*) within the larger field of mid-Heian inscription, moving beyond the contemporary discursive constructions of the literary examined in chapter 3 to consider composition and performance as concrete practices.

Although the history of education and literacy in the Heian period remains relatively understudied, the question of elite women's relationship to Chinese script has attracted very active scholarly attention. Heian discourse on writing frequently distinguishes between the limited, simplified repertoire of character forms used in *kana* phonographic writing and the larger library of "true" character forms (*mana*) used in administrative or literary Sinitic modes of inscription, and several works contain episodes that portray the use of the latter by women as unfeminine and ridiculous. The best known of these is the "rainy night discussion" of the *Tale of Genji*, where a young noble regales his friends with the humorous story of a woman who never used *kana* in her letters and corrected his *shi* poetry compositions.[1] The author of *Genji*, Murasaki Shikibu, similarly mocks her contemporary Sei Shōnagon for "littering her writings" with *mana*, and in the *Pillow Book* Sei portrays herself as conscious of the potential dangers of being branded such a show-off: despite knowing the original, she is only willing to respond to a quiz on a Tang *shi* poem with a vernacular verse in *kana* script.[2]

1. *Genji monogatari*, "Hahakigi," 1:85–88.

2. *Murasaki Shikibu nikki*, 202; trans. Bowring, *Diary of Lady Murasaki*, 54; *Makura no sōshi*, "Tō no chūjō no suzuro naru soragoto o kikite," 134–40.

Such passages have produced an image of Heian culture in which male nobles conducted affairs of state in "Chinese," while women, who were denied the same level of education, instead used the *kana* syllabary to produce masterpieces of vernacular poetry and prose. In recent years, however, scholars including Thomas LaMarre, Joshua Mostow, and Tomiko Yoda have questioned the nature and effects of this divide, undermining the image of a pervasive gender-based binary.[3] Edward Kamens points out that elsewhere in her diary, Murasaki Shikibu suggests a more ambivalent relationship to literary Sinitic. Commenting on the collection of books left by her late husband, she writes:

> Whenever my loneliness threatens to overwhelm me, I take out one or two of them to look at; but my women gather together behind my back. "It's because she goes on like this that she is so miserable. What kind of lady is it who reads Chinese books [*mannabumi*]?" they whisper. "In the past one was forbidden even to read a sutra!" "Yes," I feel like replying, "but I've never met anyone who lived longer just because they believe in taboos!" But that would be thoughtless of me. There is some truth in what they say.[4]

Murasaki Shikibu both marks herself off from her attendants' unthinking adherence to "taboos" (*monoimi*), and tacitly acknowledges their contention that her behavior is connected to her continued misfortune. Elsewhere in her diary, she records giving the imperial consort Shōshi 彰子 (988–1074) lessons in reading Bai Juyi's *Xin yuefu*, a text commonly used as an elementary primer in Heian Japan. Not wanting to be criticized for flaunting her learning, she kept these lessons secret, but when they were discovered, Shōshi's father Michinaga's reaction was to have new copies of more Chinese books presented to his daughter.[5] Such passages suggest a complex interrelationship between, on the one hand, a set of prohibitions

3. LaMarre, *Uncovering Heian Japan*, 93–115; Mostow, "Mother Tongue and Father Script"; Yoda, *Gender and National Literature*, 81–110. Other recent English-language studies on women's relationship to Chinese are Borgen, "Politics of Classical Chinese," 223–30; Heldt, "Writing Like a Man"; and Guest, "Primers, Commentaries, and Kanbun Literacy," 98–127.

4. *Murasaki Shikibu nikki*, 204; translation slightly modified from Bowring, *Diary of Lady Murasaki*, 55. See Kamens, "Terrains of Text."

5. *Murasaki Shikibu nikki*, 210.

discouraging women from reading Chinese texts or displaying overfamiliarity with Sinographs, and on the other, the impossibility of true segregation from Sinographic literacy and the social rewards that might attend knowledge of Chinese lore. Murasaki Shikibu emphasizes the peculiarity of her literacy, and its potential as an object of opprobrium, yet contemporary sources suggest she was not unique in her education.[6]

If there was a "taboo" surrounding writing, its boundaries were nebulous. To be sure, evidence from extant document signatures suggests that already by the ninth century there existed some customary discouragement of women's writing.[7] Nevertheless, Shimura Midori notes that mid-Heian sources contain repeated references to the game of *hen-tsugi* among noblewomen, in which players attempt to complete a Sinograph from which the radical has been removed.[8] Such games perhaps indicate some degree of shared knowledge of *mana* Sinographs among these women, but more importantly, suggest that such knowledge could be safely displayed only in certain socially acceptable contexts. Literacy is not a measurable quantity that can be easily separated from social mores that guide and limit its use. As David Lurie has recently emphasized in regards to the earliest examples of writing excavated in Japan, "literacy" can take many forms, predicated on a variety of relationships to and uses of text. Just as a senior noble might "compose" a petition by commissioning the services of a scholar, reading too was a skill that could be externalized: the *Pillow Book* depicts communication among aristocrats through the medium of letters sent between their ladies-in-waiting, who would then convey the contents orally to their employers.[9] Similarly, the presence of an especially educated woman such as Murasaki Shikibu must have brought others in her circle into engagement with Chinese literature.

6. Sei Shōnagon's *Pillow Book* contains numerous tales of games and wordplay, often between men and women, based on Chinese classics, histories, and poetry. Takashina no Kishi 高階貴子 (d. 996) was appointed as a palace attendant because of her education, and even submitted Chinese-style poems at palace poetry banquets, though her "excessive talent" (*amari ni zae kashikoki*) is said to have brought her unhappiness as well. *Eiga monogatari*, "Samazama no yorokobi," 1:142; *Ōkagami*, 258–59.

7. Sekiguchi, "Heian jidai no danjo," 517–24.

8. Shimura, "Heian jidai josei no mana," 25.

9. *Makura no sōshi*, "Iinikuki mono," 214.

The integral connection between reading and writing at the basis of modern literacy education did not necessarily apply in earlier cultures.[10]

Such examples of "effective literacy" demonstrate the need to reexamine literacy among male officials as well. There was not a homogenized standard of ready control of Sinographs, and certainly not of a spoken Chinese language, but rather a complex field generated through the interaction of patronage of technical abilities, a classical ideology of governance through learning, and new implementations of writing in the service of the court ritual calendar.

The Structure of the Academy

While Heian records contain some scant documentation of schools at provincial headquarters, outside of temples the only large educational institution operated in the capital. According to the preface of the *Kaifūsō*, a state-sponsored school was first established under Emperor Tenji, and the 701 Taihō Code describes a State Academy (literally "Bureau of Higher Education," Daigakuryō) under the purview of the Ministry of Ceremonial, with administrators, functionaries, and 430 students. The teachers included a head professor with two assistants, and a pair each of professors of pronunciation, calligraphy, and math. The final decades of the seventh century brought an explosion in the use of written documentation by the court, and the academy, modeled on the Tang state's Directorate of Education (and influenced by Paekche institutions as well), sought to fill the need for a literate staff of clerks and administrators.[11]

The school was centered on a core curriculum of the Chinese classics (the *Odes*, the *Changes*, the *Documents*, the *Zuo Commentary*, and the three

10. "Just as reading was linked in the medieval mind with hearing rather than seeing, writing (in the modern sense of composition) was associated with dictating rather than manipulating a pen." Clanchy, *Memory to Written Record*, 272.

11. Nothing is recorded of the Paekche education system, but Hisaki Yukio notes several direct parallels between the early Academy and Silla predecessors that hint at the influence Paekche immigrants had on the Academy curriculum. *Nihon kodai gakkō*, 49–62.

Rites), with supplementary courses in calligraphy and pronunciation, and a separate, smaller track in mathematics. As new tests and more professors were added, a four-track curriculum stabilized in the early Nara period:

1. Myōgyōdō 明經道: the central curriculum of the Academy, based on the Confucian canon, with a quota of four hundred students (hereafter, "Classics")
2. Sandō 算道: the math curriculum, with a quota of thirty students ("Math")
3. Myōbōdō 明法道: the law curriculum, focused on the court's growing body of legal codes and protocol, with a quota of ten (later twenty) students ("Law")
4. Monjōdō 文章道, later Kidendō 紀傳道: the composition curriculum, focused on Chinese histories (the *Shiji*, *Hanshu*, and *Hou Hanshu*) and belles-lettres (*Wenxuan*), with a quota of twenty students ("Letters")

By 730, the law made provision for professors and graduate students in each of these curricula.

Unsurprisingly, the question of whom exactly the academy was meant to be educating proved contentious. According to the Taihō Code, the students would be the adolescent sons of the nobility (fifth-rank and above) or immigrant-descended scribal houses (*fuhitobe*), with the remainder to be filled with lower-ranked officials' children at the discretion of the Ministry of Ceremonial. Very early, however, in 728, the academy was opened to the sons of lower and unranked officials as well, on the condition that they pass an entrance examination.[12] This was probably in reaction to lack of interest in the academy. While the law made provision for over four hundred students, that number was only approached during the academy's peak in the ninth century. From the beginning, the court seems to have struggled with a lack of incentive for academy education among the nobility, whose sons were guaranteed entrance into the bureaucracy through the *on'i* (inherited rank) system. The late eighth and

12. Kotō, "Monjō tokugōshōshi no seiritsu," 36–46. Cf. Momo, *Jōdai gakusei no kenkyū*, 35.

early ninth centuries saw repeated proclamations bestowing extra rewards on ranked nobles who passed one of the civil service examinations, or attempting to impose a kind of compulsory four-year education on children of the nobility.[13] Such efforts petered out by the end of the ninth century, unable to overcome the fundamental obstacle: the examination system was largely irrelevant to highly ranked capital posts. Whereas policy changes under the Song dynasty eventually led to the development of an "examination elite" in imperial China's state bureaucracy, the Japanese State Academy and civil service examination continued to function primarily as a technical school for low- and mid-level functionaries in the ministries, bureaus, and provincial offices of the state.[14]

The potential for access to mid-level officialdom offered by the academy was most attractive to men like Minamoto no Shitagō, who came from relatively prestigious lineages, but lacked the easy access to office afforded to sons of senior nobles. Shitagō was one of many Minamoto descended from Emperor Saga, but his father Kozoru 舉 (d. 930) never rose above the sixth rank, so Shitagō was not able to benefit from the *on'i* system. Instead, like the children of many low-ranked officials, he entered the academy in an attempt to gain access to the privileges of the fifth rank and a *zuryō* appointment. Shitagō's path through the academy demonstrates both its potentials and limitations as a mechanism of social mobility.

Shitagō began his schooling in the Shōgakuin, a kind of private dormitory for relatives of the imperial family studying at the academy.[15] It had been established in 881 by Ariwara no Yukihira 在原行平 (818–93), in imitation of the Fujiwara lineage's Kangakuin (est. 821). Such dormitories began as supplemental appendages to the academy, providing housing and some schooling to young students associated with their lineages. As they achieved official recognition and independent financial support, however, they became an integral part of the academy's institutional structure, part of the larger pattern of households and lineages assuming the state's administrative functions.[16] In the mid-Heian, the structure of the

13. Momo, *Jōdai gakusei no kenkyū*, 46–61; Hisaki, *Nihon kodai gakkō*, 146–67.
14. Hisaki, *Nihon kodai gakkō*, 323–41.
15. *Honchō monzui* 229.
16. Hisaki, *Nihon kodai gakkō*, 230–31.

academy was most directly shaped by the complex negotiations of the lineages that sponsored and relied upon it, rather than by the governmental goals that inspired its founding. For example, Shitagō's most important early sponsor, Minamoto no Takaakira (who was a maternal descendant of Shitagō's great-grandfather Sadamu 定), was also an active supporter of the Shōgakuin, petitioning the court in 963 for the dormitory to be granted the privilege of nominating students for provincial posts (in parallel with the Kangakuin).[17] The academy was established as an organ of the state bureaucracy, but Shitagō's education there would be put to use in a career defined as much by unofficial clientage as by bureaucratic duties.

The dormitories were originally dedicated to providing housing and study materials for students in the academy, but many prospective students seem to have entered the dormitories early, around the age of nine, using it as a kind of preparatory school before they officially enrolled (usually around the time of their coming-of-age, at twelve or thirteen).[18] Once a youth advanced to regular student (*gakushō* 學生) status, his formal schooling would begin. At least by the mid-Heian, however, this seems not to have involved attendance of regular lectures at the academy so much as the establishment of a private tutorial relationship with a recognized scholar.[19] Sugawara no Michizane was a professor of letters at the academy, but describes the school he ran out of his residence, a practice he inherited from his father Koreyoshi.[20] In the *Tale of Genji*, when Genji's son Yūgiri is enrolled at the academy, he is "shut up" in a room in Genji's residence, and "entrusted . . . to a learned tutor."[21]

Shitagō's early life and career in the academy are mostly unknown. In 951, when he was made a clerk in the newly established Poetry Office (Wakadokoro), he was still only a regular student at forty-one years old.[22] Given the relative paucity of information on Shitagō's early life, it might be tempting to imagine that he simply began his education very late, but it is more probable that, like the beleaguered thirty-five-year-old student Tōei in *Utsuho monogatari*, he had been unable to find advancement out

17. *Dai Nihon shiryō* ser. 1, 11:323.
18. Momo, *Jōdai gakusei no kenkyū*, 195; Hisaki, *Nihon kodai gakkō*, 219.
19. Momo, *Jōdai gakusei no kenkyū*, 260–64.
20. Borgen, *Sugawara no Michizane*, 124–40.
21. *Genji monogatari*, "Otome," 3:27; trans. Tyler, *Tale of Genji*, 383.
22. *Shitagō shū* 117.

of the academy. During his twenties, Shitagō suffered a series of losses that deprived him of a strong support network: his father died in 930; his mother in 934; and the imperial princess Kinshi, for whom he compiled the encyclopedia *Wamyō ruijushō* (discussed in the next chapter), died in 938. He had two elder brothers, but the eldest died as a young man, and the second seems to have abandoned the capital.[23]

Such connections were especially vital because in the tenth century nomination was increasingly supplanting testing as the means for advancing into official posts out of the State Academy. By the end of the ninth century, the highest-level test in each curriculum was customarily limited to graduate students (*tokugōshō* 得業生), of whom there were only ten across the entire academy. In response to this bottleneck, nomination powers were granted to each of the four curricula as well as the three most prominent dormitories to assign a handful of students each year to functionary (sixth- to eighth-rank) posts in capital or provincial offices.[24] Even the ability to sit for tests was often predicated on a nomination of some sort, so personal connections were essential to successful advancement through or out of the academy, whatever one's ability. Like the rest of the Heian bureaucracy, the academy was gradually transformed by a developing network of precedent-based prerogatives to offices passed down within family lineages.

Training in the academy was based on progression up a ladder of nominations and tests, which brought increasing potential for reward through office and rank. The letters curriculum that Shitagō pursued, summarized below, had the largest number of tests and offered the greatest opportunities for advancement.

Enrollment in the academy brought a youth the status of regular student, ostensibly part of the classics curriculum. The entrance examination (*yūgakushi* 遊學試) required the prospect to demonstrate mastery of one of the classics (generally the *Analects* or the *Classic of Filial Piety*).[25] The exact procedure is not recorded, but probably involved chanting memorized lines from the text in a pronunciation based on Tang standards of literary recitation (as will be discussed below, how near such

23. Kannotō, "Wakaki hi no Shitagō."
24. Hisaki, *Nihon kodai gakkō*, 171–73.
25. Ibid., 201–2.

recitation was to Chinese phonology is far from clear; I will refer to this register as "Sinitic" or "Sinitic-derived" pronunciation). Shitagō was not subject to this examination, however. His father's stalled career deprived him of the privileges of *on'i* rank, but the academy provided automatic admittance to both the sons and *grandsons* of nobles of fifth rank or higher.

Students officially entered the letters curriculum only when they attained the status of provisional letters student (*gimonjōshō* 擬文章生). These were set at twenty in number, and when an opening came in the ranks, regular students could be nominated by a professor to sit for the provisional letters student examination, usually called the Bureau Test (*ryōshi* 寮試). The student would be quizzed on five passages from one of the three histories in the letters curriculum (generally the *Shiji* 史記 [*Records of the Historian*, ca. 91 BCE]), needing to correctly recite three of them to pass.[26] By the twelfth century, this test became largely ceremonial, with the chapters to be tested on communicated in advance to the candidate.[27]

The goal of most students who entered the academy in the mid-Heian was probably to become one of the twenty letters students (*monjōshō* 文章生). While there were opportunities to be nominated for office out of other student levels, all letters students could expect to be assigned a post within five or six years, most commonly as a manager (*jō*) in one of the provincial headquarters.[28] The test for letters student status, usually referred to as the Ministry Test (*shōshi* 省試) because it was held by the Ministry of Ceremonial, thus functioned as a de facto official appointment examination.

The Ministry Test was normally open only to provisional letters students, but many also took the test by special permission from the sovereign. It was supposed to be held biannually in spring and autumn, but by the tenth century it seems to have been held only every two or three years. (Since letters students were awarded posts in order of seniority, there was no particular need to replace them every time the number dropped below twenty.) The number of passing grades was usually determined simply by

26. *Engi shiki* 20.524. Thus Yūgiri spends "four or five months" reading through the *Shiji* after entering the academy (*Genji monogatari*, "Otome," 3:28).

27. Momo, *Jōdai gakusei no kenkyū*, 264–68.

28. Ibid., 278–81.

the number of available slots. The test was based on poetry composition; examinees were judged on their ability to produce a poem in accordance with the assigned topic (a quotation from a classical text), length (generally six to eight couplets), and rhyme, all set by the commissioner of ceremonial. From early on, this poetry competition seems to have been treated as an opportunity for entertainment for the court. Beginning in 916, there are many instances of the Ministry Test being held in conjunction with royal excursions, where the presentation and judgment of poems serves as one of a series of events surrounding the banquet.[29]

By the end of the Heian period this test too became largely ceremonial, with the poems prepared in advance and the examinees almost all nominated by the emperor, regent, or other senior nobles. Echoing Tōei's discovery by Masayori in *Utsuho monogatari*, in the mid-Heian State Academy the selection of merit according to institutional standards was reimagined as the personal recognition of talent by the upper nobility. That examinations still retained meaning in the mid-Heian, however, we can judge by the many records of controversy and cheating surrounding them. Ivo Smits discusses a dispute in 997, in which Ōe no Masahira managed to have the failure of Ōe no Tokimune 大江時棟 (who may have been raised by Masahira) overturned.[30] As a young man, Fujiwara no Michinaga had an examiner bound and kidnapped in 988, apparently in retaliation for the failure of one of his associates.[31] Even as late as 1034, Fujiwara no Akihira, himself a former letters graduate student, was punished for altering the compositions of examinees in the middle of a test.[32]

For most students admitted into the letters curriculum, this is the path they pursued: achievement of letters student status through passing the Bureau and Ministry Tests, followed by appointment to an official post. Shitagō's own progression through the academy was delayed for many years, but once he was named a letters student in 953, he was granted a post and sixth rank in less than three years, in the spring appointments of 956. Ten years later, at the age of fifty-six, he finally achieved sufficient seniority at his post to be raised to junior fifth rank and assigned a supernumerary

29. Ibid., 270–71.
30. Smits, "Way of the Literati," 113–15.
31. Momo, *Jōdai gakusei no kenkyū*, 274.
32. Ōsone, *Ōchō kanbungaku ronkō*, 49–54.

governorship, gaining the *zuryō* office that was the primary career goal of mid-ranked officials.[33] Shitagō's path typifies the career of the academy-graduate official seeking profitable *zuryō* appointments through a combination of ability, connections, and the bureaucracy's seniority-based promotion system.

There was, however, another track through the letters curriculum, one barred to men like Shitagō. At any one time, two students in the academy were marked out as graduate letters students (*monjō tokugōshō* 文章得業生). Originally these had been chosen from among the twenty letters students, but it became increasingly common for them to be identified as scholarship students (*kyūryōshō* 給料生) through nomination already at the regular student level, marking them off from their peers. Graduate letters students were eligible to sit for the Policy Test (*hōryakushi* 方略試), the highest-level examination offered. This was an essay examination, requiring the candidate to exposit in literary-Sinitic parallel prose on two topics set by the examiner.[34]

While letters student status brought access to mid-level administrative officialdom and the potential for *zuryō* posts, men who passed the Policy Test were recognized as "scholars" (*jusha*) by the court, a prerequisite for certain posts reserved for the academic elite, including commissioner of ceremonial, palace secretary (*naiki*), tutor to the crown prince, and professor of letters. Control over these posts was fiercely guarded by lineages that had established scholarly reputations. In the tenth century, there are still records of men from outside the established lineages taking the Policy Test through special imperial dispensation, but by the eleventh century the test was effectively limited to five scholarly lineages.[35] There were thus two tracks within the letters curriculum, a general one for men seeking entrance to official posts (usually themselves the sons of mid-rank officials), and a specialized one restricted to certain families with a monopoly on scholarly posts. A similar system of graduate student status

33. Kannotō, "Anna no hen zengo." He was reassigned as the governor of Izumi Province the next year.

34. Momo, *Jōdai gakusei no kenkyū*, 281–99. See also chapter 3.

35. The descendants of Sugawara no Michizane, Ōe no Koretoki, Fujiwara no Arikuni, Fujiwara no Sanenori 藤原實範 (fl. 1023–62), and Fujiwara no Akihira. Hisaki, *Nihon kodai gakkō*, 293–96.

controlled by a few lineages was found in the other three curricula as well, though these offered fewer opportunities for non-graduate students.

As the above discussion suggests, the growing prevalence of individual tutorial relationships (often within a family) and replacement of testing by nomination attenuated both the independent power and institutional coherence of the academy. By the late Heian period, the "State Academy" was effectively a loose collective of scholarly households with established proprietary rights over the four curricula and accompanying post-nomination privileges. Nevertheless, this household-based educational network still served to reproduce the capital bureaucratic class; indeed, the attachment of certain offices to specific households through the curriculum nomination system may have allowed for more reliable transmission of practical administrative training than did the rather idealistic original curricula.[36] That the expertise of these scholarly households retained a persistent value can be seen from the regular reappearance of men from lineages such as the Nakahara and the Hino in political reformations by Go-Sanjō, Yoritomo, and the Ashikaga.[37]

Though the organizational structure of the State Academy is relatively well documented, the content of the students' education is less clear. The legal codes give us only a very sparse outline of academy education. The basic texts in each of the four curricula were decreed by law, and memorization and rote repetition in Sinitic pronunciation were considered the first step in study, with students moving on to lectures on content only after completing study with professors of pronunciation.[38] The testing system probably gives us the best sense of education's incentives and goals: in the case of the letters curriculum, the Ministry Test was based on poetry composition, highlighting the need for a class of literati bureaucrats to serve as poets at official banquets, while the Policy Test focused on the elaborate parallel prose composition used in ritual documents. The tests in the other curricula focused on Chinese and Japanese precedent (classics and law), which was the basis for decisions in the Council of State, and

36. Uesugi, *Nihon chūsei hōtaikei seiritsu*, 107–10.

37. Ibid., 115; Gomi, *Bushi to bunshi*, 55–69; Conlan, *From Sovereign to Symbol*, 77–116.

38. *Ryō no shūge* 15.449.

mathematics, which was vital to the Bureaus of Accounting and Taxation. This schematic understanding can be enriched by contemporary records and manuscript evidence of academic education, in which a few characteristics stand out: (1) early education through rote recitation in Sinitic-based pronunciation, (2) interpretation of canonical literary Sinitic texts through vernacular glossing, (3) reliance on imported Chinese commentaries as exegetical aids, and (4) an underlying assumption of the supremacy of textual authority in resolving questions of correctness. These will be discussed in turn below.

Elementary Education and Primers

The boys who began their education at dormitories like the Shōgakuin were probably taught by older students there, and spent these first years memorizing the sing-song verses of elementary primers, particularly *Mengqiu* 蒙求 (Searching from Ignorance, 746) and *Qianziwen* 千字文 (Thousand-Character Essay, early sixth century).[39] These textbooks organized elementary knowledge or vocabulary into verse, to facilitate rote memorization. Their use extended outside of the academy and its dormitories to children of the imperial household and upper nobility.[40]

The *Mengqiu* is composed of four-character phrases, each referring to a famous personage from Chinese history.[41] These episodes are arranged into alternately rhyming parallel couplets. For example, "Fan Ran grows dust, Yan Ying peels the hulls" 范冉生塵、晏嬰脱粟 refers to the

39. Ōta, "'Shibu no tokusho' kō."

40. In 878, the nine-year-old Prince Sadayasu 貞保親王 (870–924) received his first instruction in the *Mengqiu* from Tachibana no Hiromi 橘廣相 (837–90), a letters graduate, and the work appears repeatedly in records throughout the remainder of the Heian period. The first explicit reference to the *Qianziwen*'s use as child's primer in Japan is for the eight-year-old Crown Prince Sadaakira 貞明親王 (later Emperor Yōzei, r. 876–84) in 875. *Nihon sandai jitsuroku*, Gangyō 2/8/25 and Jōgan 17/4/23 (437, 361). *Qianziwen* also appears as a children's primer in *Utsuho monogatari* ("Rō no ue jō," 850).

41. The work's name derives from a passage in the *Classic of Changes*: "Obscurity is progress. It is not that I seek the young and ignorant; the young and ignorant [*meng*] seek [*qiu*] me" 蒙、亨。匪我求童蒙、童蒙求我 (*Zhouyi zhengyi* 1.8). See further Watson, *Meng ch'iu*.

stories of Fan Ran, a county magistrate in the Eastern Han who was mocked as being so poor his rice pot filled with dust, and Yan Ying, a minister of Qi in the Spring and Autumn period who lived so simply he ate unpolished rice.[42] Each couplet has some thematic link between the two figures mentioned (in the example, humble living), and each is followed by a commentary that paraphrases the original source of the episode mentioned. For students who were just beginning their reading lessons and were not yet ready to tackle the official histories, the metered text served as a mnemonic device to a great stock of illustrative anecdotes, assisting them in developing a vocabulary of reference essential to the heavily allusive style discussed in chapter 3.

The *Qianziwen* is one of the oldest and most culturally central elementary primers in East Asia, used as a calligraphy textbook all the way down to the present. Like the *Mengqiu*, *Qianziwen* is made up of four-character, alternately rhyming couplets (in this case 250 lines using 1,000 unique characters). The canonical importance of the text is best illustrated by its appearance in the *Kojiki* 古事記 (Record of Ancient Matters, 712) legend of Wani, the Paekche scholar said to have introduced continental writing and scholarship to Japan by presenting copies of the *Analects* and *Qianziwen* to Emperor Ōjin. Though anachronistic, this tale reflects the popularity of *Qianziwen* as an elementary manual for learning to read and write: examples of calligraphy practice using the work survive from as early as the first decade of the eighth century, and it was certainly widespread in the Nara period.[43]

Both of these works make use of metered, rhyming lines designed specifically for ease of recitation and memorization. But these formal qualities were more than simply an expedient for acquiring literacy or historical knowledge; the rhyming lines also served as a tool for acquiring the sound structure and rhyme rules of a Sinitic prestige dialect referred to in Japan as "Han pronunciation" (*kan'on* 漢音).[44] One manuscript of *Mengqiu* produced in the tenth century is marked throughout with red

42. *Mengqiu* 89–90; *Hou Hanshu* 81.2688–90; *Yanzi chunqiu jishi* 6.423.

43. Lurie, *Realms of Literacy*, 111–13.

44. As Christopher Nugent notes, parallel forms of instruction occurred even in Tang China, where mastering the literary language in some respects resembled learning a foreign language. *Manifest in Words*, 89–90.

ink indicating Chinese tonal values as well as some indicators of syllabic pronunciation.[45] Judging from such manuscript evidence, *Mengqiu* was just as important as an introduction to China's phonology as to its history.[46] *Qianziwen* too was memorized and recited as a method of learning the sounds of Sinographs, but it was also recited using local-language glosses of the literary Sinitic terminology. Early manuscripts indicate a peculiar recitation style in which "Han pronunciations" are read as modifiers of Japanese lexical equivalents, so that for example the line "Time and space are vast" 宇宙洪荒 becomes "*uchū no ōsora kōkō to ōi nari*" (something like "the great sky of *uchū* is immense as *kōkō*").[47] The text therefore seems to have functioned as a first introduction to the *kundoku* glossing techniques discussed in detail below.[48]

Both of these textbooks were originally composed within China, and were widely used there in similar processes of memorization, recitation, and copying.[49] The lack of locally produced "Chinese textbooks" aimed at Japanese speakers may seem surprising, but there are parallel

45. Tsukishima, *Chōshō-bon Mōgyū*, 80–84.

46. Ōta argues for the connection between *Mengqiu*'s use in Japan and the early-Heian state initiative to establish more "authentic" Chinese pronunciation in academy training. "Kangakuin no suzume," 237.

47. *Ueno-bon Chū senjimon chūkai*, 58. This method of combining Sinitic pronunciation and vernacular glosses in recitation, referred to as *monzen'yomi*, is found in manuscripts of several genres of writing, but Tsukishima Hiroshi emphasizes that it represents a small minority of Heian *kundoku* practice (*Heian jidai no kanbun kundokugo*, 277). Its use in *Qianziwen* reading is an exception for educational purposes rather than standard practice. The strength of the association between *Qianziwen* and elementary glossing practice received new evidence from the 2015 discovery of an early eighth-century wooden tablet (*mokkan*) containing a passage from *Qianziwen* glossed with phonographs giving Japanese lexical equivalents (*Mainichi shinbun*, October 29, 2016, Yamaguchi edition).

48. Two other important textbooks should be mentioned in passing: *Baiershi yong* (Hundred-Twenty Songs), a sequence of regulated verse "poems on things" (*yongwushi* 詠物詩) by the Tang poet Li Jiao 李嶠 (fl. 698–712), and Bai Juyi's *Xin yuefu*, both of which served to introduce poetic form and diction. See Steininger, "Li Jiao's *Songs*"; Smits, "Reading the *New Ballads*." By the twelfth century, *Wakan rōeishū* was similarly used as a primer for memorization. See the previous chapter and Satō Michio, *"Wakan rōeishū" eiin to kenkyū*, 157–65.

49. Fragmentary manuscripts of both works, as well as similar elementary primers, are found among the Dunhuang materials. Wang Zhongmin, *Dunhuang guji xulu*, 206–8; Tōno, "Kunmōsho." The heavy focus on early memorization and chanting continued

examples of education through a prestigious cosmopolitan script elsewhere in the classical world. In the medieval West, Latin education within Germanic and other alien language groups mostly proceeded through the use of primers written by Roman authors for native speakers of Latin. Vernacular alternatives such as Ælfric's (ca. 955–1012) Latin grammar for Anglo-Saxons emerged only gradually, and never supplanted Roman textbooks completely.[50]

On the other hand, if we compare a Heian student to his Anglo-Saxon counterpart, the lack of emphasis on grammar in his elementary education is striking. Whether in the academy, in private homes, or in temple classrooms, the earliest education seems to have focused primarily on the acquisition of vocabulary (including calligraphic reproduction) and pronunciation.[51] Medieval Latin education also began with chanting and hymns, but the first textbook was almost invariably Aelius Donatus's *Ars minor* (fourth century), which introduced the parts of speech, cases, and verb forms.[52]

Clearly, there are historical reasons for this difference, particularly the lack of a detailed program of grammatical analysis within the Chinese intellectual tradition. As in imperial Rome, where the early study of Latin took text rather than speech as the object of study, medieval Chinese scholarship pursued the orthography, meaning, and sounds of characters, not any variety of the spoken language.[53] Whereas Latin's highly inflected morphology and phonetic writing system demanded attention to problems of grammar, however, in China the isolating morphology of Sinitic and a primarily logographic writing system provided little impetus for developing a complex vocabulary of syntactic rules and categories. Instead, rules of grammar were established implicitly through the discourse

---

down to the late imperial period, on which see Elman, *Cultural History of Civil Examinations*, 260–76.

50. Hill, "Latin in Anglo-Saxon England"; Law, *Grammar and Grammarians*, 200–223.

51. Primary education in temples began with the memorized chanting of sutras. Hori, "Gakusō kyōiku seido," 591–600.

52. On sound in elementary Latin education, see Murphy, "Latin as a Second Language."

53. On the Western study of Latin as fundamentally textual, see Irvine, *Making of Textual Culture*, 3–4.

of textual commentary.[54] For non-Chinese-speaking students, problems of grammatical interpretation were particularly important; as will be seen below, Heian readers developed a complex, grammar-centered reading apparatus to fix the correct recitation of imported texts. Despite the "ungrammatical" character of elementary learning, it was seen as necessary preparation for the syntactic analysis of secondary education. Only after having built up a store of characters, sounds, and historical lore was a student considered ready to begin the process of construing the sentences of the classics under his teacher's guidance.

Glossing and Commentaries

While legal codes record the textbooks and testing system of the State Academy, they are largely silent on the details of their daily lessons, their hermeneutical principles, or the pedagogical methods pursued there. Diaries too, give us little to work with: almost all were produced by senior nobles who did not attend the academy, and they rarely mention educational matters. Instead our best source of information for how Heian readers approached reading are the documents themselves—surviving manuscripts of academic texts provide material traces of the history of their reception, including interlinear recitation guides and marginalia. A considerable number of such manuscripts, passed down within and then copied from so-called "professorial households" (*hakaseke*), survive from the twelfth century onward, but mid-Heian examples are much rarer. Nevertheless, enough survive to allow us to reconstruct a reading practice centered on the employment of Tang commentary editions to produce vernacular-based recitations.

"Reading by gloss" (*kundoku* 訓讀), a set of techniques for using the logographic properties of the Chinese writing system to read (aloud) a string of characters as an utterance in the local language, was integral to the rise of literacy in Japan from the seventh century onward.[55] *Kundoku*

54. For an overview of early Chinese grammatical discourse, see Harbsmeier, *Language and Logic*, 85–95.

55. Lurie, *Realms of Literacy*, 169–212.

functioned by establishing semantic correspondences (e.g., the character *boku* 木, associated in Chinese practice with a word meaning "tree," read as "*ki*," a Japanese word of equivalent meaning) and transferring syntactic relationships—for example, reversing the order of verb-object pairs (VO in Chinese, OV in Japanese) and assigning particles to indicate case where necessary. This form of literacy could thus "read" a literary Sinitic text through the local language—in the sources examined below, the Early Middle Japanese dialect of the Heian capital, sometimes referred to as "Yamato" speech in period documents (for simplicity's sake, I will refer nonspecifically to "Chinese" and "Japanese" languages below, with the caveat that these labels are anachronistic and ignore a great deal of linguistic diversity). For example, a phrase from *Qianziwen*, "[When you] learn of a fault, [you] must correct [it]."

知	過	必	改
know	fault	must	correct

is quoted in a 769 imperial proclamation as

ayamachi-o	*shirite-wa*	*kanarazu*	*aratame-yo*[56]
mistake-ACCUSATIVE	know-TOPIC	must	correct-EMPHATIC

Rather than providing a naturalistic translation, *kundoku* cleaves closely to the original text. The sentence produced does not aim for an idiomatic construction according to colloquial speech patterns, but represents the meaning through a limited, formalized Japanese register while maintaining the structure of the original as much as possible.

Such techniques were found around the Chinese periphery, from Turpan to Korea to Vietnam.[57] A related phenomenon observed in many of these cases is the marking up or "glossing" of a literary Sinitic text with notes and diacritics to aid in the process of construal.[58] In Japan these marks written into a text to aid in its oral performance are known as

56. *Shoku Nihongi*, 4:263.
57. Kim, *Kanbun to Higashi Ajia*, 149–64.
58. Whitman, "Ubiquity of the Gloss."

kunten 訓點. Glossing with *kunten* is a descendant of various practices that can be traced back to medieval China: marking of phrase and sentence endings; the dotting with red ink of characters with multiple readings (*poyin* 破音), which in the Tang evolved into the practice of marking characters to indicate the four tones; and interlinear commentary that provided simple definitions of difficult words in the main text. In kingdoms on the Tang periphery these techniques were adapted to record additional information to assist in interpreting texts through a local language.[59] In Japan, important forms of glossing included the use of *kana* to transcribe specific lexical translations, ordinal marks to indicate syntactic transpositions, and diacritics (*okototen*) to indicate case-marking particles and verbal suffixes needed to produce a grammatically felicitous Japanese sentence (fig. 3). Evidence suggests that both *kundoku* reading techniques and these glossing formats were imported to Japan from Korea over the seventh and eighth centuries.[60] The earliest *kunten*-annotated manuscripts that survive in Japan, from the late eighth century, are products of Buddhist temples; *kunten* glossing seems to have been adopted by the academy much later. Nara and early Heian manuscripts of non-Buddhist texts all lack *kunten*; in the tenth century, however, glossed manuscripts of texts associated with the academy curriculum begin to appear, adapting a format of diacritics originally employed by Enryakuji and other Tendai temples in the ninth century.[61]

The earliest datable example of glossing in the academy is a manuscript of a portion of Yang Xiong's biography from the *Hanshu* 漢書 (History of the Han, ca. 82). The work carries a colophon identifying it as glossed in Tenryaku 2 (948) by Fujiwara no Yoshisuke 藤原良佐, an otherwise unremarkable man who was first cousin twice-removed to Fujiwara no Arihira 藤原在衡 (892–970), a former letters student who became head of the academy in 926.[62] The *Hanshu* was part of the letters curriculum, and we can safely assume that Yoshisuke's glosses were produced as part of his study there. Yang Xiong 揚雄 (53 BCE–18 CE), the subject of this biography, was a famous writer, and the extant manuscript

59. Ishizuka, "Tonkō no katenbon," 231–37.
60. Lurie, *Realms of Literacy*, 195–204; Whitman, "Ubiquity of the Gloss," 103–12.
61. Nakada, *Kotenbon no kokugogakuteki kenkyū*, 1:386–87, 439–47.
62. Kobayashi, *Kanseki kundoku no kokugoshiteki kenkyū*, 817–20.

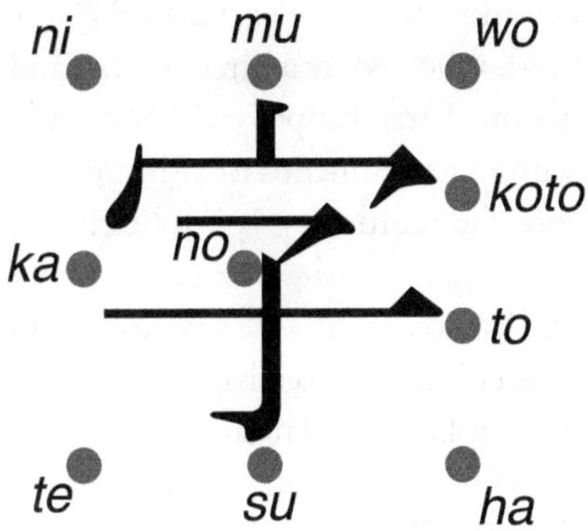

FIG. 3 A standard set of *okototen* diacritic marks. Dots around the edge of the character indicate postpositions to be added in *kundoku* recitation.

is almost completely given over to four long rhapsodies (*fu*) written by Yang, which are characterized by highly ornate descriptions of imperial palaces, outings, and ceremonies.[63]

The Tenryaku manuscript contains a startling excess of paratextual information, marked up in no fewer than five different colors of ink.[64] Much of this marking is *kunten* glossing, including punctuation marks, *okototen* diacritics indicating postpositions, and *kana*. The primary function of *kunten* as they appear in the Tenryaku manuscript is syntactic: *okototen* are applied across almost the entire text, indicating both its underlying grammatical structure and the re-orderings necessary to fashion an object-verb Japanese sentence out of a verb-object Chinese construction.[65] The four-character phrase 同符三皇 (fig. 4, A) has a dot to the upper right of the second character (indicating the accusative particle *o*) and to the

63. The biography is translated in Knechtges, *Han shu Biography*.

64. Ōtsubo Heiji divides the colors as follows: red (the primary annotation, giving punctuation, *kaeriten*, *okototen*, tone marks, most of the *kun* readings given in *kana*, and some indication of definitions through synonymous Sinographs), black (many definitions through synonymous characters, as well as some *kana*, *okototen*, and other punctuation), white (mostly *kana* used to indicate *kun* or *on* readings), yellow (*kana* readings for a few characters), and blue (tone markers for a few characters), apparently affixed in that order by the same hand. There are also *kakuhitsu* marks engraved into the paper, but the provenance of these is less clear ("Kanjo Yō Yū den").

65. This resembles the operation of *kugyŏl* glossing in Koryŏ-period Korea, which similarly emphasized syntactic re-ordering, case, and verbal conjugation over semantic translations of substantives. See the description in Whitman, "Ubiquity of the Gloss," 103–8.

upper left of the fourth character (indicating the dative particle *ni*).[66] The reader is thereby led to parse this as a verb followed by a direct object and an indirect object, "matches tally with the Three Emperors" (*fu o sankō ni onajikushi*).[67] Medieval manuscripts often use numerals to indicate such inversions (so-called *kaeriten*), but here the reordering is implicitly demanded by the indicated particles. Compared to *okototen*, *kana* giving Japanese lexical correspondences are indicated much more sparingly, and are most commonly applied to verbs with objects or to adverbs.[68] In contrast, substantives are generally not given a Japanese-language gloss, but instead read in a Sinitic-derived pronunciation. Thus the phrase 歷吉日 (LMC liajk kjit-rit, "select an auspicious day") has a *kana* gloss only for the initial verb, giving the phrase "kitsujitsu o erande" when reordered in *kundoku* (fig. 4, B).[69] A sentence is created with the Japanese verb *erabu* (select), but the object of the verb is a Sinitic-derived compound. One could compare it to the use of Latin phrases like *modus operandi* or *habeas corpus* within an English sentence, but the Sinitic elements remaining in *kundoku* were by no means all well-established loanwords that would be readily recognized by a Japanese speaker; the aural effect might be imagined as closer to a prayer to "give us our *panem quotidianum*." The glosses in the Tenryaku manuscript and other early sources demonstrate that readers of literary Sinitic texts rarely sought a complete transformation into a pure "Yamato" lexicon. Rather than "translation" that replaces the original, the goal instead was analysis of grammatical structure that assumed continued reference to the text.

Besides these *okototen* and *kana* glosses, the bulk of the remainder of the manuscript's markings indicate Sinitic (or "Han") pronunciations of characters. We find voice markings (*shōten* 聲點)—a mark in one of the four corners of a character to indicate level, rising, falling, or entering tone; homonyms written next to a character to indicate its pronunciation; and most importantly *hanzetsu* (Ch. *fanqie*) glosses, which combine two Sinographs to indicate the pronunciation of a third.[70] Such glossing

66. *Kanjo Yō Yū den zankan*, 8b.

67. English translation from Knechtges, *Wen xuan*, 2:19.

68. Kosukegawa, "Kunten no seikaku," 36.

69. *Kanjo Yō Yū den zankan*, 8b. All LMC (Late Middle Chinese) reconstructions from Pulleyblank, *Lexicon of Reconstructed Pronunciation*.

70. See the discussion of rhyme in chapter 3.

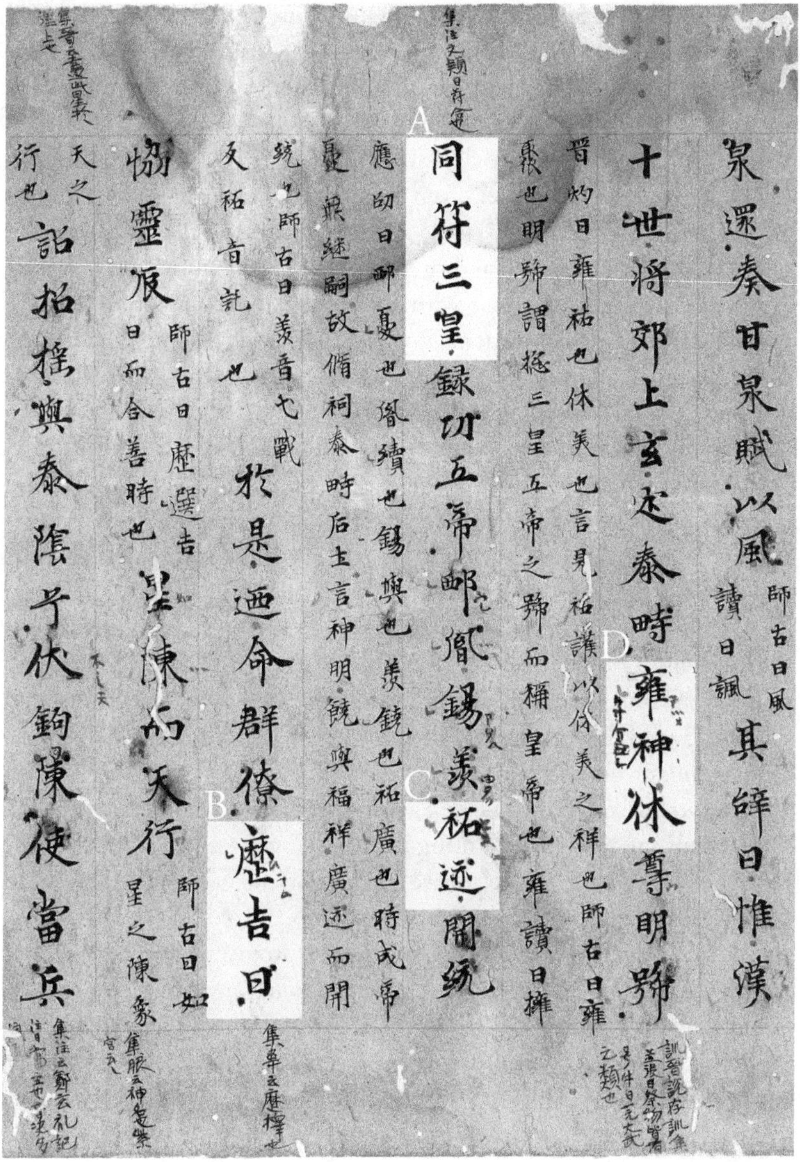

FIG. 4 Section from a *Hanshu* manuscript copy with 948 glosses added by Fujiwara no Yoshisuke. Photograph courtesy of the Kyoto National Museum, Kyoto.

techniques can be found in continental manuscripts as well, and would have been useful for the chanting of a text in Sinitic pronunciation.

There are also some examples of Sinitic-derived pronunciation indicated through *kana*; for example, next to the compound 旟旐 ("banners"), LMC jiă-trɦiawˋ, we find the *kana* 与天ウ, suggesting a pronunciation of /joteu/.[71] While relatively rare in this manuscript, *kana* glosses of Sinitic-derived pronunciations appear with increasing frequency in manuscripts of the eleventh and twelfth century. The replacement of more precise devices such as *fanqie* with *kana* indicates the predominance of *kundoku* in the Heian academy, and a concurrent decline in chanting through Sinitic pronunciation.[72] Komatsu Hideo points out that while *kundoku* pronounces many words using a Sinitic-derived pronunciation, the phonology employed in the context of a Japanese sentence (that is, surrounded by the Japanese particles and verbs employed in *kundoku*) is inevitably much closer to Japanese than that employed when a text is simply chanted through in Sinitic (just as French words like "croissant" or "hotel" are adapted to English phonology as loanwords).[73] Thus even though *kundoku* incorporates a heavy admixture of Sinitic-derived pronunciations, its widespread use had the effect of shifting the "Han pronunciation" system in Japan further away from the original Chinese sound palette, toward the looser approximations of *kana* transcription and Sino-Japanese loanwords.

The use of *kana* to indicate Sinitic pronunciations in the Tenryaku manuscript suggests that chanting in Sinitic was already declining in the tenth-century academy. The cultivation of "correct" Sinitic pronunciation had originally been one of the central operational goals of the State Academy, as is made clear by the Taihō Code's provision for professors of pronunciation, an office generally filled by continental immigrants who commanded the prestige dialect associated with the Tang bureaucracy. The need for correct pronunciation was partially motivated by the importance of international diplomacy, as Chinese apparently served as a lingua

71. *Kanjo Yō Yū den zankan*, 10b.

72. On the decline of Chinese phonology in Japan, see Sasaki Isamu, "Nihon kan'on no keishō."

73. Komatsu, "Nihon jion no shotaikei," 20–21. A better parallel might be the pronunciation of "law French" in Elizabethan England. Baker, *Manual of Law French*, 5.

franca among Japan's international contacts.[74] But anxieties about the role of language and sound in ritual efficacy also played a central role: between 792 and 806, imperial proclamations and Council of State directives called for correct, "Han pronunciation" to be used in state-sponsored recitations of the Lotus and Golden Light Sutras, as well as by students in the academy.[75] The latter, in addition to their poetic role in banquets, were obliged to serve in the biannual Memorial Rites to Confucius (*sekiten* 釋奠), where the chanting of a prayer (*shukubun* 祝文) in Sinitic took center stage.[76]

The repeated central directives suggest that the court was never satisfied with the academy's linguistic training, and after the collapse of Tang and Parhae had deprived Japan of diplomatic partners, chanting in Sinitic was increasingly replaced by *kundoku* recitation in academic and court ritual contexts, further promoting the prevalence of *kunten* glossing. One Japanese manuscript of a Tang anecdote collection contains a colophon attributing its glosses to those that Ōe no Masahira provided to Emperor Ichijō (r. 986–1011) in 1006, and around the same time Ichijō is said to have asked Ki no Tadana to gloss the *Collected Works* of the Tang poet Yuan Zhen 元稹 (779–831) with *kunten*.[77] By 987, the ceremonial First Reading Lesson (*ondokusho-hajime*) of the crown prince included use of a *tenzu* 點圖 (diagram of *okototen* glossing marks) and *kakuhitsu* 角筆 (a stylus used to indent glosses into the paper).[78] Perhaps most relevant to the current case, Yoshisuke's relative Fujiwara no Arihira gave a lecture on the *Shiji* to Emperor Suzaku in 939, and a sixteenth-century manuscript of the *Hou Hanshu* 後漢書 (History of the Later Han, ca. fifth century) attributes its glosses to his teachings.[79] These early examples suggest that *kundoku* recitation and the preparation of literary

74. See for example Sakayori, *Bokkai to kodai Nihon*, 303–9.

75. Momo, *Jōdai gakusei no kenkyū*, 126–32; Ōta, "Kangakuin no suzume," 227. The role of chanting in early Japanese ritual is taken up in depth in Abé, *Weaving of Mantra* (see especially 146–49).

76. For an introduction to the Sekiten ceremony, see I. J. McMullen, "Worship of Confucius."

77. Kobayashi, *Kanseki kundoku no kokugoshiteki kenkyū*, 29; *Gōdanshō* 5.4.

78. *Gōke shidai* 17.710. *Gōke shidai* also indicates that the use of Sinitic chanting in the Sekiten rites declined in the eleventh century. Hérail, "Lire et écrire," 268.

79. Kobayashi, *Kanseki kundoku no kokugoshiteki kenkyū*, 195.

Sinitic texts with *kunten* glossing were legitimated through the patronage of the imperial household, as academic scholarship, like other mid-Heian cultural forms, was reshaped through practices of direct service to the upper nobility.

In this context, studying meant first of all obtaining an already-glossed text, generally from one's teacher, which would be copied out by the student before he received more detailed instruction.[80] The colorful glosses of the Tenryaku manuscript vividly record this multi-stage process: the initial applications of glosses in red and black ink were followed by another annotation of the manuscript in white pigment. These white glosses provide Japanese readings for simple characters ignored in the earlier stage, and often record Sinitic-based pronunciation in *kana* with unusual lengthened vowels, all of which point to the transcription of a *kundoku* dictation of the text, probably by Yoshisuke's teacher.[81] Already by the late tenth century such glosses seem to have been regarded as a kind of "household secret" to be transmitted only within private teacher-pupil relationships, and especially within the familial lineages that dominated academic posts. This orientation toward exact reproduction of transmitted teachings encouraged a tendency toward rigidity in *kundoku* language: the lexicon found in glosses is both limited and archaic, often preserving vocabulary that had otherwise fallen out of circulation. We can see here how processes of ritualization enter the site of education, as the canonical text is sacralized through the formalization of a fixed idiom of recitation, a phenomenon returned to in more detail in the following chapter.

The lineage-based practice of transmission developed only gradually, however, and the Tenryaku manuscript still represents a very early stage in its history. The annotations are incomplete, at times even contradictory, and without the unified format we find in medieval manuscripts, suggesting the supplementary, subordinate character of *kunten* in the mid-Heian. There are no direct discussions of the status of *kundoku* as a means or object of study that survive from the period, but one highly suggestive formulation is found in *Tōzan ōrai* 東山往來 (ca. 1099–1107), a textbook

80. Momo, *Jōdai gakusei no kenkyū*, 351–57.

81. Kobayashi, "Kanjo Yō Yū den." The compound 旟旐, mentioned above as glossed with the *kana* "yo-te-u" in black ink, also has a white pigment gloss reading "yo-o̲-te-u."

in the form of a series of letters between a monk and a lay supporter.[82] In this passage, the layman asks whether sutra recitation for the purpose of acquiring merit is properly carried out in *on* 音 (Sinitic-based pronunciation) or *kun* 訓 (read into *kundoku*). His mentor answers,

> The ancient teachers explained, "Sutras in *on* reading contain many meanings. Even listening uncomprehendingly, celestial beings can attain enlightenment through their senses. This is because both Wu pronunciation and Han pronunciation [two contrasting modes of Sinitic-based pronunciation] are sacred words." Sutras in *kundoku* take one of those many meanings and put it into Yamato words. Because of this, the merit of sutras in *kundoku* is lessened. After Prince Shōtoku promulgated the sutras, he made Wu pronunciation the method of reading. I have never heard of [his using] sutras in *kundoku*. *Kundoku* can be used to get the gist of the meaning [*ichiō no gi* 一往義], but for the perpetual attainment of merit use the original [Sinitic] pronunciation [*moto no on* 本音].[83]

Here, reading in Sinitic pronunciation is valorized precisely for its indeterminacy of meaning, while the necessity of *kundoku* for comprehension becomes a sign of its limitations. The answer can be read as a discursive formalization of the dynamic of textual authority embedded within *kundoku* recitation practice, in which all performance and exegesis is secondary to an a priori textual artifact. This supplementary logic is integral to *kunten* glossing techniques, which by definition preserve access to the sacred or canonical text in its original form, even as the apparatus around it grows larger and becomes the focus of the text's actual vocalization and reception. It is not surprising then that, despite the ubiquity of *kundoku* literacy, *kunten* glossing remained almost exclusively confined to educational and recitation contexts, rather than becoming a standard form of inscription. Surviving original manuscripts of Heian Council of State directives and banquet presentation poems, for example, are all unpunctuated and lack glosses, despite the fact that they were recited primarily in *kundoku*.[84]

82. For an introduction and partial translation, see Waley, "Eleventh Century Correspondence."

83. *Tōzan ōrai*, 387–88.

84. For examples of each see Nihon Rekishi Gakkai, *Shōen hen jō*, 23, and Tōkyō Kokuritsu Hakubutsukan, *Shiika to sho*, 97.

The Tenryaku manuscript first of all, then, documents that academic literacy education was based on *kundoku* recitation as a means of syntactically parsing literary Sinitic texts through the Japanese language, and was increasingly reliant on the use of *kunten* glossing as a means to transmit these reading methods. The centrality of *kundoku* reading meant that academy education was paradoxically both fundamentally textual and inherently aural: where Murasaki Shikibu describes "listening" along with her brother's lessons (*kikinaraitsutsu*), she is in a way also *reading* the texts he would have been learning to recite.[85] If *kundoku* is the means of interpretation, however, we then have to consider its grounds in turn: on what basis were Japanese lexical equivalents and sentence structures derived from literary Sinitic text? Here we arrive at the second type of valuable evidence from the Tenryaku manuscript: the use of commentary editions.

The text of the Tenryaku manuscript derives from a Tang edition of the *Hanshu* containing commentary by Yan Shigu 顏師古 (581–645). Phrases of the original Han-dynasty text of the *History* are broken up by Yan's later commentary, written in half-size characters, which defines unusual characters and paraphrases difficult sentences. The commentary portions of the manuscript receive almost no *kunten* glossing themselves, but many of the Japanese readings glossed in *kana* in the main text are justified by reference to the Yan commentary. The phrase 歷吉日 ("select an auspicious day"), cited earlier, has *kana* recording the verb *erande* to the right side of the initial character, as well as a small hook mark to the left (fig. 4, B).[86] This corresponds to another hook mark in the following paraphrase by Yan Shigu next to the character *sen* 選, the Sinograph most commonly associated in Heian practice with the verb *erabu*.[87] Similarly, in the phrase 祏跡 ("broaden his path," fig. 4, C), the initial verb (a variant for *taku* 拓) is often used in literary Sinitic with the sense of "to open," and was therefore typically read in Heian practice with the word

85. The diary of Fujiwara no Yorinaga 藤原頼長 (1120–56) provides a relevant parallel. Yorinaga was a voracious student of the classics, but had little time to study Chinese history, so contrived to have a team of five students recite episodes from the *Nanshi* 南史 (History of the Southern Dynasties, ca. 630–50) to him while he took his meals and baths. *Taiki*, Kōji 2 (1143)/11/17 (1:104); Gotō, *Honchō kanshibun shiryōron*, 310–11.

86. *Kanjo Yō Yū den zankan*, 8b.

87. Matsumoto, "Kanjo Yō Yū den," 29–30; *Iroha jiruishō*, 256; *Ruijū myōgishō*, 67.

hiraku.[88] The Tenryaku manuscript, however, draws attention with another hook mark to a note in Yan's commentary that here it is being used in the sense of "to widen" (祏廣也). The *kana* glosses to the left of the verb, *hi . . . me*, correspond to the reading *hirome*, the verb most commonly associated in Heian documents with the Sinograph *kō* 廣 that Yan uses in his definition.[89]

Much of Yan Shigu's commentary is concerned with parsing the text's grammar. In the Tang period, Buddhist exegetes directed new attention to the syntactic and morphological differences between Sanskrit and Chinese, and contemporary classical scholarship was influenced by exposure to these sutra commentaries.[90] The Tenryaku manuscript repeatedly makes use of grammatical information in Yan's commentary to construe Japanese sentences:

> Text: 厥高慶而不可虖彊度
> Its height, alas, cannot be fully measured![91]
> Commentary: 慶、發語辭也。
> 慶 is a term of exclamation.

The Tenryaku manuscript follows Yan by reading *kei* 慶 as a cry (*sono takaki koto, aa, shikaku oehakarubekarazu*).[92] This example shows the use of descriptive linguistic terminology to explain the function of words. More commonly, however, Yan relies on paraphrase for interpretation, rather than the sort of technical vocabulary (verb, noun, predicate, object) we might associate with grammatical analysis:

88. *Iroha jiruishō*, 348.

89. *Kanjo Yō Yū den zankan*, 8b. *Ruijū myōgishō* glosses the character 廣 with the Japanese readings *hiroshi*, *hiromu*, and *hodokosu* (855).

90. Sun Liangming, *Zhongguo gudai yufaxue tanjiu*, 158–77. See, for example, in Fazang's 法藏 (643–712) *Huayanjing tanxuan ji* 華嚴經探玄記, *Taishō shinshū daizōkyō* 1733 (35:294c). It is no coincidence that the earliest *kunten*-glossed texts in both Korea and Japan are associated with Huayan Buddhism (Whitman, "Ubiquity of the Gloss," 110–11).

91. In the following three examples, the English translations of the original text are all taken or modified from Knechtges, *Wen xuan*, 2:17–23.

92. *Kanjo Yō Yū den zankan*, 11a–11b.

Text: 屬堪輿以辟壘兮
assigns to Kanyu the ramparts
Commentary: 屬、委也。以壁壘委之。
屬 means "assign." He assigns the ramparts to him.

The original clause here is a mild anastrophe, transposing the coverb phrase 以壁壘 (with the ramparts) after the verb instead of before it as is most commonly found in literary Sinitic prose. Yan clarifies this relationship by adopting the canonical word order in his paraphrase, and the Tenryaku manuscript follows Yan in combining the two clauses into a single complex sentence (*Kan'yo ni zoku-<u>suru ni</u> hekirui o motte su*, literally "in assigning to Kanyu, [he] uses the ramparts").[93]

Text: 雍神休
is protected by divine blessings
Commentary: 雍、祐也。休、美也。言見祐護以休美之祥也。
雍 means "aid." 休 means "beauty." This is to say, "He is protected because of beneficent omens."

The commentary's paraphrase interprets the character *yō* 雍 (to hold) as a passive verb, which the Tenryaku manuscript duplicates (*shinkyū ni tasuke<u>rare</u>*, fig. 4, D).[94] Much of the morphosyntactic information supplied by *kunten* we see in the Tenryaku manuscript is a direct application of the Chinese commentary tradition around the *Hanshu*.

The commentary is not the sole determining factor in the manuscript's *kana* glossing, which places a heavier emphasis than Yan Shigu on grammatical analysis over semantic definitions: many verbs that receive no mention in the commentary are simply glossed with the most commonly associated Japanese reading, and many nouns that are defined in the commentary receive no corresponding gloss. We can see here, however, how the commentary provides a vehicle for magnifying the

93. Ibid., 9a. On the predominance of preverbal *yi* phrases, see Chaofen Sun, "Adposition *yi* and Word Order."

94. *Kanjo Yō Yū den zankan*, 8b. This passage in fact has two alternative glosses indicated in the Tenryaku MS, corresponding to multiple interpretations in the commentary.

scope of *kundoku*-based literacy. Japanese practices of reading and writing with Sinographs established a network of associations between Sinographs and local vocabulary.[95] These quotidian associations were limited and perforce arbitrary, and certainly insufficient for reading complex documents written in the highest registers of literary Sinitic. However, because Chinese commentaries often worked by defining a rare character or usage through a more common one, they expanded the potential range of reading through *kundoku*. Although written in China for a Chinese-speaking audience, these commentaries functioned as the key medium for establishing the Japanese readings of *kundoku* recitation.

The Tenryaku manuscript does not, however, simply mechanically apply the readings given in Yan Shigu's commentary. After initially glossing the work in red ink using the accompanying Yan commentary, Yoshisuke seems to have returned to the manuscript and added further glosses in black ink. The alternative readings added at this stage often reflect the interpretations of other commentaries, which Yoshisuke wrote into the margins of his text. The phrase 踔夭蟜, describing warriors on the hunt, is first glossed in red ink following Yan Shigu's interpretation as *yōkyō ni hashiri*, "run through bent branches." A later, black-ink gloss adds the reading *yōkyō o koete*, "jump over bent branches," and attaches a quotation taken from another commentary defining the initial verb as "cross over" (*yu* 踰) rather than "run" (*sō* 走).[96]

The use of commentaries was at the center of academy teaching from its origins. The Taihō Code already specifies one or two commentaries for each of the classics, upon which lectures were to be based (the Zheng Xuan 鄭玄 and Wang Bi 王弼 commentaries on the *Changes*, for example).[97] The interpretations recorded in medieval manuscripts of texts in the classics curriculum overwhelmingly rely on these commentaries, as well as the gloss collection *Jingdian shiwen* 經典釋文 (ca. 589). The curriculum in letters, however, did not yet exist at the time of the Taihō

95. Kobayashi, "Shokiyō kanji no kun."

96. *Kanjo Yō Yū den zankan*, 34a. The commentary Yoshisuke referenced for his alternative reading, which he labels here only with the character 集, has been variously identified with *Wenxuan jizhu* 文選集注, a collection of commentaries to the *Wenxuan*, and *Hanshu gujin jiyi* 漢書古今集義, a seventh-century commentary on the *Hanshu*. See Hanabusa, "Monzen kan dai 98"; Kosukegawa, "Monzen tekisuto," 9–11.

97. *Ryō no shūge* 15.448.

Code, and later sources like the *Engi shiki* 延喜式 (Procedures of the Engi Era, 927) show no evidence that officially approved commentaries were ever designated for its main texts (the first three Chinese dynastic histories and the *Wenxuan*). The Tenryaku manuscript suggests that at least within the letters curriculum, students made catholic use of a range of available commentaries in formulating their interpretations.[98]

By contrast, Kosukegawa Teiji notes that the manuscript shows no evidence of any extensive use of dictionaries as a tool for interpretation. There are a few marginal glosses derived from the rhyme dictionary *Yupian* 玉篇 (Jade Tablets, ca. 543), but these exclusively refer to the sounds of characters, rather than semantic distinctions.[99] Insofar as the manuscript annotations can guide us, Yoshisuke's study of this text seems to have proceeded as: (1) the acquisition of the original chapter accompanied by Yan Shigu's commentary; (2) the insertion of glosses in red ink to aid in reciting the text in *kundoku*, based on Yan Shigu's commentary, and likely copied from a manuscript provided by his teacher; (3) marginal insertion in black ink of quotations from other commentaries regarding alternative interpretations of certain problematic passages, along with glosses indicating corresponding alternative *kundoku* readings where applicable; (4) the insertion in white ink of glosses transcribing a teacher's dictation of the text in *kundoku*, with close attention to the aural qualities of the recitation (such as Sinitic-derived pronunciations).

Both the historical record and manuscript evidence suggest that the State Academy developed a mode of education centered on applying interlineal commentary to a canonical text, a set of practices encouraged by the historical circumstances of the Heian. Through the Nara period, continental immigrants (or their immediate descendants) were often employed in the academy, at least as professors of pronunciation, but by the late Heian even this post was simply filled through the scholarly families.[100] Just as recitation in "Han pronunciation" was gradually crowded out by *kundoku* reading, the absence of Chinese-speaking interpreters (or a mature domestic interpretive tradition) must have made textual authority all

98. Matsumoto, "Kanjo Yō Yū den."
99. Kosukegawa, "Tenkyo no mondai," 40–42.
100. Momo, *Jōdai gakusei no kenkyū*, 302.

the more paramount. In the Tenryaku manuscript, we see how imported commentaries are marshaled and compared to arrive at an authoritative reading of the text adapted to the local language environment.

Truth and Method in the Academy

Heian scholars produced personal literary collections, official state chronicles, dictionaries and encyclopedias, and innumerable occasional documents, but no original commentaries or treatises on the canonical works studied in the State Academy (in sharp contrast to the large body of doctrinal scholarship produced in Japanese monasteries). For this reason, it is difficult to reconstruct scholarly method and standards of proof as they were understood by academy scholars, but here again early manuscripts provide the most useful evidence. Many early Japanese manuscripts of academic texts contain marginalia that do not directly quote a Chinese commentary, but refer rather to the instructions of a teacher, an ancestor, or generic transmitted teachings (*shisetsu* 師説). These annotations can include notes about textual variations or the Sinitic pronunciation of characters, but are mostly focused on questions of meaning. Based on names, dates, and texts mentioned in medieval marginalia, Kobayashi Yoshinori postulates that much of this discourse derives from academy lectures in the mid- to late ninth century.[101] The methodology seen in these transmissions emphasizes textual authority, precedent-based rules rather than historical verification, and the preservation of multiple parallel explanations.

Many of these annotations confirm the view given above, that pedagogy in the academy and associated scholarly lineages was centered on application of commentaries. An eleventh-century manuscript of the *Shiji* is accompanied throughout by the commentary of Pei Yin 裴駰 (fl. 438), but marginalia often introduce alternative explanations. When a general is assigned to the locale Xiliu 細柳, Pei's commentary locates it "on the north bank of the Wei." On the verso of the manuscript, however,

101. Kobayashi, *Kanseki kundoku no kokugoshiteki kenkyū*, 645–77.

we find a long "transmitted teaching" comparing three different explanations of the place name, the sources of which can be traced to another *Shiji* commentary by Sima Zhen 司馬貞 (fl. early eighth century), as well as commentaries on the *Hanshu*.[102]

This methodology shows an essential continuity with textually oriented Buddhist scholarship from the same period. A mid-Heian example is *Guketsu getenshō* 弘決外典鈔 (991), a commentary on Zhanran's 湛然 (711–82) exegesis of the Tiantai meditation treatise *Mohe zhiguan* 摩訶止觀 (Great Calming and Contemplation, 594), purportedly authored by Prince Tomohira. Tomohira was educated by the academy graduate Yoshishige no Yasutane, and he draws repeatedly on academic commentaries such as Pei Yin's and Sima Zhen's to supplement Zhanran.[103] Despite the rise of esoteric ritual and Kūkai's attack on doctrinal Buddhism, exegetical scholarship employing academic sources and citation formats continued to thrive in the monastic community through the Heian and onward.[104]

The reliance on the authority of prior texts is a defining feature running through the scholarly and literary productions of academy graduates. By comparison, European scholarship in late antiquity places a much heavier weight on abstracted rules of usage, which thereby frequently come into conflict with the authority of actual ancient texts.[105] As the discussion of erudition in poetic composition in chapter 3 suggested, in the Heian academy no usage rule was ever immune to invalidation by a contrary example of classical precedent. In the 997 Ministry Test scandal mentioned above, Ōe no Masahira justified all the apparent flaws and errors in his relative's composition by reference to a long string of earlier poems by Japanese and Chinese authors, effectively refuting the general aesthetic principles that his opponent Ki no Tadana sought to bring to bear. Unable to produce examples of poems that had failed the test, Tadana lost out to Masahira's appeal to precedent.[106] The authority of prior usage,

102. *Kōbun hongi dai 10*, 51; Kobayashi, *Kanseki kundoku no kokugoshiteki kenkyū*, 660–61.

103. Kōno, "*Guketsu getenshō* no hōhō," 67–71.

104. Abé, "Scholasticism, Exegesis, and Ritual Practice," 192–96; Yamazaki Makoto, *Chūsei gakumonshi*, 485–91.

105. Snare, "Practice of Glossing," 453.

106. Konishi, *"Bunkyō hifuron" kō*, 2:71–77.

while not absolute, was the ground upon which any assessment of competing truth claims had to begin.

This is perhaps unsurprising in regards to the letters curriculum, but evidence suggests the classics and law curricula functioned much the same. An 877 eclipse provides one convenient instance to see these scholarly strategies side by side: upset with the Bureau of Yin-Yang's failure to give advance notice of a solar eclipse calculated to occur at night (that is, not visible from Japan), the court ordered the professors of classics, letters, and law to submit reports on whether a nighttime eclipse required the suspension of court business. The assembled professors provided three different answers. The classics scholars' report begins by citing a passage of text, commentary, and sub-commentary dealing with a nighttime eclipse from the standard Tang edition of the *Spring and Autumn Annals Guliang Commentary* (*Chunqiu Guliang zhuan* 春秋穀梁傳, ca. second century BCE), followed by another quotation on eclipses from the *Record of Rites*. However, unable to find any distinction in the classics between daytime and nighttime eclipses, they conclude court business should be suspended in either case. The law professor's report produces quotations of text and commentary regarding eclipses from the administrative code, and conversely concludes that since these texts all refer to daytime activity, a nighttime eclipse should not necessitate a response. The report of the letters scholars first quotes the same *Guliang Commentary* passage as had the classics report, but then dismisses it by noting that although the ancients had no way of predicting eclipses, such predictions were now possible. It turns instead to the Tang Kaiyuan Code, which calls for eclipses to be announced to the throne, finally arguing that all eclipses should be announced beforehand and court business suspended for any occurrence of an eclipse, day or night.[107] The letters scholars clearly lacked a basis for argument within their own textual purview of histories and belles-lettres, but perhaps for that reason freely juxtaposed texts in both classical and legal canons.

As Kristina Buhrman argues, this "debate" can be understood as a performance of court power over the technicians of the Bureau of Yin-Yang.[108]

107. Hamada, *Heianchō Nihon kanbungaku*, 510–38. The original text of the three reports is recorded in *Nihon sandai jitsuroku*, Gangyō 1/4/1 (399–401).

108. Buhrman, "Stars and the State," 140–43.

The court employed academy scholars to draw on textual authority, thereby countermanding the secret traditions of the bureau (cited as "writing on the bureau's walls" by one of their representatives). Thus, rather than read too much into the different rhetorical strategies pursued by the day's assembled academics—the tendency toward establishment of one authoritative interpretive tradition in the classics curriculum versus the more diverse comparison of different registers of text in the letters curriculum, for example—it is more important to emphasize their shared reliance on the transmitted canon as the basis of both (written) usage and (social, especially ritual) practice.

The methods of academy scholarship show clear continuities with the "elucidation" (*yishu*, J. *giso* 義疏) commentaries of sixth- and seventh-century China. These works are characterized by a catholic openness to differing explanations, assembling the different interpretive traditions that have accreted around a canonical text without passing final judgment on their relative merits or seeking historical evidence from other kinds of documents outside the tradition.[109] John Makeham, discussing Huang Kan's 皇侃 (488–545) commentary on the *Analects*, refers to this as the "accommodation strategy": the textual canon is flattened, so that no one proposition has more explanatory value or significance than another.[110] In the same manner, even though academy scholarship is based on the authority of canonical texts and precedent, the method of citation tends to encourage the papering over of contradictions in service of an a priori truth, rather than inductive conclusions based on the comparison of competing claims.

To borrow Anthony Grafton's terminology, the interpretive framework of academic scholarship is rhetorical rather than historical. "Meaning" is parsed in terms of the usage rules related to individual words, rather than in relationship to a recoverable historical truth.[111] The scholars

109. Qiao, *Gisogaku suibō shiron*, 45–46.

110. Makeham, *Transmitters and Creators*, 123–27. As Makeham makes clear, for Huang and many other medieval Chinese scholars, this attitude was dependent on a conception of transcendental truth beyond the reach of language. See also Mou, *Zhushizhai conggao*, 323–31. David McMullen's summary of canonical scholarship in the early Tang emphasizes both the impulse for comprehensive summary of earlier debates and an inclusive tolerance for mutually exclusive interpretations (*State and Scholars*, 71–79).

111. Grafton, "Renaissance Readers and Ancient Texts," 618–19.

assembled in the eclipse debate show no consciousness of Duke Zhuang of Lu as a real figure whose behavior could be reconstructed; his historical presence has been entirely abstracted away into a set of relationships with the canon of ritual precedent. The text here is a vehicle for pedagogy or an object to be imitated in ritual and in the composition of formally correct documents, and the distinction between the citation of a historical incident and an exemplary literary usage is collapsed.

Essential Knowledge

While the central government often propagandized for the value of classical learning to ministers of state, for the most part the State Academy functioned as a technical training ground for mid- to low-level bureaucrats. Despite repeated attempts to induce the upper nobility to send their sons to the academy, these children tended to receive their education at home. It is true that this private education was heavily influenced by the pedagogical methods of the academy, as nobles often employed academy-trained scholars as tutors. However, the textual authority that underwrote classical learning exercised only limited influence over the decision-making and political maneuvering of the central oligarchy. The mid- to late Heian brought a growing emphasis on an alternative body of knowledge, centered on court ritual, which challenged scholarly authority by drawing on the charismatic legitimacy of revered ancestors and genealogical transmission.

The origins of the private tutorial system, which eventually spread throughout the senior nobility, seem to lie in the imperial household. The Taihō Code already makes provision for two tutors (*gakushi*) to the crown prince, but no concurrent position existed for a sitting emperor. By the end of the ninth century, however, imperially sponsored lecture duties (*jitō* 侍讀 or *jikō* 侍講) developed into a semi-official post, usually filled by a professor of letters.[112] Official histories record at least four official lectures on classical texts carried out by academy professors for Emperor Ninmyō (r. 833–50), and the accession of two successive child emperors in

112. Hisaki, *Nihon kodai gakkō*, 348–51.

the late ninth century may have encouraged the formalization of the imperial lecturer post.[113] The code-defined duties of academy professors do not include lectures for the palace, and they are mentioned only sporadically before the mid-ninth century, but by the second half of the Heian period they were increasingly ceremonialized as an official recognition essential to a household's scholarly status.

The appointment of a professor as a private tutor was quickly imitated by other lineages within the upper nobility. The office of "lecturer to the regent" would eventually gain a quasi-official status, but other mid-Heian elites similarly were educated by academy-graduate tutors.[114] Fujiwara no Kintō, for example, a Northern Branch Fujiwara and eventual senior noble, studied under Takaoka no Sukeyuki 高丘相如 (fl. 960–92), a former letters student who held sixth and seventh-ranked offices in the central bureaucracy.[115] Such tutorial relationships extended into and overlapped with other sorts of scholarly and scribal service.[116] This redefinition of professors' social role away from work in the academy and large public rituals (such as the Sekiten), toward smaller ceremonies centered on the person of the emperor and commissioned service for the upper nobility, mirrors the larger transformation of ritual space discussed in chapter 2.

For sons of the senior nobles, formal education in the Chinese classics was begun at the age of thirteen or fourteen with a ceremony, the *fumihajime*, wherein a student would receive first instruction from an academic on what was usually a historical work such as the *Shiji*, mimicking the path of students preparing to sit for the Bureau Test.[117] Shitagō describes a celebration for Fujiwara no Sanenobu 藤原誠信 (964–1001), the adolescent son of a Northern Branch senior noble, on his completion of the

113. The encyclopedia *Nichūreki* 二中歴 (ca. thirteenth century), compiled from early twelfth-century sources, lists tutors to the crown prince and imperial lecturers together in one list, without any distinction between them (2.39–40).

114. A list of lecturers to the Regent House can be found in *Nichūreki* 2.40–41.

115. *Gōdanshō* 5.30.

116. Satō Michio notes that elites turned to academic tutors for correction and assistance with banquet poetry compositions. *"Wakan rōeishū" eiin to kenkyū*, 219.

117. Momo, *Jōdai gakusei no kenkyū*, 401. This should not be confused with the *dokushohajime* ceremony observed by imperial princes, which took place at a much younger age and used the *Classic of Filial Piety*.

first volume of the *Hou Hanshu*.[118] Such private tutorial relationships often extended well past adolescence: the senior noble Fujiwara no Yukinari 藤原行成 (972–1027) received private lessons on the *Odes* and *Documents* from academy professors in his thirties.[119]

Reading the canon, however, required an initial basic grounding in Sinographic literacy. Like junior students in the academy's dormitories, privately educated children first began their education through recitation of primers such as *Mengqiu*. Whereas academy students seem to have relied exclusively on imported Chinese works, however, in this context we find several examples of tutors compiling original primers to aid in their charges' education. A year or two before Shitagō's celebration for the young Sanenobu, Minamoto no Tamenori 源爲憲 (d. 1011), a letters graduate who studied under Shitagō, produced an encyclopedia called *Kuchizusami* 口遊 (Singing to Yourself, 970) for the same boy. The textbook is divided into nineteen categories aimed at the education of a future official, each of which contains several "stanzas," for example:

> Sun, Moon, Stars. (These are called the Three Lights, also called the Three Celestials.)
>
> Hie, Hira, Ibuki, Kanmine, Atago, Kinpu, Katsuragi. (These are called the Seven High Mountains.)[120]

Tamenori presents these limericks as replacements for the popular songs the boy currently sings to himself in his play.[121]

Almost four decades later, Tamenori was again called upon to produce a textbook for a young heir, this time Fujiwara no Yorimichi 藤原

118. *Shitagō shū* 242. The Nishi Honganji MS quoted is missing the initial syllable of *Go-Kanjo* (History of the Later Han), but this can be emended by the Bōmon no tsubone MS (p. 198). See also *Shūi wakashū* 271.

119. *Gonki*, Chōhō 4 (1002)/5/1 and Chōhō 6 (1004)/3/21 (1:258, 2:8).

120. *Kuchizusami chūkai*, 36, 62. The text enclosed in parentheses is parenthetical in the original.

121. The categories are Celestial Movements, Seasons, Eras, Topography, Provinces, Agriculture, the Capital, Residences, Scriptures, Humanity, Office, Geomancy, Medicine, Dining, Literature, Music, Arts, Fauna, Miscellaneous. The only surviving manuscript of the work (the Shinpukuji MS) has two additional sections at the end that are probably later additions. Ury provides an excellent overview of the work and its image of the Heian intellectual world ("Chinese Learning and Intellectual Life," 348–52).

頼通 (992–1074), the sixteen-year-old son of Michinaga, then at the height of his power. The work, *Sezoku genbun* 世俗諺文 (Popular Maxims and Their Sources, 1007), collects widely cited maxims such as "A woman makes herself up for one who appreciates her" or "[Rushing around] like your head is on fire."[122] Tamenori's goal is to match each such saying with a source in Buddhist scripture or Chinese literature, sometimes finding questionable "sources" even for what are likely sayings of local origin.[123] Like his teacher Shitagō's encyclopedia *Wamyō ruijushō*, discussed in chapter 5, Tamenori's *Sezoku genbun* represents an attempt to establish continuity between local vernacularizations and borrowings from Chinese and their textual origins, reaffirming the academy's logic of textual primacy in the face of usage that exceeded these demarcations.

Even though the path of literacy acquisition and higher education remained essentially faithful to the academy model through the Heian, new creations like Tamenori's textbooks point to a growing consciousness in the tenth century of that model's inadequacy to the duties of senior nobles and their sons. The career path of such men, which advanced through the Chamberlain's Office and the Council of State, bore no relation to the typical academy graduate's clambering through bureaucratic posts in pursuit of a lucrative governorship. Just as the top scholars could no longer expect to advance to senior noble status, the duties of senior nobles seemed to have little to do with the classical scholarship passed down in scholarly lineages. Furthermore, the academy's maintenance of a textual standard based on canonical literary works had obvious limitations: while documents in orthodox literary Sinitic remained important to court ritual, the bulk of administration and law was handled through more vernacularized forms of Sinographic writing that regularly violated the grammar and usage of the received canon (a problem discussed further in the next chapter).

Fujiwara no Tadazane 藤原忠實 (1078–1162), regent in the early twelfth century, quotes Ōe no Masafusa, a proud representative of the Ōe scholarly lineage, on the difference between academic and upper-noble

122. *Sezoku genbun*, 84, 166. Examples of Heian citations of these maxims can be found in *Makura no sōshi*, "Shiki no mizōshi no nishiomote no tatejitomi no moto nite," 103; *Konjaku monogatari shū* 17.33.

123. See Kōno, "Minamoto no Tamenori sen *Sezoku genbun*."

education: "There is no profit to a regent composing poetry [*shi*]. Official functions [*kuji* 公事] are what are important. The way to have him study is to give him a scroll of thirty sheets, put someone like [Professor of Letters Ōe no] Michikuni beside him, and have him write out things like 'I will present myself forthwith' or 'Today the weather was clear. I was summoned to the palace.' If there is a character he does not know, have him ask [Michikuni]. If he just writes out two scrolls like that, he will be scholar enough [*uruseki gakushō nari*]."[124] Masafusa implies that composition in literary genres is irrelevant to an upper noble, whose literacy education should be focused on producing letters and household records.

Masafusa's remarks have the edge of sarcasm, but perhaps a great deal of truth. His emphasis on court functions accords with a growing body of discourse surrounding the proper disposition of ceremony (most often referred to as *senrei* 先例 or *kojitsu* 故實 in contemporary documents). The court's ritual calendar multiplied rapidly in the ninth century, and a mid-Heian senior noble like Fujiwara no Tadahira devoted much of his energies to regulating the often-competing claims of precedent, ritual purity, and unforeseen accident.[125] The instructions left by Tadahira's son Morosuke for his descendants urge them to consult a calendar each morning upon rising, to be aware of any such events or festivals.[126] Education in the proper observance of ceremony was especially crucial among the highest-ranked nobility. As depicted in *Kagerō nikki*, the future regent Fujiwara no Kaneie shows little interest in his son Michitsuna's 道綱 (955–1020) upbringing until the year before his coming of age, when he begins regularly bringing the boy to his manor to observe his father's daily business and prepare for the upcoming ceremony.[127]

Fujiwara no Sanenobu, the youth tutored by Shitagō and Tamenori, would ironically grow up to be a negative example of the importance of ceremony in the careers of the upper nobility. The son of a prime minister, and nephew to three different regents, Sanenobu should have advanced quickly through the ranks of the senior nobles. Instead, contemporary diaries record repeated instances of his failure to observe the proper

124. *Chūgaishō*, 312–13.
125. Piggott, "What Did a Regent Do?," 45–52.
126. *Kujō ushōjō yuikai*, 118.
127. Umemura Keiko, "Fujiwara no Michitsuna boshi," 70–75.

protocols at court ceremonies such as the Harvest Festival (Niinamesai) and Buddha's Birthday Rite (Kanbutsue).[128] Many of these episodes seem to pivot on his inability to handle liquor. Tamenori's encyclopedia emphasizes the importance of alcohol to courtier duties, listing rules for drinking games and spells to protect one on an inebriated trip home, but they were of no use to the adult Sanenobu, who was involved in brawls and once vomited on a precious folding screen at the regent's annual New Year's Reception.[129] His father was able to intervene on his behalf, once refusing to leave the home of Michinaga unless Sanenobu was made an advisor (*sangi*) on the Council of State, but after his death Sanenobu's career stalled.[130] The late Heian historical tale *Ōkagami* 大鏡 (The Great Mirror) records that Sanenobu died from rage when his younger brother (the supremely poised Tadanobu of Sei Shōnagon's *Pillow Book*) was promoted to counselor (*chūnagon*) ahead of him.[131] For Sanenobu, at least, the inability to maintain ceremonial protocol proved to be a literally fatal flaw.

The education for court service Masafusa sets out for his prospective regent is not based on classics or poetry, but letters and record-keeping, both of which hint at important developments in literacy education. Though Chinese epistolary collections circulated in Japan at least from the Nara period, in the eleventh century locally compiled collections of exemplary letters such as *Unshū shōsoku* and *Tōzan ōrai* began to appear.[132] Oftentimes arranged in a yearlong calendar of festivals and ceremonies, letters in these epistolary handbooks (*ōraimono*) introduced young students to the ritual calendar, social etiquette, and a local idiom of epistolary prose that broke from literary Sinitic models to incorporate Japanese-language-based usage. By the late Heian period, some of these elementary textbooks even circulated with *kunten* glossing, applying to local texts

128. *Shōyūki*, Shōryaku 1 (990)/11/24–26 (1:241); *Gonki*, Shōryaku 3/4/8 (1:3).

129. *Kuchizusami chūkai*, 200, 47; *Shōyūki*, Eiso 1 (989)/1/14 (1:154–55); *Ōkagami*, 229–30.

130. *Shōyūki*, Eien 2 (988)/2/28 (1:139).

131. *Ōkagami*, 227–29. This account is supported by *Gonki*, Chōhō 3 (1001)/9/3 (1:221).

132. Ishikawa, *Ko ōrai ni tsuite no kenkyū*, 63–74. Rütterman, "Concept of Epistolary Etiquette," traces the prescriptive discourses surrounding letter writing from ancient to early modern Japan.

pedagogical methods previously reserved for the academic and Buddhist canons.[133]

Masafusa's mention of diary-keeping similarly reflects the surging importance of records among the senior noble households, evident from the mid-tenth century onward. Such diaries were vital tools in maintaining authority within the Council of State. In the mid-Heian, the scions of the elite increasingly advanced to high rank automatically, and took seats on the council at a young age (Sanenobu, for example, was named an advisor at twenty-five, and Michinaga's son Yorimichi was appointed directly to counselor at eighteen, without even passing through an advisor post). In this context, household records were an essential body of knowledge for young men with little to no previous official experience, and they preserved this information against the possibility of a break in transmission were a father to die early.[134] In the mid-Heian, knowledge of ritual and administrative precedents came to be recognized as a specialized body of expertise, transmitted within household lineages and consolidated into precedent manuals such as Fujiwara no Kintō's *Hokuzanshō* 北山抄 (Northern Mountains Miscellany, ca. 1020). Medieval anecdotal literature contains countless tales of men esteemed for their erudition (*yūsoku* 有職) in this area. When Masafusa disparages poetry in favor of ceremony for a regent's education, he is tacitly acknowledging the independent authority this field of knowledge had established by the late Heian.

This is not to say, however, that the ideology of classical learning propagated by the academy ever died out completely. Genji's insistence that studying the classics is a foundation for governing the realm (discussed in chapter 2) is echoed a century and a half later in the prime minister Fujiwara no Koremichi's 藤原伊通 (1093–1165) textbook for the young Emperor Nijō (r. 1158–65): classical learning (*gakumon*) is desirable in a sovereign, "not simply for composing verse, but for employing ministers," and these ministers in turn should be men who have "sought to learn the way to govern the realm (*yo osamaru*)."[135] If anything, the restructuring of

133. Tsukishima, "Kōzanji-bon koōrai," 467.

134. Morita, *Ōchō seiji*, 207–10. For a contemporary espousal of the importance of daily record-keeping, see *Kujō ushōjō yuikai*, 116.

135. *Taikai hishō*, 14.

political power in the late Heian and Kamakura brought renewed interest from elites in classical learning as a tool (or justification) for governance.[136] Nevertheless, while citations of the classics are sometimes brought out as rhetorical window dressing in Heian political debates, such instances are far outnumbered by references to ceremonial precedent.[137] Study of canonical literary Sinitic texts persisted as a model of education, but new forms of knowledge increasingly assumed the bulk of cultural authority in officials' daily lives.

Conclusion

The pedagogical model institutionalized in the State Academy, beginning with memorization through chanting and moving on to interpretation through *kundoku*, was the most widely used basis for literacy training, both in and outside the academy. The privileged sons of senior nobles, who had no incentives to enter the academy themselves, were nevertheless trained by academy graduates using the same texts and methods. As time passed, this model spread further: at least by the thirteenth century, adolescents at temples around the archipelago began their study of literacy by chanting from the same set of primers that had been used by Heian officials.[138] By the late medieval period, the sons of powerful warrior clans often had their primary schooling at temples, exposing them to the same tradition.[139] The academy's ideology of clas-

136. Ōsone, "Chūsei kanbungaku no shosō," discusses such examples as Kujō Kanezane's political consultations with the classics scholar Kiyohara no Yorinari 清原頼業 (1122–89), and Hōjō Masako's commission of the letters scholar Sugawara no Tamenaga 菅原爲長 (1158–1246) to produce a *kana* translation of the *Zhenguan zhengyao* 貞觀政要 (709–12). See also Ashikaga, *Kamakura Muromachi jidai*, 90–106 and passim.

137. On rhetorical use of classical texts in the late Heian, see Kojima Kogorō, *Kuge bunka no kenkyū*, 101–44.

138. Ōta, "'Shibu no tokusho' kō"; Gotō, *Honchō kanshibun shiryōron*, 201–12; Fukushima, "Kamakura chūki no kyō, Kamakura," 8. Note, however, that such primers were in use in Chinese monasteries already in the Tang dynasty, suggesting that the continuity between academic and monastic education goes back much further. See Galambos, "Confucian Education in a Buddhist Environment."

139. Yūki, "Chūsei jiin no sezoku kyōiku."

sical learning, with its text-based epistemology and emphasis on citation as the basis of judgment, was thus widely inculcated across the Heian nobility and officialdom, and would play a major role in the later development of Japanese intellectual history.

A more difficult question is to what degree this education had broader implications for mid-Heian conceptualizations of knowledge and truth. Was academic literacy training a "constitutive discipline"—not just one field of knowledge among many, but a mediating structure that shaped its epoch's entire epistemological order—as Martin Irvine posits was the case for "grammatical" literacy in the European Middle Ages?[140] The historian Ikeda Genta advanced one such argument by suggesting that the tenth-century rise of ritual precedent as a discrete body of knowledge was based on an understanding of "the source text as absolute authority" (*honmon shijō shugi*) shared with academic scholarship.[141] For him, the courtier diaries and protocol manuals of Council of State debates are a mirror image of the Chinese classics cited as authorities in the State Academy.

Ikeda's view does seem in harmony with the arguments of scholars that have posited the mid-Heian as a crucial turning point in the development of document-based law in Japan. Watanabe Shigeru, for example, notes that it is only in the early eleventh century that we begin to find records of disputes over the disposition of property centered on conflicts between a written will and oral instructions, as the transfer of property through a written document was still rare as late as the tenth century.[142] However, Ikeda's argument clearly overstates the authority of written records per se in matters of court ritual. As noted above, the central importance of precedent in mid-Heian governance led to a widespread practice of diary-keeping among the upper nobility, as well as the compilation of ritual manuals derived from such diaries. Yet the nature of precedent complicated the value of such works: almost by definition, any situation could have multiple relevant cases available for citation, so decision-making

140. Irvine, *Making of Textual Culture*, 2–8, 334.

141. Ikeda, *Nara Heian jidai no bunka*, 266–70.

142. Watanabe Shigeru, *Kodai chūsei no jōhō dentatsu*, 84–98. For an overview of scholarship on the "textualisation" of the mid-Heian, see Fröhlich, *Written Word in Medieval Japan*, 70–76.

could only proceed through analysis and argument to establish the superiority of one precedent over another.[143] The mere recorded fact was rarely enough to settle an argument, and the need for charismatic forms of authority to establish relative value instead led senior nobles to rely heavily on transmitted oral teachings (*kuden* 口傳).[144] Particularly from the time of Fujiwara no Tadahira and his children Saneyori 實賴 (900–970) and Morosuke, courtiers displayed an increased awareness of the importance of maintaining ritual practices ascribed to particular precursors, such as Tadahira's father Mototsune 基經 (836–91), and later Tadahira himself.[145] Manuals of precedent such as Minamoto no Takaakira's *Saikyūki* 西宮記 (Record of the Western Palace, before 982) were widely consulted, but they could be corrected by a noble who possessed access to direct oral transmissions.[146] Because these precedents derived value from a lineage-based exclusivity, the specific content of the teachings was at times less important than their difference from other traditions.[147]

Thus, rather than the appeal to a shared, canonical text we see in academy scholarship, court precedent depended on a socially recognized transmission from a ritual authority to one or more heirs. While these epistemologies contrast, they need not necessarily be opposed. On the contrary, just as the use of diaries and manuals of court precedent often seems to imitate the citation practices of academy scholarship, so the scholarly households of the mid-Heian academy began to emphasize the linear transmission of distinctive bodies of secret knowledge. In the medieval period, this model of inherited authority came to extend across almost all

143. On the complex nature of appeals to precedent in Heian governmental procedure, see Satō Shin'ichi, *Nihon no chūsei kokka*, 50–55; Ryūfuku, "Heian chūki no 'rei.'"

144. For examples of citation of *kuden*, see *Shōyūki*, Shōryaku 4 (993)/1/27 (1:259); *Shunki*, Eishō 3 (1048)/3/20 (335).

145. Takeuchi, *Ritsuryōsei to kizoku seiken*, 2:482–89.

146. *Shōyūki*, Chōwa 2 (1013)/7/5 (3:123); *Gōke shidai* 1.59. The authority of textually transmitted knowledge could be undercut by the perception of a break in oral transmission (Ogawa, "Chi to chi," 167–68).

147. Sanesuke criticizes Fujiwara no Kintō, like himself part of the Ononomiya line descended from Fujiwara no Saneyori, for his use of ritual procedures transmitted in the rival Kujō line—or more precisely, it is through such criticism that Sanesuke establishes the distinction between the two lines. *Shōyūki*, Kannin 2 (1018)/3/19 (5:6); Kojima Kogorō, *Kuge bunka no kenkyū*, 173–74.

spheres of cultural production, as "houses" developed specialized renown in fields ranging from astrology to kickball (*kemari*).[148]

Although diaries and other written guides to court precedent served to extend or supplement the charismatic authority of household lineages, they lacked the inherent textual authority ascribed to works within the classical canon. This is to say that while academic models of knowledge and truth were still fundamental to literacy, and thus textual culture in the mid-Heian, the realm of court ritual was not primarily text-based. Instead, houses vied against one another for cultural authority by emphasizing the exclusivity of their lineage transmission.

The Heian State Academy institutionalized a model of literacy based on the exegesis of a central canon, using the Chinese commentarial tradition as a means to interpret these texts and generate authoritative vocalizations of them in the Japanese-language-based idiom of *kundoku*. Academic training reproduced a highly educated subclass of officials—identified as "scholars," "Confucians," or "poets"—who were recognized as uniquely qualified to serve as tutors to the young and drafters of ornate ritual documents. The activities of these men in turn reaffirmed the legitimacy of the classics, but as this chapter has shown, the nature of those activities, and thus of textual engagement, was reshaped by social realities. The mid-Heian shift from practices of examinations, ceremonies, and Sinitic pronunciation in favor of personal nominations, private tutoring, and *kundoku* recitation entailed a change in the lived experience of the classical canon's meaning. Even though almost all Heian discourse on education still insists on the primacy of study of the Chinese classics, there are hints of an increasing awareness of the limitations of the realm of knowledge delineated by academic scholarship. The restricted, ritual use of literary Sinitic poetry and parallel prose provided poor justification for the enormous efforts required to master them, while the bulk of quotidian administration was carried out through hybrid, vernacular-influenced

148. Ratcliff, "Cultural Arts in Service," 3–10; Stone, *Original Enlightenment*, 110–14. Whereas discourse of "secret teachings" can already be found in the tenth century in arenas such as musical technique or esoteric Buddhist ritual, the crucial transformation in the late Heian is the linking of this transmission to the patrilineal inheritance of office. On the transmission of household diaries to the "heir" (*chakushi*) beginning in the late eleventh century, see Takahashi Hideki, *Nihon chūsei no ie to shinzoku*, 111–17.

forms of Sinographic writing that bore little resemblance to the texts studied in the academy.

These were not, however, two unrelated modes of reading and writing. The reliance on *kundoku*-based literacy both inside and outside the academy meant there was an essential continuity between the classical studies of professors and the record-keeping of regents. The use of *kundoku* glossing as the basis for interpretation and recitation meant that the reception of Chinese texts inevitably brought them into intertextual relationships with literature in "Yamato" genres such as *waka*, while writers, whether they employed the *kana* syllabary, orthodox literary Sinitic, or something in between, similarly had frequent recourse to quotation and adaptation of classical learning. The next chapter takes up the fraught distinction between orthodox literary Sinitic and hybrid modes of Sinographic writing, examining several works in which Heian assumptions about writing's referential capacity come to the fore. Rather than the ideology of classical learning as the engine of knowledge-making, these texts instead reveal precisely the limits of textual authority and legitimacy, as classically trained officials sought to engage in new and productive ways with local subject matter.

FIVE

Reading Out Loud

Literary Writing and Oral Performance

The aesthetics of Heian literary composition were based on comprehensive standards of appropriate content and formal beauty derived primarily from Six Dynasties and Tang anthologies and manuals. As the previous chapter demonstrated, however, the reading method of *kundoku*, through which literary Sinitic texts were recited in a hybrid idiom of Japanese, dominated the State Academy, and this provided the primary reception medium of literary Sinitic throughout the Heian period. This chapter takes up the question of how *kundoku* literacy interacted with and reshaped the aesthetics of mid-Heian composition in orthodox literary Sinitic genres and beyond. After introducing the ubiquity of *kundoku* recitation and reception, the chapter takes up the ramifications of this practice for the *bunshō* idiom of ornamented literary Sinitic discussed in previous chapters, first by examining a liminal genre of donation documents that shift between different written styles, and second by unraveling the contradictory relationship between script and language presented in a Heian encyclopedia of Japanese terms. The pervasive use of *kundoku* recitation blurred many of the core formal principles of literary Sinitic genres, but through careful regulation of correct recitation practice, *kundoku* paradoxically served to re-differentiate literary writing and its innate value at a different level of apprehension.

Breaking *Bun*

> Whenever a document is drafted, a table of contents should also be made listing the year, month, and office, and bound around a rod. These will be put into storage every fifteen days. Drafts of royal proclamations are stored separately. Copies of proclamations, reports to the throne, appointments and demotions . . . should be stored in perpetuity. All other documents should be examined and culled every three years, with a record made of their contents.
>
> —Yōrō (ca. 720) State Documentation Code (*Kushiki ryō*)

As already observed in chapter 3, the establishment of new forms of administration beginning in the late seventh century unleashed a torrent of legal codes, calendars, histories, directives, registries, and other documents onto the previously illiterate Yamato state. The most widely used modern academic term for the eighth-century polity, the "code-based state" (*ritsuryō kokka*), defines this period in terms of its use of documents, and passages like the above from the administrative code have encouraged exaggerated images of a state bureaucracy whose devotion to documentation was "unmatched in the ancient world."[1]

Nevertheless, despite this expansion of writing's use, evidence suggests that ancient Japan retained a powerful emphasis on the audible even as it adopted continental methods of document-based governance.[2] The early administrative code portrays a world of perfect documentation and written communication, but in practice Nara officials were ready to allow that, "when the matter cannot all be written down, the messenger can supply the details."[3] The Yamato state modified the Tang bureaucratic model (perhaps in deference to limited literacy rates among the nobility), so that decision-making within offices tended to proceed through the

1. Ishimoda, *Nihon kodai kokkaron*, 1:42.

2. Perhaps the most influential proponent of this view was Hayakawa Shōhachi. See *Nihon kodai kanryōsei no kenkyū*, 299–325. On orality and governance in the Nara period, see also Bender, "Performative Loci."

3. *Ryō no shūge* 18.554, quoted in Watanabe Shigeru, *Kodai, chūsei no jōhō dentatsu*, 171. The language here alludes to a statement attributed to Confucius in the *Changes*, "What is written does not exhaust all of what is said; what is said does not exhaust all of what is meant." See Owen, *Readings in Chinese Literary Thought*, 31–32.

reading aloud of a document by a functionary, with a decision pronounced orally by the official in charge, rather than circulating documents through various levels of an office and obtaining written approval separately from each level.[4] Mid-Heian records of court ceremony suggest the powerful ritual force retained by the spoken word: names and titles were summoned, proclamations read, songs sung, music played, poems recited. At major palace events, the master of ceremonies was responsible for so many summons and cries (*ishō*) that he licked salt throughout to keep his voice from cracking.[5]

This emphasis on oral audience overlapped with the culture of recitation-based literacy discussed in the previous chapter, in which youths were trained to read through rote memorization and vocal repetition. In pre-print cultures across the world, oral recitation seems to have been the default mode of reading.[6] Japanese sources record reading aloud of such diverse materials as fictional tales, esoteric Buddhist ritual liturgy, imperial edicts, and lawsuits.[7] Such practices do not preclude the possibility of silent reading, and beginning in the late eighth century there is some evidence of silent reading in government procedures. However, throughout the Heian, oral recitation remained common in official settings. This may be due in part to the inertia of established custom, but there were practical motives as well, especially when the contents of a document needed to be communicated to a large assembly quickly. The Heian can thus be characterized as a transitional period, with newer silent reading practices only gradually supplanting an older culture of vocalized recitation.[8]

4. Yoshikawa, *Ritsuryō kanryōsei no kenkyū*, 198–207. Nara epigraphic materials also show some evidence of central directives being transmitted to district-level officials orally, without transfer of documentation. Kanegae, "Kōtō dentatsu no shosō," 20–24.

5. *Gōke shidai* 1.50, 1.59.

6. On recitation as the typical mode of reading in Tang China, see Nugent, *Manifest in Words*, 132–34. On script as "sounds needing hearing" in the West, see Clanchy, *Memory to Written Record*, 268–74, 287.

7. Fröhlich, *Written Word in Medieval Japan*, 33–35. Tamagami Takuya's so-called "*monogatari ondoku ron*" (theory of the oral recitation of tales) has had an enormous impact on literary scholarship since the 1960s. See Masuda, "Monogatari ondokuron no yukue," and Richard Okada, *Figures of Resistance*, 173–82.

8. Yoshikawa, *Ritsuryō kanryōsei no kenkyū*, 232–58. While literary scholars have tended to emphasize the relative modernity of silent reading, cognitive research suggests

The widespread use of oral recitation does not imply that such performance was simple or taken for granted; the ability to correctly recite a written text—to ritualize the written word through grand oral performance in a ceremonial context—was highly valued among officials. The social value of recitation ability is given material expression in the rewards presented to lecturers at religious ceremonies, which could include silk, clothing, or a personal item belonging to the sponsor, and most importantly, promotion up the ecclesiastical ladder.[9] The court's ceremonies of governance also frequently demanded training in particular recitation methods that might be handed down across generations.[10] Belletristic texts constituted another arena where the importance of correct recitation was felt very keenly. One of the central episodes of *Utsuho monogatari* concerns the protagonist Nakatada's discovery of a storehouse of his grandfather Toshikage's books, including a collection of Toshikage's poetry he presents and reads to the reigning emperor:

> [The emperor] commanded, "Add glosses yourself and read it aloud to me," so [Nakatada] placed [Toshikage's collection] on the desk and read it. He did not read as loudly as he would when serving as reader at events like the blossom-viewing banquets. It was seven or eight sheets of writing. At the end, [the emperor] had him read it once in *kundoku* and once in Sinitic pronunciation [*hitotabi wa kuni, hitotabi wa koe ni*], and had him chant [the lines] the emperor found delightful. Because in each case a man with a wonderful voice was chanting, it was delightful and moving, and even the listening emperor shed tears.[11]

---

that readers make continuous parallel use of phonological and lexical routes for information processing, calling into question a categorical distinction between audible and silent reading. Dehaene, *Reading in the Brain*, 38–41.

9. See, respectively, *Rihō ō ki*, Jōhei 1 (931)/9/24 (54); *Midō kanpaku ki*, Kankō 4 (1007)/8/11 (1:229); *Sakeiki*, Kannin 2 (1018)/12/18 and Chōgen 1 (1028)/12/30 (74, 258).

10. Watanabe Shigeru, *Kodai, chūsei no jōhō dentatsu*, 23–24. On the social prestige of correct recitation in the Kamakura period, see Conlan, "Traces of the Past."

11. *Utsuho monogatari*, "Kurabiraki chū," 535. For an extended analysis of this scene in relation to reading practice in the tenth century, see Nakada, *Kotenbon no kokugogakuteki kenkyū*, 1:5–34.

Chapter 4 detailed the various methods by which *kundoku* reading techniques were used in the interpretation of literary Sinitic texts, but such exegesis was not purely internal and theoretical; *kundoku* recitation of Sinographic texts was often a public act, and sometimes a command performance.

The episode of Nakatada's recitation accentuates the importance of Japanese-based *kundoku* alongside Sinitic-derived "Han pronunciation" for appreciation of literature. This may even be a somewhat anachronistic depiction on the part of *Utsuho monogatari* (which, like the *Tale of Genji*, often seems to nostalgically depict social practices several decades out of date by the time of its authorship): as discussed in the previous chapter, Sinitic-based pronunciation was already a declining practice in the tenth century, with recitation in *kundoku* becoming the norm. Whereas Sinitic pronunciation is consistent with reception of literary Sinitic poetry in Tang China and across East Asia, *kundoku* vocalization is more problematic. The formal qualities of literary Sinitic—tonal prosody, meter, and rhyme—all depend on auditory attributes of the recitation language, and would be obscured to one degree or another in *kundoku*. The growing reliance on *kundoku* recitation of literary Sinitic texts in the mid-Heian would seem to directly undermine the heavy emphasis on formal ornament discussed in chapter 3, which was premised on recitation through correct Sinitic pronunciation.[12] Even as they continued to adhere to Sinitic-based formal principles, Heian writers could not help but react to the central role *kundoku* recitation had come to play in literary reception, composing with the knowledge that a poem might be praised or disparaged for formal qualities only apparent in one or the other of two possible linguistic registers.

The importance of oral recitation is invoked explicitly in *Sakumon daitai*, the composition manual introduced in chapter 3. It begins with ten rules of poetry composition, which mostly cover the components of topic exposition, rhyme, parallelism, and tonal prosody integral to orthodox

12. But cf. Matsuura Tomohisa's contrarian suggestion that precisely by their removal from the realm of perception, the auditory patterns of literary Sinitic could be abstracted into a purely conceptual formalism, and thereby assigned a kind of "metaphysical value." "Jōdai kanshibun," 24.

literary Sinitic. The tenth rule, however, explains the importance of "popular traditions" (*zokusetsu* 俗説):

> Popular traditions are instructions that are passed down according to custom. According to these traditions, when composing poetry, one must not only consider the topic and avoid maladies, but also be careful of the broken sentences [*habun* 破文] and the tonal composition [*chōsei* 調聲]. This is because if the *habun* is difficult to read, the words will be circuitous and the meaning unclear. If one is not attentive to the tonal composition, it will be difficult to chant.

Sakumon daitai notes that it is not enough to follow prohibitions on certain tonal arrangements ("avoid maladies") and observe the rhetorical patterns of topical exposition; one must also anticipate the concrete oral performance of the poem. While "tonal composition" refers to patterns of tonal prosody heard in Sinitic pronunciation, the term *habun* refers to *kundoku*; examples can be found in Nara applications for monastic ordination, in which the applicant's ability to read a sutra in either Sinitic pronunciation (*on*) or *habun* is often specified.[13] Both types of recitation were skills demanding training: just as chanting in Sinitic required careful attention to tonal prosody and an alien phonology, chanting in *kundoku* could employ pitch, elongated syllables, and vibrato to achieve a dramatic or euphonic performance.[14] When, in *Utsuho monogatari*, the impoverished scholar Tōei's talent is discovered by Masayori, it is as much a result of the beauty of Tōei's voice, "ringing like a Koma bell," as the content of the poem he is chanting.[15]

Sakumon daitai goes on to give three examples of "violations" that could cause one to "be laughed at." First are the phrases *shumon* 朱門 (vermillion gate) and *sekigan* 赤雁 (red goose) which can be taken as euphemisms for female and male genitalia, respectively. The second is the phrase *hatsu shika* 發枝柯 (opening among the branches), a description of flowers that sounds "like a monk delivering a spell" when chanted in

13. See, for example, *Dai Nihon komonjo hennen monjo*, 8:162. For *chōsei* as a term for tonal prosody, see *Bunkyō hifuron*, "Ten," 28–32.

14. Aoyagi, "Shi hikō kō."

15. *Utsuho monogatari*, "Matsuri no tsukai," 230.

Sinitic pronunciation. The final example is the phrase *kan mutan* 感無端 (my emotions have no limit), which read aloud sounds "like a poor man complaining that he lacked even a scrap of paper"—in the *kundoku* reading implied here, *kan hashi nashi*, the Sino-Japanese word *kan* (LMC kam') sounds similar to the Japanese word for paper (*kami*), while the reading for 端, *hashi*, means "border/limit" but also "scrap/shred" in Japanese.[16]

Like *Utsuho*'s description of Nakatada's performance, *Sakumon daitai*'s warning of the potential for ridicule accompanying recitation emphasizes its social context. The post of reader (*kōji* 講師) at a poetry banquet, mentioned in the *Utsuho* passage, is one example of several such ritual roles that required an appealing performance of the target text in *kundoku* recitation. The early twelfth-century *Gōdanshō* contains commentary on several famous couplets taken from banquet poems that describe the tasks faced by such readers:

酔中賞翫欲其奈	Drunk I toy with [the flowers] in admiration, but what shall I do?
未得將心地忍之	My heart cannot just bear [their beauty].

—From a palace banquet, [on the topic] "Enjoying Half-Opened Blossoms," Emperor Daigo

The old man [Ōe no Masafusa] said, "Though they studied it, the reader and his assistant did not accord with his majesty's intention [in reading] the second line of this final couplet. [The emperor] announced this and the scholars were humbled."

誰知秋昔爲情盛	Who could know how the autumn evening makes my thoughts overflow?
三五晴天徹夜遊	With a clear sky on the fifteenth, we will revel through the night.

—"The Moon's Image Floats in an Autumn Pool," Ōe no Asatsuna, Tei[ji'in Palace]

The old man told me, "Long ago there was a wicked man who informed Asatsuna that Ōe no Koretoki often said Asatsuna was a talented poet, but a weak scholar. Hearing this, and knowing that Koretoki would certainly

16. *Sakumon daitai*, 16–17.

> be the reader at the Teiji'in poetry banquet, Asatsuna crafted this couplet, hoping he could get Koretoki to read it incorrectly. However, [Koretoki] recited it just as the lines were intended [to be read], and Asatsuna was greatly impressed. 昔 means 'evening,' and 爲 means 'to cause.'"[17]

The first couplet employs an unusual construction, "just bear it" 地忍之, taken from the *Hanshu*. The character *chi* 地, which generally means "ground" or "earth," is here used to indicate the nearly homophonous adverb *tei* 第 meaning "only" or "just."[18] In the second episode, the character *seki* 昔, which is almost always read *mukashi* (long ago, ancient times) in *kundoku*, is used with the recondite sense of "evening."[19] The character *i* 爲, most often read as *tame* (because) or *su* (to do), is used instead in a causative construction (usually translated by the suffix *-shimu* in *kundoku*). Both anecdotes emphasize the difficulty and the extreme erudition required to produce an on-the-spot *kundoku* reading of a banquet poem, revealing a crucial but unwritten improvisational element to Heian literary Sinitic.

If the discussion in the previous chapter emphasized the practical function of *kundoku* as a hermeneutic device and basis for literacy, passages like the above make clear the formal restrictions necessary to ensure its success as a vehicle of performance. *Kundoku* functioned through establishing equivalencies between Sinographs and Japanese language, but this target language of recitation was neither self-evident nor uncontested. Like the Suma fishermen who "chirp" earnestly at Genji, the Heian archipelago possessed a range of dialects and, as Torquil Duthie has recently argued, the centralized state needed to posit and enact a shared, "literate vernacular" to serve as the voice of its "imperial imagination."[20] Moreover, the effort to mimic directly the grammatical structures of a literary Sinitic

17. *Gōdanshō* 4.4 and 4.68.

18. *Hanshu* 74.3146. The character 地 is listed under the word *tada* (only) in *Iroha jiruishō*, with 地忍 provided as an example phrase (136).

19. This definition, which is found in the dictionary *Guangya* 廣雅 (ca. 227), is quoted by Li Shan in *Wenxuan* 27.16a. The *kundoku* reading *yoru* is assigned to this character in *Iroha jiruishō* and *Ruijū myōgishō*.

20. *Genji monogatari*, "Suma," 2:214; Duthie, *"Man'yōshū" and the Imperial Imagination*, 206–15. On linguistic diversity in Japan, see Shibatani, *Languages of Japan*, 185–214.

original introduced creolized locutions into *kundoku*, further divorcing its language from natural speech. The Yamato "vernacular" through which *kundoku* operated was thus not an a priori register defined by a set speech community, but a "historical process" (to borrow Sheldon Pollock's formulation), retrospectively recognized through intertwined practices of performance and writing.[21] The anxiety surrounding *kundoku* recitation reveals the tension between its twin responsibilities to two different symbolic codes, each of which was subject to modification and negotiation.

Like any prescriptive linguistic discourse, *Sakumon daitai* is forced to mediate the inevitable discrepancies between a fixed canon of exemplars and the infinite potential of practical application. The underlying impossibility of a truly comprehensive standard was of course multiplied many times in a linguistically alien periphery, so distant from the Tang court whose usage (or the imagination thereof) was universalized into the principles of literary ornament discussed in chapter 3. These contradictions were not limited to the gaps between Tang formal standards and *kundoku* recitation practices, but appeared on a variety of levels: How to narrate and name local phenomena not found in Chinese model texts? On whose authority to determine the correct reading of a character in "Han pronunciation"? Can and should spoken registers of Japanese discourse be inscribed in writing? Heian officials were forced to confront such problems repeatedly as they sought to harness the technology of writing to a variety of ends. Their answers to these questions are key to understanding the role of literary Sinitic genres in the mid-Heian as well as the long-term development of the interdependent relationship between this mode of inscription and the growing practice of writing in phonographic *kana*.

Literary Form and *Kundoku* Reception

The discussions of parallel prose and poetic genres in chapters 2 and 3 were largely based on exemplars of literary writing retrospectively defined by anthologists. But what determines the categories and scope of literature?

21. Pollock, *Language of the Gods*, 23.

Why does *Honchō monzui* contain so many prefaces, memorials, and prayers as opposed to other genres? To flip the question on its head, what determines whether a particular application of writing needs to be "patterned," conforming to the formal regulations and rhetorical strategies of this standard? This chapter first approaches this problem by taking up a genre that occupied an ambiguous position in the Heian literary sphere, commendation documents attesting to the donation of property to a temple or other institution. In the mid-Heian, practices differed on the need for literary ornament in commendations, as well as the nature of such ornamentation. Extant documents show the complex interaction of formal principles, performance practices, and practical utility.

Donations to temples are one of the most common religious practices across premodern East Asia. As in medieval China, the Heian laity frequently sought merit or favorable alliances by donating goods, income, or land to a temple. Particularly in the case of land, such donations were generally effected through a document testifying to the commendation. The earliest known such declaration dates to 749, but Nara and early Heian sources generally refer to these documents as *ganmon* (prayer texts), a generic term for prayers at Buddhist services.[22] It is only in the mid-Heian that we start to see references to "commendations" (*senyūbun* 施入文 or *yosebumi*) as a distinct category of document, perhaps in response to the increasing number of commendations to non-Buddhist institutions, such as shrines or noble households.[23] Consistent with the *ganmon* genre, most surviving early Heian examples of commendations are in a dense parallel prose style, incorporating elaborate rhetoric and tonal prosody patterns. However, starting in the late tenth century, a new kind of commendation contract that made no attempt to conform to parallel prose or any Tang literary model began to appear, adopting instead a

22. For the 749 commendation, see *Tōdaiji monjo* 864–3 (9:146–48). For references to commendations as *ganmon*, see *Tōdaiji monjo* 564 (2:405–7); *Kanke bunsō, Kanke kōshū* 644–45 and 667.

23. *Heian ibun* 164 (1:156); *Tōdaiji monjo* 476 (2:107); *Shōyūki*, Jian 3 (1023)/11/19 (6:232). Symptomatic of the transition is a 953 declaration of the property of Kinchōkokuji in Ise Province, which uses the term *ganmon* throughout to refer to donation documents, but has a district certification (*gunpan*) attached that refers to these documents as *senyūbun*. *Heian ibun* 265 (1:387–95). From the Kamakura period onward, *kishinjō* 寄進狀 becomes the standard term.

strictly contractual idiom that frequently deviated from literary Sinitic standards. This type of commendation became increasingly commonplace: a thirteenth-century set of templates (*kakiyō*) for various types of documents presents a short *ganmon* in allusive parallel prose, but its examples of commendations are both in a brief, unornamented idiom.[24] In the mid-Heian period, whether or not a commendation was literary—whether it required rhetorical decoration or was simply a verified and witnessed list—was open to question. Because of this ambiguity, tenth-century commendation documents show more clearly than conventional belletristic genres the multilayered operations attendant on local applications of an authoritative and unitary literary idiom.

Examples of commendations in parallel prose tend to run long, but a 933 document declaring the donation of tax income (*fuko*) by Fujiwara no Tadahira to Daigoji (a temple associated with the recently deceased Emperor Daigo, who had been emperor through most of Tadahira's career) provides a relatively brief example:

> I humbly donate the tax income of forty-five households.
>
> Twenty households of Shinano. Twenty-five households of Sanuki.
>
> Regarding the above, last winter heaven's benefice unexpectedly descended, my rank advanced to the first grade. Quietly considering how this new favor exceeds my worth, I became aware this was the previous ruler's continued blessing. At this, unable to repress the hidden urging of my heart, I humbly bowed at his gravesite and spread my prayer mat. Long ago I served in the palace of Penglai, where frosted spears lined up before the throne; now I gaze upon the color of the pines and cypresses, and green weeds fill the walls. My tears, falling unrestrained, have all unaware dampened my collar.
>
> The temple he created is called Daigoji. It [lies] near the site of his mountain grave, but we have yet to complete the merit of its construction.[25] Therefore I will divert part of my newly acquired households, adding my sincere resolve to the hall. Though this dust and dew [i.e., my labors] be faint,

24. *Jurin shūyō*, 365, 373, 378. The manual seems to have been assembled by a lower-ranked provincial official in Kii Province. Takeuchi, "Heian makki no ōraimono," 525.

25. Construction on the famous five-story pagoda at Daigoji began in 931 in honor of Daigo, but was not completed until 951. There is a missing character in the text that I have supplied as "lies" in the translation.

how could the mountains and rivers reject it? I wish through the sincerity of pine and bamboo to somehow multiply the adornment of this hermitage. Humbly declared.

Jōhei 3, tenth month, third day, Junior First Rank Minister of the Left Fujiwara no Tadahira[26]

奉施入封戸卌五烟

信濃廿戸　讃岐廿五戸

右去冬、天慈猥降、爵昇一品。閑思新寵之過分、追知先朝之餘恩。爰難抑心懷之暗催、敬拜陵園而展席。昔陪蓬萊之宮、霜戟列陛、今望松柏之色、綠蕪滿墻。淚之亂落、不覺濕襟。

御願道場號醍醐寺。近山陵之側、未畢土木之功。仍割新加之戸邑、添忠志於堂構。塵露雖微、山河豈厭。願以松筠之誠、聊增蘭若之飾。敬白。

承平三年十月三日　　從一位行左大臣藤原朝臣忠平

The rhetorical style of this piece is identical to *ganmon* from the same period. The declaration conforms to strict meter and displays simple tonal patterns, interspersing scriptural language with rhetoric taken from Tang verse: the line "Now I gaze upon the color of the pines and cypresses,/Green weeds fill the walls," for example, borrows phrasing from one of Bai Juyi's *Xin yuefu* to describe the desolation of Daigo's tomb.[27] The document testifies to the legal transfer of tax income to the temple, but its ornamentation is consistent with ritual recitation as an assembly prayer (see chapter 2).

Tadahira's commendation emphasizes his personal gratitude toward Emperor Daigo; he had risen to minister of the left under Daigo, and became regent with the accession of Daigo's eight-year-old son Suzaku. Standing at the pinnacle of the nobility, the regent Tadahira had ready access to specialist scribes to draft his documents. In this case, he most likely commissioned Ōe no Asatsuna (a State Academy graduate who would be made professor of letters the next year) to write this prayer, as

26. *Daigoji shin yōroku* 7.370–71. The text is corrupt, and I have made the following emendations: 席] 度; 霜戟列陛] 霜載列階 (cf. *Quan Tangshi* 1.8); 之色] 之邑; 忠志] 中志. A similar early commendation can be found in *Chōya gunsai* 17.431–432.

27. "Lingyuan qie" 陵園妾, *Bai Juyi ji jianjiao* 4.238–41. Ironically, this source for Tadahira's eulogy is a pointed critique, in which Bai Juyi describes the tragic fate of palace ladies-in-waiting forced to serve out their days at the mausoleum of a dead emperor.

Asatsuna also composed Tadahira's memorials of resignation around the same period.[28] The formal features of the document—especially the observance of tonal prosody and incorporation of classical language that make it "literary"—therefore are heavily dependent on the social position of its sponsor. The question that naturally follows from this is what options to commend property existed for donors who lacked this access to an academy-trained composer.

A document preserved in Tōdaiji gives some sense of the way in which the academic prose style might be imperfectly imitated. This commendation was presented to Tōdaiji in 958 by Tachibana no Motozane 橘元實, an otherwise unknown low-ranked official from the small, mountainous province of Iga, east of Nara (fig. 5).[29] In it, he describes how the forest of Tamataki has been controlled by his family for generations and is the gravesite of his ancestors. However, he is no longer able to resist council directives that have permitted logging on the land for construction at Tōdaiji and other locations:

> Since I had no power to make a complaint over my private grief, the trees were eventually cleared away, the gravesite became a bare field. This curse will surely fall on Motozane and my descendants. Nothing could be better than to donate [the land] in perpetuity to this monastery, allowing my ancestors to achieve enlightenment's path as well as saving Motozane from their destructive curse. Therefore, I make this commendation as described. If in the future anyone should violate this wish, the gods of heaven and earth, the Four Heavenly Kings and other dharma-protecting deities will punish that person: In this life he will encounter the disaster of pestilence and lose all his descendants. In the next life he will fall into the suffering of the three paths and be born in a land without buddhas.[30]
>
> 無力愁申私歎之間、樹木漸切掃、墳墓作露地。其祟彌可有元實幷子孫之身。不若永奉施入伽藍、令得先祖菩提之道、兼免元實禍殃之祟。仍施入如件。若後代之人破此願者、天神地祇四王護法現罰其人、現在遭疾疫災横、永斷子孫、後生墮三途苦處、生無仏土。

28. *Honchō monzui* 100–103.

29. A Tōdaiji record identifies Motozane as a "landholder of Iga Province" 伊賀國住人. *Dai Nihon shiryō* ser. 1, 10:596.

30. *Tōdaiji monjo* 478 (2:112). Emendations: 現罰] 見罰; 無仏土] 無仏在. The three paths refer to rebirth as a hell-being, a hungry ghost, or an animal.

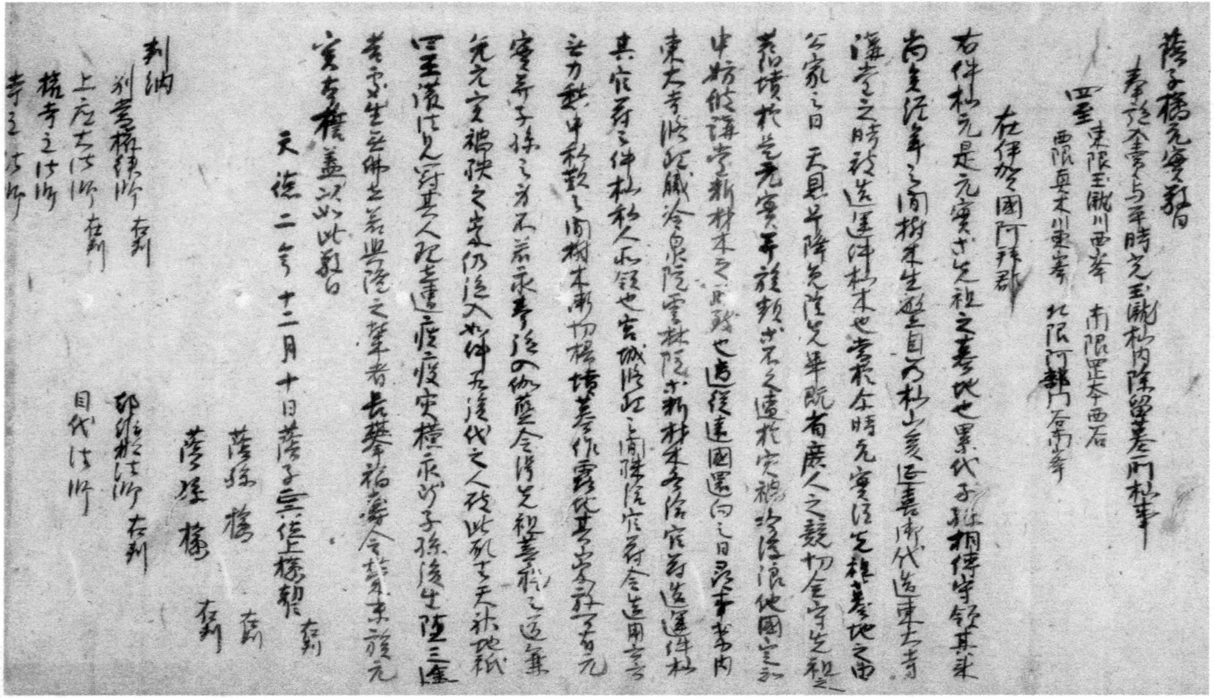

FIG. 5 A copy of Tachibana no Motozane's 958 commendation, which was held in the archives of Tōdaiji's Tōnan'in together with a Council of State directive from the next year recognizing Tōdaiji's claim over Tamataki. Photograph courtesy of the Office of the Shōsōin Treasure House, Nara.

The writer sometimes adopts parallel constructions (underlined in the excerpt), but the couplets show no awareness of tonal prosody, and often are not even true syntactic parallels. Nor does the document employ the poetic vocabulary found in Tadahira's commendation or the works in *Honchō monzui*.

Such deviations from the formal orthodoxy exhibited by Tadahira's commendation and *ganmon* of the period can be read in at least two ways. One interpretation is based on the uneven distribution of technical knowledge: the scribe who composed this document may have had less extensive training in the literary Sinitic prose tradition. There are several odd constructions (oftentimes reflecting Japanese grammar) in the piece, and it is not difficult to imagine that Motozane's household in Iga did not have ready access to a scholar of the type employed by Tadahira. The effort by a less educated periphery to imitate scribal techniques of the elite suggests what Amino Yoshihiko has characterized as the aspirational pull the formal standards of the capital exerted on the broader literate community.[31] This model implies a unipolar spectrum of literacy and correctness, with a capital-based standard at the top to which others seek to cleave as best they can.

Yet if we consider Tadahira and Motozane's documents in terms of a primarily aural reception environment, the differences between them are much less striking. In an oral, *kundoku* recitation, many of the formal features missing from Motozane's document, such as tonal prosody, would not be perceptible anyway, so the differences between Tadahira's and Motozane's commendations would have been largely elided. As explained above, *kundoku* recitation practice entailed the positing of a prestigious, unitary vernacular marked by the incorporation of Sinitic-derived locutions and archaic Japanese vocabulary. However, the formalization of this "high vernacular" idiom meant that it could be imitated irrespective of any actual relationship to a literary Sinitic original. Parallel constructions, for example, recited in a *kundoku* idiom would in this sense "sound like" literature, even if the corresponding inscription failed to accord to the metrical, grammatical, and/or phonic parallelism of literary Sinitic parallel prose. The style in Motozane's document is almost identical to that found in the contemporaneous war tale *Shōmonki* 將門記 (Record of

31. Amino, *Rethinking Japanese History*, 123–43.

Masakado, mid-tenth century); almost a third of this text is made up of parallel couplets, but these observe no tonal prosody and contain frequent deviations from Sinitic syntax.[32] Rather than simply a matter of education, examples like these suggest that the mid-Heian understanding of the formal requirements of literary inscription were being reshaped through performance practices.

A parallel example of compromise between Tang literary standards and *kundoku*-based reception can be seen in another portion of the composition manual *Sakumon daitai*. As detailed in chapter 3, the rules of *kudaishi* composition held that all five characters of the "topic phrase" must appear in the first couplet of a poem; according to *Sakumon daitai*, however, one of these characters can also be replaced by another with the same *kundoku* reading. In the example given, the Sinograph *gan* 顔 in the topic phrase is switched out for *men* 面 within the poem's opening couplet: the characters have different Sinitic pronunciations, and subtly different meanings, but are both commonly glossed in *kundoku* with the reading *omote* (face).[33] Here *kundoku* recitation practice warps the rules of correct composition. If the passages discussed at the beginning of this chapter mostly address anxieties surrounding incorrect recitation, documents like Motozane's commendation instead suggest the compositional opportunities that a reception environment based on *kundoku* recitation could provide scribes, loosening through reinterpretation the rigid formulations of literary patterning.

These two possible explanations, a lack of education and an understanding of the literary transformed by *kundoku* performance, are not mutually exclusive, and the most likely scenario is that both are at work in Motozane's commendation. The document suggests the combination of a reception context in which many of the formal characteristics of literary Sinitic parallel prose were rendered irrelevant or invisible, but an educational environment in which the orthodox model was credited with ritual efficacy. Though the writer of this document may have lacked the classical education necessary to craft a ritual text consistent with orthodox examples, he had no doubt seen and especially heard *ganmon*, and knew that was the format appropriate to this occasion. The result is a

32. Rabinovitch, *Shōmonki*, 53–62.

33. *Sakumon daitai*, 50; Tsukishima, *Kunten goi shūsei*, 2:350–51.

literary discourse that cannot be explained purely through appeal to either text-based continental models or local linguistic norms, but that rather seeks to strategically position itself within the space opened up by their interaction.

The Limits of Literature

While Motozane's document incorporates a large number of formal infelicities, it is still recognizable as an imitation of the orthodox parallel prose seen in Tadahira's commendation. Beginning in the late tenth century, however, an alternative format of commendation appears. Where earlier commendations emulated the *bunshō* style of ornate parallel prose, this new format employs a strictly contractual idiom, detailing legal conditions and consequences:

> The above ten locales are donated as specified. However, though I have no children other than daughters, if there are any monks among the descendants of those daughters, they should be made [the estate's] administrator. If any other party should obstruct this, disaster will occur; he may be punished for his crime through his residence burning down. Therefore, the income from these estates and pastures should be delivered to the temple household and assigned to the temple's use. Therefore, I record this for after my passing.[34]
>
> 已上拾箇處施入如件。但自女子外無他子、件女子々孫之中有僧、以彼可令爲別當。若他人成其妨者、自災禍出來、在所令燒亡蒙罪歟。仍莊牧等地子納院家、可宛院用。仍爲没後記。

From the eleventh century onward, commendations became widely used as a means of guaranteeing property claims, as temples and noble households amassed enormous estates through power-sharing agreements with

34. *Kōyasan monjo* 1925 (8:447). This is a 1277 copy of a 1001 document. Other examples similar in format can be found in *Dai Nihon shiryō* ser. 1, 12:38; *Heian ibun* 373, 596 and 677 (2:508, 750, 3:812–13).

local overseers.[35] Commendation documents thus became crucial evidence in property disputes in the medieval period (which is why so many survive), and this development in the function of commendations coincides with a rejection of the literary idiom. Examples like the above follow the basic outlines of earlier commendations, beginning with a list of items or explanation of property boundaries (*shishi* 四至) to be "humbly donated" (奉施 or 奉寄), but instead of parallel couplets and classical allusions we find plain legal language.

Many of the commendations in this newer, contractual mode are signed by provincial residents, so it may be tempting to explain this development through variations in levels of education, but the evidence suggests otherwise. The document quoted above, for one, is signed by Taira no Korenaka 平惟仲 (944–1005), a senior noble at the time of the donation. Korenaka came from a scholarly family, and even served as head of the State Academy for a year.[36] He certainly had the means to produce or have produced a commendation in the *bunshō* idiom Tadahira had used. In fact, there is at least one example of commendations in both the literary style and the newer contract style being commissioned by the same person, the regent Fujiwara no Tadazane.[37] These men had material access to the more elaborate prose style we see in Tadahira's contract, so the rejection of parallel prose is not simply a matter of insufficient education. Instead, we see parallel sets of generic conventions for commendations existing side by side. It is soon after the appearance of this new format, in the early eleventh century, that distinct terms for commendation contracts become more common in contemporary documents, with commendations recognized as a genre separate from prayer texts. In the eleventh century, commendations both with and without literary orna-

35. Nagahara, "*Shōen-Kokugaryō* System," provides an English-language explanation of the creation of estates (*shōen*) through commendation, but is now somewhat dated. For an overview of recent research on commendation as means of guaranteeing property, see Kamakura, "Shōensei seiritsu shiron."

36. Korenaka's younger brother Narimasa 生昌 appears in a famous episode in the *Pillow Book*, as the object of Sei Shōnagon's mockery. He refers to himself as "an old letters student" (*furuki shinji*). *Makura no sōshi*, "Daijin Narimasa ga ie ni," 34.

37. *Chūyūki*, Kōwa 4 (1102)/10/13 (4:229); *Chōya gunsai* 7.175–76. For other examples of "orthodox" and "deviant" Sinographic writing produced by the same person, see Tsukishima, *Heian jidai no kanbun kundokugo*, 29–34.

mentation are produced, but both types are referred to as *yosebumi* or *senyūjō* interchangeably.

In some ways Korenaka's commendation is a mode of inscription radically different from Tadahira's. Writing in the *bunshō* idiom demanded accordance with standards of both legibility and aesthetics generalized from Tang examples. Korenaka's commendation, by contrast, not only abandons parallelism, but incorporates Japanese vocabulary freely, and makes little effort to conform to Chinese syntax. Though written entirely in Sinographs, the document only gestures at the linguistic features of Chinese, often getting no further than placing the verb in front of the object. Phrases like *onnago yori hoka ni* 自女子外, *onozukara saika shuttai* 自災禍出來, or *in no yō ni atsu-beshi* 可宛院用 make clear that the scribe's use of writing is based in Japanese usage, abandoning the canonical standard of literary Sinitic we saw in Tadahira's commendation. We find many of the same sorts of deviant constructions in Motozane's commendation (e.g., the character *shin* 申, "to declare," used as the humilific auxiliary verb *-mōsu*, or the character *yū* 有 used where we would expect *zai* 在, both characters normally read *ari* in *kundoku* recitation), but whereas in the latter these might appear to be exceptional glitches within a sincere attempt at producing orthodox writing, Korenaka's commendation persistently uses Sinographs in accordance with Japanese linguistic structures.

This extension of the logographic properties of the Chinese writing system—associating Sinographs with Japanese lexemes on a mostly one-to-one basis—was integral to the spread of literacy in ancient Japan. Official or ritually potent writings in the *bunshō* idiom, such as those found in *Honchō monzui*, are often indistinguishable from compositions by early Tang literati, but when the primary goal was utilitarian information transfer, and both writer and intended reader spoke a variety of Japanese, the tendency was to rely on *kundoku* readings to compose sentences based on Japanese usage, without consideration of their legibility if read as literary Sinitic. The excavated wooden tablets (*mokkan*) that provide the most direct evidence on writing in the seventh and eighth centuries are generally characterized by this "*kundoku*-based everyday style."[38] Use of this everyday style of logographic writing continued

38. Lurie, *Realms of Literacy*, 190–94.

through the Heian period in letters, records, and directives, only gradually losing ground to primarily phonographic forms of *kana* writing over the course of the medieval and early modern periods. What might appear at first glance to be "Chinese" is replete with local vocabulary and vestiges of Japanese syntax, including object/verb transpositions, redundant characters, and honorific language. The logographic use of Sinographs formed the core of literacy in classical and medieval Japan, but quotidian writing rarely conformed to strict classical standards or Chinese-language legibility. In this respect, the "errors" in Motozane's or Korenaka's commendations are not in the first instance mistakes betraying inadequate command of literary Sinitic, but rather side effects of the practical use of logographic characters as a medium of communication in a Japanese-language environment.

The form of orthography found here is in some ways a reversal of the *kundoku* reading method discussed in the previous chapter: instead of using the Japanese language to read out imported Chinese texts, the same logographic relationships are marshaled to adapt elements of Japanese discourse into Sinographic writing. There are a few important modifications, however. Imported literary Sinitic texts display an enormous vocabulary, and many words are used in multiple senses, so that *kundoku* recitation necessitates flexibility: in tenth- and eleventh-century manuscripts, the character *ko* 固 is usually glossed with the adjective *katashi* (hard) or the adverb *makoto ni* (truly), but sometimes with the verb *katamu* (harden) or the noun *katame* (guard), a typical assortment.[39] Use of *kundoku* as a method of writing, on the other hand, encouraged the development of a much more limited palette of one-to-one correspondences between Japanese lexemes and Sinographs.[40] For example, the dictionary *Iroha jiruishō* (twelfth century) lists fifty-six different Sinographs that might receive the *kundoku* reading *miru* (to see/look).[41] If we examine a quotidian Heian document such as Fujiwara no Michinaga's diary,

39. Tsukishima, *Kunten goi shūsei*, 2:541, 567–69, 7:214.

40. On this phenomenon of so-called "fixed readings" (*teikun*), see Kobayashi, "Shokiyō kanji no kun," and Minegishi Akira, "Kanji no teikun ni tsuite."

41. *Iroha jiruishō*, 315. Conversely, in literary Sinitic texts verbs of seeing are almost exclusively glossed as *miru*, while synonymous Japanese vocabulary such as *nagamu* or *furisaku* seems to have never been used in *kundoku*.

however, almost none of these appear, and *miru* is written exclusively with the Sinograph *ken* 見 (or occasionally *ran* 覽). This limited array of characters meant that documents in the everyday style were correspondingly easy to read.[42] No extant manuscripts of Heian courtier diaries contain any of the glossing with *kunten* found in manuscripts of imported texts, indicating that they were readily legible to literate officials.[43]

Such strong connections between Sinographs and Japanese words should not mislead us into taking the everyday style as a transcription of idiomatic, conversational language. Sinographic texts were susceptible to vocalization as a Japanese utterance, but not necessarily to *one and only one* possible vocalization. In most cases, the primary goal was conveyance of information, not exact transcription.[44] Furthermore, the establishment of *kundoku* associations could be highly conditional, with the same Japanese word written differently by different groups, even within capital society (not to speak of the linguistic variety of Japonic dialects across the archipelago).[45] Finally, although the everyday style incorporates numerous constructions based on spoken Japanese, the mediation of classics-centered literacy education often produces hybrid forms and circumlocutions that were as alien to conversational Japanese as they were to literary Sinitic. Like the performative language of classics recitation also produced through *kundoku*, though to a lesser degree, the language of contracts such as Korenaka's is stilted, marked off from conversational speech.

As detailed above, in the *kundoku* recitation of literary Sinitic texts, the combination of frequent use of compounds read in "Han pronunciation," a lexicon of archaic Japanese preserved in the transmission of *kundoku* techniques, and recitation venues that called for grandiose performance led to the creation of a hybrid idiom that was "vernacular" in its positing of communal reception, yet unmistakably distinguished from

42. Mid-Heian courtier diaries use a far smaller range of characters than literary works from the same period. Asano, *Heian jidai shikijisō*, 160–66.

43. Minegishi Akira, "Kirokutai," 170.

44. For a trenchant critique of the limits of Kobayashi's *teikun* paradigm, see Komatsu, *Kokugoshigaku kiso ron*, 248–74.

45. Yamamoto Shingo provides examples of words consistently written differently in the Sinographic documents of Heian court officials and Buddhist monks. *Hyōbyaku ganmon no buntai*, 580–89.

everyday speech. However, other types of everyday, non-literary inscription circulated through practices that, while employing functionally similar forms of *kundoku* literacy, posited a different relationship between script and vocalization, allowing for the transcription or incorporation of Japanese terminology and constructions outside of canonical literary Sinitic. Thus, the language of literary Sinitic *kundoku* recitation is differentiated, not only from recitation in Sinitic pronunciation, but also from another register of Japanese discourse inscribable through the everyday style—a lexicon of "colloquial" language at home in both oral and written quotidian usage. In this respect the language of *kundoku* recitation resembles Dante's "high vernacular" (*vulgare illustre*), which paradoxically is shared and recognized among all Italians, yet can be traced back to no particular region of the country since the populace of each possesses unacceptable impurities in their actual speech; at the root of both is a fundamental imaginative break positing the existence of a unifying standard of elegance that is defined by its identification and rejection of an indecorous counterpart.[46]

The emergence of contractual commendations in the mid-Heian does not derive from some sort of degradation of the older, *ganmon*-based format, but rather a shift in generic consciousness that led to the abandoning of one style of writing (literary) for another (everyday), the two of which already possessed a long parallel history within Japan.[47] This shift was doubtless motivated by the growing use of commendations in the field of law, which had its own vocabulary grounded in customary, colloquial usage. Through the mid-Heian, property transfers, including wills, were conducted by oral testimony. Deeds from this period do not themselves effect the transfer but rather testify to witnessing the essentially oral act, so that the witnesses could be summoned at a later date to confirm the fact if necessary. Watanabe Shigeru suggests that it is only during the mid-Heian that document wills gradually transition from the exception (for cases when property moves "outside the family," such as donation to a temple) to the rule.[48] In such cases, where the written

46. Dante, *De vulgari eloquentia*, 2–3, 38–41.

47. On the early history of the two styles, see Lurie, *Realms of Literacy*, 214–25.

48. Watanabe Shigeru, *Kodai, chūsei no jōhō dentatsu*, 84–126. The same transition from oral act to sealed document can be observed in medieval English wills. Clanchy, *Memory to Written Record*, 256.

document is predicated on an oral pronouncement, the need to be faithful to the exact terms of the original agreement must have encouraged the use of colloquial terminology in writing.

Parallel phenomena are in fact common in other medieval cultures. Following the Norman Conquest, legal documents in England were almost all written in Latin through the thirteenth century. Despite this shift, however, the Domesday Book (1086) as well as later legal treatises and court memoranda are littered with English terminology for property, crimes, and social positions.[49] We are sometimes told that in Heian Japan Chinese was the language of religion and law, but in contrast with the cosmopolitan standard of literary Sinitic used in ritual, law tended toward the vernacular.[50] Nevertheless, this local "colloquial" is not a preexisting stratum of pure Yamato speech. The language of property and law found in mid-Heian commendations instead shows a complex hybridity incorporating local inventions and re-appropriations of literary Sinitic terminology. Terms such as *shobun* 處分 (disposition [of property]) or *rusudokoro* 留守所 (local office [of an absentee governor]) suggest the ways that "colloquial" language was not transcribed by but instead created through the everyday style of inscription.

Such colloquial legal terminology is almost completely absent from commendations written in parallel prose. Eleventh- and twelfth-century commendation documents generally display either colloquial legal terminology or the decorative patterning of parallel prose, not both, suggesting an antithetical relationship between literary form and legal discourse. The use of commendations as a means of establishing ownership claims pulled such documents out of the realm of ritual, where the literary ornamentation of prayer texts facilitated the cycle of symbolic exchange, and into the lawsuit, where evidentiary goals necessitated the reproduction of customary terminology alien to orthodox literary Sinitic. The "mistakes" in Motozane's and especially Korenaka's commendations preserve longstanding, orally based legal practices and language.

49. Woodbine, "Language of English Law," 405, 416–19.

50. Not coincidentally, the transmission of Tang legal discourse to Japan made heavy use of Chinese vernacular language as an interpretive medium, fossils of which are preserved in the Nara administrative codes. Kuranaka, "Risturyō, bukkyō, bungaku," 35–38.

Through *kundoku* literacy, all three of the documents discussed above are equally legible in some form of Japanese-based vocalization, but while the ornamented literary Sinitic of Tadahira's prayer demanded recitation in the high vernacular of ritual performance, Korenaka's commendation incorporates another register of discourse associated with the colloquial speech of everyday use. The close identification of literary writing with a limited idiom of elegant language meant that the growing incentive to incorporate vernacular legal terminology into commendations thus encouraged a concomitant abandonment of literary, parallel prose. Such examples show that through the practice of literary inscription, Heian writers were confronted not simply with "translation" problems between the Japanese and Chinese languages, but rather undertook a complex negotiation of the relationship between script and speech that served both to mark off a realm of the "vernacular" and to differentiate levels within it. The next section will take up one of the most explicit Heian examinations of this set of problems in the pages of a tenth-century encyclopedia, to show how literary language came to be defined through a contradictory union of Tang exemplars and vernacular speech.

The Princess's Encyclopedia

Compared to alphabetic scripts, or the heavy admixture of *kana* in modern Japanese prose, the use of Sinographs alone to write Japanese logographically may feel counterintuitive or inherently limited. Certainly, from the beginning writers on the archipelago often resorted to transcribing certain words—proper names, or names of native fauna—using Sinographs for their sound values instead of their meaning. The same technique had been adopted by early propagators of Buddhist sutras in China, who sometimes transliterated Sanskrit terms with Sinographs instead of translating their meaning (for example, the Sanskrit *bodhi*, a term for enlightenment, transcribed as 菩提 [Middle Chinese bɔdɛj] using two characters originally representing the name of a plant and the verb "to carry").[51] The use of

51. Early Middle Chinese reconstruction from Pulleyblank, *Lexicon of Reconstructed Pronunciation*. The term *bodhi* appears in the *Da zhidu lun* 大智度論 (Commentary on

modified Sinographs as Japanese phonographs—the shorthand syllabary of *kana*—was only gradually adapted to more prosaic idioms. A few examples of letters and petitions written mostly in *kana* survive from the mid-eighth century onward, but it was not until the mid-Heian that substantial prose texts came to be produced in *kana*.[52]

As we have seen above, throughout the Heian, logographic writing remained the default mode of inscription in most contexts. Even so, some forms of language could throw up severe hurdles to written communication:

> When Councilor [Ōe no] Koretoki first became a chamberlain, he prepared for planting the emperor's garden by writing out the names of the flowers, but was laughed at for writing many in *kana*. Hearing this, Koretoki said, "If I wrote their real graphs [*jitsuji* 實字], no one could read them." Later, the emperor summoned Koretoki and had him prepare a list of the garden plants to examine, saying he should use Sinographs [*kanji* 漢字]. Koretoki drew up the list on the spot, but the others could not read even one of the names, and quickly begged Koretoki's help. He said, "This is why I used *kana* the other day, so what did you laugh at me for?"[53]

As discussed in the previous chapter, *kunten* glossing focused on syntactic relationships and tended to translate verbs into vernacular equivalents. The names of things—proper names, but also plants, animals, and other objects of mundane experience—could be much more difficult. How to know which of a hundred flowers in a Chinese encyclopedia corresponds to the one in your yard? The anecdote of Koretoki's gardening reflects the ineluctable reappearance of local language and the difficulty of establishing reliable equivalencies with orthodox literary Sinitic usage.

---

the Great Perfection of Wisdom, trans. early fifth century) as an example of the difference in morphology between the languages of China (Qin) and those of India (Sindhu) in which "graphs [*sic*] combine to make a word." *Taishō shinshū daizōkyō* 1509 (25:380).

52. In literary history, Ki no Tsurayuki's 紀貫之 (d. 945) ca. 905 preface to the *Kokin wakashū* and ca. 935 *Tosa nikki* 土佐日記 (Tosa Diary) are often pointed to as the first datable works of *kana* prose.

53. *Kojidan* 6.40. *Makura no sōshi* contrasts the "adorable" appearance of the flower *kamatsuka* (unidentified) with how "unpleasant" its name is written out in characters. "Kusa no hana wa," 120.

Wamyō ruijushō (Categorical Miscellany of Yamato Names) is an encyclopedia from this context, a peculiar lexicographical assembly whose entries attempt to bridge the gap between vernacular language and the literary Sinitic canon. According to the compiler Minamoto no Shitagō's preface, the work was commissioned by Emperor Daigo's daughter, Princess Kinshi 勤子内親王 (904–38), to address the inadequacies and unreliability of contemporary dictionaries of Japanese vocabulary. The preface explains that Kinshi, in mourning for her late father Daigo, has given up music and now passes the time with painting and calligraphy. She has thus developed an interest in the "myriad names of things," but is frustrated by the lack of information about "Yamato names" in Chinese anthologies (*Wenguan cilin*) and encyclopedias (*Baishi liutie shilei* 白氏六帖事類, "Mr. Bai's Six-Fascicle Encyclopedia," ninth century). She knows of a few Japanese books that deal with "questions about the everyday world": the *Benshiki ryūjō* 辨色立成 (Handbook for Distinguishing Appearances) and *Yōshi Kango shō* 楊氏漢語抄 (Mr. Yō's Lexicon of Chinese), two eighth-century dictionaries of Sinographs with short definitions combining literary Sinitic glosses and Japanese translations; *Honzō wamyō* 本草和名 (Materia Medica with Yamato Names), a 918 revision of the Chinese *Xinxiu bencao* 新修本草 (659) glossed with Japanese translations for the various plants; and the *Nihongi shiki* 日本紀私記 (Private Notes on the *Nihon shoki*), a set of expository notes (mostly focused on *kundoku* reading) produced in conjunction with official lectures in 904 on the *Nihon shoki* 日本書紀 (Chronicle of Japan; 720), Japan's oldest official history.[54] These works are, however, too short, too specialized in their purview, unclear in their sources, or riddled with falsehoods. Shitagō is tasked with sifting out the reliable information to resolve her confusion.

The encyclopedia is arranged in hierarchically nested sets under broad categories of Heaven and Earth, Humans, the Body, the Arts, Buildings, Vehicles, Clothing, etc. A typical entry consists of a headword, a citation of a definition or a usage of the term from a Chinese text (most frequently a rhyming dictionary such as the *Tangyun* 唐韻, 751), and commentary

54. Information on these sources can be found in the footnotes to the translation of the preface in Appendix B.

noting a Sinitic pronunciation and a Japanese *kundoku* reading, usually labeled as a "Yamato name" (*wamyō* or *yamatona* 和名).[55]

> Aurora: The *Tangyun* states, Aurora <pronounced KA,[56] Yamato name *kasumi*> means a reddish cloud.[57]
>
> 霞。唐韻云、霞〈胡加反。和名、賀須美〉赤氣雲也。

This entry for the word *kasumi* (mist) cites the definition and *fanqie* pronunciation guide for the Sinograph *ka* 霞 (LMC xɦja:) from the *Tangyun*, and interpolates into it the Japanese translation *kasumi* (both the Sinitic pronunciation and Yamato name are written as double-column interlinear commentary, enclosed with angle brackets here). The work thus affirms a one-to-one correspondence between an item of literary Sinitic vocabulary and a vernacular word (transcribed syllabically in phonographs). The entry also makes clear the immediate problem of any translingual dictionary: lexical items in different languages rarely allow for one-to-one correspondence. The association of the Japanese word *kasumi* with the Sinograph *ka* 霞 was well established by Shitagō's day, but the primary sense of the word in canonical Chinese texts, the reddish haze of dawn and dusk, only partially overlapped with the semantic field of *kasumi* in Japanese.

The intended application of Shitagō's work is not entirely clear. It assigns "Yamato" readings to Sinographs, but its categorical organization limits its utility as a reference dictionary for readers: the contemporary *Shinsen jikyō* 新撰字鏡 (Newly Selected Mirror of Characters) and the

55. The *Wamyō ruijushō* has a complicated textual history: there are two main lineages of the text, one in ten volumes and a larger one in twenty, but both seem to have circulated in parallel already in the mid-Heian, and extant manuscripts are late or incomplete. I use examples from entries that show no significant difference between the two lineages, relying on Mabuchi, *Koshahon "Wamyō ruijushō" shūsei*, but for ease of reference cite the widely published *Senchū Wamyō ruijushō*, an edition of the ten-volume text.

56. Here and below, all pronunciation guides are represented as *kan'on* readings, following the late Heian *kana* transcriptions in the Heian *Mengqiu* MS known as "Chōshō-bon Mōgyū" (see Tsukishima, *Chōshō-bon Mōgyū*, and Numoto, "Goon kan'on bunrui hyō"). As in this case, many of the pronunciations are given in the *fanqie* (J. *hanzetsu*) format, where the first character indicates the initial consonant, and the second the syllable's rhyme.

57. *Senchū Wamyō ruijushō* 1.22a.

late Heian *Ruijū myōgishō* 類聚名義抄 (Categorical Miscellany of Names and Meanings), by contrast, are both organized by character shape, for quickly looking up an unknown character. Fujiwara no Yukinari records lending the encyclopedia to his eleven-year-old son Yoshitsune 良經 (1001–58) along with the elementary textbook *Kuchizusami*, suggesting that the work was primarily viewed as a primer for reading through, rather than a reference work to be consulted at need.[58]

Each entry is based upon a definition or usage example, almost always cited from a Chinese source. These make up the bulk of each entry, while the "Yamato names" are consigned to double-column annotation, visually presented as a supplement to the Sinitic pronunciation guides. Nevertheless, it is the Japanese words that actually organize the work, as entries such as the following make clear:

> Skylark: Cui Yuxi's *Dietary Classic* states, The skylark resembles a sparrow, only larger. <[Yamato name is] *hibari*.> *Yōshi Kango shō* states, Oriole <Pronounced SAUKAU. The reading is the same as above>.[59]
>
> 雲雀。崔禹錫食經云、雲雀似雀而大〈比波里〉楊氏漢語抄云、鶬鶊〈倉庚二音。訓上同〉。

Here we have two different literary Sinitic compounds (referring in fact to two different birds) brought together into one entry because they are translated by the same *kundoku* reading in earlier sources. The Japanese terminology of *Wamyō ruijushō* is largely harvested from the earlier dictionaries mentioned in the preface, so the compilation of Chinese source citations would have been Shitagō's most extensive task as editor, but in many cases their definitional value is almost nil:

> Quail: *Tangyun* states, Quail <Pronounced BU. *Kango shō* states, Bunting is *shitoto*>, the name of a bird.[60]
>
> 鵐鳥。唐韻云、鵐〈音巫。漢語抄云、巫鳥、之止止〉鳥名也。

58. *Gonki*, Kankō 8 (1011)/11/20 (2:207–8). *Kuchizusami* is discussed in the previous chapter.

59. *Senchū Wamyō ruijushō* 7.27a.

60. Ibid. 7.17a.

The earlier Japanese dictionary *Kango shō* uses the Sinographs 巫鳥 (literally "shaman bird") to write the word *shitoto* (bunting), an orthographic usage that appears in *Nihon shoki*.[61] Rather than citing *Nihon shoki*, however, Shitagō finds a bird listed in *Tangyun* whose Sinograph coincidentally contains the same sound-element, 巫, and provides that as the entry's source, based entirely on the orthographic coincidence (the character 䳜 is extremely rare, but classical dictionaries alternately define it as a kind of sparrow or quail).

While the citations Shitagō provides are sometimes definitional, they supply meaning only incidentally. Instead, their primary function is to establish the limits of standard orthography, locating the inscription of "Yamato names" within a unified, trans-regional sphere of writing. As he explains in his introduction, Shitagō is very aware that Sinographic orthography in Japan is plagued by "errors," which the encyclopedia seeks to correct:

> Cedar. *Glosses on the Erya* states, Cedar <Pronounced SAN, or alternatively SEN. [The reading] *sugi* is found in *Nihongi shiki*. Editor's note: popularly the character 椙 is used, but this is incorrect. 椙 is pronounced UN and means "pillar." This is found in the *Tangyun*.> resembles pine. It grows south of the Yangtze, and can be used in boat construction.[62]
>
> 杉。爾雅音義云、杉〈音衫、一音纖。須岐、見日本紀私記。今案、俗用椙字、非也。椙於粉反、柱也。見唐韻〉似松、生江南、可以爲船材矣。

The character 椙, frequently used in Heian documents to write the name of the local *sugi* (Japanese cedar, *Cryptomeria japonica*) tree, is defined as "pillar" in Chinese dictionaries, so Shitagō instead offers the character 杉 (in Tang usage, a generic term for tall conifers such as *Cunninghamia lanceolata*) as the "correct" orthography. Many entries, however, reveal the

61. *Nihon shoki*, 3:397. The original rationale behind this orthography is far from clear, but two pieces of evidence—the appearance in *Kogo shūi* of a kind of shaman with the same name, and the mysterious word *kōnaishitoto* カウナイシトヽ in *Ruijū myōgishō*—suggest that the bird was associated with the divinatory practices of religious figures called *kannagi*. See *Kogo shūi*, 53, 112; *Ruijū myōgishō*, 1170.

62. *Senchū Wamyō ruijushō* 10.96b.

difficulties Shitagō encountered in trying to achieve a neat correspondence between the Japanese vernacular and orthodox literary Sinitic usage:

> Cuckoo: *Man'yōshū* states, Cuckoo <read as *yobukodori*>.[63]
> 喚子鳥。萬葉集云、喚子鳥〈其讀與不古止里〉。

The *yobukodori* is a bird that appears in ancient song (generally thought to correspond to the cuckoo, modern Japanese *kakkō*). Rather than cite a Chinese source as in most entries, Shitagō here provides a citation from a *waka* collection. The orthography of the header is also exceptional: the morphemes of the name *yobukodori* are roughly homophonous with "calling child bird" in Japanese, and here the word is written with three Sinographs combined for the sound value of their respective *kundoku* readings: 喚 ("call," *yobu*), 子 ("child," *ko*), and 鳥 ("bird," *tori*). The compound is a local application of Sinographs that cannot be found in the literary Sinitic canon.

In the preface to the encyclopedia, Shitagō acknowledges the necessity of resorting to such "provisional characters" (*kaji* 假字). He defends this expedient by referring to Xu Shen's 許慎 *Shuowen jiezi* 說文解字 (ca. 121), one of the earliest and most canonical Chinese dictionaries, which identifies "borrowed orthography" (*kasha*, Ch. *jiajie* 假借) as one of the six forms of Sinograph etymology. In Xu Shen's scheme, borrowing seems to refer to the process by which pictographic characters were adapted to write homophonous words of a more abstract nature, the latter not easily communicated through images—the character for the negative *wu* 無 (not have), for example, can be traced back to a depiction of a person dancing, originally used to write a homophonous word meaning "dance."[64] Shitagō further points out that similar methods were used in China for the transcription of Sanskrit words, but despite these authoritative precedents, he clearly has reservations regarding such "provisional" forms of orthography:

63. Ibid. 7.18b.

64. For a lucid discussion of Xu Shen's six categories of etymology, see Qiu, *Chinese Writing*, 151–63. For two recent arguments connecting Japanese writing and *kundoku* to Xu Shen's paradigm, see Lurie, *Realms of Literacy*, 334–42; Saitō, *Kanji sekai no chihei*, 80–92.

Scow. *Shiming* states, A long [boat] with a shallow hull is called a scow <Pronounced TAI. Editor's note: [Yamato name is] *hirata*, popularly [the characters] 平田舟 are used>.[65]

艜。釋名云、艇薄而長者曰艜〈當蓋反、與帶同。今案比良太、俗用平田舟〉。

In this case, Shitagō has located a definition in a Chinese dictionary that seems to describe a type of boat called a *hirata* or *hiratabune* in Japanese, thus establishing a connection with the rather obscure Sinograph 艜. He supplies an editor's note, however, admitting that in practice, people tend to use the Sinographs 平田舟 instead. These characters literally mean "flat rice-paddy boat," but their individual *kundoku* readings can be combined to form *hira-ta-bune*. The characters in popular usage are much more elementary, and simple to parse with even basic *kundoku* literacy, but form a nonsensical compound if read as literary Sinitic, making another "error" Shitagō's encyclopedia is compelled to correct.

In this last example, the conflict between "popular" usage and Shitagō's orthodoxy is made explicit. This is an exceptional case, however. In most instances, Shitagō silently elides the realities of customary practice at odds with the canon of literary Sinitic authorities:

Golden Ox. The "Record of Yidu" states, At Golden Ox Shallows a man pulls a golden ox <*Benshiki ryūjō* calls it *ameuji*>.[66]

黄牛。宜都記云、黄牛灘、有人牽黄牛〈辨色立成云、阿女宇之〉。

The term *ameuji* refers to a kind of amber-colored ox with auspicious connotations, used in certain geomantic rituals in the Heian period. They are mentioned repeatedly in Fujiwara no Michinaga's diary, but often he resorts to the orthography 天牛 (literally "sky ox"), based on the conventional association of the character *ten* 天 with the *kundoku* reading *ame* (sky).[67] Such examples of Sinographs employed primarily for the sounds

65. *Senchū Wamyō ruijushō* 3.58a.

66. Ibid. 7.80b.

67. The character *kō* 黄 (yellow) has no such association with the reading *ame*. This example is discussed in Minegishi Akira, "Kanji no teikun," 55.

(rather than the meaning) of their Japanese *kundoku* readings, what David Lurie calls "vernacular phonographs," are ubiquitous in quotidian writing, but violate the orthographic standards *Wamyō ruijushō* seeks to establish.[68]

Efforts to regulate customary usage and legitimate particular orthographies were not new to the tenth century. As Lurie notes, both *Kojiki* and *Nihon shoki* reject the use of vernacular phonographs in transcribing *waka* poetry in order to "maintain more formal registers" of inscription.[69] A particularly visible locus of anxiety over the proper inscription of language can be found in place names. These naturally are not susceptible to translations or expedient equivalencies in the way the common nouns found in *Wamyō ruijushō* are, and the question of how they were to be inscribed was not trivial.[70] In the eighth-century *shi* anthology *Kaifūsō*, phonographic transcriptions of Japanese place names, some including vernacular phonographs, appear frequently in titles, and occasionally even within the body of poems:

- "Pursuing the immortal's path,/I accompany him to the banks of Yoshino" 欲訪神仙迹、追從吉野潯.
- "The clouds wrap round Mifune Valley" 雲卷三舟谷.
- "Hie is truly a divine mountain" 裨叡寔神山.[71]

Such examples are already exceptional within the collection. More common is the replacement of a local toponym with a Chinese analogue:

68. Of course, there is usually a residual semantic component as well: we might imagine that the *ameuji*'s ritual use influenced Michinaga's "heaven cow" orthography, while conversely the character *u* 雨 (rain) is never employed in this context, despite its homophonous *kundoku* reading, *ame*. A parallel problem to such vernacular phonographs occurs with so-called *kokuji*, domestically invented characters not found in the Chinese corpus (e.g., 鰯 for *iwashi*, the sardine). These too Shitagō only resorts to when unable to locate another attested orthography for the word.

69. Lurie, *Realms of Literacy*, 266.

70. The twenty-volume recension of *Wamyō ruijushō* is itself one of the most important sources for Heian place names, but as the date of this expansion is not clear, I have not treated these in the analysis.

71. *Kaifūsō* 48, 80, and 105.

- "Flowering plants float across Yao Lake" 瑤水花藻陳.
- "Unexpectedly blessed with an imperial command,/I accompanied his carriage to springtime Shanglin" 不期逐恩詔、從駕上林春.[72]

Here the lake and garden of the imperial residence are granted elegant sobriquets. By the ninth century, reference to places through descriptive epithets ("the villa by the River," "the Great Lake"), or by an adopted Chinese name (such as a series of poems on Heyang/Kaya 河陽) had become standard, with the name of the event's actual location confined to the prose title statement (*hashizukuri*) before the poem.[73] In mid-Heian *shi* and parallel prose, only place names derived from literary Sinitic vocabulary (such as those of temples and certain official residences) appear unaltered in the body text. Local names are replaced by convenient continental equivalents (Luoyang for the capital is a ubiquitous example), or altered to fit conventions of literary Sinitic inscription (province names are shortened and the suffix *shū* 州, "state," added, so that Owari 尾張 for example becomes Bishū 尾州).[74]

Nor was this attention to toponym orthography limited to the realm of poetry. A 713 order demanded that all districts and townships use two auspicious Sinographs to write their name, and at the end of the century Emperor Kanmu (r. 781–806) ordered that the province Yamashiro be written 山城 ("mountain castle") instead of 山背 ("back of the mountains") to provide a suitably noble location for his new capital of Heian ("tranquil peace").[75] The most famous examples involve the name of the

72. Ibid. 14 and 18. On the treatment of Japanese place names in *Kaifūsō*, see also Denecke, "Bilingual Landscapes."

73. See for example *Bunka shūreishū* 1, 8, and 96–99. This remained standard practice through the early modern period. See, e.g., Miura, *Shitetsu*, 154–55.

74. A parallel phenomenon is the so-called "Tang names" (*tōmei*) used in place of conventional official post titles within poetry and other literary contexts. See Kudō, "Heianchō ni okeru kanshoku tōmei."

75. Kobayashi, "Heijōkyū mokkan," 167; Denecke, *Classical World Literatures*, 169. In the early ninth century, Emperor Saga broke with prior tradition by naming his newborn son Masara, written with the characters 正良 ("correct" and "good"). Whereas previous imperial princes were called by the surname of their nurse, hereafter all would be assigned a name written with two auspicious Sinographs. Hashimoto Yoshihiko, *Heian kizoku*, 237–39.

state itself, as Nippon, "the source of the sun," was adopted in correspondence with the Tang empire, and the older name of Yamato came to be written using the character *wa* 和 (peaceful) instead of the homophonous ethnonym 倭 found in early Chinese sources.[76]

Wamyō ruijushō's efforts at orthographic correctness thus continue a central ideological project of early Japan, part of a current in the East Asian intellectual tradition focused on the moral obligation for correct inscription and the ritual ramifications of signs.[77] The projection of a universalized formal standard, with its most immediate basis in Tang norms, is furthermore consistent with the prescriptive discourse of *bunshō* examined in chapter 3. However, because *Wamyō ruijushō* is an encyclopedia of "Yamato names," its discursive purview cannot be limited simply to classical standards of writing, but must venture into questions of the relationship between local speech and script; the perhaps inadvertent consequence of Shitagō's project is to subject the realm of "vernacular" language posited by *kundoku* logography to new and destabilizing questions.

As seen in the above entries, *Wamyō ruijushō* generally seeks to establish a one-to-one relationship between a Japanese word and a Sinograph, fixing a kind of authoritative orthography. However, certain entries display a troubled ambiguity regarding the referential significance of the "Yamato names" themselves:

> Scales: *Tangyun* states, Scales <Pronounced RIN. [Yamato name is] *irokuzu*. Popularly called *iroko*.> are the shell of fish.[78]
> 鱗。唐韻云、鱗〈音鄰。以呂久都。俗云伊呂古〉魚甲也。

If we think of the "Yamato names" supplied by *Wamyō ruijushō* simply as translations into a preexisting vernacular, the distinction here between *irokuzu* and *iroko* is unclear. Entries like the following, however, suggest consciousness of a divide between the language of reading (*kundoku* recitation) and the language of everyday speech:

76. On the history of Japan's name, see Kōnoshi, *"Nihon" to wa nani ka*.
77. On the "rectification of names" in the early Japanese state, see Abé, *Weaving of Mantra*, 310–15, and Hérail, *Cour du Japon*, 52–55.
78. *Senchū Wamyō ruijushō* 8.31a.

Madness: The *Tang Administrative Code* states, Madmen and drunkards are ineligible for posts in the Imperial Guard <癲 is pronounced TEN. 狂 is read as *taburu*. Popularly called *monogurui*>.

癲狂。唐令云、癲狂酗酒、皆不得居侍衞之官〈癲音天。狂訓太布流。俗云毛乃久流比〉。

Ascent: *Tangyun* states, ascent <Pronounced SIYO. . . . The "Rhapsody on Pheasant Shooting" in *Wenxuan* has "flap their wings" [read as] *hafuru*. Popularly called *hatsutsu*> is taking flight.

飛翥。唐韻云、翥〈音恕. . . . 文選射雉賦云、軒翥、波布流。俗云波都々〉飛擧也。

Fruit: *Tangyun* states, [according to] *Shuowen* [*jiezi*], in the trees it is called hanging-fruit <Also written with the character 菓. *Nihongi shiki* calls it *konomi*. Popularly called *kudamono*>, on the ground it is called melon.[79]

果蓏。唐韻云、説文、木上曰果〈字或作菓。日本紀私記云古乃美。俗云久太毛乃〉地上曰蓏。

In these examples, Shitagō first provides a Japanese reading derived from *kundoku* recitation practices applied to canonical texts from China and Japan, but then supplements this reading with another translation based on popular or colloquial (*zoku* 俗) usage. The language of Shitagō's "Yamato names" is first and foremost the language of *kundoku* recitation, but many of the terms employed therein were archaic or rarified.[80] Entries such as the above expose the gap Shitagō perceived between the recitation idiom and colloquial speech, which necessitated the intervention of a supplementary explanation.

Shitagō's conception of the colloquial illustrates the complex conditions regulating the linguistic range of *kundoku*. As detailed in chapter 4, academy texts glossed in the mid-Heian display marked tendencies in

79. Ibid. 2.68a, 7.48b, 9.56a.

80. On the category of *zoku* in *Wamyō ruijushō*, see especially Tsukishima, "*Wamyō ruijushō* no wakun," and Ōtomo and Eguchi, "*Wamyō ruijushō* no sei-zoku-tsū." There is a tantalizing parallel in the distinction of "folk names" 俗云 from "local names" 郷名 in the Koryŏ botanical text *Hyangyak kugŭppang* 鄉藥救急方 (Prescriptions of Local Botanicals for Emergency Use, ca. 1236). See Suh, "Herbs of Our Own Kingdom," 406–10.

the readings they record, tending to limit vernacular translation to verbs and the addition of particles, while substantives were most often read in a Sinitic-derived pronunciation. Within *kundoku* recitation, compounds read in Sinitic enhanced the performative impact through the retention of certain auditory qualities (such as alliteration or assonance).[81] Furthermore, as depicted in *Wamyō ruijushō* and confirmed by extant manuscripts, even when vernacular translations were employed in *kundoku*, the restricted Japanese lexicon used was itself often highly archaic, implying that immediate auditory comprehensibility was not necessarily the primary motivation.[82]

Although the concept of vernacular translation as it is now understood implies a functional replacement of the original text, *kundoku* recitation certainly does not; the canonical text is present and unchanged, even as it is transformed through its projection into an auditory register. Furthermore, the distance preserved between *kundoku* language and conversational speech indicates that these practices also cannot be understood as pursuing a fundamentally interpretive goal, parsing a Chinese text for the comprehension of a Japanese audience. Certainly, as the Tenryaku manuscript discussed in chapter 4 shows, the production of a vernacular reading relied on a series of interpretive decisions. Nevertheless, the efforts by Shitagō and others to regulate the language of recitation, marking off correct "Yamato" readings from a wider lexographical network connecting Sinographs with the vernacular, suggest that as *kundoku* became systematized through education (and externalized in *kunten*-glossed manuscripts), academic recitation developed its own independent and performance-oriented principles.[83]

81. On the preservation of Chinese auditory effects through the use of *on'yomi* within *kundoku*, see Ōta, "Kangakuin no suzume," 234–35.

82. On archaic language in *kundoku*, see Tsukishima, *Heian jidai no kanbun kundokugo*, 58–74, 128–81. Shitagō relies on official lectures on the *Nihon shoki* for many of his readings because the rarified language of these lectures differed from typical academy and Buddhist *kundoku* practice in its effort to utilize an exclusively Yamato lexicon, thereby providing many more of the nouns Shitagō's encyclopedia focuses on. Kōnoshi Takamitsu provides a useful analysis of the "fictionality" of *Nihon shoki* recitation's archaistic language. *Hensōsareru "Nihon shoki,"* 185–202.

83. The connection of *kundoku* to recitation performance rather than individual comprehension is also suggested by the tendency to refrain from glossing portions of the text that were not vocalized in recitation. This can be seen in the commentary sections

In this sense, rather than serving as a local replacement or exegesis of a foreign text, *kundoku* functions as a necessary preliminary step giving life to the text. Recitation is not the endpoint of interpretation but instead "a prerequisite for meaning since it is the text-as-read which is the object of interpretation."[84] The practices surrounding recitation in early Japan suggest a complex structure of recapitulation, in which Sinographic texts were given audible form in a "vernacular" utterance that was both the product of a process of interpretation (externalized through *kunten* and committed to memory, or assembled by the reader from patterns acquired in the study of canonical texts) as well as itself the object of supplementary explication through a freer and more colloquial idiom. Many Heian-period ceremonies are structured around a deferred moment of interpretation; public recitation of a text in *kundoku* was almost always followed by an "explication" of some sort, such as the *rongi* 論議 of the biannual Sekiten ceremony or the *seppō* 説法 at the conclusion of Buddhist assemblies.[85] This pattern is consistent with Maurice Bloch's characterization of the "formalization" of authoritative language. Ceremonies are able to exert authority through an artificial code dependent on repetition and restriction of communicative freedom. Because formalized speech is thus "impoverished," it needs to be supplemented by other forms of communication.[86] The apparent limitations of *kundoku* when viewed from a modern conception of "translation" are not coincidental flaws, but integral to its function as ritualized linguistic performance, drawing upon and reinforcing the authority of valorized texts.

To summarize, *Wamyō ruijushō*'s survey of local "names" constructs a discourse of legitimation. Surveying the multifaceted possibilities of

of the Tenryaku MS, but also the table (*biao* 表) and treatise (*shu* 書 or *zhi* 志) volumes of Chinese dynastic histories, which were not lectured upon. Hiranaka, "Yonezawa no Sōhan Zengo Kanjo," 13.

84. Irvine, *Making of Textual Culture*, 70.

85. *Engi shiki* 20.521–22; Komine, *Chūsei hōe bungeiron*, 284. The contents of an assembly's explication corresponded to the preceding prayer text (ibid., 27–28). Kanegae Hiroyuki finds a similar process of ceremonial recitation followed by colloquial explanation in the promulgation of Nara-period directives from the capital to the provinces ("Kōtō dentatsu no shosō"). Examples of the recitation-comment structure in later literature are discussed in Horton, "Japanese Spirit and Chinese Learning," 167, 172.

86. Bloch, introduction to *Political Language and Oratory*, 12–17, 26.

inscription on Heian Japan (where a commendation document might as easily be written in Tang-style parallel prose or a local legal idiom illegible as Chinese), the dictionary defines through exclusion a field of correct, universalized orthography and prestigious, ceremonial speech. Just as the orthography Shitagō mobilizes corresponds to the canonical standard of usage found in Heian *bunshō* writing, script's relationship to speech is circumscribed within the realm of formalized recitation. The media of this orthography and language—Chinese classics and dictionaries, national histories, and official lectures—locate the regulation of representational authority squarely within the pedagogical traditions of the State Academy, where Shitagō and other Heian scholars were trained. In its inscription and again in its recitation, a literary Sinitic document thus entails a reaffirmation of this difference, the production of a distinction that simultaneously is overseen by and validates one group of officials within court society.

Conclusion: The Audible Literary

Writing in early Japan was aurally experienced through a multilayered mechanism of vocalization practices, employing both Sinitic prestige dialects and more or less standardized idioms of formal Japanese. Among these, *kundoku* recitation into a rarified "vernacular" was the primary form of reception for both imported and domestic texts in literary Sinitic. As seen in *Sakumon daitai*, such reading practices could in turn undermine or transform the aesthetics of *bunshō* compositional practice, as auditory features of Sinitic pronunciation were lost. The mid-Heian rejection of ornamental literary Sinitic for legalistic commendations, however, shows the limits of the "vernacularization" of *bunshō*: rather than freely incorporating legal terminology, literary prose was abandoned in favor of the everyday style. The reasons for this are suggested by the legitimating rationales employed in *Wamyō ruijushō*, which defines correct orthography and recitation in opposition to colloquial usage. It is not that addressing legal concerns per se precludes the use of literary ornament, but rather that the literary is differentiated precisely by the systematic exclusion of a negatively defined realm of common (*zoku*) language in both inscription and recitation.[87]

Kundoku recitation can be understood as a ritualization of the (canonically authorized) written word, emphasizing or inventing its difference from other modes of language. As historians of writing have argued, technologies of inscription, literacy pedagogy, and the tendency of written forms to become self-replicating patterns all encourage a persistent disjuncture between written language (sometimes called a "grapholect") and oral language, even if the writing is in a colloquial mother tongue.[88] In the case of literary Sinitic's use in Heian Japan, the linguistic gap between inscription and quotidian speech could hardly be larger, but *kundoku* "glossing" reopens the potential for equivalency between the two, and even allows a limited form of transcription of colloquial speech through the "everyday style" seen in Korenaka's commendation and numerous other mid-Heian documents.[89] The ritualized practices of recitation, however, counteract this potential, re-inscribing the difference between script and speech at a different level by employing a rarified and sometimes archaic vernacular, marked by its deviation from the colloquial. The ornamented idiom of *bunshō* inscription demanded recitation through a similarly formalized register of "vernacular" language, for it was in ritual performance that the text could coordinate symbolic exchanges among sponsor, reader, and audience.

The blurring of the definitions of correct and literary inscription occasioned by *kundoku* literacy, once opened up, could never be completely restored. *Kundoku* recitation was based on the principle of a preexisting literary Sinitic text performed in a high vernacular, but the audible aesthetic of such recitation could then be reverse-engineered for mimicry and appropriation in documents far outside the prescriptive

87. Shitagō's formulation in this sense mirrors Kukai's distinction between patterned literature (*bunshō*) and "common language" (see chapter 3).

88. Ong, *Orality and Literacy*, 105–8.

89. Extant early examples of "vernacular" Japanese prose are filled with peculiar circumlocutions and other seemingly unnatural constructions, which have often been analyzed as examples of "translationese" or Chinese influence. For a thoughtful essay problematizing distinctions between "colloquial" and "translated" constructions in early Japanese documents, see Okumura, "Hanasu koto to kaku koto."

boundaries of orthodox literary Sinitic genres. Thus we find works such as Motozane's commendation incorporating parallelism as formal decoration. While other formal characteristics of the literary (rhyme, tonal prosody, literary allusion) were difficult to convey in *kundoku* recitation, parallel constructions retained a peculiar rhythm that marked them off from ordinary speech.

Examining the idiom of formal *kundoku* recitation as a prestige dialect at variance with common usage suggests important parallels with developments elsewhere in East Asia. Partially in response to a growing awareness of linguistic variation during the political upheavals and migrations of the early middle ages, Chinese literati such as Yan Zhitui 顏之推 (531–ca. 591) developed linguistic standards dependent on a "determinant logic of textual authority," in which "spoken language itself is generated by a prior textuality."[90] Rhyme dictionaries such as the *Qieyun* are the most obvious example of a discourse of prescriptivism that fostered a rarified, standardized system of pronunciation. John Phan has recently argued that such works catalyzed the development of a "self-conscious Sinitic diglossia" across medieval China and peripheral regions like Annam (Vietnam), with an artificial set of pronunciations, distinguished from spoken Chinese dialects, employed in belletristic writing and other prestigious cultural venues.[91] Unlike Annam, Heian Japan lacked a significant Sinophone community, but there too this split is echoed in the ninth-century state's denigration of established Sinitic-based pronunciation traditions in favor of "Han pronunciation" (*kan'on*). As Günther Wenck long ago observed, "Han pronunciation" was less a living phonological system than a political concept, with roots in early Heian contestation among the imperial household, Nara temples, and new sects such as Tendai.[92] In the mid-Heian, the earlier pronunciation traditions came to be referred to as "Wu pronunciation" (*goon* 呉音), borrowing a

90. Connery, *Empire of the Text*, 40–41.

91. Phan, "Lacquered Words," 175–238. Going back further, Martin Kern has suggested that the "elegant standard speech" (*yayan* 雅言) mentioned in the *Analects* refers to an idealized *koiné* employed in ritual speech by educated elites across the various regions of the Warring States, in conscious contradistinction to local language ("Early Chinese Poetics," 51–53). See also Saitō, *Kanji sekai no chihei*, 110–12.

92. Wenck, *Japanische Phonetik*, 1:306–12.

derogatory Tang term for the southern dialects that deviated from Chang'an standards.[93]

It is therefore telling that the entries of Shitagō's encyclopedia are so frequently derived from rhyming dictionaries, the primary vehicle for linguistic orthodoxy in and around China. *Wamyō ruijushō*'s elucidation of correct readings reveals an extension of this logic of authority to the realm of the Yamato vernacular, as scholars demonstrated their command over the text through ceremonial forms of recitation. The performance of a formalized register of speech legitimated both texts and their interpreters. In the *Tale of Genji*, academy professors are characterized through their peculiar speech, larded with antiquated terms and Chinese compounds; to observing courtiers, this incomprehensible patois is often risible, but for the professors it must have served as the display of their mastery over the language of the classics.[94] The conflict of values here reflects an ongoing negotiation over the social authority of canonical texts.

Heian writing in literary Sinitic genres presents us with a paradox: on the one hand *kundoku* recitation practices firmly seat the production and reception of this literature in a Japanese language environment—in certain respects, this work is just as "vernacular" as the *Tale of Genji* and other works based on *kana* inscription. But at the same time, the *bunshō* aesthetic of Heian poetry and parallel prose is defined through its rejection of the registers of ordinary speech. The ubiquity of *kundoku* recitation meant that even texts that conformed exactly to Tang aesthetic principles (and even texts imported from abroad) were bound up in networks of intertextuality extending through two linguistic and literary traditions. However, as the discussions of *Gōdanshō* and *Sakumon daitai* that opened this chapter demonstrated, such ambiguity was more often perceived as a problem than exploited for its creative potential. By contrast with poetic and parallel prose genres, quotidian records and letters were characterized by the free intermingling of Chinese and Japanese vocabulary and syntactic forms, but only in the context of an "everyday style" that abandoned

93. Tōdō, *Chūgoku gogaku ronshū*, 74–79. On the distinction between "Han pronunciation" and "Wu pronunciation" (or "Yamato pronunciation" [*waon*]) as a form of self-authorization by groups within Heian society, see also Komatsu, "Nihon jion no shotaikei."

94. Tsukishima, *Heian jidai no kanbun kundokugo*, 811–20.

the possibility of literary ornament. The anxiety surrounding this underlying hybridity is reflected in sustained efforts to demarcate appropriate *kundoku* techniques and thereby secure a realm of literary language whose legibility and auditory manifestation were as stable as was depicted in dictionaries. Even as the routinization of *kundoku* recitation pulled literary Sinitic out of the orbit of Tang aesthetic principles, recitation practice was regulated through homologous principles of legitimacy that differentiated it from ordinary speech, preserving the authority of the written word.

CONCLUSION

The Changing Purview of Literary Sinitic

In the layout of this study, I have sought to gradually magnify the texture of the lived practice of literary Sinitic in the mid-Heian period. Chapters 1 and 2 introduced the role of composition and performance in a network of exchange that organized the social relationships of capital officialdom, then explored how new modes of ritualization through exclusivity redefined composition in literary Sinitic as a kind of technical expertise supplied by lower ranking officials as service to senior nobles and the emperor. Chapters 3 and 4 demonstrated how scholar-officials responded to their increasingly precarious position in the weakening bureaucracy, first in the rhetorical strategies of their formal compositions, through which they sought to differentiate themselves in a field of competitors and establish links with potential patrons, and second in their role as authorities on classical Chinese learning, which they plied as tutors to the upper nobility. As chapter 4 shows, mastery of a literary Sinitic text was demonstrated through vocalization in a hybrid idiom of Japanese, *kundoku*. Chapter 5 returns to the space of ritual performance to consider the ramifications of this mode of reception; by strictly regulating the lexicon and delivery of *kundoku* recitation, scholars sought to legitimate both canonical classics and the formal genres of ornamented literary Sinitic (*bunshō*), whose composition was their portfolio within capital society.

The order of this analysis risks implying a mechanistic relationship between social structures and resulting formal or literary effects; it is important therefore to reemphasize the contrary dynamics by which the status distinctions laid out in chapter 1 are created through compositional and performative acts analyzed in later chapters. As detailed in chapters 4 and 5, the mid-Heian witnessed the decline of forms of Sinitic recitation that had been actively promoted by the state in the eighth and ninth centuries, and reception through *kundoku* increasingly became the accepted norm for almost all literary Sinitic genres. However, as the discussion in chapter 5 makes clear, the purely technical matrix of equivalencies between two different languages does not explain the complex tendencies and taboos apparent in actual *kundoku* recitation practice. Instead, the language of *kundoku* (like any speech act) implies within it a specific site of audience, here linked to the particular uses of literary Sinitic among mid-Heian officialdom. The peculiar, rarified language of *kundoku* served both to project a grandiose textual authority into banquets and funerals, and conversely to legitimate the ritual documents themselves. Thus, turning this study on its head and beginning instead from analysis of literacy and inscription likewise leads inevitably back to the problem of the nature of ritual space and its role in establishing hierarchies within officialdom, suggesting the dialectic of what Bourdieu called "structured structures."[1]

The thrust of this argument is that Heian literary Sinitic cannot be separated from the sites and modes of presentation through which it was actualized. Documents in literary Sinitic were largely produced through the patronage-based exchange relationships that academy-educated officials established with the upper nobility. Literary Sinitic writing that fell outside such relationships—we might think of the ninth-century court chronicles or the formal experiments of Kūkai—gradually tended to wither away. Instead, conceptions of the "literary" (*bunshō*) were limited to a few favored genres of parallel prose and poetry that had widely recognized performance venues. The recitation practices attendant on these venues thus became the arena in which literature's linguistic status was negotiated. Heian scholars theorized a discursive sphere of Sinographic text and *kundoku* recitation through a unipolar model of the relationship between script and speech, in which writing necessarily manifested in its appropriate vocalization, but colloquial speech was only indirectly susceptible to transcription. This paradigm served as a crucial basis for

1. *Theory of Practice*, 72.

literature's authority, limiting its use in practical realms like law, but accentuating its connection to a ritual realm removed from quotidian life.

This monograph has focused on a specific historical moment, the early tenth through late eleventh centuries, in order to facilitate a synchronic treatment of the processes by which literary writing was imagined and differentiated within a wider field of scribal practice. Nevertheless, the paradigm of *bunshō* established in the mid-Heian, which posited a field of ritually efficacious language defined by its twin identification with a (primarily textual) idiom of ornamented literary Sinitic and a (primarily aural) register of refined Japanese speech, would continue into the medieval period, with important ramifications for both the literary Sinitic genres examined in this study and the larger history of writing in Japan.

The lingering force of and gradual challenges to this paradigm can be seen most clearly in the discourse of place—the most explicit engagement with the local particular—as it was articulated in literary Sinitic genres such as poetry. As indicated in chapter 5, an ideology of orthographic correctness limited the direct transcription of local names, which instead were replaced by continental analogues or provided a more decorous orthography. Concurrently, the maintenance of universalized prescriptive standards and the valuation of erudite allusions together tended to encourage a de-individuation of local space, figuring it typologically through invocation of classical precursors. In the numerous eleventh- and twelfth-century poems on excursions to suburban temples collected in *Honchō mudaishi* 本朝無題詩 (Non-Topic-Line Poetry of This Court, ca. 1163), poets describe majestic views of the Luo (Kamo River) and Mount Song (Higashiyama) from Chōrakuji east of the capital; an imperial excursion to the Byōdōin, south of the Uji River, prompts the question, "Why should [King] Wen of Zhou have [travelled] north of the Wei?"[2] Locales could echo or even surpass classical exemplars, but remain largely confined to an established vocabulary of representational tropes. The particular—the ceremony, banquet, or excursion

2. *Honchō mudaishi* 532 and 3.

which we, the poets and revelers, attend—is figured as an iteration of a universal type.[3]

In the medieval period, composition in literary Sinitic genres was increasingly dominated by Zen monks, who carried out scribal roles both within the Gozan monastic network and for powerful military officials and aristocrats. Literary history has tended to emphasize the discontinuity between the scholarly traditions of the capital nobility (which are often characterized as petering out into obscurity by the end of the Heian period) and the new texts and ideas at the center of the Gozan cultural efflorescence, seen as directly influenced by more recent continental developments, such as Song learning.[4] There is certainly no disputing the epochal influx of new models and aesthetics in the fourteenth and fifteenth centuries, but the concurrent abandonment of earlier traditions has been somewhat exaggerated. Both *Wakan rōeishū* and *Honchō monzui*, for example, circulated widely in medieval monasteries, respectively as an elementary literacy primer and a template for the composition of letters and prayer texts.[5] Gozan monks also made use of the interpretive traditions that were passed down by noble scholarly lineages: a manuscript of the *Lunyu jijie* 論語集解 (Collected Explanations of the Analects, 242), copied in 1331 by the influential Zen master Kokan Shiren 虎關師錬 (1278–1347), contains colophons showing that its text and *kunten* glosses derive from Kiyohara no Noritaka 清原教隆 (1199–1265), a prominent classics scholar; similarly, an extant copy of the *Wenxuan*, printed in the Southern Song and imported to Japan, contains glosses inserted in the early fifteenth century by a Kenninji monk that originally derived from a text owned by the letters professor Fujiwara no Atsuchika 藤原敦周 (1119–83).[6] Despite the important role played in Zen monasteries by both immigrant monks from the continent and Japanese monks who had travelled

3. There were important exceptions to this tendency, such as Ōe no Masafusa's literary, yet highly particularistic records of local customs and supernatural mysteries. See Bialock, *Eccentric Spaces, Hidden Histories*, 184–85.

4. For a recent discussion of discontinuity in the history of literary Sinitic in Japan, see Smits, "Minding the Gaps," 93–95.

5. Gotō, *Honchō kanshibun shiryōron*, 113–15, 201–12.

6. Yamamoto Nobuyoshi et al., *Shinshitei jūyō bunkazai*, 215; Horikawa, "Kuge no gakumon to Gozan." Another extant Song edition of the *Shiji* contains glosses added by the Rinzai monk Gesshū Jukei 月舟壽桂 (1470–1533), deriving from a copy that had been

to the Ming empire to study, *kundoku* recitation remained central to education in temples across the archipelago, and actively drew upon scholarly traditions developed in the State Academy.

In this context, it is not surprising to find that medieval literary Sinitic largely maintains the same strategies for representation of local space. Consider the following poem by the Kenninji monk Kōsei Ryūha 江西龍派 (1375–1446):

城南尋去年花	Seeking Last Year's Blossoms South of the City
玄都千樹漲車塵	The thousand trees of the Mysterious Metropolis billowed with wagon dust;
榮辱悲歡旦暮新	Glory and shame, grief and joy are turned over in a day.
贏得渭南三四屋	But I've found three or four houses south of the Wei,
去年花對去年人	Where last year's blossoms face last year's men.[7]

In Kōsei's poem, a trip "south of the city"—perhaps Fushimi or Uji south of Kyoto—to see the blossoms calls to mind the familiar trope of the eternal renewal of flowers contrasted with the ephemerality of human life.[8] In this case, Kōsei specifically refers to a famous poem by Liu Yuxi 劉禹錫 (772–842), which describes sightseers clamoring to see the blossoming peach trees of the Daoist abbey Mysterious Metropolis (Xuanduguan), all of which had been planted and grown up during Liu's decade-long exile from Chang'an. The poem was often quoted in the *shihua* 詩話 (talks on poetry) collections that circulated among Gozan monks as a parable on life's vicissitudes, since the poem was said to have itself led to Liu being almost immediately banished again from the capital, not to see the blossoms again for another thirteen years.[9] Kōsei's paean to the humbler but less treacherous glories of

glossed by one Fujiwara no Hidefusa 藤原英房 (fl. 1334), like Atsuchika a distant descendant of Fujiwara no Akihira. Ozawa Kenji, "Nanka-bon *Shiki* kaisetsu."

7. *Chūka jakuboku shishō* 94.

8. For a canonical Tang poem contrasting the aging of "last year's men" with the renewal of flowers, see Can Shen's 岑參 (d. 770) "Song on the Blossoming Trees at the Home of Vice-Director Wei" 韋員外家花樹歌, *Quan Tangshi* 199.2058.

9. See, for example, the twelfth-century collection *Shihua zonggui qianji* 31.309.

this unnamed village superimposes the geography of Chang'an over Kyoto and its environs. Gozan writers like Kōsei incorporated a new rhetorical lexicon, drawing on authors such as Su Shi 蘇軾 (1037–1101) that were unknown or ignored in the Heian period, but their compositional principle of "no word without a source" (*shukkyo nakereba mochiizaru*) was essentially consistent with the classicism of Heian *kudaishi*.[10]

At the same time, shifts in the sites and audience of poetic composition were encouraging more deviation from canonical models. Most important was the tendency, already visible in *Wakan rōeishū*, to juxtapose the composition and performance of *shi* with the Japanese genre of *waka*. Beginning in the tenth century there are records of events in which participants were invited to compose in either form at their discretion (*wakan nin'i* 和漢任意), and the medieval period brought new formats in which lines of literary Sinitic and Japanese poetry were matched against each other (*shiika-awase*) or linked in sequence (*wakan renku* 和漢聯句).[11] In some cases, tropes from *waka* came to be directly incorporated into literary Sinitic genres, but more commonly such compositional modes encouraged a smoothing away of contradictions between the two traditions in favor of a seamless continuity.[12] A consciousness of *waka* poetics is visible in this poem by Chūgan Engetsu 中巖圓月 (1300–1375):

遊渡月橋看嵐山花	Visiting Togetsukyō Bridge to View the Blossoms of Arashiyama
痴雲向晚襯花垂	Toward dusk the torpid clouds sagged over the blossoms,
預惜明朝雨打稀	And I was sorry the morning rain would dash all but a few.
扶老來看寺門外	I doddered out of the temple gates to see them,
橋欄倚遍不知歸	And leaning upon the bridge rail I never thought to return.[13]

10. The epigram is from a sixteenth-century composition manual attributed to Sakugen Shūryō 策彦周良 (1501–79). See Horikawa, *Zoku Gozan bungaku kenkyū*, 287.

11. *Honchō monzui* 350; Horikawa, *Shi no katachi*, 79–101; Ōtani, "Hajimete no dokusha."

12. Some examples of *waka* tropes passing into Japanese literary Sinitic are discussed in Miki, *Heian shiika no tenkai*.

13. *Gozan bungaku shū*, 90–91.

From one perspective, the poem is a pastiche of canonical Chinese models, with almost every phrase traceable to anthologies that circulated widely among the Gozan temples.[14] At the same time, by engaging with an established *waka* topos—the cherry blossoms of Arashiyama (Storm Mountain), in danger of destruction by the mountain's eponymous winds—the poem establishes a specific locale populated by the mountain and its flowers, the Togetsukyō (Moon-Crossing Bridge) over the Katsura River, and the temple (almost certainly Tenryūji, where Chūgan lived 1356–59) that faces them.[15]

Medieval writing in literary Sinitic genres of poetry and parallel prose adopted a new canon of continental exemplars, emphasized continuities with Japanese poetic forms, and engaged with Zen philosophy's critique of discursive representation and writing in particular; all of these developments tended to subvert the paradigm of authoritative, primary script and formal vernacular, secondary recitation that had defined *bunshō* in the Heian period. In the early modern period, this definition was subject to overt challenge. Whereas for Heian writers literary Sinitic could be universalized as a trans-historic standard with its own inherent laws, the early modern philologist Ogyū Sorai 荻生徂徠 (1666–1728) inverted the primacy of script over speech, arguing that, "*Bunshō* is none other than the [spoken] language [*gogen* 語言] of the Chinese."[16] As chapter 5 showed, the regulation of *kundoku* recitation generated a register of rarified, hybrid speech for the oral evocation of canonical texts whose value transcended any regional linguistic differences. Sorai, on the other hand, characterized Chinese antiquity and Tokugawa Japan as linguistic unities in a relationship of mutual exclusivity, and rejected the use of *kundoku*

14. For example, the phrase "the rain will dash [the blossoms], thinning them out" is from a poem by the revered poet Du Fu 杜甫 (712–70), and the phrase "leaning against the railing" appears with a slightly different orthography in an anonymous poem lamenting rain scattering the flowers collected in the Yuan anthology *Lianzhu shige* 聯珠詩格 (1300). "San jueju," 三絶句, *Quan Tangshi* 227.2452; "Xi hua" 惜花, *Yakuchū Renju shikaku*, 120.

15. The most well-known *waka* on the topic is probably Minamoto no Sanetomo's 源實朝 (1192–1219) "Deep in spring, the cherry of Storm Mountain—when I looked to see them bloom they'd already scattered" (*haru fukami arashi no yama no sakurabana saku to mishi ma ni chirinikeru kana*, *Fūga wakashū* 241). For Chūgan's time at Tenryūji, see Tamamura, *Gozan zensō denki shūsei*, 453–54. For a treatment of "Japanese" elements in Gozan poetry, see Pollack, *Fracture of Meaning*, 111–33.

16. Saitō, *Kanji sekai no chihei*, 61–67.

for its elision of this difference. Naoki Sakai has argued that Sorai collapsed the definitional opposition between text and speech, apprehending both as verbal acts whose "authenticity" demonstrated the writer's success or failure in inhabiting the idealized interiority of antiquity.[17]

For this reason, Sorai condemned what he saw as the frequent deviations from canonical literary Sinitic standards in the writings of other Tokugawa scholars, labeling these as "Japanese propensities" (*washū* 和習) in need of correction.[18] The same underlying assumptions regarding language, mutatis mutandis, are at work in the nativist scholar Motoori Norinaga's 本居宣長 (1730–1801) criticism of the "faux Chineseness" (*kanbun-buri*) of his contemporaries' vernacular writing as a "dirty trick" to impress the unlearned. Language derived from Chinese (even calques based on Chinese expressions such as "welcome the spring," *haru o mukau*) had no place in Norinaga's "elegant writing."[19] For both men, the postulation of a linguistically unified collectivity and consequent discovery of the classical tradition's "Chineseness" justified a strict delineation of purified textual realms, whose empirical basis was projected into the ancient past (of either China or Japan). In practice, Sorai's rejection of the *bunshō* paradigm demanded an even stricter imitation of Chinese models in literary composition (especially Tang writers in the case of *shi*). Ironically, however, it was the particularization of deviations from orthodoxy as a peculiarly local phenomenon—the transformation of Shitagō's "popular usage" into Sorai's "Japanese propensities"—that allowed later writers to perform a conceptual inversion, authorizing a vernacular and iconoclastic mode of ornamented literary Sinitic.

Here again, discourse on place becomes the most visible node of contention: the shifting winds are suggested by the 1757 *Shōko bensei* 稱呼辨正 (Correction of Appellations), which assembles arguments against the convention of replacing local names with elegant sobriquets that had been mainstream poetic practice since the ninth century.[20] By

17. Sakai, *Voices of the Past*, 217–39.

18. On the history of *washū* discourse, see Kanda, "Washū no dangi"; Kojima Noriyuki, *Kango shōyō*, 243–73.

19. *Tamaarare*, 515, 490.

20. On *Shōko bensei* and toponyms in Edo *shi*, see Hu, "Chimei hyōki."

the late eighteenth century, the scholar Yamamoto Hokuzan 山本北山 (1752–1812) was condemning Sorai's reverence for Tang literary authorities as "imitation and plagiarism," and promoting a poetics of spontaneous expression based on the poet's "innate sensibility" (*seirei*, Ch. *xingling* 性靈). Hokuzan's polemics took place within the context of critical debates in late imperial China—he drew his theories largely from the writings of Yuan Hongdao 袁宏道 (1568–1610), and his followers were further inspired by Yuan Mei 袁枚 (1716–97)—but their effects increasingly led Sinographic verse in Japan away from transnational poetic norms.[21] Poets intent on demonstrating their free expression of a genuine "sensibility" sought out subject matter and vocabulary that could deviate dramatically from the Tang models espoused by Sorai, most famously in Rai Sanyō's 頼山陽 (1780–1832) odes to celebrated medieval warriors.[22] In 1786, the Edo poet Ichikawa Kansai 市河寛齋 (1749–1820) published the sequence *Hokurika* 北里歌 (Songs of the North Quarter), which vividly describes the contemporary New Yoshiwara district:

曲坂長堤起晩埃	Up the long dike's curving path, they kick up the evening dust,
無人不道觀燈回	There's not a one who doesn't say he's off to see the lanterns.
黃昏火點家々樹	At dusk the flames are lit, each house its own tree,
一夕秋風花盡開	For a single night, in the autumn wind every flower blooms.[23]

Kansai's description of customers walking along the Nihonzutsumi embankment to the Tamagiku Lantern Festival, held every autumn in Yoshiwara, still consciously inhabits a long tradition centered on Tang and Song

21. On Hokuzan's poetic theories, see Ibi, *Edo shiikaron*, 64–89. For Yuan Hongdao's advocacy of "innate sensibility," see Chou, *Yüan Hung-tao*, 44–48.

22. On San'yō and late Edo trends toward "nativizing" Sinographic poetry, see the essays and translations by Haruo Shirane and Peter Flueckiger in Shirane, *Early Modern Japanese Literature*, 910–24.

23. *Hokurika*, 18. For a selection of other poems from this sequence, see the translations by Mark Borer in Jones and Watanabe, *Edo Anthology*, 465–76.

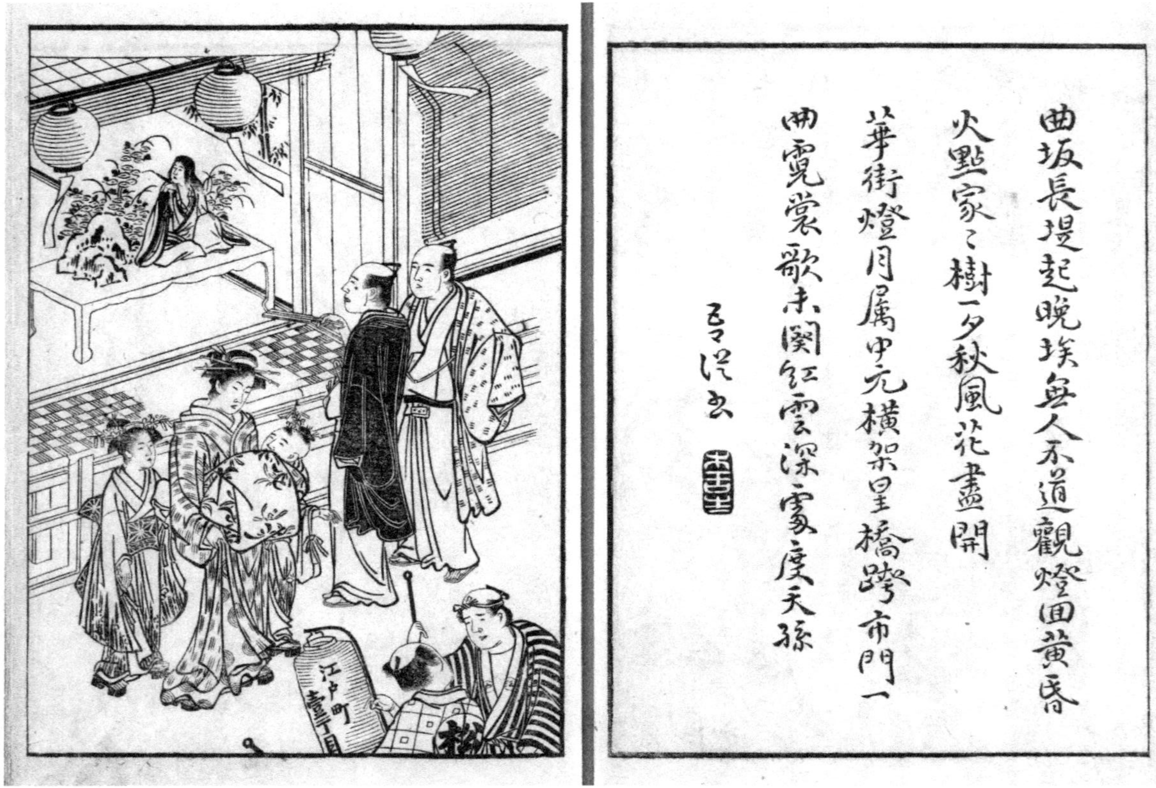

FIG. 6 An illustration of passersby examining a Yoshiwara teahouse doll display for the Tamagiku Lantern Festival, by Isoda Koryūsai (1735–90), from *Songs of the North Quarter*. Photograph courtesy of the National Diet Library, Tokyo.

exemplars—the poem's second line quotes the same Liu Yuxi poem alluded to by Kōsei above. However, where the earlier poems mostly invoked universal and eternal types as a medium for representing a lived moment of particular experience that was shared by a group of poet-revelers, Kansai's sequence, which was published by a Nihonbashi bookseller with accompanying illustrations, instead seeks to elicit from his indeterminate reading audience the sense of recognition of a persistent local space (fig. 6). Rather than group composition, Kansai's connection to his posited readers is based on their shared inhabitation of and identification with a local urban milieu, comparable to but distinguished from continental counterparts. Followers of his such as Kikuchi Gozan 菊池五山 (1769–1855) similarly used the *shi* form as reportage, a poetic counterpart to the print depictions of the "floating world" produced by contemporary artists such as Torii Kiyonaga 鳥居清長 (1752–1815).[24]

The engagement with local images, themes, and topoi in literary Sinitic is not itself new to the early modern period, or even a phenomenon particular to Japan, but a structural component of a classicist mode of composition characterized by the continuous reconciliation of eternal exemplars to inevitable deviation, in Tang Chang'an as much as in eighteenth-century Edo. What changes in the Edo period is rather the conceptualization of the relationship of the local particular to these canonical authorities: if the ritualized patterning of Heian *bunshō* is defined against quotidian writing and speech, late Edo writers treated literary precursors as simply the quotidian of another time and place, justifying their own embrace of new rhetoric and language.[25] As discussed above, medieval authors often incorporated *waka* topoi into literary Sinitic compositions that nevertheless strove to remain consistent with canonical precedent. By contrast, as Hino Tatsuo astutely notes, for writers of the early nineteenth century a *shi* poem on the subject of *sakura* could function as a deliberate rehearsal of "Japanese propensities," in which local deviation from the classical tradition itself became both an aesthetic goal and a means of cultural self-identification.[26] This new valorization of a Sinographic aesthetic now

24. Fujikawa, *Edo kōki no shijintachi*, 105.

25. On one Qing scholar's view of the strange language found in Japanese-composed *shi*, see Guo, *Hanshi yu hexi*, 37–74, 202–24.

26. Hino, "Sakura to Nihon kinsei kanshi," 459–60.

particularized instead of universal would become a key touchstone in the unprecedented popularity of literary Sinitic composition in the nineteenth century. Poems on the teahouses of Fukagawa or Minamoto generals reversed the polarity of Heian literary hybridity, trading authority for breadth of content, as a supple idiom of local literary Sinitic found new outlets in an era of revolutionary change.

The brief and schematic history sketched above follows the body of this study in emphasizing the regulatory force of the *bunshō* paradigm, which responded to the ambiguous hybridity of Heian composition in literary Sinitic genres by demarcating registers of ornamented inscription and majestic vocal performance in order to differentiate and legitimate the literary. It is, however, important to emphasize the treacherous foundations of this ideological project, which could never truly eliminate the fecund potential for cross-linguistic signification inherent in *kundoku* literacy. In many ways, the scholars of the Heian State Academy were the flag-bearers of prescriptive orthodoxy in literature, which justified their own fragile place within capital officialdom, but it is in their writings that we find the most direct engagement with the contradictions inherent in this paradigm of the vernacular literary. Here again Minamoto no Shitagō draws this crux into sharpest focus.

Shitagō is known for his formal experimentalism in many genres, including sequences of *waka* poems in the shape of a *sugoroku* game board or beginning with each of the forty-eight syllables of the *kana* syllabary, and some of his works similarly push the boundaries of literary Sinitic forms. A striking example of hybridization is the satire "High Phoenix: A Song to Mock Fraternizing between the Distinguished and Lowly" 高鳳刺貴賤之同交歌. The song appears to mock a mid-ranked palace official named Takahashi ("high bridge"), here given the mocking sobriquet "High Phoenix":

高鳳高鳳彼誰人子	High Phoenix, High Phoenix, whose child is he?
正六位下孫、從七位上子	Grandson of a sixth-rank, son of a seventh.
待年官於志摩國	He waits for his post in Shima Prefecture,

期月俸於内膳司	And hopes for a salary in the palace kitchens.[27]
口是木訥	He's got the mouth of a simpleton—
天鼓之聲頻鳴	His voice rumbles away like thunder;
才是土偶	And all the talent of a marionette—
地望之胤最卑	This scion of promise is low as can be.
訪其帶於腰間	Take a look at the belt around his waist:
則出雲石老	The Izumo agates are aging.
尋其韈於足下	Consider the socks on his feet:
亦信濃布穿	The Shinano cloth is worn through.
初參藏人所之朝	The morning he first entered the Chamberlain's Office,
布袴招責	His hemp trousers invited attack.
偸過帶刀陣之夕	One evening he snuck past the barracks of the Prince's Guard,
烏帽取嘲	But his cap drew their ridicule.
昔有高鳳	Long ago there was a High Phoenix
讀書傳賢士之名	Who was famed as a sage through his studies.[28]
今有高鳳	This High Phoenix today
障文注愚老之字	Has "old fool" written on his excuse letter.[29]
高鳳高鳳、名同性異	High Phoenix! High Phoenix! Same name, different nature![30]
昔賢人今愚哉愚哉	Long ago a sage, but today how stupid! How stupid!

27. Kakimura Shigematsu surmised from these lines that "High Phoenix" is a play on the surname Takahashi, as this household held control of the Imperial Kitchen (*naizenshi*) through inherited posts, and its members were also regularly assigned the governorship of Shima. *Honchō monzui chūshaku*, 1:131.

28. The story of the original "High Phoenix," Gao Feng, is found in the "Biographies of Recluses," *Hou Hanshu* 83.2768–70.

29. 障文 (*sawaribumi?*) is a problematic phrase. The one other attestation I have located seems to refer to a missive explaining why the writer is unable to participate in a palace function. *Chūyūki*, Kōwa 4 (1102)/4/11 (4:161).

30. The language here alludes to the madman Jie Yu who accosts Confucius, saying "Phoenix! Phoenix! How your virtue has declined!" *Analects* 18.5 (*Lunyu zhushu* 18.73).

何啻壁上張文冊人	How could there only be examinees' names on the wall?[31]
不足言、不足嘲	Not worth speaking of, not worth mocking,
共恥白物之入青雲	We're ashamed at a "white idiot" flying among the blue clouds.[32]

While not a piece of regulated verse, the "song" format Shitagō has chosen here was fairly popular among Tang poets.[33] Unlike most Heian composition, however, this piece seems to revel in violations of Tang literary models: place names (Izumo, Shima, Shinano) and bureaucratic offices (Kurōdodokoro, Tachihaki no jin) appear in the quotidian orthography of the everyday style, instead of the Sinified equivalents favored in elegant composition. Most drastically, in the final line, 白物 is clearly the Japanese word *shiremono* (idiot), here written using characters meaning "white" (*shiro*) and "thing" (*mono*).[34] The compound is meaningless in literary Sinitic, so that the line only makes sense in a *kundoku* recitation. But even here, the author still maintains principles of literary patterning with a parallel construction that contrasts the *shiremono* with "blue clouds," a common figure in classical Chinese texts for the lofty circles frequented by great men.[35]

Literacy based in *kundoku* creates an environment in which phrases from the Chinese tradition like "heavenly drum" (an epithet for thunder)

31. This line is corrupt in the extant manuscripts. The emendation and tentative reading here are suggested by Kinpira Tadashi in the Shin Nihon koten bungaku taikei edition of *Honchō monzui*.

32. *Honchō monzui* 43. Another translation of this text can be found in Rabinovitch and Bradstock, *Dance of the Butterflies*, 177–78.

33. The "song" 歌 was a somewhat free-form style with changing rhyme and sometimes line lengths (though most examples are primarily heptasyllabic), apparently growing out of the *yuefu* tradition. The most famous example is perhaps Bai Juyi's "Changhen ge" 長恨歌 (Song of Lasting Sorrow, *Bai Juyi ji jianjiao* 12.659–81), but see also Li Bai's "Xiangyang ge" 襄陽歌 (*Quan Tangshi* 29.421–22) or Bai Juyi's "Huazhu ge" 畫竹歌 (*Bai Juyi ji jianjiao* 12.651–54).

34. *Sezoku genbun*, one of the primers by Shitagō's student Tamenori discussed in chapter 4, includes the proverb *kasu wa shiremono* (lenders are fools), in which the same characters are glossed with this reading (184).

35. See for example *Shiji* 61.2127: "Though the folk of villages and alleyways may strive to establish a reputation, unless one serves one of the *nobles of the blue clouds*, how can [this reputation] possibly be passed down to later generations?"

can intermingle freely with vernacular Japanese vocabulary. This underlying hybridity was an integral element of mid-Heian literary culture. Nevertheless, it is no accident that this piece is a humorous one. While the potential for fluid juxtaposition was always there, the prescriptive force of Tang models and the regulation of *kundoku* recitation as a performance of textual orthodoxy meant that embrace of the vernacular in literary Sinitic genres would tend to be read first of all as farce. Shitagō was deeply interested in the relationship between language and script, but his experiments were primarily couched in the medium of aesthetic *play*, and this tendency extends across other mid-Heian examples as well.[36] Conversely, in poetic prefaces and other commissioned documents, his usage accords with a universalized aesthetic that all but effaces the presence of local particularity. In this respect, compositions like the above are exceptions proving the rule: even as *kundoku* literacy undermined Tang aesthetic principles, countervailing forces generated new forms of prescriptivism that maintained the distinctiveness of literary writing.

Nevertheless, Shitagō's peculiar song suggests important ramifications for how we understand Heian literary Sinitic and the place of the mid-Heian in Japanese literary history. As stated in the introduction of this book, the reuse of images, plot elements, and language from Chinese works is ubiquitous in the classics of Heian *kana* poetry and prose, and modern scholarship has often sought to understand this phenomenon through a narrative of native tradition, foreign influence, and sublimating synthesis. This narrative is dependent on a specifically modern understanding of national culture (and even the place of Japan in the global order), but has a deeper history as well, for the discovery of translations, adaptations, and references to the Chinese tradition has occupied scholarship on *monogatari* and *waka* from the beginning of the commentarial tradition.[37] Just as Heian discourse surrounding *bunshō* emphasized its

36. Robert Borgen documents a similar form of punning on vernacular sexual vocabulary through homophonous Chinese compounds in an eleventh-century burlesque. "Heian Love," 274.

37. The earliest commentaries on the *Tale of Genji*, *Genji shaku* 源氏釋 (ca. 1160) and Fujiwara no Teika's *Okuiri* 奥入 (ca. 1233), are both primarily concerned with identifying precedents and sources, including numerous passages from canonical Chinese works. For prototypical modern discourse of cultural "assimilation," see the discussion of Japan's importation of continental culture as an "emptying of self" (*onore o munashūshite*)

difference from "ordinary" speech or script, *kana*-based literary genres too were often realized through highly codified language, and in the case of *waka* even limited to a largely fixed lexicon that excluded Sino-Japanese vocabulary. However, such lexical restrictions never precluded the adoption into vernacular forms of themes and figures from the Chinese canon (sometimes absorbed secondhand through the medium of local composition in literary Sinitic). By contrast, the adaptation of local tropes and terms into orthodox literary Sinitic genres was much more limited, largely precluded by the socially inscribed functions, prescriptive aesthetics, and codified recitation practices discussed in the chapters above.

These conditions combined to channel the underlying potentials of Heian literary culture into specific forms. In the medieval period, works like *The Tale of the Heike* that fuse the vocabulary and rhetoric of *kundoku* parallel couplets with the seven-five rhythm of Japanese prosody are a result of hybrid interaction, but the direction and limits of this development could be forecast from mid-Heian materials. In this context, Shitagō's song, with all its puerile insults, suggests a path not taken, a vision of a Sinographic literary still situated within the Chinese literary tradition that nevertheless embraces the reality of *kundoku*-based reception, treating recitation in the vernacular as a locus of possibility, rather than the source of anxiety we see depicted in *Sakumon daitai* and other technical discourse of the period. If the embrace of the quotidian in late Edo-period *shi* is motivated by recognition of an essential difference from the foreign other, toppling the universal applicability of classical models, Shitagō's experiments instead present a vision of literary form that obviates linguistic difference, not through consolidation to a homogenous unity, but rather as inscribed textual patterns whose potency extends across the diverse realms of speech. His work is a particularly vivid example of the continuous contestation of literature's definition at work in the commission, form, and performance of mid-Heian texts.

in the 1937 *Fundamentals of Our National Polity*. Ministry of Education, *Kokutai no hongi*, 97.

APPENDIX A

Selections from *Sakumon daitai*

Sakumon daitai, discussed in chapters 3 and 5, is a manual for composing in the *bunshō* genres of regulated verse and parallel prose. Produced in several stages, the original core text seems to have been written by and for officials, but it later circulated widely in medieval Buddhist monasteries, where genres like the prayer text (*ganmon*) and dedication (*hyōbyaku* 表白) applied literary rhetoric to religious devotions. The manual gives instructions and examples for composition in the most important genres of prose and poetry, focusing especially on regulations of rhyme, tonal prosody, rhetorical parallelism, and proper exposition of a set topic (*dai*).

The contents of *Sakumon daitai* tie it to a specific point in literary history. The manual follows in the footsteps of Kūkai's early ninth-century *Bunkyō hifuron*, but where the latter was edited together from several Tang manuals of poetic composition, *Sakumon daitai* draws most of its examples from local authors, and the poetics described have begun to exhibit deviations from continental practice.[1] Most importantly, the manual shows the early stages of the *kudaishi* (topic-line poetry) genre, a form of regulated verse with specific rules for topical exposition that arose in the tenth century and became the uncontested standard for composition on formal occasions in the late Heian (see chapter 3). For prose genres, we can see the growing emphasis on "alternating parallel lines" (*kakku*) that characterizes the major genres of Heian literary Sinitic prose, such

1. Some manuscripts of *Sakumon daitai* in fact append large chunks of quotation from *Bunkyō hifuron*. On *Bunkyō hifuron*, see Bodman, "Poetics and Prosody."

as prefaces (*jo*), petitions (*sōjō*), and prayers. Many examples cited in the text were written by scholar-officials active during the late ninth through tenth centuries, including Sugawara no Michizane, Ki no Haseo 紀長谷雄 (845–912), Sugawara no Fumitoki, and Yoshishige no Yasutane. The manual is thus an artifact of literary Sinitic composition's institutionalization in mid-Heian Japan, whereby direct study of Tang models was gradually supplanted by a canon of domestic products.

Sakumon daitai survives today in a variety of very different manuscripts, a testament to its status as practical tool to be freely altered, rather than a canonical text to be preserved untouched. The oldest surviving version of the text is found in a manuscript deriving from the Kanchiin of Tōji (Kyoto), and now held in the Tenri Central Library (Nara). It dates to the late Kamakura period, but seems to preserve a late Heian recension of the text. The text can be divided into five sections:

I. "Preface"

II. Essentials of Composition

III. Essentials of Prose

IV. Fundamental Form of Poetry

V. Assorted Poetic Examples

Section II, a set of ten rules relating exclusively to poetic composition (not prose), seems to be the original *Sakumon daitai*. It is attributed to Minamoto no Shitagō in several manuscripts, and probably dates to the tenth century. Sections III, IV, and V are clearly by a different author, and were probably added to the manual sometime in the mid- to late eleventh century, perhaps by a Shingon monk.[2] This revision expanded the text to include detailed instructions for parallel prose composition (section III),

2. See Ozawa Masao, "Sakumon daitai no kisoteki kenkyū"; Gotō, "Honbun kaidai." Many standard reference works attribute *Sakumon daitai* to Fujiwara no Munetada 藤原宗忠 (1062–1141), based on a colophon preserved in certain manuscripts of the work (see e.g. Yamagishi, *Nihon kanbungaku kenkyū*, 250–54). However, as Ozawa first noted, Munetada's colophon properly refers to a further revision and expansion of the work beyond the five sections listed above, and thus represents a later version of the text than that found in the Kanchiin manuscript.

as well as further instructions and examples for poetry (sections IV and V). At the same time, the preface to a tenth-century rhyming dictionary, *Wachū setsuin* 倭注切韻 (*Qieyun* with Japanese Annotations), by Ōe no Asatsuna, was grafted onto the beginning of the text (section I), presumably because of its argument for the importance of poetic composition. The appendix below includes a complete translation of section II, as well as selected articles from section V relevant to the arguments in chapters 3 and 5. The translation is based on the Kanchiin manuscript, but I have made some reference to other manuscripts in the notes.[3]

Essentials of Composition

1. CONSIDERING THE TOPIC (*dai*)

Generally speaking, the way of poetry is to first consider the topic, and only then dip one's brush. There are different lengths of poem, and there are substantial and empty topics. [Lines] taken from the classics that contain profound principle are called substantial topics [*jitsudai* 實題].[4] [Lines] concerning natural scenery that are purely decorative are called empty topics [*kyodai* 虛題]. There are also binary [*sōkan* 雙關] topics, wherein two objects appear side by side within a topic.[5]

2. PENTASYLLABIC POETRY

Pentasyllabic poetry is the name for that in which the upper line is five graphs [*ji* 字], the bottom line is five graphs, and together ten graphs make a couplet [*shō* 章]. The *Tianbaoji* has

3. Manuscript sources are cited in the bibliography. I have occasionally corrected corruptions in the Kanchiin MS based on Ozawa Masao's edited edition ("Sakumon daitai no kisoteki kenkyū"). For a commentary on the text, see Ozawa Masao, "Sakumon daitai chūkai."

4. Topics quoting from the Confucian classics were primarily used in the Ministry Test to determine letters students (see chapter 4).

5. See the "Binary Form" entry, p. 242.

萬里人南去	Ten-thousand leagues a man goes south,
三春雁北飛	Through three months of spring the geese fly north.
不知何歲月	I don't know when it will be
得與汝同歸	That I can return with you.[6]

3. HEPTASYLLABIC POETRY

Heptasyllabic poetry is the name for that in which the upper line is seven graphs, the bottom line is seven graphs, and together fourteen graphs make a couplet. *Bai Juyi's Collected Works* has

柳無氣力條先動	The willows are lifeless but their branches begin to move,
池有波文冰盡開	While the pond surface ripples as the ice melts away.
今日不知誰計會	I don't know who planned this today:
春風春水一時來	The spring wind and spring water all at once arrived.[7]

4. TERMS FOR LINES

The terms for different lines, regardless of whether it is pentasyllabic or heptasyllabic verse, are *hokku* 發句 [opening couplet] for the head, *kyōku* 胸句 [breast couplet] for the next, *yōku* 腰句 [waist couplet] for the next, and *rakku* 落句 [completing couplet] for the next and final. [A poem with] head, tail, breast, and waist is called *shiin* 四韻 [four rhyme] or

6. This poem, on the topic "In the South, Composing on Geese" ("Nanzhong yong yan shi" 南中詠雁詩), is attributed to the Tang historian and poet Wei Chengqing 韋承慶 (d. 709) in *Quan Tangshi* 46.557. The poem is also quoted in *Wakan rōeishū* 317. The *Tianbaoji* 天寶集 is a lost work, probably a Tang collection of verse. The title appears in the bibliographies *Nihonkoku genzai shomokuroku* 日本國現在書目錄 (ca. 891) and *Tsūken nyūdō shomokuroku* (twelfth century), though not in the bibliographies of the Tang histories.

7. "Fu xi chi" 府西池, *Bai Juyi ji jianjiao* 28.1971.

chōku 長句 [long lines]. [A poem] that only has the two head and tail couplets is called *ichizetsu* 一絶 [one break] or *zekku* 絶句 [broken lines].[8]

Higashiyama MS: A popular mnemonic device divides octaves into Subject Matter [*daimoku*], Topic Decomposition [*hadai*], Classical Anecdote [*honmon*], and Divulgence of Feeling [*jukkai*].[9] Subject Matter is the speaking of the topic's name in the opening couplet.[10] Topic Decomposition is breaking up the meaning of the topic in the breast couplet.[11] Classical Anecdote is to describe a classical source in the waist couplet.[12] Divulgence of Feeling is to describe one's inner thoughts in the completing couplet.[13] However, the classical anecdote need not necessarily appear in the waist couplet. Based on the quality of the lines, anecdote can be used wherever is most convenient (often people employ such [a rearrangement] because of a superlative couplet). If one has a classical anecdote that accords with the topic, one should use it wherever is most expedient among the breast and waist couplets. If one has a brilliant [classical anecdote] couplet, one should use it in the breast couplet, and the topic's entire meaning will appear. If [the anecdote] is poorly done, it should be used in the waist couplet, and [at least] it will somewhat preserve the [standard] poetic form. Figural couplets are sometimes placed in the waist couplet.[14] As for quatrains, it is considered skillful when the sense of the poem is not confined to the beginning or end, but the different parts complement each other. There is more than one possible form: one should learn from [Bai Juyi's] *Collected Works*.

8. The Chisan MS adds the line, "Nevertheless, from here on we will use broken lines [as examples] to discuss four rhymes [as well]." *Sakumon daitai* generally refers to eight-line poems as *shiin* and four-line poems as *zekku*, but I will use the terms "octave" and "quatrain" below for the sake of clarity.

9. This terminology is discussed in chapter 3.

10. That is, the five characters of the topic line are incorporated into the words of the couplet.

11. The topic line is restated using synonyms, metaphors, or other obscure language.

12. The content of the topic line is referred to obliquely using literary or historical allusion.

13. This is a description of the poet's reaction to the topic or the occasion of composition.

14. Figural imagery (*nisemono*) is further described below.

5. POETIC MALADIES

There are eight maladies in poetry. The most important to avoid are these four maladies: Level Head [*heitō* 平頭], Raised Tail [*jōbi* 上尾], Wasp's Waist [*hōyō* 蜂腰], and Crane's Knee [*kakushitsu* 鶴膝].[15] Level Head is when the first or second graph of the top line in a couplet is the same tone as the corresponding graph of the lower line. (It is not considered a malady for the first graph of both lines to be level tone.) Raised Tail is when the fifth and tenth graphs [i.e., the line-final syllables of a couplet] have the same tone. (It is not considered a malady when the opening couplet rhymes internally.)[16] Wasp's Waist is when, in any line, the second and fifth graphs share the same tone. (In the case of level tone, it is not considered a malady.) Crane's Knee is when the fifth and fifteenth graph [i.e., line-final syllables of the first and third lines] share the same tone.[17] (One should particularly avoid this when using a variant-tone rhyme.)[18] The Level Head, Raised Tail, Wasp's Waist, and Crane's Knee for heptasyllabic verse can be extrapolated from the principles for pentasyllabics.

6. PARALLELISM

There are eight types of parallelism in poetry. The most frequently used are color parallels, number parallels, and sound parallels. Color parallels are those of the sort that have "red and blue" in the upper line and "white and black" in the lower. Number parallels are those of the sort that have "three-thousand" in the upper line and "ten-thousand" in the lower. Sound parallels are those of the sort that have the graph "immortal" in

15. The remaining four of the standard "eight poetic maladies" are Large Rhyme 大韻 and Small Rhyme 小韻, which have to do with using rhyming words within a single couplet, and Side Knot 旁紐 and Direct Knot 正紐, which have to do with alliteration and sound duplication. For a detailed description, see Bodman, "Poetics and Prosody," 298–320.

16. Normally only the even-number lines of a poem rhyme (viz. the last syllable of each couplet), but the last syllable of the first line may rhyme as well. *Sakumon daitai* refers to this as "internal rhyme."

17. Chisan MS interpolates language indicating that the Level Head malady is no longer avoided, while the Raised Tail and Wasp's Waist maladies have become very important to avoid.

18. Text corrected based on the Ōsu MS.

the upper line and "ten-thousand" in the lower. The graph "immortal" 仙 [LMC sian] sounds similar to the graph "thousand" 千 [LMC ts^{h}ian], so it can form a parallel with the graph "ten-thousand" 萬. Besides these, the names of natural phenomena, flora, and fauna are also used as parallels. Within color parallels, one may use "raven" for black, or "snow" for white.[19] Within number parallels, one may treat the graph "double" 雙 as two, and the graph "alone" 孤 as one. One does not seek parallelism in the opening and completing couplets, nor in quatrain-form poems.[20]

7. COMPOSING THE TONES

Tonal composition is the proper placement of level tones [*hyōshō* 平聲] and variant tones [*tashō* 他聲].[21] The three tones—rising, falling, and entering—besides the level tone are called variant tones. Therefore the mnemonic for pentasyllabics goes:

●●○○●
○○●●○ (for the opening couplet)
○○○●●
●●●○○ (for the completing couplet)[22]

Unless it would bring about the Level Head malady, the first graph of each line can be either level or variant without any problem (heptasyllabics can follow this rule too).

The mnemonic for heptasyllabics goes:

19. Sentence interpolated from the Higashiyama and Chisan MSS.

20. Chisan MS adds here: "In octaves, one seeks parallelism in the breast and waist couplets. [The principles for] longer poems can be extrapolated from this. Looking through the quatrains in various collections, it is quite rare to discover one with parallelism in either the opening or completing couplet."

21. Regulated verse depends on a regular alternation between level tones and tones of the other three categories, often grouped together under the label "deflected" or "oblique" tones (Ch. *zesheng* 仄聲), and here referred to as "variant" or "other" tones.

22. Here and below an empty circle indicates a level tone (indicated by the character 平 in the original MS), while a filled-in circle indicates a deflected tone (indicated by the character 他 in the MS).

○○●●○○●	(in cases where the couplet uses internal rhyme, the fifth graph instead will take a variant tone, and the seventh graph a rhyme)
●●○○●●○	(for the opening couplet)
●●○○○●●	
○○●●●○○	(for the completing couplet)[23]

8. PRONUNCIATION GUIDES

All graphs have a corresponding pronunciation guide [*han'on* 反音, also written 翻音]. A pronunciation guide is made up of two graphs.[24] Therefore the mnemonic chant says, "Tone is determined by the second [graph], clarity and weight are determined by the first."[25] In the level tone, the light sound is 東 [east, LMC təwŋ], the heavy is 同 [same, LMC tɦəwŋ]. In the entering tone, the light is 德 [virtue, LMC təə̆k], and the heavy is 獨 [alone, LMC tɦəwk].[26] All derive their weight and clarity from the first graph of the pronunciation guide. The reason I only give the level and entering tones here is that heavy sounds in the rising tone are equivalent to a falling tone, and light sounds in the falling tone are equivalent to a rising tone, so the two are difficult to distinguish.[27]

23. The Chisan MS is much more extensive, giving separate charts for quatrains and octaves with both pentasyllabic and heptasyllabic lines, with internal rhyme variants indicated for all four possibilities as well.

24. The Chinese commentarial and lexicographical traditions often made use of *fanqie* (J. *hanzetsu*) annotations, which combine two characters to indicate the reading of a third (one character for the opening consonant, and a second for the vowel and final). See chapter 3.

25. The terms weight (*keijū* 輕重) and clarity (*seidaku* 清濁) can refer to various qualities in early Chinese poetics, but most commonly to aspiration and voicing in consonants.

26. The pairs given contrast voiceless and voiced initials in Early Middle Chinese, but in LMC (upon which Japanese *kan'on* recitation practices seem to have been based), the voiced obstruents were replaced by murmured articulation (Pulleyblank, *Middle Chinese*, 67, 163). Thus, for example, in *katakana* transcriptions based on older, Buddhist recitation practices (so-called *goon*), 同 is given as /dou/, but in the newer *kan'on* recitation influenced by LMC, it became /tou/.

27. On the confusion between rising and falling tones in Japanese recitation traditions, see Mabuchi, *Nihon ingakushi no kenkyū*, 1:428–37.

9. RHYME

Most poems use a level-tone rhyme. Whether pentasyllabic or heptasyllabic, the final graph of the second line [of each couplet] will have the same rhyme. If one mistakenly makes use of two similar rhymes, this is called transgressing rhyme, and people mock it. An example of this is using the character "blue" 青 [LMC ts^{h}iajŋ] in a poem with the rhyme "clear" 清 [LMC ts^{h}iajŋ].[28]

10. POPULAR TRADITIONS[29]

Popular traditions are instructions that are passed down according to custom. According to these traditions, when composing poetry, one must not only consider the topic and avoid maladies, but also be careful of the *kundoku* reading and composing the tones. This is because if the *kundoku* is difficult to read, the words will be circuitous and the meaning unclear. If one is not attentive to the tonal composition, it will be difficult to chant. Or, if one violates a [linguistic] taboo, one will be laughed at. Examples of these are "vermillion gate" and "red goose" [*shumon sekigan* 朱門赤雁], "opening among the branches" [*hatsu shika* 發枝柯], or "my emotions have no limit" [*kan mutan* 感無端].

Someone used the phrase "opening among the branches" in a poem about flowers, but when he chanted the poem in Sinitic pronunciation, it sounded like a monk delivering a spell. Another man's poem used the phrase "my emotions have no limit," but read aloud it sounded like a poor man complaining that he lacked even a scrap of paper. Examples like these must be avoided.

28. According to Pulleyblank's reconstruction, the pronunciation of these two characters was no longer distinguishable in LMC, but they originally had a different medial, and were still classified as different rhymes in dictionaries such as *Guangyun* 廣韻 (1008).

29. This passage is discussed in detail in chapter 5.

The pentasyllabic mnemonic chant goes (Two and Four are different, Two and Nine match):[30]

○○●●○ (internal rhyme)
○●●○○
○●○○●
●○●●○
○○○●●
○●●○○
●●○○●
○○●●○

The heptasyllabic mnemonic chant goes (Two and Four are different, Two and Six match):

○○●●●○○ (internal rhyme)
●●○○●●○
●●○○○●●
○○●●●○○
○○●●○○●
●●○○●●○
●●○○○●●
○○●●●○○ (pinched two)[31]

30. That is, in the ten characters of a pentasyllabic couplet, the tones of the second and fourth syllables must contrast (one level, one deflected), while the second and ninth must accord.

31. There is a description of "pinching the two" 捻二 in the Higashiyama MS: "Starting from the second graph of the first line, read the poem sideways [that is, the second syllable of each line]. If the poem begins with a level tone, the order goes as ○●●○○●●○. The order for poems beginning from a variant tone can be deduced from this. This is called 'Pinching the Two.'"

Assorted Poetic Examples

SETTING THE TOPIC [*shutsudai* 出題]:

The poetry of the Tang accords with [external] things and vocalizes [the poet's] intentions; they have never used topic lines [*kudai* 句題]. Our court was much the same prior to the Jōgan era [859–77], but for a long time now has preferred topic lines. ("Topic lines" are lines taken from an old pentasyllabic or heptasyllabic poem that conform to the occasion. One may also use a new [invented] topic [*shindai* 新題].)[32]

PREDETERMINING THE RHYME [*rokuin* 勒韻]:[33]

Poems without a topic line [*mudaishi* 無題詩] often use pre-selected rhymes, but an example of a topic-line poem that uses pre-selected rhymes is [the piece] on the topic "Early Spring Brings a Light Chill" 春淺帶輕寒, which had the pre-selected rhymes 初, 餘, 魚, and 虛. This piece is by Sugawara no Michizane.[34]

IN THE OPENING COUPLET, USING A DIFFERENT CHARACTER WITH THE SAME READING [*yomi* 讀] IN PLACE OF A CHARACTER FROM THE TOPIC:

The opening couplet always contains all the graphs in the topic [phrase]. These cannot be altered, but [an exception of] this sort is Minamoto no Fusaakira's poem on the topic "Spring Rains Wash the Flowers' Faces" 春雨洗花顏, [in which the line] "Why do the thin drops of spring rain fall so often?/To pass across a flower's face and wash away the red dust" 春雨何因細脚頻、爲過花面洗紅塵 replaces *gan* 顏 with *men* 面.[35]

32. On the transition in the Heian period from quoted to invented topic lines, see Denecke, "Kudaishi no tenkai."

33. Literally, "reining in the rhyme." In this type of composition, popular at banquets, not only the rhyme syllable to be observed, but the exact words to end each couplet are set for the composing poets.

34. *Kanke bunsō, Kanke kōshū* 445.

35. See the discussion of this passage in chapter 5. The original poem is lost, but another couplet from it, along with a couplet on the same topic by Ki no Haseo, are together preserved in *Shinsen rōeishū kōhon to sakuin* 74–75.

FORM WITH TOPIC DECOMPOSITION [*hadai*]:

Sugawara [no Fumitoki]'s poem on the topic "Palace Warblers Twitter in the Dawn Light" 宮鶯囀曉光 reads, "Moonlight falls on the western tower, a song among the flowers;/Lamplight fades in the central pavilion, a tune in the bamboo" 西樓月落花間曲、中殿燈殘竹裏音.[36] In this [line] every graph is an exposition of the topic.[37]

FORM WITH FIGURAL IMAGERY [*nisemono* 似物]:[38]

[An example of] this is Sugawara [no Michizane]'s poem on the topic "With the Sky Clear, We Recognize the Visiting Geese" 天淨識賓鴻, which reads, "On a zither inlaid with green jade, the bridges stand aslant;/Across paper colored with blue moss are written a few lines" 碧玉裝箏斜立柱、青苔色紙數行書.[39]

BINARY [*sōkan*] FORM:

Sugawara [no Fumitoki]'s poem on the topic "Pipes and Strings Are Soft among the Sounds of Autumn" 秋聲脆管絃 reads, "The echo of falling leaves scrambles to accompany the lone bamboo,/The hum of the tall pines is light with the seven strands" 落葉響隨孤竹亂、長松韻逐七絲輕.[40] This couplet is written with the "pipes" and "strings" [of the topic phrase] divided into the upper and lower lines; each couplet is like this.[41]

36. The remainder of the poem is lost. This couplet is included in *Wakan rōeishū* 71.

37. See the discussion of this couplet in chapter 3.

38. *Nisemono* as a term for visual analogy in *waka* poetry can be found in Minamoto no Toshiyori's 源俊頼 (1055–1129) composition manual *Toshiyori zuinō* 俊頼髓脳 (early twelfth century). Toshiyori gives examples such as describing cherry blossoms as clouds or falling snow, or autumn leaves as brocade, among others (78).

39. Each line describes an image comparable to geese flying across the sky. *Kanke bunsō, Kanke kōshū* 379; *Wakan rōeishū* 322.

40. A line from the *Tentoku 3-nen dairi shiawase*, 364.

41. Instead of having the whole topic restated in each line, the customary *hadai* technique, the topic phrase is divided into component parts that are spread between the two lines of a couplet. In this case "the sounds of autumn" appears as "echo of falling

FORM USING PARALLELISM WITHIN A SINGLE LINE:

[An example of] this is Ōe no Mochitoki's poem written on an autumn evening that reads, "The forest foliage is entirely given over to desolate shades,/The ninth month barely retains but two more days' light" 林叢唯任蕭條色、九月纔殘二日光.[42] The graphs "forest foliage" and "desolate," as well as "ninth month" and "two days" are in a parallel relationship.[43]

SOUND PARALLELISM:[44]

[An example of] this is Ōe [no Asatsuna]'s poem on the topic "With Their Scents Jumbled, the Flowers Cannot Be Recognized" 香亂花難識, which reads, "If this is not the Hundredfold Blend seeping from its burner,/It must be sandalwood sunk beneath the waves" 若非百和籠中透、定是栴檀浪底沈.[45] The graphs "hundred" 百 and "sandalwood" 栴 form a parallel by virtue of their sound.[46]

leaves" in the first line and "hum of the tall pines" in the second, but "pipes and strings" is divided, so that the first line refers to woodwinds ("lone bamboo") and the second line to strings ("seven threads"). On this technique see Satō Michio, *Heian kōki Nihon kanbungaku*, 191–97.

42. The end of the ninth month is the last day of autumn. The remainder of this poem is lost.

43. The compounds *rinsō* 林叢 ("woods and grasses") and *shōjō* 蕭條 (a mimetic word for a lonely or desolate state) can be taken as parallel because the two characters of the latter compound would literally mean "wormwood" and "branches" when read individually, and thus correspond to the plants of the first compound.

44. See also the "Parallelism" subsection in "Essentials of Composition," pp. 236–37.

45. The "Hundredfold Blend" is a blend of incense. Sandalwood is a fragrant wood used for various implements, but Asatsuna's imagery here is instead suggestive of aloeswood, called "sunken incense" (沈香 or 沈水). The remainder of this poem is lost, but Asatsuna's preface at the same occasion (at the manor of Prince Shigeakira, probably during the 940s), is preserved in *Honchō monzui* 297.

46. The character "sandalwood" (LMC tʂian) sounds similar to the character "thousand" 千 (LMC tsʰian), which makes a neat parallel with "hundred."

OBLIQUE PARALLELISM [*sokutai* 側對]:

Taira no Sukemoto's poem on the topic "The Full Moon is Bright as a Mirror" 滿月明如鏡 reads, "The radiance is so pure I cannot tell it from green copper's forging,/When the light scatters I further fear the hundredfold refining has dispersed it" 光清不辨青銅冶、影散更疑百錬消.[47] "Green" 青 and "hundred" 百 form a parallel.[48]

IN THE CASE OF NUMBER PARALLELISM, THE PARALLELISM NEED NOT BE SO STRICT IN THE SECOND GRAPHS [OF THE TWO CORRESPONDING COMPOUNDS]:

Ōe [no Asatsuna]'s poem on Wang Zhaojun reads, "A single cry from a Hu horn, her dream after the frost;/Ten-thousand leagues from the Han palace, her heart before that moon" 胡角一聲霜後夢、漢宮萬里月前腸.[49] "Single cry" and "ten-thousand leagues" are parallel.[50]

47. Bronze ("green copper") was the customary material for mirrors in ancient East Asia, and the "hundred-times refined mirror" is an image from Jin-dynasty sources that was popularized in Japan through Bai Juyi's poem of the same name, part of the *Xin yuefu* sequence (*Bai Juyi ji jianjiao* 4.204–5). The remainder of this poem is lost, but a couplet from a poem on the same topic by Sugawara no Fumitoki is preserved in *Wakan rōeishū* 249.

48. "Green" (the first character in the compound *seidō*, meaning "bronze") forms a parallel with "hundred" 百 because a portion of the latter character can be read as "white" 白, making a color parallel. Oblique parallelism apparently refers to parallels derived from isolated parts of the actual characters used. See the description in *Bunkyō hifuron*, "Tō," 345–48.

49. Wang Zhaojun was a Han dynasty beauty given as consort to a Xiongnu ruler. "Hu" is a term for Central Asian peoples like the Xiongnu. The image here seems to be that Zhaojun is woken from her sleep by the cold and the horn's sound, and looks up to see the moon, thinking of home far away. This couplet, along with the remainder of the poem, is collected in *Wakan rōeishū* 699–702.

50. The point seems to be that even though the words "cry" and "league" do not form any meaningful opposition, because they are part of compounds beginning with numbers, the two compounds achieve "number parallelism." The Chisan MS has the final sentence as "'One' and 'ten-thousand' are parallel, while 'cry' and 'league' are not parallel."

DIRECTIONAL PARALLELISM:

Oe [no Asatsuna]'s poem on "Relating My Thoughts among the Mountains" 山中述懐 reads, "The moon sinks over Shang Mountain, their autumn beards are white;/Waves rise in Ying River, his left ear is cleansed" 商山月落秋鬂白、潁水波揚左耳清.[51] "Autumn" corresponds to the west, and thus makes a parallel with "left."[52]

51. *Fusōshū kōhon to sakuin* 25. The Four White-Haired Recluses of Mount Shang fled from society during the Qin dynasty, and refused Liu Bang's request for service after the advent of the Han. The sage Xu You 許由 is supposed to have washed out his ears in the Ying River when Emperor Yao asked him to take the throne (Huangfu Mi's *Gaoshi zhuan* 高士傳, quoted in Zhang Shoujie's commentary to *Shiji* 61.2121–22).

52. The Chisan MS has this sentence as "'Autumn' corresponds to west and 'left' to east, therefore they make a pair." In traditional "Five Phases" cosmology, autumn corresponds to the direction west (metal element, white color, etc.), and left is identified with east in numerous classical sources. See e.g. the commentaries quoted in *Wenxuan* 3.9b; *Shangshu zhengyi* 16.111.

APPENDIX B

Preface to *Wamyō ruijushō*

The preface to Minamoto no Shitagō's *Wamyō ruijushō*, discussed in chapter 5, provides a discussion of language and script almost unique among Heian sources in its detail and explicitness. It is written in an elaborate and highly allusive parallel prose, and in preparing the translation that follows I have relied on the copious notes in Kariya Ekisai's *Senchū wamyō ruijushō*, but in the interest of brevity do not note individual instances below.[1] The text of the preface shows very little variation among the extant manuscripts, with the exception of one manuscript held in the Nagoya Museum, which has numerous variants and may represent a preliminary draft of the preface.[2] I have only noted variants in the Nagoya manuscript in places where its text sheds light on problems of interpretation in the standard text. For the sake of clarity, I have broken up the translation into sections based on the structure of Shitagō's argument.

1. I have also benefitted from the translation in Takahashi Tadayuki and Takahashi Hisako, *Nihon no kojisho*, 20–32.
2. Nagoya-shi Hakubutsukan, *Wamyō ruijushō*.

If I may speak of the fourth princess of the Enchō reign,[3] her gentle virtue was established early, and her beauty is like a flower. The banks of her breast engulf Huyang, and the shores of her breath enfold Shanyin.[4] At the age of only seven, she was first presented to the late emperor. Because of her appearance, cheerful demeanor, and grace in in all things, the late emperor was particularly fond of her. He therefore bestowed on her a cither from the royal storehouses, and personally taught her its melodies. The princess is naturally perceptive, and learns on the first attempt. In a year or two, she was able to achieve wondrous music; from the thirteen strings rang out new sounds. Since the clouds mourned and the rivers choked at the mountain tomb of Daigo,[5] she has long avoided the moonlight at the Wei palace-gates, and has not brushed the dust from her Qin cither. The only occasional relief she finds in her retirement are the amusements of writing and painting. Here, the marvel of making flies from ink dots has nearly alighted on her folding-screen;[6] her skill to spin around the simurgh with a brush is also adept at scattering dew.[7] She has managed to distinguish the eight styles of writing,[8] and already inquires about the myriad names of things.

竊以延長第四公主、柔德早樹、淑姿如花。呑湖陽於胸陂、籠山陰於氣岸。年纔七歳、初謁先帝。先帝以其姿貌言笑、毎事都雅、特鍾愛焉。即賜御府箏、手教授其譜。公主天然聰高、學不再問。一二年

3. Kinshi was the fourth princess of the Emperor Daigo, whose reign names were Engi and Enchō. She was married to Minister of the Right Fujiwara no Morosuke.

4. Huyang and Shanyin are both place names, but also names of princesses who appear in the Chinese official histories. The language here is unusual, but seems to indicate that Kinshi's virtue surpasses these two earlier figures. The Nagoya MS has "Shanyin is embarrassed for its chilly lands, Huyang begs pardon for its meager virtue" 山陰慙其地寒、湖陽謝以德薄. On this phrase, see also Honma, *Ōchō kanbungaku hyōgen ronkō*, 148–50.

5. The temple where her father the late emperor was interred.

6. Reference to the story of Cao Buxing 曹不興 (fl. early third century), whose skill was such that flies he painted were mistaken for real ones by the Wu emperor Sun Quan. The story is recounted in an excerpt from the lost text *Wulu* 呉錄 quoted in Pei Songzhi's commentary to *Record of the Three Kingdoms* (*Sanguozhi* 63.1425).

7. "Spin the simurgh" and "dripping dew" are terms commonly used in calligraphy manuals such as the *Bishi lun* 筆勢論, which circulated in Japan by the late ninth century (Kobase, *Nihonkoku genzaisho mokuroku*, 6).

8. The eight different scripts listed in *Shuowen jiezi* 15[*shang*].2a.

間、能究妙曲、十三絃上、更秦新聲。自醍醐山陵、雲愁水咽、永辭魏闕之月、不拂奏箏之塵。時々慰幽閑者、書畫之戲而已。於是因點成蠅之妙、殆上屏風、以筆廻鸞之能、亦巧垂露。漸辨八體之字、豫訪萬物之名。

Her majesty said:

> I have heard those who think to gather mustard diligently investigate principles and facts; those who hope to break the cassia bough compete to pluck literary flowers.[9] But as for Yamato names, they are abandoned and ignored. Therefore, though [I have] one hundred cases of the *Institute of Literature and Grove of Lyrics*,[10] thirty volumes of *Mr. Bai's Encyclopedia*,[11] these merely provide poetic [*fūgetsu*] amusements, but are inadequate to everyday [*sezoku*] uncertainties. Those [books] that can answer these questions are the *Handbook for Distinguishing Appearances*,[12] *Mr. Yō's Lexicon of Chinese*,[13] *Materia Medica with Yamato Names,* compiled according to imperial decree by the Imperial Doctor Fukane no Sukehito,[14] *Private Notes on the Nihon shoki* by Supernumerary Governor of Yamashiro Province Yatabe no

9. "Gathering mustard" and "breaking the cassia bough" are here allusions to civil service examinations that focused on either elucidation of the classics or literary composition. See *Hanshu* 75.3159; *Jinshu* 52.1443.

10. *Wenguan cilin*, a Tang literary anthology in 1000 *juan* compiled under the direction of Xu Jingzong 許敬宗 (592–672).

11. A Tang encyclopedia attributed to Bai Juyi, more commonly referred to as *Baishi liutie* 白氏六帖.

12. *Benshiki ryūjō* appears in the *Nihonkoku genzaisho mokuroku*, but little is known about the work besides what appears in *Wamyō ruijushō*. It is thought to have been a categorically arranged dictionary compiled in Japan. The Nagoya MS also includes here a text called *Hōgen yōmoku* 方言要目.

13. *Yōshi Kango shō*. The authorship of this text is unknown, though according to Shitagō it was compiled in the early eighth century (see below). The name Yō is speculatively associated with the surname Yagi 楊貴 by Kamei ("Yagi-shi ni tsuki," 69), the eighth-century figure Yako no Muzane 陽胡眞身 by Ōta ("Sonkeikaku sankanbon Iroha jiruishō," 150), and Lin suggests an immigrant (*toraijin*) lineage from the continent with the surname Yang ("Nara jidai no jisho," 307)—though given the localizations that were frequently applied to the names of such immigrant lineages, these possibilities are not mutually exclusive.

14. *Honzō wamyō*. This 918 work is based on the Chinese *Xinxiu bencao*.

Kinmochi,[15] and so on. However, from the Yōrō era [717–24] we have only ten chapters of Yō's commentary, and the work selected in Engi [901–23] only deals with medicinal herbs. The three volumes of Yatabe's *Private Notes* are full of archaic language, but few Yamato names; the eighteen sections of the *Handbook for Distinguishing Appearances* and Yō's commentary have different titles but the same content. All of these works have strengths and weaknesses. As for the other *Lexicons of Chinese*,[16] it is not known who compiled them. People call these "Grade-A Books" or call them "Practice Books." "Grade A" is a term of open-mouthed praise,[17] "practice" refers to memorization and recitation. The popular understanding is divided, and neither [explanation] is clear.[18] In addition, the terms recorded lack proper definitions and are mixed with falsehoods, such as when octopus [*tako*] becomes 鮹, freshwater fish [*hae*] becomes 鰉 , sacred pine [*sakaki*] becomes 榊, or washbasin [*hanisō*] becomes 椋.[19] Collect the best explanations from among these various authorities, so that I may begin my writing without any doubts.

其教曰、我聞思拾芥者、好探義實、期折桂者、競採文華。至于和名、棄而不屑。是故雖一百帙文舘詞林、三十卷白氏事類、而徒備風月之興、難決世俗之疑。適可決其疑者、辨色立成、楊氏漢語抄、大醫博士深根輔仁奉勅撰集和名本草、山州員外刺史田公望日本紀私記等也。然猶養老所傳、楊説纔十部、延喜所撰、藥種只一端。田氏私記一部三卷、古語多載、和名希存。辨色立成十有八章、與楊家説、名異實同。編錄之間、頗有長短。其餘漢語抄、不知何人撰。世謂之甲書、或呼爲業書。甲則開口裒揚之名、業是服膺誦習之義。俗説兩端、未詳其一矣。又其所撰錄名、音義不見、浮僞相交。海蛸爲鮹、河魚爲鰉、祭樹爲榊、澡器爲椋等是也。汝集彼數家之善説、令我臨文無所疑焉。

15. The *Nihongi shiki* is attributed to Yatabe no Kinmochi (fl. 904–36) in the thirteenth-century bibliography *Honchō shojaku mokuroku* 本朝書籍目錄, but the version cited by Shitagō in *Wamyō ruijushō* does not otherwise survive.

16. That is, other editions besides the "Mr. Yō" commentary edition mentioned earlier.

17. The phrase 開口裒揚 here is quite unusual. I follow Takahashi and Takahashi in taking the third character as a variant of 褒 (*Nihon no kojisho*, 27), which seems to be supported by the entry in *Ruijū myōgishō* (744).

18. The Nagoya MS includes at this point the sentence: "When I ventured to examine this matter, I found that it was neither *kōsho* 甲書 nor *gōsho* 業書, but rather a mispronunciation of *goshō* 語抄."

19. These are presented as examples of "mistaken" orthography.

My late father was honored to be one of the princess's maternal relatives,[20] so I was able to see the marvel of her calligraphy. My old mother too served under the princess's beneficent influence, thus I was able to receive her gentle command. My firm refusal was not accepted: in the end she employed me to edit [the text]. Whether it be text from the *Lexicon of Chinese*, or an explanation circulating among the populace, first I quote classical sources and authoritative explanations, affixing [the words] to their commentary. If a classical source cannot be found, I simply quote the *Handbook for Distinguishing Appearances*, *Mr. Yō's Lexicon of Chinese*, or the *Private Notes on the Nihongi*, or cite the phonetic orthography used in the *Classified History of the Country*, the *Collection of Myriad Ages*, or the three *Procedures*:[21] The water animals have the *ashika* [sea lion], the highland birds have the *inaōsedori*;[22] among plants the *ominaeshi* [golden lace], among seaweed the *ogonori* [gracilaria].[23] As for terms such as *ogonori* 於期菜, is it not the case that among the so-called Six Classes [of writing],[24] number five is called borrowing? Where the thing lacks a graph, we indicate it through the sound [of another character]. The Sanskrit terms in Buddhist scriptures are also like this. It is not without precedent, so I have made use of this [method] here. There are also Sinitic pronunciations that have been adopted into the vernacular [*zoku*].[25] Although they are not Yamato names, nevertheless they must be used: names for stones like "magnet" or "alum," names for incense like "sinking

20. Kinshi's mother Shūshi 周子 (d. 935) was cousin to Shitagō's father—their respective fathers were both sons of Minamoto no Sadamu 源定 (816–63), a first-generation Saga Genji.

21. *Ruijū kokushi* (892), a categorically organized historical encyclopedia edited by Sugawara no Michizane; *Man'yōshū*, a poetic anthology; and the *Kōnin shiki*, *Jōgan shiki*, and *Engi shiki*, successive promulgations of court procedure.

22. A legendary bird that appears in *waka* poetry.

23. All of these are examples of names written with characters used for the phonetic value of their *kun* readings to write Japanese words (ex: *ashika*, 葦鹿), as opposed to being represented with either phonetic *kana* transcriptions (阿之加) or semantic equivalents drawn from literary Sinitic (海驢).

24. Introduced by Xu Shen in the *Shuowen jiezi*. For a discussion of this passage, see chapter 5.

25. That is, Chinese compounds that have been adopted as loan words into Japanese speech, so that the characters do not have vernacular equivalents like most of the entries in Shitagō's dictionary.

incense" and "floating incense";[26] monk's implements like censers and the *khakkhara* staff, artist's tools like safflower rouge and lead powder. There may also be cases where common people know that something is an error but are unable to correct it, such as: the character 鮏 [fishy-smelling] misused for "salmon" [*sake*], the character 椙 [pillar] read as "cedar" [*sugi*], the pronunciation of "blacksmith" [*tan'ya* 鍛冶] taken to be *kaji*,[27] the name of the "spoon worm" [*ii*] written as 蛦.[28] In instances of this sort, I have noted my assessment, illuminating somewhat the accounts of the ancients, recounting briefly the rumors of the streets.

僕之先人幸忝公主之外戚、故僕得見其草隸之神妙。僕之老母亦陪公主之下風、故僕得蒙其松容之教命。固辭不許、遂用修撰。或漢語抄之文、或流俗人之說、先擧本文正說、各附出於其注。若本文未詳、則直擧辨色立成、楊氏漢語抄、日本紀私記、或擧類聚國史、萬葉集、三代式等所用之假字。水獸有葦鹿之名、山鳥有稻負之號、野草之中女郎花、海苔之屬於期菜等是也。至如於期菜者、所謂六書法、其五曰假借、本無其字、依聲託事者乎。内典梵語、亦復如是。非無所據、故以取之。或復有以其音用于俗者、雖非和名、既是要用。石名之磁石礬石、香名之沈香淺香、法師具之香爐錫杖、畫師具之燕脂胡粉等是也。或復有俗人知其訛謬、不能改易者。鮏訛爲鮭、椙讀如杉、鍛冶之音誤涉鍜治、蝙蛞之名僞用蛜蛦等是也。若此之類、注加今案。聊明故老之說、略述閭巷之談。

To sum up, I hope it will be close to common usage and convenient to use, so at a moment of forgetfulness, [the answer] will be readily available. I have sought to avoid multiple names and alternate terms, or deep and complex definitions that could cause confusion when reading. First come heaven and earth, next human affairs, lastly the trees and grasses. I have arranged it in ten volumes, each volume divided into chapters, each chapter divided into topics. [With altogether] twenty-four chapters and 148

26. Two types of incense made from agarwood.

27. The rather obscure characters for "blacksmith" resemble characters that could be read *ka-chi* in Sino-Japanese, leading to a false etymological interpretation based on the native word for "blacksmith," *kaji*.

28. These characters were used for their Chinese sound value to represent the Japanese word *ii*, a type of marine worm, but their meaning is different in Chinese texts.

topics, it is called the *Categorical Miscellany of Yamato Names.*[29] Long ago a man said: The gossip in the street and back-alley rumors are yet worth investigating.[30] Although my learning is indeed wanting, nevertheless my annotations all proceed from the ancient classics and histories of Yamato and Han. However, to correct errors and repair deficiencies is beyond the reach of my talent. I am ashamed before the princess's august gaze within, and mortified by the laughter of wiser men without.

總而謂之、欲近於俗、便於事、臨忽忘如指掌。不欲異名別號、義深旨廣、有煩于披覽焉。上擧天地、中次人物、下至草木。勒成十卷、々中分部、々中分門。廿四部、百廿八門。名曰和名類聚抄。古人有言、街談巷説、猶有可採。僕雖誠淺學、而所注緝、皆出自前經舊史倭漢之書。但刊謬補闕、非才分所及。内慙公主之照覽、外愧賢智之盧胡耳。

29. These numbers (of volumes, chapters, and topics) are all different in the prefaces that appear in twenty-volume manuscripts of the work.

30. A modified quotation from Cao Zhi's "Yu Yang Dezu shu" 與楊德祖書, *Wenxuan* 42.14a. The term "street gossip and alley rumors" 街談巷説 derives from the *Hanshu* description of *xiaoshuo* 小說 miscellaneous narratives (30.1745).

Bibliography

Primary Sources

Bai Juyi ji jianjiao. Edited by Zhu Jincheng. Shanghai: Shanghai guji chubanshe, 1988.

Bunka shūreishū. Compiled by Fujiwara no Fuyutsugu, Sugawara no Kiyokimi, Nakao ō, Isayama no Fumitsugu, Shigeno no Sadanushi, and Kuwabara no Haraka. In *Kaifūsō, Bunka shūrei shū, Honchō monzui*. Edited by Kojima Noriyuki. Nihon koten bungaku taikei 67. Tokyo: Iwanami shoten, 1964.

Bunkyō hifuron. Compiled by Kūkai. In *Kōbō Daishi Kūkai zenshū*, vol. 5, edited by Kōzen Hiroshi. Tokyo: Chikuma shobō, 1986.

Chōya gunsai. Compiled by Miyoshi no Tameyasu. In *Shintei zōho kokushi taikei*, vol. 29 pt. 1.

Chuci buzhu. Annotated by Hong Xingzu. Edited by Bai Huawen, Xu Denan, Li Rulian, and Fang Jin. Zhongguo gudian wenxue jiben congshu. Beijing: Zhonghua shuju, 1983.

Chūgaishō. By Nakahara no Moromoto. In *Gōdanshō, Chūgaishō, Fukego*. Edited by Gotō Akio, Ikegami Jun'ichi, and Yamane Taisuke. Shin Nihon koten bungaku taikei 32. Tokyo: Iwanami shoten, 1997.

Chūka jakuboku shishō. Compiled by Nyogetsu Juin. In *Chūka jakuboku shishō, Yunoyama renkushō*. Edited by Ōtsuka Mitsunobu, Ozaki Yūjirō, and Asakura Hisashi. Shin Nihon koten bungaku taikei 53. Tokyo: Iwanami shoten, 1995.

Chuxueji. Compiled by Xu Jian et al. 2 vols. Beijing: Zhonghua shuju, 1962.

Chūyūki. By Fujiwara no Munetada. Edited by Tōkyō Daigaku Shiryō Hensanjo. 6 vols. Dai Nihon kokiroku. Tokyo: Iwanami shoten, 1993–.

Chūyūki burui shihai kanshishū. In *Toshoryō sōkan: Heian Kamakura mikan shishū*, edited by Kunaichō Shoryōbu, 47–108. Tokyo: Meiji shoin, 1972.

Dai Nihon komonjo hennen monjo. Edited by Tōkyō Daigaku Shiryō Hensanjo. 25 vols. Tokyo: Tōkyō Teikoku Daigaku, 1901–40.

Dai Nihon shiryō. Edited by Tōkyō Daigaku Shiryō Hensanjo. 398 vols. in 12 series. Tokyo: Tōkyō Daigaku shuppankai, 1901–.

Daigoji shin yōroku. Compiled by Gien. Edited by Daigoji Bunkazai Kenkyūjo. 2 vols. Kyoto: Hōzōkan, 1991.

Denshi kashū chū. By Shimada no Tadaomi. Edited by Kojima Noriyuki. 3 vols. Ōsaka: Izumi shoin, 1991–94.

Eiga monogatari. Edited by Yamanaka Yutaka, Ikeda Naotaka, Akiyama Ken, and Fukunaga Susumu. 3 vols. Shinpen Nihon koten bungaku zenshū 31–33. Tokyo: Shōgakkan, 1995–98.

Engi shiki. Compiled by Fujiwara no Tokihira, Fujiwara no Tadahira, et al. In *Shintei zōho kokushi taikei*, vol. 26.

Fūga wakashū. Compiled by Retired Emperor Kōgen. In *Shinpen kokka taikan*, 1:553–99. Tokyo: Kadokawa shoten, 1983–92.

Fusōshū kōhon to sakuin. Compiled by Ki no Tadana. Edited by Tasaka Junko. Fukuoka: Tōka shobō, 1985.

Genji monogatari. By Murasaki Shikibu. Edited by Abe Akio, Imai Gen'e, Akiyama Ken, and Suzuki Hideo. 6 vols. Shinpen Nihon koten bungaku zenshū 20–25. Tokyo: Shōgakkan, 1994–98.

Gōdanshō. By Fujiwara no Sanekane. In *Gōdanshō, Chūgaishō, Fukego*. Edited by Gotō Akio, Ikegami Jun'ichi, and Yamane Taisuke. Shin Nihon koten bungaku taikei 32. Tokyo: Iwanami shoten, 1997.

Gōke shidai. Compiled by Ōe no Masafusa. In *Shintō taikei, chōgi saishi hen 4*. Edited by Watanabe Naohiko. Tokyo: Shintō taikei hensankai, 1991.

Gonki. By Fujiwara no Yukinari. 2 vols. Zōho shiryō taisei 4–5. Kyoto: Rinsen shoten, 1965.

Gozan bungaku shū, Edo kanshi shū. Edited by Yamagishi Tokuhei. Nihon koten bungaku taikei 89. Tokyo: Iwanami shoten, 1966.

Hanshu. Compiled by Ban Gu, Ban Zhao, and Ma Xu. Beijing: Zhonghua shuju, 1962.

Heian ibun. Edited by Takeuchi Rizō. 14 vols. Tōkyōdō shuppan, 1963.

Hokurika. By Ichikawa Kansai. In *Yoshiwara shi shūsei*, edited by Saita Sakura [Asakawa Seiichirō], 5–58. Taihei Bunko 22. Tokyo: Taihei shooku, 1993.

Hokuzanshō. Compiled by Fujiwara no Kintō. In *Dairi gishiki hoka 4-shu gōhon*. Edited by Zōtei Kojitsu Sōsho Henshūbu. Zōtei kojitsu sōsho 4. Tokyo: Yoshikawa kōbunkan, 1928.

Honchō monzui. Compiled by Fujiwara no Akihira. Edited by Ōsone Shōsuke, Kinpira Tadashi, and Gotō Akio. Shin Nihon koten bungaku taikei 27. Tokyo: Iwanami shoten, 1992.

Honchō mudaishi zenchūshaku. Edited by Honma Yōichi. 3 vols. Tokyo: Shintensha, 1992–94.

Honchō reisō kanchū. Compiled by Takashina no Moriyoshi. Edited by Kawaguchi Hisao, Honchō Reisō o Yomu Kai. Tokyo: Benseisha, 1993.

Hōsō shiyōshō. In *Gunsho ruijū*, vol. 6 (Ritsuryō bu), 71–136. Tokyo: Zoku gunsho ruijū kanseikai, 1932.

Hou Hanshu. Compiled by Fan Ye. 12 vols. Beijing: Zhonghua shuju, 1965.

Huainan honglie jijie. Compiled by Liu An. Edited by Feng Yi and Qiao Hua. 2 vols. Beijing: Zhonghua shuju, 1989.

Iroha jiruishō. In *Iroha jiruishō kenkyū narabi ni sakuin. Honbun, sakuin hen*. Edited by Nakada Norio and Minegishi Akira. Tokyo: Kazama shobō, 1964.

Ise monogatari. In *Taketori monogatari, Ise monogatari, Yamato monogatari, Heichū monogatari*. Edited by Katagiri Yōichi, Fukui Teisuke, Takahashi Shōji, and Shimizu Yoshiko. Shinpen Nihon koten bungaku zenshū 12. Tokyo: Shōgakkan, 1994.

Jinshu. Compiled by Fang Xuanling. 10 vols. Beijing: Zhonghua shuju, 1974.

Jōgen 2-nen sanjō sadaijin Yoritada senzai utaawase. In *Utaawase shū*. Edited by Hagitani Boku and Taniyama Shigeru. Nihon koten bungaku taikei 74. Tokyo: Iwanami shoten, 1965.

Jurin shūyō. In *Zoku gunsho ruijū*, vol. 31 pt. 2, 354–88. Tokyo: Zoku gunsho ruijū kanseikai, 1926.

Kagerō nikki. By Michitsuna no Haha. In *Tosa nikki, Kagerō nikki*. Edited by Kikuchi Yasuhiko, Kimura Masanori, and Imuta Tsunehisa. Shinpen Nihon koten bungaku zenshū 13. Tokyo: Shōgakkan, 1995.

Kaifūsō. In *Kaifūsō, Bunka shūrei shū, Honchō monzui*. Edited by Kojima Noriyuki. Nihon koten bungaku taikei 67. Tokyo: Iwanami shoten, 1964.

Kanjo Yō Yū den zankan. Kyōto Teikoku Daigaku Bungakubu eiin kyūshōhon 2. Kyoto: Kyōto Teikoku Daigaku bungakubu, 1935.

Kanke bunsō, Kanke kōshū. By Sugawara no Michizane. Edited by Kawaguchi Hisao. Nihon koten bungaku taikei 72. Tokyo: Iwanami shoten, 1966.

Kankenshō. Naikaku Bunko Collection, *Jū* 004-0001. National Archives of Japan, Tokyo.

Keikokushū. Compiled by Yoshimine no Yasuyo, Minabuchi no Hirosada, Sugawara no Kiyokimi, Yasuno no Fumitsugu, Abe no Yoshihito, and Shigeno no Sadanushi. In *Gunsho ruijū* 8 (Bunpitsu bu), 490–554. Tokyo: Zoku gunsho ruijū kanseikai, 1932.

Kōbun hongi dai 10. Tokyo: Kichō kotenseki kankōkai, 1954.

Kogo shūi. Compiled by Inbe no Hironari. Edited by Nishimiya Kazutami. Tokyo: Iwanami shoten, 1985.

Kojidan. Compiled by Minamoto no Akikane. In *Kojidan, Zoku kojidan*. Edited by Kawabata Yoshiaki and Araki Hiroshi. Shin Nihon koten bungaku taikei 41. Tokyo: Iwanami shoten, 2005.

Konjaku monogatari shū. Edited by Mabuchi Kazuo, Kunisaki Fumimaro, and Inagaki Taiichi. 4 vols. Shin Nihon koten bungaku zenshū 35–38. Tokyo: Shōgakkan, 1999–2002.

Kōyasan monjo. 8 vols. In *Dai Nihon komonjo*, vol. 1. Edited by Tōkyō Daigaku Shiryō Hensanjo. Tokyo: Tōkyō Daigaku shuppankai, 1904–7.

Kuchizusami chūkai. By Minamoto no Tamenori. Edited by Yōgaku no Kai. Tokyo: Benseisha, 1997.

Kugyō bunin. 5 vols. In *Shintei zōho kokushi taikei*, vols. 53–57.

Kujō ushōjō yuikai. By Fujiwara no Morosuke. In *Kodai seiji shakai shisō*, edited by Yamagishi Tokuhei, Takeuchi Rizō, Ienaga Saburō, and Ōsone Shōsuke, 115–22. Nihon shisō taikei 8. Tokyo: Iwanami shoten, 1979.

Kunaichō Shoryōbu zō shijoshū. Edited by Ōsone Shōsuke and Satō Michio. In *Wakan hikaku bungaku kenkyū no shomondai*, vol. 8 of *Wakan hikaku bungaku sōsho*, edited by Wakan Hikaku Bungakkai. Tokyo: Kyūko shoin, 1988.

Kyūreki. By Fujiwara no Morosuke. Edited by Tōkyō Daigaku Shiryō Hensanjo. Dai Nihon kokiroku. Tokyo: Iwanami shoten, 1958.

Lunyu zhushu. Annotated by Xing Bing. In *Shisanjing zhushu*, edited by Ruan Yuan, 2:2453–536. Beijing, Zhonghua shuju, 1980.

Makura no sōshi. By Sei Shōnagon. Edited by Matsuo Satoshi and Nagai Kazuko. Shinpen Nihon koten bungaku zenshū 18. Tokyo: Shōgakkan, 1997.

Mengqiu. By Li Han. In *Mōgyū kochū shūsei.* 3 vols. Edited by Ikeda Toshio. Tokyo: Kyūko shoin, 1987.

Midō kanpaku ki. By Fujiwara no Michinaga. Edited by Tōkyō Daigaku Shiryō Hensanjo. 3 vols. Dai Nihon kokiroku. Tokyo: Iwanami shoten, 1952–54.

Murasaki shikibu nikki. In *Izumi shikibu nikki, Murasaki shikibu nikki, Sarashina nikki, Sanuki no suke nikki.* Edited by Fujioka Tadaharu, Nakano Kōichi, Inukai Kiyoshi, and Ishii Fumio. Shin Nihon koten bungaku zenshū 26. Tokyo: Shōgakkan, 1994.

Nan Qishu. Compiled by Xiao Zixian. 3 vols. Beijing: Zhonghua shuju, 1972.

Nanshi. Compiled by Li Yanshou. 6 vols. Beijing: Zhonghua shuju, 1975.

Nichūreki. In *Shintei zōho shiseki shūran*, vol. 5. Edited by Tsunoda Bun'ei and Gorai Shigeru. Kyoto: Rinsen shoten, 1967.

Nihon kiryaku. 2 vols. In *Shintei zōho kokushi taikei*, vols. 10–11.

Nihon sandai jitsuroku. Compiled by Fujiwara no Tokihira, Sugawara no Michizane, Ōkura no Yoshiyuki, and Mimune no Masahira. In *Shintei zōho kokushi taikei*, vol. 4.

Nihon shiki: Honbun to sōsakuin. Compiled by Ichikawa Kansai. Edited by Takashima Kaname. 3 vols. Tokyo: Bensei shuppan, 2003.

Nihon shiki shūi. Edited by Gotō Akio. Tokyo: Yoshikawa kōbunkan, 2000.

Nihon shoki. Compiled by Toneri Shinnō. Edited by Kojima Noriyuki, Naoki Kōjirō, Nishimiya Kazutami, Kuranaka Susumu, and Mōri Masamori. 3 vols. Shinpen Nihon koten bungaku zenshū 2–4. Tokyo: Shōgakkan, 1994–98.

Ōkagami. Edited by Tachibana Kenji and Katō Shizuko. Shinpen Nihon koten bungaku zenshū 34. Tokyo: Shōgakkan, 1996.

Quan Tangshi. Compiled by Cao Yin et al. 25 vols. Beijing: Zhonghua shuju, 1960.

Rihō ō ki. By Shigeakira Shinnō. Edited by Yoneda Yūsuke and Yoshioka Masayuki. Shiryō sanshū. Tokyo: Zoku gunsho ruijū kanseikai, 1974.

Rōei Gōchū. Attributed to Ōe no Masafusa. In *Wakan rōeishū kochūshaku shūsei*, edited by Itō Masayoshi, Kuroda Akira, and Miki Masahiro, 1:1–296. Kyoto: Daigakudō shoten, 1997.

Ruijū kudaishō zenchūshaku. Edited by Honma Yōichi. Osaka: Izumi shoin, 2010.

Ruijū myōgishō. Edited by Masamune Atsuo. Tokyo: Kazama shobō, 1968.

Ryō no shūge. Annotated by Koremune no Naomoto. 2 vols. In *Shintei zōho kokushi taikei*, vols. 23–24.

Saikyūki. Compiled by Minamoto no Takaakira. Edited by Zōtei Kojitsu Sōsho Henshūbu. 2 vols. Zōtei kojitsu sōsho 39–40. Tokyo: Yoshikawa kōbunkan, 1931.

Sakeiki. By Minamoto no Tsuneyori. Zōho shiryō taisei 6. Kyoto: Rinsen shoten, 1965.

Sakumon daitai cited editions:

Chisan Archive MS	In "Chisan Shoko-zō 'Sakumon daitai' honkoku to kaidai." Edited by Yamazaki Makoto. *Kokubungaku Kenkyū Shiryōkan chōsa kenkyū hōkoku* 24 (2003): 67–90.
Higashiyama Imperial Archive MS	In "Sakumon daitai no gensho keitai ni tsuite—furoku Higashiyama Bunko-bon *Bunpitsu daitai* honkoku." Edited by Yamazaki Makoto. *Kokubungaku Kenkyū Shiryōkan chōsa kenkyū hōkoku* 23 (2002): 331–74.
Kanchiin MS	In *Heian shibun zanpen*. Tenri Toshokan zenpon sōsho, Washo no bu 57. Tokyo: Yagi shoten, 1984. (Unless otherwise noted, this is the version quoted.)
Ōsu Archive MS	In *Kanbungaku shiryōshū*, 285–312. Edited by Kokubungaku Kenkyū Shiryōkan. Shinpukuji zenpon sōkan 12. Kyoto: Rinsen shoten, 2000.

Sandai gyoki itsubun shūsei. Edited by Tokoro Isao. Tokyo: Kokusho kankōkai, 1982.

Sanguozhi. Compiled by Chen Shou. 5 vols. Beijing: Zhonghua shuju, 1962.

Seiji yōryaku. Compiled by Yoshimune (Koremune) no Tadasuke. In *Shintei zōho kokushi taikei*, vol. 28.

Senchū Wamyō ruijushō. Annotated by Kariya Ekisai. In *Shohon shūsei Wamyō ruijushō: Honbun hen*. Edited by Kyōto Daigaku Bungakubu Kokugogaku Kokubungaku Kenkyūshitsu. Kyoto: Rinsen shoten, 1968.

Sezoku genbun. By Minamoto no Tamenori. In *Heian shibun zanpen*, 63–196. Tenri Toshokan zenpon sōsho, Washo no bu 57. Tokyo: Yagi shoten, 1984.

Shangshu zhengyi. Annotated by Kong Yingda. In *Shisanjing zhushu*, edited by Ruan Yuan, 1:109–258. Beijing, Zhonghua shuju, 1980.

Shihua zonggui qianji. Compiled by Ruan Yue. Edited by Zhou Benchun. Beijing: Renmin wenxue chubanshe, 1987.

Shiji. Compiled by Sima Qian. 10 vols. Bejing: Zhonghua shuju, 1959.

Shikyō ruijū. Compiled by Kibi no Makibi. In *Kodai seiji shakai shisō*, edited by Yamagishi

Tokuhei, Takeuchi Rizō, Ienaga Saburō, and Ōsone Shōsuke, 43–48. Nihon shisō taikei 8. Tokyo: Iwanami shoten, 1979.

Shinsen rōeishū kōhon to sakuin. Compiled by Fujiwara no Mototoshi. Edited by Kawamura Teruo and Satō Michio. Tokyo: Miyai shoten, 1994.

Shintei zōho kokushi taikei. Edited by Kuroita Katsumi. 66 vols. Tokyo: Yoshikawa kōbunkan, 1929–66.

Shitagō shū. By Minamoto no Shitagō, cited editions:

Bōmon no tsubone MS	In *Heian shikashū* 3, 59–236. Reizei-ke Shiguretei sōsho 16. Tokyo: Asahi shinbunsha, 1995.
Nishi Honganji MS	In *Shinpen kokka taikan*, 3:98–104. Tokyo: Kadokawa shoten, 1983–92.

Shoku Nihongi. Compiled by Sugano no Mamichi et al. Edited by Aoki Kazuo, Sasayama Haruo, Inaoka Kōji, and Shirafuji Noriyuki. 5 vols. Shin Nihon koten bungaku taikei 12–16. Tokyo: Iwanami shoten, 1989–98.

Shōyūki. By Fujiwara no Sanesuke. Edited by Tōkyō Daigaku Shiryō Hensanjo. 11 vols. Dai Nihon kokiroku. Tokyo: Iwanami shoten, 1959–86.

Shūi wakashū. Attributed to Retired Emperor Kazan. Edited by Komachiya Teruhiko. Shin Nihon koten bungaku taikei 7. Tokyo: Iwanami shoten, 1990.

Shunki. By Fujiwara no Sukefusa. Zōho shiryō taisei 7. Kyoto: Rinsen shoten, 1965.

Shuowen jiezi. Compiled by Xu Shen. Edited by Chen Changzhi. Beijing: Zhonghua shuju, 1963.

Sonpi bunmyaku. Compiled by Tōin Kinsada. 4 vols. In *Shintei zōho kokushi taikei*, vols. 58–60.

Taiheiki. Edited by Hasegawa Tadashi. 4 vols. Shin Nihon koten bungaku zenshū 54–57. Tokyo: Shōgakkan, 1998.

Taikai hishō. By Fujiwara no Koremichi. In *Gunsho ruijū*, vol. 18 (Zatsu bu), 1–17. Tokyo: Zoku gunsho ruijū kanseikai, 1939.

Taiki. By Fujiwara no Yorinaga. 3 vols. Zōho shiryō taisei 23–25. Kyoto: Rinsen shoten, 1965.

Taiping yulan. Compiled by Li Fang et al. 4 vols. Beijing: Zhonghua shuju, 1960.

Taishō shinshū daizōkyō. Edited by Takakusu Junjirō and Watanabe Kaigyoku. 85 vols. Tokyo: Taishō issaikyō kankōkai, 1924–32.

Teishin-kō ki. By Fujiwara no Tadahira. Edited by Tōkyō Daigaku Shiryō Hensanjo. Dai Nihon kokiroku. Tōkyō: Iwanami shoten, 1956.

Tentoku 3-nen dairi shiawase. In *Heianchō utaawase taisei*, edited by Hagitani Boku, 1:362–65. Zōho shinteiban (rev. enl. ed.). Kyoto: Dōmeisha shuppan, 1995.

Tentoku 4-nen dairi utaawase. In *Utaawase shū*. Edited by Hagitani Boku and Taniyama Shigeru. Nihon koten bungaku taikei 74. Tokyo: Iwanami shoten, 1965.

Tōdaiji monjo. 21 vols. In *Dai Nihon komonjo*, vol. 18. Edited by Tōkyō Daigaku Shiryō Hensanjo. Tokyo: Tōkyō Daigaku shuppankai, 1944–.

Toshiyori zuinō. By Minamoto no Toshiyori. In *Karon shū*. Edited by Hashimoto Fumio, Ariyoshi Tamotsu, and Fujihira Haruo. Shin Nihon koten bungaku zenshū 87. Tokyo: Shōgakkan, 2002.

Tōzan ōrai. By Jōshin. In *Nihon kyōkasho taikei: Ōrai hen*, edited by Ishikawa Ken, 1:367–422.Tokyo: Kōdansha, 1968.
Tsūken nyūdō zōsho mokuroku. In *Gunsho ruijū*, vol. 28 (Zatsu bu), 188–200. Tokyo: Zoku gunsho ruijū kanseikai, 1932.

Ueno-bon Chū senjimon chūkai. Annotated by Li Xian. Edited by Kurota Akira, Gotō Akio, Tōno Haruyuki, and Miki Masahiro. Osaka: Izumi shoin, 1989.
Unshū shōsoku. Attributed to Fujiwara no Akihira. In *Gunsho ruijū*, vol. 9 (Shōsoku bu), 390–437. Tokyo: Zoku gunsho ruijū kanseikai, 1928.
Utsuho monogatari (zen). Edited by Muroki Hideyuki. Rev. ed. Tokyo: Ōfū, 2001.

Wakan rōeishū. Compiled by Fujiwara no Kintō. Edited by Ōsone Shōshuke and Horiuchi Hideaki. Shinchō Nihon koten shūsei 61. Tokyo: Shinchōsha, 1983.
Wenxin diaolong jiaozheng. By Liu Xie. Edited by Wang Liqi. Shanghai: Shanghai guji chubanshe, 1980.
Wenxuan: Fu kaoyi. Annotated by Li Shan. Taibei: Yiwen yinshuguan, 2003.

Xijing zaji. Attributed to Ge Hong. In *Yan Danzi, Xijing zaji.* Gu xiaoshuo congkan. Beijing: Zhonghua shuju, 1985.

Yakuchū Renju shikaku. Annotated by Kashiwagi Jotei. Edited by Ibi Takashi. Tokyo: Iwanami shoten, 2008.
Yanzi chunqiu jishi. Attributed to Yan Ying. Edited by Wu Zeyu. 2 vols. Xinpian zhuzi jicheng 1. Beijing: Zhonghua shuju, 1982.

Zhouyi zhengyi. Annotated by Kong Yingda. In *Shisanjing zhushu*, edited by Ruan Yuan, 1:5–108. Beijing, Zhonghua shuju, 1980.
Zhuangzi jishi. Edited by Guo Qingfan. 4 vols. Beijing: Zhonghua shuju, 1961.
Zizhi tongjian. Compiled by Sima Guang. 10 vols. Beijing: Zhonghua shuju, 1956.

Secondary Sources

Abé, Ryūichi. "Scholasticism, Exegesis, and Ritual Practice: On Renovation in the History of Buddhist Writing in the Early Heian Period." In *Heian Japan: Centers and Peripheries*, edited by Mikael Adolphson, Edward Kamens, and Stacie Matsumoto, 179–211.
———. *The Weaving of Mantra: Kūkai and the Construction of Esoteric Buddhist Discourse.* New York: Columbia University Press, 1999.
Adolphson, Mikael, Edward Kamens, and Stacie Matsumoto, eds. *Heian Japan: Centers and Peripheries.* Honolulu: University of Hawai'i Press, 2007.
Althusser, Louis. *Lenin and Philosophy and Other Essays.* Translated by Ben Brewster. New York: Monthly Review Press, 1972.
Amino Yoshihiko. *Rethinking Japanese History.* Translated by Alan S. Christy. Ann Arbor: University of Michigan Center for Japanese Studies, 2012.

Aoyagi Takashi. "Shi hikō kō." *Tōkyō Seitoku kokubun* 26 (2003): 127–37.

Asano Toshihiko. *Heian jidai shikijisō no kanji, kango no juyō ni tsuite no kenkyū*. Osaka: Izumi shoin, 2011.

Ashikaga Enjutsu. *Kamakura Muromachi jidai no jukyō*. Tokyo: Nihon koten zenshū kankōkai, 1932.

Baker, John H. *Manual of Law French*. 2nd ed. Aldershot, UK: Scolar Press, 1990.

Bataille, Georges. "The Notion of Expenditure." In *Visions of Excess: Selected Writings, 1927–1939*, edited by Allan Stoekl, translated by Allan Stoekl with Carl R. Lovitt and Donald M. Leslie, Jr., 116–29. Minneapolis: University of Minnesota Press, 1985.

Batten, Bruce L. "Provincial Administration in Early Japan: From *Ritsuryō kokka* to *Ōchō kokka*." *Harvard Journal of Asiatic Studies* 53, no. 1 (1993): 103–34.

Baudrillard, Jean. *The Mirror of Production*. Translated by Mark Poster. St. Louis: Telos Press, 1975.

Bell, Catherine. *Ritual Theory, Ritual Practice*. New York: Oxford University Press, 1992.

Bender, Ross. "Performative Loci of the Imperial Edicts in Nara Japan, 749–770." *Oral Tradition* 24, no. 1 (2009): 249–68.

Bialock, David. *Eccentric Spaces, Hidden Histories: Narrative, Ritual, and Royal Authority from "The Chronicles of Japan" to "The Tale of the Heike."* Stanford: Stanford University Press, 2007.

Bloch, Maurice. Introduction to *Political Language and Oratory in Traditional Society*, 1–28. London: Academic Press, 1975.

Bodman, Richard Wainwright. "Poetics and Prosody in Early Medieval China: A Study and Translation of Kūkai's *Bunkyō hifuron*." Ph.D. diss., Cornell University, 1978.

Bokenkamp, Stephen Robert. "The *Ledger on the Rhapsody*: Studies in the Art of the T'ang *fu*." Ph.D. diss., University of California, Berkeley, 1986.

Bol, Peter. *"This Culture of Ours": Intellectual Transitions in T'ang and Sung China*. Stanford, CA: Stanford University Press, 1992.

Borgen, Robert. "Heian Love: Domestic and Imported." *Nihon kanbungaku kenkyū* 4 (2009): 257–86.

———. "The Politics of Classical Chinese in the Early Japanese Court." In *Rhetoric and the Discourses of Power in Court Culture: China, Europe, and Japan*, edited by David R. Knechtges and Eugene Vance, 199–238. Seattle: University of Washington Press, 2005.

———. *Sugawara no Michizane and the Early Heian Court*. Honolulu: University of Hawai'i Press, 1986.

Bourdieu, Pierre. *Outline of a Theory of Practice*. Translated by Richard Nice. Cambridge: Cambridge University Press, 1977.

Bowring, Richard, trans. *The Diary of Lady Murasaki*. London: Penguin, 1996.

Branner, David. "The Sui-Tang Tradition of *Fǎnqiè* Phonology." In *History of the Language Sciences: An International Handbook on the Evolution of the Study of Language from the Beginnings to the Present*, edited by Sylvain Auroux, 36–46. Berlin: W. de Gruyter, 2000.

———. "Tonal Prosody in Chinese Parallel Prose." *Journal of the American Oriental Society* 123, no. 1 (2003): 93–119.

Brower, Robert H., and Earl Miner. *Japanese Court Poetry*. Stanford, CA: Stanford University Press, 1961.

Brownstein, Michael C. "From *Kokugaku* to *Kokubungaku*: Canon Formation in the Meiji Period." *Harvard Journal of Asiatic Studies* 47, no. 2 (1987): 435–60.

Buhrman, Kristina. "The Stars and the State: Astronomy, Astrology, and the Politics of Natural Knowledge in Early Medieval Japan." Ph.D. diss., University of Southern California, 2012.

Carter, Steven D. *Householders: The Reizei Family in Japanese History*. Cambridge, MA: Harvard University Asia Center, 2007.

Ceugniet, Atsuko. *L'office des études supérieures au Japon du VIIIe au XIIe siècle et les dissertations de fin d'études*. Geneva: Librarie Droz, 2000.

Chino Kaori. "Gender in Japanese Art." In *Gender and Power in the Japanese Visual Field*, edited by Joshua S. Mostow, Norman Bryson, and Meribeth Graybill, 17–34. Honolulu: University of Hawai'i Press, 2003.

Chou, Chih-p'ing. *Yüan Hung-tao and the Kung-an School*. Cambridge: Cambridge University Press, 1988.

Clanchy, M. T. *From Memory to Written Record: England, 1066–1307*. 3rd ed. Chichester, West Sussex, UK: John Wiley & Sons, 2013.

Conlan, Thomas. *From Sovereign to Symbol: An Age of Ritual Determinism in Fourteenth Century Japan*. Oxford: Oxford University Press, 2011.

———. "Traces of the Past: Documents, Literacy, and Liturgy in Medieval Japan." In *Currents in Medieval Japanese History: Essays in Honor of Jeffrey P. Mass*, edited by Gordon M. Berger, Andrew Edmund Goble, Lorraine F. Harrington, and G. Cameron Hurst III, 19–50. Los Angeles: Figueroa Press, 2009.

Connery, Christopher Leigh. *The Empire of the Text: Writing and Authority in Early Imperial China*. Lanham, MD: Rowman & Littlefield Publishers, 1998.

Dante Alighieri. *De vulgari eloquentia*. Edited and translated by Steven Botterill. Cambridge: Cambridge University Press, 1996.

Dehaene, Stanislas. *Reading in the Brain: The Science and Evolution of a Human Invention*. New York: Viking Penguin, 2009.

De Man, Paul. "Shelley Disfigured." In *Deconstruction and Criticism*, edited by Harold Bloom, Paul De Man, Jacques Derrida, Geoffrey Hartman, and J. Hillis Miller. New York: Seabury Press, 1979.

Denecke, Wiebke. "Bilingual Landscapes: Divided Pleasures at Yoshino Palace in Early Japanese and Sino-Japanese Poetry." In *Minds of the Past: Representations of Mentality in Literary and Historical Documents of Japan and Europe*, edited by Takami Matsuda, Kenji Yoshitake, Masato Izumi, and Michio Sato, 165–89. Tokyo: Centre for Integrated Research on the Mind, Keio University, 2005.

———. "Chinese Antiquity and Court Spectacle in Early *Kanshi*." *Journal of Japanese Studies* 30, no. 1 (2004): 97–122.

———. *Classical World Literatures: Sino-Japanese and Greco-Roman Comparisons*. Oxford: Oxford University Press, 2013.

———. "Kudaishi no tenkai: Kanshi kara washi e." In *Kudaishi kenkyū*, edited by Satō

Michio, 47–88. Tokyo: Keio University Centre for Integrated Research on the Mind, 2007.

———. "'Topic Poetry Is All Ours': Poetic Composition on Chinese Lines in Early Heian Japan." *Harvard Journal of Asiatic Studies* 67, no. 1 (2007): 1–49.

Dien, Albert E. "Civil Service Examinations: Evidence from the Northwest." In *Culture and Power in the Reconstitution of the Chinese Realm, 200–600*, edited by Scott Pearce, Audrey Spiro, and Patricia Ebray. Cambridge, MA: Harvard University Asia Center, 2001.

Ditter, Alexei. "Genre and the Transformation of Writing in Tang Dynasty China (618–907)." Ph.D. diss., Princeton University, 2009.

Downer, G. B., and A. C. Graham. "Tone Patterns in Chinese Poetry." *Bulletin of the School of Oriental and African Studies* 26, no. 1 (1963): 145–48.

Duthie, Torquil. *"Man'yōshū" and the Imperial Imagination in Early Japan*. Leiden: Brill, 2014.

Elman, Benjamin. *A Cultural History of Civil Examinations in Late Imperial China*. Berkeley: University of California Press, 2000.

Endō Motoo. *Chūsei ōken to ōchō girei*. Tokyo: Tōkyō Daigaku shuppankai, 2008.

Esaka Yukiko. "Kansai Daigaku Toshokan-zō Ikuta-bon *Wakan rōeishū* to Rōei Gōchū." *Chūko bungaku* 86 (2010): 40–54.

Farris, William Wayne. *Daily Life and Demographics in Ancient Japan*. Ann Arbor: Center for Japanese Studies, University of Michigan, 2009.

———. "Famine, Climate, and Farming in Japan, 670–1100." In *Heian Japan: Centers and Peripheries*, edited by Mikael Adolphson, Edward Kamens, and Stacie Matsumoto, 275–304.

———. *Heavenly Warriors: The Evolution of Japan's Military, 500–1300*. Cambridge, MA: Council on East Asian Studies, Harvard University, 1992.

Fröhlich, Judith. *Rulers, Peasants and the Use of the Written Word in Medieval Japan: Ategawa no shō 1004–1304*. Bern: Peter Lang, 2007.

Fujikawa Hideo. *Edo kōki no shijintachi*. Toyō bunko 816. Tokyo: Heibonsha, 2012.

Fujiwara Katsumi. "Genji monogatari to Hakushi bunshū: Suetsumuhana-maki no 'Jūfu' no in'yō o tegakari ni." In *"Genji monogatari" to kanbungaku*, vol. 12 of *Wakan hikaku bungaku sōsho*, edited by Wakan Hikaku Bungakkai, 103–19. Tokyo: Kyūko shoin, 1993.

———. "Osana-koi to gakumon: Otome no maki." In *Naidaijin, Kashiwagi, Yūgiri*, edited by Murofushi Shinsuke and Uehara Sakukazu, 283–92. Jinbutsu de yomu "Genji monogatari" 16. Tokyo: Benseisha, 2006.

Fukui Toshihiko. "Heianchō ni okeru jige." In *Heian kizoku no seikatsu*, edited by Yūseidō Henshūbu, 41–47. Tokyo: Yūseidō shuppan, 1985.

Fukushima Kinji. "Kamakura chūki no kyō, Kamakura ni okeru kanseki juyōsha-gun: *Kankenshō* to *Kyūreishū* no aida." *Kokuritsu Rekishi Minzoku Hakubutsukan kenkyū hōkoku* 175 (2013): 1–14.

Furuse Natsuko. *Nihon kodai ōken to gishiki*. Tokyo: Yoshikawa kōbunkan, 1998.

Galambos, Imre. "Confucian Education in a Buddhist Environment: Medieval Manuscripts and Imprints of the *Mengqiu*." *Studies in Chinese Religions* 1, no. 3 (2015): 269–88.

Gentz, Joachim. "Zum Parallelismus in der chinesischen Literatur." In *Parallelismus Membrorum*, edited by Andreas Wagner, 241–69. Fribourg: Academic Press, 2007.

Gomi Fumihiko. *Bushi to bunshi no chūseishi*. Tokyo: Tōkyō Daigaku shuppankai, 1992.

Gotō Akio. *Heianchō kanbun bunken no kenkyū*. Tokyo: Yoshikawa kōbunkan, 1993.

———. *Heianchō kanbungaku ronkō*. Tokyo: Ōfūsha, 1981.

———. "Honbun kaidai." In *Heian shibun zanpen*, 3–5. Tenri Toshokan zenpon sôsho, Washo no bu 57. Tokyo: Yagi shoten, 1984.

———. *Honchō kanshibun shiryōron*. Tokyo: Bensei shuppan, 2012.

Grafton, Anthony. "Renaissance Readers and Ancient Texts: Comments on Some Commentaries." *Renaissance Quarterly* 38, no. 4 (1985): 615–49.

Grapard, Allan G. "Religious Practices." In *Heian Japan*, edited by Donald H. Shively and William H. McCullough, 517–75.

Guest, Jennifer. "Primers, Commentaries, and Kanbun Literacy in Japanese Literary Culture, 950–1250 CE." Ph.D. diss., Columbia University, 2013.

Guo Ying. *Hanshi yu hexi: Cong "Dongying shixuan" dao Riben de shige zijue*. Xiamen, Fujian: Xiamen Daxue chubanshe, 2013.

Hamada Kan. *Heianchō Nihon kanbungaku no kitei*. Tokyo: Musashino shoin, 2006.

Hanabusa Hideki. "'Monzen kan dai 98' ni tsuite." In *Obi Hakushi taikyū kinen Chūgoku bungaku ronshū*, edited by Obi Hakushi Taikyū Kinen Ronbunshū Henshū Iinkai, 379–408. Tokyo: Daiichi gakushūsha, 1976.

Harbsmeier, Christoph. *Language and Logic*. Vol. 7, pt. 1 of *Science and Civilization in China*. Edited by Joseph Needham. Cambridge: Cambridge University Press, 1998.

Hashimoto Fumio. *Ōchō wakashi no kenkyū*. Tokyo: Kasama shoin, 1972.

Hashimoto Yoshihiko. *Heian kizoku*. Tokyo: Heibonsha, 1986.

Hayakawa Shōhachi. *Nihon kodai kanryōsei no kenkyū*. Tokyo: Iwanami shoten, 1986.

Hayashiya Tatsusaburō. *Kodai kokka no kaitai*. Tokyo: Tōkyō Daigaku shuppankai, 1957.

Heldt, Gustav. *The Pursuit of Harmony: Poetry and Power in Early Heian Japan*. Ithaca, NY: Cornell University East Asia Program, 2008.

———. "Writing Like a Man: Poetic Literacy, Textual Property, and Gender in the *Tosa Diary*." *Journal of Asian Studies* 64, no. 1 (2005): 7–34.

Hérail, Francine. *La cour du Japon à l'époque de Heian aux Xe et XIe siècles*. Paris: Hachette, 1995.

———. "Lire et écrire dans le Japon ancient." In *Paroles à dire, paroles à écrire: Inde, Chine, Japon*, edited by Viviane Alleton, 253–74. Paris: Editions de l'Ecole des hautes études en sciences sociales, 1997.

———. "De la place et du rôle des gouverneurs de province à l'apogée de l'époque Heian." In *Autour de Genji monogatari* (Special issue of *Cipango*), edited by Sumie Terada, 291–355. Paris: Publications Langues O', 2008.

Herder, Johann Gottfried. *Philosophical Writings*. Translated by Michael N. Forster. Cambridge: Cambridge University Press, 2002.

Hightower, James Robert. "Some Characteristics of Parallel Prose." In *Studies in Chinese Literature*, edited by John L. Bishop, 108–41. Cambridge, MA: Harvard University Press, 1965.

Hill, Joyce. "Learning Latin in Anglo-Saxon England: Traditions, Texts, and Techniques."

In *Learning and Literacy in Medieval England and Abroad*, edited by Sarah Rees Jones, 7–29. Turnhout, Belgium: Brepols Publishers, 2003.

Hino Tatsuo. "Sakura to Nihon kinsei kanshi: Washū ni tsuite." In *Edo no jugaku*, vol. 1 of *Hino Tatsuo chosakushū*, 442–69. Tokyo: Perikansha, 2006.

Hiranaka Reiji. "Yonezawa no Sōhan Zengo Kanjo ni tsuite." In *Kokuhō "Kanjo" Sō Keigenbon*, vol. 1, 1–24. Kyoto: Hōyū shoten, 1977.

Hisaki Yukio. *Nihon kodai gakkō no kenkyū*. Tokyo: Tamagawa Daigaku shuppanbu, 1990.

Honma Yōichi. *Ōchō kanbungaku hyōgen ronkō*. Osaka: Izumi shoin, 2002.

———. "*Ruijū kudaishō* kenkyū oboegaki: Kaisetsu ni kaete." In *Ruijū kudaishō zenchūshaku*, 42–76.

Hori Ichirō. "Waga kuni gakusō kyōiku seido." In *Hori Ichirō chosakushū*, 3:547–692. Tokyo: Miraisha, 1978.

Horikawa Takashi. "Kuge no gakumon to Gozan." Paper presented at the Spring Meeting of the Chūsei Bungakukai, Tokyo, May 23, 2015.

———. *Shi no katachi, shi no kokoro: Chūsei Nihon kanbungaku kenkyū*. Chūsei bungaku kenkyū sōsho 12. Tokyo: Wakakusa shobō, 2006.

———. *Zoku Gozan bungaku kenkyū: Shiryō to ronkō*. Tokyo: Kasama shoin, 2015.

Horkheimer, Max, and Theodor W. Adorno. *Dialectic of Enlightenment: Philosophical Fragments*. Edited by Gunzelin Schmid Noerr. Translated by Edmund Jephcott. Stanford, CA: Stanford University Press, 2002.

Horton, H. Mack. "Japanese Spirit and Chinese Learning: Scribes and Storytellers in Pre-modern Japan." In *The Ethnography of Reading*, edited by Jonathan Boyarin, 156–79. Berkeley: University of California Press, 1993.

———. *Traversing the Frontier: The "Man'yōshū" Account of a Japanese Mission to Silla in 736–737*. Cambridge, MA: Harvard University Asia Center, 2012.

Hotate Michihisa. *Heian ōchō*. Tokyo: Iwanami shoten, 1996.

Hu Zhengyi. "Chimei hyōki kara miru kanshi no tsukurikata: Kobunjiha o chūshin ni." *Kokugo kokubun* 82, no. 11 (2013): 32–51.

Huang Shaoguang. "Nara Heianchō Nihon kanshi no shiritsuteki kenkyū." Ph.D. diss., Tōkyō Gaikokugo Daigaku, 2003.

Hurst, G. Cameron. "*Kugyō* and *Zuryō*: Center and Periphery in the Era of Fujiwara no Michinaga." In *Heian Japan: Centers and Peripheries*, edited by Mikael Adolphson, Edward Kamens, and Stacie Matsumoto, 66–101.

Ibi Takashi. *Edo shiikaron*. Tokyo: Kyūko shoin, 1998.

Ikeda Genta. *Nara Heian jidai no bunka to shūkyō*. Kyoto: Nagata bunshōdō, 1977.

Imai Gen'e. "Kageyu shōkō Fujiwara no Arikuni den: Ichi keishi-sō bunjin no shōgai." In *Imai Gen'e chosakushū*, 8:270–303. Tokyo: Kasama shoin, 2005.

Inoue Kōji. "Daijōkan benkankyoku no jitsumu shokuin no hensen to sono haikei." *Ritsumeikan bungaku* 564 (March 2000): 65–126.

Inoue Yutaka. "Utsuho monogatari no sakusha no mondai: Minamoto no Shitagō setsu o chūshin to shite." In *"Utsuho monogatari" shinron*, edited by Utsuho Monogatari Kenkyūkai, 285–316. Tokyo: Koten bunko, 1958.

Irvine, Martin. *The Making of Textual Culture: "Grammatica" and Literary Theory, 350–1100*. Cambridge: Cambridge University Press, 1994.

Ishikawa Ken. *Ko ōrai ni tsuite no kenkyū: Jōsei chūsei ni okeru shotō kyōkasho no hattatsu.* Tokyo: Kōdansha, 1949.

Ishimoda Shō. *Nihon kodai kokkaron.* 2 vols. Tokyo: Iwanami shoten, 1973.

———. "Utsuho monogatari ni tsuite no oboegaki: Kizoku shakai no jojishi to shite no." In *Ishimoda Shō chosakushū,* 11:1–38. Tokyo: Iwanami shoten, 1990.

Ishizuka Harumichi. "Tonkō no katenbon." In *Tonkō kanbun bunken,* vol. 5 of *Kōza Tonkō,* edited by Ikeda On, 229–61. Tokyo: Daitō shuppansha, 1992.

Iso Mizue. *Setsuwa to ongaku denshō.* Osaka: Izumi shoin, 2000.

Itō Shingo. *Muromachi sengokuki no kuge shakai to bunji.* Tokyo: Miyai shoten, 2012.

Jones, Sumie, and Kenji Watanabe, eds. *An Edo Anthology: Literature from Japan's Mega-City, 1750–1850.* Honolulu: University of Hawai'i Press, 2013.

Kakimura Shigematsu. *Honchō monzui chūshaku.* Rev. ed. 2 vols. Tokyo: Fuzanbō, 1968.

Kamakura Saho. "Shōensei seiritsu shiron no shindankai e mukete." *Rekishi hyōron* 622 (February 2002): 60–73.

Kamei Takashi. "Yagi-shi ni tsuki gogaku no tachiba kara." *Nihon rekishi* 217 (June 1966): 68–74.

Kamens, Edward. "Terrains of Text in Mid-Heian Court Culture." In *Heian Japan: Centers and Peripheries,* edited by Mikael Adolphson, Edward Kamens, and Stacie Matsumoto, 129–52.

Kanda Kiichirō. "Washū no dangi." In *Kanda Kiichirō zenshū,* 9:105–20. Kyoto: Dōhōsha shuppan, 1984.

Kanegae Hiroyuki. "Kōtō dentatsu no shosō: Kōtō dentatsu to tennō, kokka, minshū." *Rekishi hyōron* 574 (February 1998): 16–28.

Kannotō Akio. "Minamoto Shitagō den danshō: Anna no hen zengo made no kannin to shite no Shitagō." *Atomi Gakuen Joshi Daigaku kokubungaku kahō* 12 (1984): 55–62.

———. "Minamoto Shitagō den danshō: Wakaki hi no Shitagō o megutte." *Atomi Gakuen Joshi Daigaku kokubungaku kahō* 9 (1981): 1–12.

Kern, Martin. "Early Chinese Poetics in the Light of Recently Excavated Manuscripts." In *Recarving the Dragon,* edited by Olga Lomová, 27–72. Prague: Karolinum Press, Charles University in Prague, 2003.

———. "Ritual, Text, and the Formation of the Canon: Historical Transitions of 'Wen' in Early China." *T'oung Pao* 87, nos. 1–3 (2001): 43–91.

Kido Yūko. "Heian shijo no keishiki: Jikenku no kakuritsu ni tsuite." *Gobun kenkyū* 69 (1990): 12–24.

Kiley, Cornelius J. "Estate and Property in the Late Heian Period." In *Medieval Japan: Essays in Institutional History,* edited by John Hall and Jeffrey Mass, 109–24. Stanford, CA: Stanford University Press, 1974.

———. "Provincial Administration and Land Tenure in Early Heian." In *Heian Japan,* edited by Donald H. Shively and William H. McCullough, 236–340.

Kim Moonkyong. *Kanbun to Higashi Ajia: Kundoku no bunkaken.* Tokyo: Iwanami shoten, 2010.

Knechtges, David R., trans. *The Han shu Biography of Yang Xiong (53 B.C.–A.D. 18).* Tempe: Center for Asian Studies, Arizona State University, 1982.

———, trans. *Wen Xuan, Or, Selections of Refined Literature*. 3 vols. Princeton, NJ: Princeton University Press, 1982–.

Kobase Keikichi, ed. *Nihonkoku genzaisho mokuroku kaisetsukō*. Tokyo: Komiyama shoten, 1956.

Kobayashi Yoshinori. *Heian Kamakura jidai ni okeru kanseki kundoku no kokugoshiteki kenkyū*. Tokyo: Tōkyō Daigaku shuppankai, 1967.

———. "Heijōkyū mokkan no kanji yōhō to Kojiki no yōjihō." In *Jōdai bungaku kōkyū: Ishii Shōji hakushi kiju kinen ronshū*, edited by Ishii Shōji, Itō Haku, and Watase Masatada, 136–70. Tokyo: Hanawa shobō, 1978.

———. "Jōdai ni okeru shokiyō kanji no kun no keitai." *Kokugo to kokubungaku* 47, no. 10 (1970): 50–80.

———. "Kanjo Yō Yū den Tenryaku 2-nen ten ni okeru ichionsetsu jion no chōonka ni tsuite." In *Kokugoshi e no michi*, edited by Doi Sensei Shōju Kinen Ronbunshū Kankōkai, 1:34–50. Tokyo: Sanseidō, 1981.

Kojima Kogorō. *Kuge bunka no kenkyū*. Tokyo: Ikuhōsha, 1942.

Kojima Noriyuki. *Kango shōyō*. Tokyo: Iwanami shoten, 1998.

Komatsu Hideo. *Kokugoshigaku kiso ron*. Tokyo: Kasama shoin, 1973.

———. "Nihon jion no shotaikei." In *Nihon Kanjionshi ronshū*, edited by Tsukishima Hiroshi, 13–38. Tokyo: Kyūko shoin, 1995.

———. *Nihongo shokishi genron*. Rev. ed. Tokyo: Kasama shoin, 2000.

Komine Kazuaki. *Chūsei hōe bungeiron*. Tokyo: Kasama shoin, 2009.

Kon Masahide. "Heian chū/kōki kara Kamakuraki ni okeru kanshi un'ei no tokushitsu: Kuraryō o chūshin ni." *Shigaku zasshi* 99, no. 1 (1990): 1–36.

———. "Ōchō kokka chūō kōki no kōzō to tokushitsu: Daijōkan to Kurōdodokoro." *Hisutoria* 145 (December, 1994): 148–73.

Konishi Jin'ichi. *"Bunkyō hifuron" kō*. 3 vols. Kyoto: Ōyashima shuppan, 1948–53.

———. *The High Middle Ages*. Vol. 3 of *A History of Japanese Literature*, translated by Aileen Gatten and Mark Harbison, edited by Earl Miner. Princeton: Princeton University Press, 1991.

Kōno Kimiko. "Minamoto no Tamenori sen *Sezoku genbun* ni miru kango to kanseki no juyō." In *Higashi Ajia no Konjaku monogatari shū: Hon'yaku, hensei, yogen*, edited by Komine Kazuaki, 419–43. Tokyo: Bensei shuppan, 2012.

———. "Tomohira shinnō *Guketsu getenshō* no hōhō." In *Umi o wataru Tendai bunka*, edited by Yoshihara Hiroto and Wang Yong, 49–80. Tokyo: Bensei shuppan, 2008.

Kōnoshi Takamitsu. *Hensōsareru "Nihon shoki."* Tokyo: Tōkyō Daigaku shuppankai, 2009.

———. *"Nihon" to wa nani ka: Kokugō no imi to rekishi*. Tokyo: Kōdansha, 2005.

Kornicki, Peter F. *The Book in Japan: A Cultural History from the Beginnings to the Nineteenth Century*. Leiden: Brill, 1998.

———. "A Note on Sino-Japanese: A Question of Terminology." *Sino-Japanese Studies* 17 (2010). http://chinajapan.org/articles/index.php/sjs/article/view/21/25.

Kosukegawa Teiji. "Monzen tekisuto to shite mita Ueno-bon Kanjo Yō Yū den Tenryaku 2-nen ten." *Kuntengo to kunten shiryō* 94 (September 1994): 156–92.

———. "Ueno-bon Kanjo Yō Yū den kunten no seikaku." *Kuntengo to kunten shiryō* 77 (March 1987): 28–50.

———. "Ueno-bon Kanjo Yō Yū den Tenryaku 2-nen ten ni okeru tenkyo no mondai ni tsuite." *Kuntengo to kunten shiryō (Kinen tokushū)* (1998): 132–151.

Kotō Shinpei. "Monjō tokugōshōshi no seiritsu." *Shirin* 74, no. 2 (1991): 34–72.

Kudō Shigenori. "Heianchō kanshibun ni okeru engo kakekotoba-teki hyōgen." In *Chūko bungaku to kanbungaku 1*, vol. 3 of *Wakan hikaku bungaku sōsho*, edited by Wakan Hikaku Bungakkai, 203–24. Tokyo: Kyūko shoin, 1986.

———. "Heianchō ni okeru kanshoku tōmei no bungakuteki sokumen." *Gobun kenkyū* 66 (June 1989): 33–40.

———. *Heianchō ritsuryō shakai no bungaku*. Tokyo: Perikansha, 1993.

Kuranaka Shinobu. "Ritsuryō, bukkyō, bungaku no kōsaku: Tōdai kōgo goi 'ganmen' o meguru kōsetsu no ba." *Nihon bungaku* 60, no. 5 (2011): 31–39.

Kuroda Akira. *Chūsei setsuwa no bungakushiteki kankyō*. Osaka: Izumi shoin, 1987.

Kuroita Nobuo. *Heian ōchō no kyūtei shakai*. Tokyo: Yoshikawa kōbunkan, 1995.

Kyōraku Mahoko. "Heiankyō ni okeru toshi no tensei." *Nihonshi kenkyū* 415 (March 1997): 3–27.

LaMarre, Thomas. *Uncovering Heian Japan: An Archaeology of Sensation and Inscription*. Durham, NC: Duke University Press, 2000.

Law, Vivien. *Grammar and Grammarians in the Early Middle Ages*. London: Longman, 1997.

Lee Yeounsuk. *The Ideology of Kokugo*. Translated by Maki Hirano Hubbard. Honolulu: University of Hawai'i Press, 2010.

Lewis, Mark Edward. *Writing and Authority in Early China*. Albany: State University of New York Press, 1999.

Lin Zhongpeng. "Nara jidai no jisho *Kangoshō* oyobi sono shūroku goi ni tsuite." In *Higashi Ajia no kanseki isan: Nara o chūshin to shite*, edited by Kōno Kimiko and Wang Yong, 305–20. Tokyo: Bensei shuppan, 2012.

Lowe, Bryan. "Rewriting Nara Buddhism: Sutra Transcription in Early Japan." Ph.D. diss., Princeton University, 2012.

Lurie, David. *Realms of Literacy: Early Japan and the History of Writing*. Cambridge, MA: Harvard University Asia Center, 2011.

Mabuchi Kazuo. *Koshahon "Wamyō ruijushō" shūsei*. 3 vols. Tokyo: Bensei shuppan, 2008.

———. *Nihon ingakushi no kenkyū*. Rev. ed. 3 vols. Kyoto: Rinsen shoten, 1984.

Mair, Victor H. "Buddhism and the Rise of the Written Vernacular in East Asia: The Making of National Languages." *Journal of Asian Studies* 53, no. 3 (1994): 707–51.

Makeham, John. *Transmitters and Creators: Chinese Commentators and Commentaries on the Analects*. Cambridge, MA: Harvard University Asia Center, 2003.

Mass, Jeffrey P. "The Kamakura Bakufu." In *Medieval Japan*, vol. 3 of *The Cambridge History of Japan*, edited by Kozo Yamamura, 46–88. Cambridge: Cambridge University Press, 1990.

Masuda Shigeo. "Chokusen wakashū to wa nani ka." In *Kokinshū to sono zengo*, vol. 2 of *Waka bungaku ronshū*, ed. "Waka bungaku ronshū" Henshū Iinkai, 41–66. Tokyo: Kazama shobō, 1994.

———. "Monogatari ondokuron no yukue." *Nihon bungaku* 31, no. 5 (1982): 34–42.

Matsumoto Mitsutaka. "Kanjo Yō Yū den Tenryaku 2-nen ten ni okeru kundoku no hōhō." *Kokugogaku* 128 (March 1982): 28–40.

Matsuura Tomohisa. "Jodai kanshibun ni okeru rinen to yōshiki." In *Nihon jōdai kanshibun ronkō*, vol. 3 of *Matsuura Tomohisa chosakusen*, 5–27. Tokyo: Kenbun shuppan, 2004.

———. "Rikuchō shintaishi kara Tōdai kintaishi e." In *Chūgoku shibun no gengogaku*, vol. 1 of *Matsuura Tomohisa chosakusen*, 44–82. Tokyo: Kenbun shuppan, 2003.

Mauss, Marcel. *The Gift*. Translated by W. D. Halls. London: Routledge, 1990.

McCullough, Helen Craig. *Brocade by Night: "Kokin wakashū" and the Court Style in Japanese Classical Poetry*. Stanford, CA: Stanford University Press, 1985.

———, trans. *Ōkagami, The Great Mirror: Fujiwara Michinaga (966–1027) and His Times*. Princeton, NJ: Princeton University Press, 1980.

McCullough, William H. "The Heian Court, 794–1070." In *Heian Japan*, edited by Donald H. Shively and William H. McCullough, 20–96.

McMullen, David. *State and Scholars in T'ang China*. Cambridge: Cambridge University Press, 1988.

McMullen, I. J. "The Worship of Confucius in Ancient Japan." In *Religion in Japan: Arrows to Heaven and Earth*, edited by Peter F. Kornicki and I. J. McMullen, 39–77. Cambridge: Cambridge University Press, 1996.

Mesheryakov, Alexander N. "On the Quantity of Written Data Produced by the *Ritsuryō* State." *Japan Review* 15 (2003): 187–99.

Mikawa Kei. *Insei no kenkyū*. Tokyo: Rinsen shoten, 1996.

Miki Masahiro. *Heian shiika no tenkai to Chūgoku bungaku*. Osaka: Izumi shoin, 1999.

———. *"Wakan rōeishū" to sono kyōju*. Tokyo: Benseisha, 1995.

Minegishi Akira. "Heian jidai ni okeru kanji no teikun ni tsuite." *Kokugo to kokubungaku* 61, no. 10 (1984): 44–60.

———. "Kirokutai." In *Buntai*, vol. 10 of *Iwanami kōza Nihongo*, 161–223. Tokyo: Iwanami shoten, 1977.

Minegishi Yoshiaki. *Heian jidai waka bungaku no kenkyū*. Tokyo: Ōfūsha, 1965.

Ministry of Education. *Kokutai no hongi*. Tokyo: Monbushō, 1937.

Mitamura Masako. "Utsuho monogatari no ronri: Shukusai no jikan to nichijō no jikan to." In *Shoki monogatari bungaku no ishiki*, vol. 2 of *Ronshū chūko bungaku*, edited by Chūko Bungaku Kenkyūkai, 177–99. Tokyo: Kasama shoin, 1979.

Miura Baien. *Shitetsu*. In *Nihon shiwa sōsho*, edited by Ikeda Roshū, 7:47–230. Tokyo: Bunkaidō, 1920 (orig. pub. 1786).

Momo Hiroyuki. *Jōdai gakusei no kenkyū*. Rev. ed. Vol. 1 of *Momo Hiroyuki chosakushū*. Kyoto: Shibunkaku shuppan, 1994.

———. "Kaidai." In *Shōyūki*, edited by Tōkyō Daigaku Shiryō Hensanjo, 11:179–200. Dai Nihon kokiroku. Tokyo: Iwanami shoten, 1986.

Mori Kimiyuki. *Zaichō kanjin to bushi no seisei*. Tokyo: Yoshikawa kōbunkan, 2013.

Morita Tei. *Ōchō seiji*. Rekishi shinsho 20. Tokyo: Kyōikusha, 1979.

———. "Toward Regency Leadership at Court." Interpreted by Joan R. Piggott. In *Capital and Countryside in Japan, 300–1180: Japanese Historians in English*, edited by Joan R. Piggott, 209–26.

Morris, Ivan. *The World of the Shining Prince: Court Life in Ancient Japan*. New York: Knopf, 1964.

Mostow, Joshua. *At the House of Gathered Leaves: Shorter Biographical and Autobiographical Narratives from Japanese Court Literature*. Honolulu: University of Hawai'i Press, 2004.

———. "Mother Tongue and Father Script: The Relationship of Sei Shōnagon and Murasaki Shikibu to Their Fathers and Chinese Letters." In *The Father-Daughter Plot: Japanese Literary Women and the Law of the Father*, edited by Rebecca L. Copeland and Esperanza Ramirez-Christensen. Honolulu: University of Hawai'i Press, 2001.

Motoori Norinaga. *Tamaarare*. In *Motoori Norinaga zenshū*, 5:463–517. Tokyo: Chikuma shobō, 1970 (orig. pub. 1792).

Mou Runsun. *Zhushizhai conggao*. Beijing: Zhonghua shuju, 1987.

Murai Yasuhiko. *Heian kizoku no sekai*. Tokyo: Tokuma shoten, 1968.

———. "Zuryō: Ōchō no akuyaku." *Kokubungaku: kaishaku to kyōzai no kenkyū* 17, no. 11 (1972): 82–88.

Murase Toshio. *Kokinshū no kiban to shūhen*. Tokyo: Ōfūsha, 1971.

Muroki Hideyuki. *"Utsuho monogatari" no hyōgen to ronri*. Tokyo: Wakakusa shobō, 1996.

Murphy, James J. "The Teaching of Latin as a Second Language in the 12th Century." *Historiographia linguistica* 7 (1980): 159–74.

Nagahara Keiji. "Landownership under the *Shōen-Kokugaryō* System." *Journal of Japanese Studies* 1, no. 2 (1975): 269–96.

Nagase Yumi. "Ichijō-chō bunjin no kanshoku/ikai to bungaku." In *Ochō bungaku to kanshoku/ikai*, edited by Hinata Kazumasa, 245–74. Heian bungaku to rinsetsu shogaku 4. Tokyo: Chikurinsha, 2008.

Nagoya-shi Hakubutsukan, ed. *Wamyō ruijushō*. Nagoya-shi Hakubutsukan shiryō sōsho 2. Nagoya: Nagoya-shi Hakubutsukan, 1992.

Nakada Norio. *Kotenbon no kokugogakuteki kenkyū*. Rev. ed. 2 vols. Tokyo: Benseisha, 1979.

Nakagomi Ritsuko. *Heian jidai no zei-zaisei kōzō to zuryō*. Tokyo: Azekura shobō, 2013.

Nakahara Toshiaki. *Chūsei ōken to shihai kōzō*. Tokyo: Yoshikawa kōbunkan, 2005.

Nakamura Keiji. *Gi Shin Nanbokuchō ni okeru kōbunsho to bunsho gyōsei no kenkyū*. Tokyo: Heisei 10–12-nendo Kagaku Kenkyūhi Hojokin kenkyū seika hōkokusho, 2001.

Nakano Kōichi. *"Utsuho monogatari" no kenkyū*. Tokyo: Musashino shoin, 1981.

Nihon Rekishi Gakkai. *Enshū komonjosen: Shōen hen jō*. Tokyo: Yoshikawa kōbunkan, 1980.

Nishiyama Mika. "Utsuho monogatari 'mono' ga miseru sōkanzu: 'Saizōyo' ni himerareta onnatachi no kensei to tōsō." In *"Genji monogatari" no kotoba to shintai*, edited by Mitamura Masako, 144–67. Tokyo: Seikansha, 2010.

Nugent, Christopher M. B. *Manifest in Words, Written on Paper: Producing and Circulating Poetry in Tang Dynasty China*. Cambridge, MA: Harvard University Asia Center, 2010.

Numoto Katsuaki, ed. "Goon kan'on bunrui hyō." In *Nihon kanjionshi ronshū*, edited by Tsukishima Hiroshi, 121–243. Tokyo: Kyūko shoin, 1995.

Ogawa Takeo. "Chi to chi: Sekkanke no kuji no setsu o megutte." In *Kenryoku to bunka*, edited by Inseiki Bunka Kenkyūkai, 151–80. Inseiki bunka ronshū 1. Tokyo: Shinwasha, 2001.

Ōida Yasuhiko. *"Utsuho monogatari" no sekai*. Tokyo: Kazama shobō, 2002.

Okada, H. Richard. *Figures of Resistance: Language, Poetry, and Narrating in "The Tale of Genji" and Other Mid-Heian Texts*. Durham, NC: Duke University Press, 1991.

———. Review of *Uncovering Heian Japan: An Archaelogy of Sensation and Inscription. Harvard Journal of Asiatic Studies* 64, no. 1 (2004): 184–200.

———. "Translation and Difference." *Journal of Asian Studies* 47, no. 1 (1988): 29–40.

Okada Yoshio. "Minamoto no Shitagō oyobi dō Tamenori nenpu." In *Okada Yoshio shū*, vol. 7 of *Setsuwa bungaku kenkyū sōsho*, edited by Kuroda Akira and Yutani Yūzō, 17–72. Tokyo: Kuresu shuppan, 2004.

Okumura Eizō. "Hanasu koto to kaku koto no aida." *Kokugo to kokubungaku* 68, no. 5 (1991): 11–22.

———. "Kana monjo no seiritsu izen." In *Jōdai*, vol. 1 of *Nihon bungaku Nihongo: ronshū*, edited by Hamada Keisuke, 225–48. Tokyo: Kadokawa shoten, 1978.

———. "Kana monjo no seiritsu izen, zoku: Shōsōin kana monjo, otsushu o megutte." *Man'yō* 99 (1978): 37–58.

Ong, Walter J. *Orality and Literacy: The Technologizing of the Word.* London: Routledge, 1982.

Ono Yasuo. *Heianchō Tenryakuki no bundan*. Tokyo: Kazama shobō, 2008.

Ooms, Herman. *Imperial Politics and Symbolics in Ancient Japan: The Tenmu Dynasty, 650–800*. Honolulu: University of Hawai'i Press, 2009.

Ōsone Shōsuke. "Chūsei kanbungaku no shosō: Tenkanki ni okeru kanbungaku." In *Ōsone Shōsuke Nihon kanbungaku ronshū*, 1:207–19. Tokyo: Kyūko shoin, 1998.

———. "Kanbuntai." In *Ōsone Shōsuke Nihon kanbungaku ronshū*, 1:407–48. Tokyo: Kyūko shoin, 1998.

———. *Ōchō kanbungaku ronkō*. Tokyo: Iwanami shoten, 1994.

Ōta Shōjirō. "Kangakuin no suzume wa naze *Mōgyū* o saezutta ka." In *Ōta Shōjirō chosakushū*, 1:218–35. Tokyo: Yoshikawa kōbunkan, 1991.

———. "'Shibu no tokusho' kō." In *Ōta Shōjirō chosakushū*, 1:236–46. Tokyo: Yoshikawa kōbunkan, 1991.

———. "Sonkeikaku sankanbon Iroha jiruishō kaisetsu." In *Ōta Shōjirō chosakushū*, 4:150–89. Tokyo: Yoshikawa kōbunkan, 1992.

Ōtani Masao. "Hajimete no dokusha no tame ni: Wakan renku hiroiyomi." *Ajia yūgaku* 95 (January 2007): 18–28.

Ōtomo Shin'ichi, and Eguchi Yasuo. "*Wamyō ruijushō* no sei-zoku-tsū." In *Goi no kenkyū*, edited by Satō Kiyoji, 91–112. Kokugo ronkyū 1. Tokyo: Meiji shoin, 1986.

Ōtsu Tōru. *Michinaga to kyūtei shakai*. Nihon no rekishi 6. Tokyo: Kōdansha, 2001.

———. *Ritsuryō kokka shihai kōzō no kenkyū*. Tokyo: Iwanami shoten, 1993.

Ōtsubo Heiji. "Kanjo Yō Yū den Tenryaku-ten kaidokubun." *Okayama Daigaku Hōbungakubu gakujutsu kiyō* 36 (1975): 37–59.

Owen, Stephen. *The Late Tang: Chinese Poetry of the Mid-Ninth Century*. Cambridge, MA: Harvard University Asia Center, 2006.

———. *The Poetry of the Early T'ang*. New Haven, CT: Yale University Press, 1977.

———. *Readings in Chinese Literary Thought*. Cambridge, MA: Council on East Asian Studies, Harvard University, 1992.

———. *Traditional Chinese Poetry and Poetics: Omen of the World*. Madison, WI: University of Wisconsin Press, 1985.

Ozawa Kenji. "Nanka-bon *Shiki* kaisetsu." In *Shiki*, edited by Koten Kenkyūkai, 12:501–22. Koten Kenkyūkai Sōsho, Kanseki no bu 28. Tokyo: Kyūko shoin, 1998.

Ozawa Masao. "Sakumon daitai chūkai." *Chūkyō Daigaku bungakubu kiyō* 19, no. 2 (1984): 189–220; no. 3/4 (1985): 113–74.

———. "Sakumon daitai no kisoteki kenkyū." *Setsurin* (Aichi Kenritsu Joshi Daigaku) 11 (1963): 1–81.

Phan, John Duong. "Lacquered Words: The Evolution of Vietnamese under Sinitic Influences from the 1st Century BCE through the 17th Century CE." Ph.D. diss., Cornell University, 2013.

Piggott, Joan R. *The Emergence of Japanese Kingship*. Stanford, CA: Stanford University Press, 1997.

———. "What Did a Regent Do? Fujiwara no Tadahira in the 930s." In *Teishinkōki: The Year 939 in the Journal of Regent Fujiwara No Tadahira*, edited by Joan R. Piggott and Yoshida Sanae, 23–78. Ithaca, NY: East Asia Program, Cornell University, 2008.

———, ed. *Capital and Countryside in Japan, 300–1180: Japanese Historians in English*. Ithaca, NY: East Asia Program, Cornell University, 2005.

Plaks, Andrew H. "Where the Lines Meet: Parallelism in Chinese and Western Literatures." *CLEAR* 10, no. 1/2 (1988): 43–60.

Pollack, David. *The Fracture of Meaning: Japan's Synthesis of China from the Eighth through the Eighteenth Centuries*. Princeton, NJ: Princeton University Press, 1986.

Pollock, Sheldon I. *The Language of the Gods in the World of Men: Sanskrit, Culture, and Power in Premodern India*. Berkeley: University of California Press, 2006.

Pulleyblank, Edwin G. *Lexicon of Reconstructed Pronunciation in Early Middle Chinese, Late Middle Chinese, and Early Mandarin*. Vancouver: UBC Press, 1991.

———. *Middle Chinese: A Study in Historical Phonology*. Vancouver: University of British Columbia Press, 1984.

Qiao Xiuyan [Hashimoto Hidemi]. *Gisogaku suibō shiron*. Tōkyō Daigaku Tōyō Bunka Kenkyūjo kenkyū hōkoku. Tokyo: Hakuhōsha, 2001.

Qiu Xigui. *Chinese Writing*. Translated by Gilbert L. Mattos and Jerry Norman. Berkeley: Society for the Study of Early China, University of California, 2000.

Rabinovitch, Judith N. *Shōmonki: The Story of Masakado's Rebellion*. Tokyo: Monumenta Nipponica, Sophia University, 1986.

———. "Wasp Waists and Monkey Tails: A Study and Translation of Hamanari's *Uta no Shiki* (*The Code of Poetry*, 772), Also Known as *Kakyō Hyōshiki* (*A Formulary for Verse Based on The Canons of Poetry*)." *Harvard Journal of Asiatic Studies* 51, no. 2 (1991): 471–560.

Rabinovitch, Judith N., and Timothy R. Bradstock, trans. *Dance of the Butterflies: Chinese Poetry from the Japanese Court Tradition*. Ithaca, NY: East Asia Program, Cornell University, 2005.

Ratcliff, Christian. "The Cultural Arts in Service: The Careers of Asukai Masaari and His Lineage." Ph.D. diss., Yale University, 2007.

Ruppert, Brian. *Jewel in the Ashes: Buddha Relics and Power in Early Medieval Japan*. Cambridge, MA: Harvard University Asia Center, 2000.

Rütterman, Markus. "'So That We Can Study Letter-Writing': The Concept of Epistolary Etiquette in Premodern Japan." *Japan Review* 18 (2006): 57–128.

Ryūfuku Yoshitomo. "Heian chūki no 'rei' ni tsuite." In *Ronshū chūsei no mado*, edited by Chūsei No Mado Dōjin, 245–92. Tokyo: Yoshikawa kōbunkan, 1977.

Saitō Mareshi. *Kanji sekai no chihei: Watashitachi ni totte moji to wa nani ka*. Tokyo: Shinchōsha, 2014.

Sakai, Naoki. "Modernity and Its Critique: The Problem of Universalism and Particularism." In *Postmodernism and Japan*, edited by Masao Miyoshi and H. D. Harootunian, 93–122. Durham, NC: Duke University Press, 1989.

———. *Voices of the Past: The Status of Language in Eighteenth-Century Discourse*. Ithaca, NY: Cornell University Press, 1991.

Sakaki, Atsuko. *Obsessions with the Sino-Japanese Polarity in Japanese Literature*. Honolulu: University of Hawai'i Press, 2006.

Sakayori Masashi. *Bokkai to kodai no Nihon*. Tokyo: Azekura shobō, 2001.

Sansom, George Bailey. *A History of Japan: To 1334*. Stanford, CA: Stanford University Press, 1958.

Sasaki Isamu. "Nihon kan'on no keishō messhō ni tsuite: Kan'on no kokugoka no ichisokumen." *Kokugo kokubun* 734 (October, 1995): 11–19.

Sasaki Muneo. "The Court-Centered Polity." Interpreted by Joan R. Piggott. In *Capital and Countryside in Japan*, edited by Joan R. Piggott, 227–44.

Satō Atsuko. "Masayori-ke no seiritsu, 'ie' no sekai no keisei: Utsuho monogatari Fujiwara no kimi no maki no shisō." *Nihon bungaku* 34, no. 6 (1985): 1–11.

Satō Michio. "'Bunshō' to 'saigaku': Heian kōki no yōrei kara sono tokushitsu o saguru." *Ajia yūgaku* 162 (March 2013): 133–42.

———. *Heian kōki Nihon kanbungaku no kenkyū*. Tokyo: Kasama shoin, 2003.

———. *Mikawa Hōraiji kyūzō Ryakuō 2-nen shosha "Wakan rōeishū" eiin to kenkyū: Kenkyū hen*. Tokyo: Bensei shuppan, 2014.

Satō Shin'ichi. *Nihon no chūsei kokka*. Tokyo: Iwanami shoten, 1983.

Satō Yasuhiro. *Nihon chūsei no reimei*. Kyoto: Kyōto Daigaku gakujutsu shuppankai, 2001.

Schafer, Edward H. "Fusang and Beyond: The Haunted Seas to Japan." *Journal of the American Oriental Society* 109, no. 3 (1989): 379–99.

Sekiguchi Yūko. "Heian jidai no danjo ni yoru moji (buntai) tsukaiwake no rekishiteki zentei: 9-seiki no monjo no shomei o tegakari ni." In *Nihon ritsuryōsei ronshū*, edited by Sasayama Haruo Sensei Kanreki Kinenkai, 2:505–54. Tokyo: Yoshikawa kōbunkan, 1993.

Shibatani, Masayoshi. *The Languages of Japan*. Cambridge: Cambridge University Press, 1990.

Shimura Midori. "Heian jidai josei no mana kanseki no gakushū: 11-seiki goro o chūshin ni." *Nihon rekishi* 457 (June 1986): 22–38.

Shirane, Haruo. *The Bridge of Dreams: A Poetics of "The Tale of Genji."* Stanford, CA: Stanford University Press, 1987.

———. "Curriculum and Competing Canons." In *Inventing the Classics: Modernity, National Identity, and Japanese Literature*, edited by Haruo Shirane and Tomi Suzuki, 220–49. Stanford, CA: Stanford University Press, 2000.

———, ed. *Early Modern Japanese Literature: An Anthology, 1600–1900*. New York: Columbia University Press, 2002.

———, ed. *Traditional Japanese Literature: An Anthology, Beginnings to 1600*. New York: Columbia University Press, 2007.

Shively, Donald H., and William H. McCullough, eds. *Heian Japan*. Vol. 2 of *The Cambridge History of Japan*. Cambridge: Cambridge University Press, 1999.

Shizunaga Takeshi. "Haku Kyoi no fūyushi." In *Haku Kyoi no bungaku to jinsei*, vol. 2 of *Haku kyoi kenkyū kōza*, edited by Ōta Tsugio, 141–62. Tokyo: Benseisha, 1993.

Smits, Ivo. "Minding the Gaps: An Early Edo History of Sino-Japanese Poetry." In *Uncharted Waters: Intellectual Life in the Edo Period*, edited by Anna Beerens and Mark Teeuwen, 93–108. Leiden: Brill, 2012.

———. "Reading the *New Ballads*: Late Heian *Kanshi* Poets and Bo Juyi." In *Wasser-Spuren: Festschrift für Wolfram Naumann zum 65. Geburtstag*, edited by Stanca Scholz-Cionca, 169–84. Wiesbaden, Germany: Otto Harrassowitz, 1997.

———. "Song as Cultural History: Reading *Wakan rōeishū*." *Monumenta Nipponica* 55, no. 2 (Summer 2000): 225–56; no. 3 (Autumn 2000): 399–427.

———. "The Way of the Literati: Chinese Learning and Literary Practice in Mid-Heian Japan." In *Heian Japan: Centers and Peripheries*, edited by Mikael Adolphson, Edward Kamens, and Stacie Matsumoto, 105–28.

Snare, Gerald. "The Practice of Glossing in Late Antiquity and the Renaissance." *Studies in Philology* 92, no. 4 (1995): 439–59.

Soga Yoshinari. *Ōchō kokka seimu no kenkyū*. Tokyo: Yoshikawa kōbunkan, 2012.

Sorensen, Joseph T. *Optical Allusions: Screens, Paintings, and Poetry in Classical Japan (ca. 800–1200)*. Leiden: Brill, 2012.

Steininger, Brian. "Li Jiao's *Songs*: Commentary-Based Reading and the Reception of Tang Poetry in Heian Japan." *East Asian Publishing and Society* 6, no. 2 (2016): 103–29.

———. "Poetic Ministers: Literacy and Bureaucracy in the Tenth-Century State Academy." Ph.D. diss., Yale University, 2010.

Stone, Jacqueline I. *Original Enlightenment and the Transformation of Medieval Japanese Buddhism*. Honolulu: Kuroda Institute, University of Hawai'i Press, 1999.

Suh, Soyoung. "Herbs of Our Own Kingdom." *Asian Medicine* 4 (2008): 395–422.

Sun, Chaofen. "Adposition *yi* and Word Order in Classical Chinese." *Journal of Chinese Linguistics* 19 (1991): 202–20.

Sun Liangming. *Zhongguo gudai yufaxue tanjiu*. Beijing: Shangwu yinshuguan, 2002.

Takahashi Hideki. *Nihon chūsei no ie to shinzoku*. Tokyo: Yoshikawa kōbunkan, 1996.

Takahashi Tadayuki, and Takahashi Hisako. *Nihon no kojisho: Jobun, batsubun o yomu*. Tokyo: Taishūkan shoten, 2006.

Takahashi Tōru. "Utsuho monogatari: Hajimari no sekai no sōzōryoku." In *Shoki monogatari bungaku no ishiki*, vol. 2 of *Ronshū chūko bungaku*, edited by Chūko Bungaku Kenkyūkai, 155–76. Tokyo: Kasama shoin, 1979.

Takeuchi Rizō. "Heian makki no ōraimono ni arawareta shōen." In *Takeuchi Rizō chosakushū*, 7: 519–36. Tokyo: Kadokawa shoten, 1998.

———. *Ritsuryōsei to kizoku seiken*. 2 vols. Tokyo: Ochanomizu shobō, 1957–58.

Takigawa Kōji. *Tennō to bundan: Heian zenki no kōteki bungaku*. Osaka: Izumi shoin, 2007.

Tamai Chikara. *Heian jidai no kizoku to tennō*. Tokyo: Iwanami shoten, 2000.

Tamamura Takeji. *Gozan zensō denki shūsei*. Tokyo: Kōdansha, 1983.

Tambiah, Stanley Jeyaraja. *Culture, Thought, and Social Action: An Anthropological Perspective.* Cambridge, MA: Harvard University Press, 1985.

Teiser, Stephen [Tai Shiwen]. "Shilun zhaiwen de biaoyanxing." *Dunhuang Tulufan yanjiu* 10 (2007): 295–307.

Terauchi Hiroshi. *Zuryōsei no kenkyū.* Tokyo: Hanawa shobō, 2004.

Tian, Xiaofei. *Beacon Fire and Shooting Star: The Literary Culture of the Liang.* Cambridge, MA: Harvard University Asia Center, 2007.

Toda Yoshimi. "Kyōto and the Estate System in the Heian Period." Interpreted by Janet R. Goodwin. In *Capital and Countryside in Japan*, edited by Joan R. Piggott, 245–79.

———. *Shoki chūsei shakaishi no kenkyū.* Tokyo: Tōkyō Daigaku shuppankai, 1991.

Tōdō Akiyasu. *Chūgoku gogaku ronshū.* Tokyo: Kyūko shoin, 1987.

Tōkyō Kokuritsu Hakubutsukan. *Shiika to sho: Nihon no kokoro to bi; Tokubetsuten.* Tokyo: Tōkyō Kokuritsu Hakubutsukan, 1991.

Tōno Haruyuki. "Kunmōsho." In *Tonkō kanbun bunken*, vol. 5 of *Kōza Tonkō*, edited by Ikeda On, 401–38. Tokyo: Daitō shuppansha, 1992.

Tsuda Kiyoshi. "*Kaifūsō* no hyōsoku ni tsuite." *Kokugakuin zasshi* 82, no. 1 (1981): 76–91.

Tsukishima Hiroshi. *Heian jidai no kanbun kundokugo ni tsukite no kenkyū.* Tokyo: Tōkyō Daigaku shuppankai, 1963.

———. "Kōzanji-bon koōrai no bunkengakuteki kenkyū." In *Kōzanji-bon koōrai, hyōbyakushū*, vol. 2 of *Kōzanji shiryō sōsho*, edited by Kōzanji Tenseki Monjo Sōgō Chōsadan, 437–69. Tokyo: Tōkyō Daigaku shuppankai, 1972.

———. *Kunten goi shūsei.* 9 vols. Tokyo: Kyūko shoin, 2007–9.

———. "*Wamyō ruijushō* no wakun ni tsuite." *Kuntengo to kunten shiryō* 25 (1963): 28–60.

———, ed. *Chōshō-bon Mōgyū.* Tokyo: Kyūko shoin, 1990.

Tyler, Royall, trans. *The Tale of Genji.* New York: Penguin Books, 2001.

Uesugi Kazuhiko. *Nihon chūsei hōtaikei seiritsu shiron.* Tokyo: Azekura shobō, 1996.

Umemura Keiko. "Fujiwara no Michitsuna boshi to Kaneie no seikatsu." In *Josei to bunka*, edited by Ningen Bunka Kenkyūkai, 3:57–80. Tokyo: Hakuba shuppan, 1984.

Umemura Takashi. *Nihon kodai shakai keizaishi ronkō.* Tokyo: Hanawa shobō, 2006.

Ury, Marian. "Chinese Learning and Intellectual Life." In *Heian Japan*, Donald H. Shively and William H. McCullough, 341–89.

Van Zoeren, Steven. *Poetry and Personality: Reading, Exegesis, and Hermeneutics in Traditional China.* Stanford, CA: Stanford University Press, 1991.

Verschuer, Charlotte von. *Across the Perilous Sea: Japanese Trade with China and Korea from the Seventh to the Sixteenth Centuries.* Translated by Kristen Lee Hunter. Ithaca, NY: East Asia Program, Cornell University, 2006.

———. "Life of Commoners in the Provinces: The *Owari no gebumi* of 988." In *Heian Japan: Centers and Peripheries*, edited by Mikael Adolphson, Edward Kamens, and Stacie Matsumoto, 305–28.

Waley, Arthur. "An Eleventh Century Correspondence." In *Études d'orientalisme, publiées par le Musée Guimet à la mémoire de Raymonde Linossier*, 2:531–62. Paris: E. Leroux, 1932.

Wang Li. *Hanyu shilüxue*. Hong Kong: Zhonghua shuju, 1976.

Wang, Yugen. "*Shige*: The Popular Poetics of Regulated Verse." *T'ang Studies* 22 (2004): 81–125.

Wang Zhongmin. *Dunhuang guji xulu*. Beijing: Zhonghua shuju, 2010 (first pub. 1958).

Watanabe Hideo. "Ganmon: Heianchō no tsuizen ganmon o chūshin ni." In *Shōdō no bungaku*, vol. 8 of *Bukkyō bungaku kōza*, edited by Itō Hiroyuki, Imanari Genshō, and Yamada Shōzen, 132–59. Tokyo: Benseisha, 1995.

Watanabe Naohiko. *Nihon kodai kan'i seido no kisoteki kenkyū*. Rev. ed. Tokyo: Yoshikawa kōbunkan, 1978.

Watanabe Shigeru. *Kodai, chūsei no jōhō dentatsu: Moji to onsei, kioku no kinōron*. Tokyo: Yagi shoten, 2010.

Watson, Burton, trans. *Meng ch'iu: Famous Episodes from Chinese History and Legend*. Tokyo: Kodansha International, 1979.

Webb, Jason P. "In Good Order: Poetry, Reception, and Authority in the Nara and Early Heian Courts." Ph.D. diss., Princeton University, 2005.

Wen Yiduo. "Leishu yu shi." In *Tangshi zalun*. Shanghai: Shanghai guji chubanshe, 1998.

Wenck, Günther. *Japanische Phonetik*. 4 vols. Wiesbaden, Germany: Harrassowitz, 1954–59.

Whitman, John. "The Ubiquity of the Gloss." *SCRIPTA* 3 (2011): 95–121.

Wixted, John Timothy. "*Kanbun*, Histories of Japanese Literature, and Japanologists." *Sino-Japanese Studies* 10, no. 2 (1998): 23–31.

———. "The *Kokinshū* Prefaces: Another Perspective." *Harvard Journal of Asiatic Studies* 43, no. 1 (1983): 215–38.

Woodbine, George E. "The Language of English Law." *Speculum* 18, no. 4 (1943): 395–436.

Wu Shengxiong. "You 'Fengtong Yuan Cheng caizi Heyuanyuan fu' de gelü lun Yuan Shun dui hanyu shengdiao de zhangwo." *Zhongguo xueshu niankan* 29 (2007): 167–90.

Yamagishi Tokuhei. *Nihon kanbungaku kenkyū*. Tokyo: Yūseidō shuppan, 1973.

Yamamoto Nobuyoshi, Ōyama Jinkai, Yuyama Ken'ichi, Ōtsuka Hideaki, and Adachi Naoya, eds. *Shinshitei jūyō bunkazai: Kaisetsuban*. Vol. 7, *Shoseki, tenseki, komonjo*. Tokyo: Mainichi shinbun, 1981.

Yamamoto Shingo. *Heian Kamakura jidai ni okeru hyōbyaku ganmon no buntai no kenkyū*. Tokyo: Kyūko shoin, 2006.

Yamashita Shin'ichirō. *Nihon kodai no kokka to kyūyosei*. Tokyo: Yoshikawa kōbunkan, 2012.

Yamazaki Akira. "Ōe no Masafusa no ganmon ni miru *Meikō zatsuroku* no juyō." *Chūko bungaku* 88 (2011): 81–95.

Yamazaki Makoto. *Chūsei gakumonshi no kitei to tenkai*. Osaka: Izumi shoin, 1993.

———. "Sakumon daitai no gensho keitai ni tsuite—furoku Higashiyama Bunko-bon *Bunpitsu daitai* honkoku." *Kokubungaku Kenkyū Shiryōkan chōsa kenkyū hōkoku* 23 (2002): 331–74.

Yoda, Tomiko. *Gender and National Literature: Heian Texts in the Constructions of Japanese Modernity*. Durham, NC: Duke University Press, 2004.

Yoshida Sanae. "Aristocratic Journals and the Courtly Calendar." In *Teishinkōki: The Year 939 in the Journal of Regent Fujiwara No Tadahira*, edited by Joan R. Piggott and Yoshida Sanae, 8–21. Ithaca, NY: East Asia Program, Cornell University, 2008.

Yoshikawa Shinji. *Ritsuryō kanryōsei no kenkyū*. Tokyo: Hanawa shobō, 1998.

Yu, Pauline. "Poems for the Emperor: Imperial Tastes in the Early Ninth Century." In *Rhetoric and the Discourses of Power in the Court Culture*, edited by David R. Knechtges and Eugene Vance, 73–93. Seattle: University of Washington Press, 2005.

Yūki Rikurō. "Chūsei jiin no sezoku kyōiku ni kansuru ichikōsatsu." In *Kyōikugaku ronshū*, edited by Nihon Kyōiku Gakkai, 1:247–57. Tokyo: Meguro shoten, 1951.

Zhang Dihua. *Leishu liubie*. Shanghai: Shangwu yinshuguan, 1958.

Index

Page numbers for figures are in italics.

Harvard East Asian Monographs
(most recent titles)

310. Rachel DiNitto, *Uchida Hyakken: A Critique of Modernity and Militarism in Prewar Japan*
311. Jeffrey Snyder-Reinke, *Dry Spells: State Rainmaking and Local Governance in Late Imperial China*
312. Jay Dautcher, *Down a Narrow Road: Identity and Masculinity in a Uyghur Community in Xinjiang China*
313. Xun Liu, *Daoist Modern: Innovation, Lay Practice, and the Community of Inner Alchemy in Republican Shanghai*
314. Jacob Eyferth, *Eating Rice from Bamboo Roots: The Social History of a Community of Handicraft Papermakers in Rural Sichuan, 1920–2000*
315. David Johnson, *Spectacle and Sacrifice: The Ritual Foundations of Village Life in North China*
316. James Robson, *Power of Place: The Religious Landscape of the Southern Sacred Peak (Nanyue 南嶽) in Medieval China*
317. Lori Watt, *When Empire Comes Home: Repatriation and Reintegration in Postwar Japan*
318. James Dorsey, *Critical Aesthetics: Kobayashi Hideo, Modernity, and Wartime Japan*
319. Christopher Bolton, *Sublime Voices: The Fictional Science and Scientific Fiction of Abe Kōbō*
320. Si-yen Fei, *Negotiating Urban Space: Urbanization and Late Ming Nanjing*
321. Christopher Gerteis, *Gender Struggles: Wage-Earning Women and Male-Dominated Unions in Postwar Japan*
322. Rebecca Nedostup, *Superstitious Regimes: Religion and the Politics of Chinese Modernity*
323. Lucien Bianco, *Wretched Rebels: Rural Disturbances on the Eve of the Chinese Revolution*
324. Cathryn H. Clayton, *Sovereignty at the Edge: Macau and the Question of Chineseness*
325. Micah S. Muscolino, *Fishing Wars and Environmental Change in Late Imperial and Modern China*
326. Robert I. Hellyer, *Defining Engagement: Japan and Global Contexts, 1750–1868*
327. Robert Ashmore, *The Transport of Reading: Text and Understanding in the World of Tao Qian (365–427)*
328. Mark A. Jones, *Children as Treasures: Childhood and the Middle Class in Early Twentieth Century Japan*
329. Miryam Sas, *Experimental Arts in Postwar Japan: Moments of Encounter, Engagement, and Imagined Return*
330. H. Mack Horton, *Traversing the Frontier: The* Man'yōshū *Account of a Japanese Mission to Silla in 736–737*

331. Dennis J. Frost, *Seeing Stars: Sports Celebrity, Identity, and Body Culture in Modern Japan*
332. Marnie S. Anderson, *A Place in Public: Women's Rights in Meiji Japan*
333. Peter Mauch, *Sailor Diplomat: Nomura Kichisaburō and the Japanese-American War*
334. Ethan Isaac Segal, *Coins, Trade, and the State: Economic Growth in Early Medieval Japan*
335. David B. Lurie, *Realms of Literacy: Early Japan and the History of Writing*
336. Lillian Lan-ying Tseng, *Picturing Heaven in Early China*
337. Jun Uchida, *Brokers of Empire: Japanese Settler Colonialism in Korea, 1876–1945*
338. Patricia L. Maclachlan, *The People's Post Office: The History and Politics of the Japanese Postal System, 1871–2010*
339. Michael Schiltz, *The Money Doctors from Japan: Finance, Imperialism, and the Building of the Yen Bloc, 1895–1937*
340. Daqing Yang, Jie Liu, Hiroshi Mitani, and Andrew Gordon, eds., *Toward a History beyond Borders: Contentious Issues in Sino-Japanese Relations*
341. Sonia Ryang, *Reading North Korea: An Ethnological Inquiry*
342. Shih-shan Susan Huang, *Picturing the True Form: Daoist Visual Culture in Traditional China*
343. Barbara Mittler, *A Continuous Revolution: Making Sense of Cultural Revolution Culture*
344. Hwansoo Ilmee Kim, *Empire of the Dharma: Korean and Japanese Buddhism, 1877–1912*
345. Satoru Saito, *Detective Fiction and the Rise of the Japanese Novel, 1880–1930*
346. Jung-Sun N. Han, *An Imperial Path to Modernity: Yoshino Sakuzō and a New Liberal Order in East Asia, 1905–1937*
347. Atsuko Hirai, *Government by Mourning: Death and Political Integration in Japan, 1603–1912*
348. Darryl E. Flaherty, *Public Law, Private Practice: Politics, Profit, and the Legal Profession in Nineteenth-Century Japan*
349. Jeffrey Paul Bayliss, *On the Margins of Empire: Buraku and Korean Identity in Prewar and Wartime Japan*
350. Barry Eichengreen, Dwight H. Perkins, and Kwanho Shin, *From Miracle to Maturity: The Growth of the Korean Economy*
351. Michel Mohr, *Buddhism, Unitarianism, and the Meiji Competition for Universality*
352. J. Keith Vincent, *Two-Timing Modernity: Homosocial Narrative in Modern Japanese Fiction*
354. Chong-Bum An and Barry Bosworth, *Income Inequality in Korea: An Analysis of Trends, Causes, and Answers*
355. Jamie L. Newhard, *Knowing the Amorous Man: A History of Scholarship on* Tales of Ise
356. Sho Konishi, *Anarchist Modernity: Cooperatism and Japanese-Russian Intellectual Relations in Modern Japan*
357. Christopher P. Hanscom, *The Real Modern: Literary Modernism and the Crisis of Representation in Colonial Korea*

358. Michael Wert, *Meiji Restoration Losers: Memory and Tokugawa Supporters in Modern Japan*
359. Garret P. S. Olberding, ed., *Facing the Monarch: Modes of Advice in the Early Chinese Court*
360. Xiaojue Wang, *Modernity with a Cold War Face: Reimagining the Nation in Chinese Literature Across the 1949 Divide*
361. David Spafford, *A Sense of Place: The Political Landscape in Late Medieval Japan*
362. Jongryn Mo and Barry Weingast, *Korean Political and Economic Development: Crisis, Security, and Economic Rebalancing*
363. Melek Ortabasi, *The Undiscovered Country: Text, Translation, and Modernity in the Work of Yanagita Kunio*
364. Hiraku Shimoda, *Lost and Found: Recovering Regional Identity in Imperial Japan*
365. Trent E. Maxey, *The "Greatest Problem": Religion and State Formation in Meiji Japan*
366. Gina Cogan, *The Princess Nun: Bunchi, Buddhist Reform, and Gender in Early Edo Japan*
367. Eric C. Han, *Rise of a Japanese Chinatown: Yokohama, 1894–1972*
368. Natasha Heller, *Illusory Abiding: The Cultural Construction of the Chan Monk Zhongfeng Mingben*
369. Paize Keulemans, *Sound Rising from the Paper: Nineteenth-Century Martial Arts Fiction and the Chinese Acoustic Imagination*
370. Simon James Bytheway, *Investing Japan: Foreign Capital, Monetary Standards, and Economic Development, 1859–2011*
371. Sukhee Lee, *Negotiated Power: The State, Elites, and Local Governance in Twelfth-Fourteenth China*
372. Foong Ping, *The Efficacious Landscape: On the Authorities of Painting at the Northern Song Court*
373. Catherine L. Phipps, *Empires on the Waterfront: Japan's Ports and Power, 1858–1899*
374. Sunyoung Park, *The Proletarian Wave: Literature and Leftist Culture in Colonial Korea, 1910–1945*
375. Barry Eichengreen, Wonhyuk Lim, Yung Chul Park, and Dwight H. Perkins, *The Korean Economy: From a Miraculous Past to a Sustainable Future*
376. Heather Blair, *Real and Imagined: The Peak of Gold in Heian Japan*
377. Emer O'Dwyer, *Significant Soil: Settler Colonialism and Japan's Urban Empire in Manchuria*
378. Martina Deuchler, *Under the Ancestors' Eyes: Kinship, Status, and Locality in Premodern Korea*
379. Joseph R. Dennis, *Writing, Publishing, and Reading Local Gazetteers in Imperial China, 1100–1700*
380. Catherine Vance Yeh, *The Chinese Political Novel: Migration of a World Genre*
381. Noell Wilson, *Defensive Positions: The Politics of Maritime Security in Tokugawa Japan*
382. Miri Nakamura, *Monstrous Bodies: The Rise of the Uncanny in Modern Japan*
383. Nara Dillon, *Radical Inequalities: China's Revolutionary Welfare State in Comparative Perspective*

384. Ma Zhao, *Runaway Wives, Urban Crimes, and Survival Tactics in Wartime Beijing, 1937-1949*
385. Mingwei Song, *Young China: National Rejuvenation and the* Bildungsroman, *1900-1959*
386. Christopher Bondy, *Voice, Silence, and Self: Negotiations of Buraku Identity in Contemporary Japan*
387. Seth Jacobowitz, *Writing Technology in Meiji Japan: A Media History of Modern Japanese Literature and Visual Culture*
388. Hilde De Weerdt, *Information, Territory, and Networks: The Crisis and Maintenance of Empire in Song China*
389. Elizabeth Kindall, *Geo-Narratives of a Filial Son: The Paintings and Travel Diaries of Huang Xiangjian (1609–1673)*
390. Matthew Fraleigh, *Plucking Chrysanthemums: Narushima Ryūhoku and Sinitic Literary Traditions in Modern Japan*
391. Hu Ying, *Burying Autumn: Poetry, Friendship, and Loss*
392. Mark E. Byington, *The Ancient State of Puyŏ in Northeast Asia: Archaeology and Historical Memory*
393. Timothy J. Van Compernolle, *Struggling Upward: Worldly Success and the Japanese Novel*
394. Heekyoung Cho, *Translation's Forgotten History: Russian Literature, Japanese Mediation, and the Formation of Modern Korean Literature*
395. Terry Kawashima, *Itineraries of Power: Texts and Traversals in Heian and Medieval Japan*
396. Anna Andreeva, *Assembling Shinto: Buddhist Approaches to Kami Worship in Medieval Japan*
397. Felix Boecking, *No Great Wall: Trade, Tariffs, and Nationalism in Republican China, 1927–1945*
398. Chien-Hsin Tsai, *A Passage to China: Literature, Loyalism, and Colonial Taiwan*
399. W. Puck Brecher, *Honored and Dishonored Guests: Westerners in Wartime Japan*
400. Miya Elise Mizuta Lippit, *Aesthetic Life: Beauty and Art in Modern Japan*
401. Brian Steininger, *Chinese Literary Form in Heian Japan: Poetics and Practice*
402. Lisa Yoshikawa, *Making History Matter: Kuroita Katsumi and the Construction of Imperial Japan*
403. Michael P. Cronin, *Osaka Modern: The City in the Japanese Imaginary*
404. Soyoung Suh, *Naming the Local: Medicine, Language, and Identity in Korea since the 15th Century*
405. Yoon Sun Yang, *From Domestic Women to Sensitive Young Men: Translating the Individual in Early Colonial Korea*
406. Michal Daliot-Bul and Nissim Otmazgin, *The Anime Boom in the United States: Lessons for Global Creative Industries*
407. Nathan Hopson, *Ennobling the Savage Northeast: Tōhoku as Japanese Postwar Thought, 1945–2011*